The Genealogist's Companion & Sourcebook

The Genealogist's Companion & Sourcebook

E M I L Y A N N E C R O O M

BETTERWAY BOOKS
CINCINNATI, OHIO

The Genealogist's Companion & Sourcebook. Copyright © 1994 by Emily Anne Croom. Printed and bound in the United States of America. All rights reserved. No part of this book may be reproduced in any form or by any electronic or mechanical means including information storage and retrieval systems without permission in writing from the publisher, except by a reviewer, who may quote brief passages in a review or by the purchaser of the book, who may reproduce the blank forms in the Appendix for personal use. Published by Betterway Books, an imprint of F&W Publications, Inc., 1507 Dana Avenue, Cincinnati, Ohio 45207. (800) 289-0963. First edition.

Other fine Betterway Books are available from your local bookstore or direct from the publisher.

98   97   96   6   5   4

Library of Congress Cataloging-in-Publication Data
Croom, Emily Anne
  The genealogist's companion & sourcebook / by Emily Anne Croom.
      p. cm.
  Includes bibliographic references and index.
    ISBN 1-55870-331-4
    1. United States—Genealogy—Handbooks, manuals, etc. I. Title. II. Title: Genealogist's companion and sourcebook.
CS47.C75 1994
929'.1'072073—dc20   93-46365
                                                               CIP

Edited by Donna K. Collingwood
Interior design/cover design by Sandy Conopeotis

ABOUT THE AUTHOR

Emily Anne Croom is a member of the National Genealogical Society and conducts workshops and classes in genealogy.

She also speaks to genealogy societies and is an active researcher and writer on the subject. Her previous books include *Unpuzzling Your Past: A Basic Guide to Genealogy* (Betterway Books, 1989) and five privately printed family genealogies.

She lives in Houston, Texas.

FOREWORD

"Where do I go from here? What do I do now?" Have you ever asked these questions when you ran into a brick wall in your research?

Many records are waiting to be found, if we just knew where to look. The recorders in the past—the county clerk, the minister, the ship captain, the census enumerator, the newspaper editor, and perhaps even a neighbor—may have recorded exactly what we want to know. Our challenge is finding what they wrote. Of course, some of these now valuable records were thrown out as trash, were lost in floods, or went up in flames. Especially that bane of Southern research, the burned courthouse, proves to be a real obstacle to research and requires creative thinking to find alternate sources for the answers it may have contained.

This book focuses on American (United States) research materials outside of private family sources, i.e., Bible entries, letters, and interviews. Readers who want to review the use of these important foundation sources and basic research methods are encouraged to refer to guides such as *Unpuzzling Your Past: A Basic Guide to Genealogy*, available in book stores and libraries as well as from the publisher, Betterway Books, 1507 Dana Avenue, Cincinnati, OH 45207.

The first chapter on cluster (or whole family) genealogy may seem elementary to those readers who are old hands at this game. Many genealogists, however, fail to realize the great usefulness of this method until well into their research. Then they have to backtrack to pick up key relatives or neighbors whom they missed by concentrating only on the "target" ancestor. To make searches more effective and more efficient, I urge readers to think more about this approach from the very beginning.

Part of this book concentrates on special places for research, such as courthouses and public, university, and law libraries, as well as the genealogical sources available there and how to use them. The book also discusses sources, such as maps, newspapers, census records, military records, passenger lists, and church records, which are available for use in many research libraries and archives collections. Of course, it is one thing to know about a source but another to know how or where to find it. This book tries to guide the reader to the record: where it is available for use, for purchase, or for rent. Many materials are also available through interlibrary loan at local public libraries or through photoduplication services from publishers, archives, or libraries.

Some of us need encouragement to try new avenues of research. We genealogists often become interested in new sources when we hear about someone else's success in using them. That is why I have included examples and case studies from my own research or that of friends. It is the real-life examples that make sources inviting.

In our rushed existence, we tend to want instant rewards and immediate success. Sometimes, we are lucky enough to experience those quick results and unexpected discoveries in genealogy. However, I constantly must remind myself of my favorite Shakespeare quotation: "Though patience be a tired mare, yet she will plod on."

Throughout the writing of this book, I have spoken and corresponded with many librarians, archivists, researchers, and publishers throughout the country, to whom I am most grateful for answers, explanations, and clarifications. I would especially like to thank Tom Kallsen of the University of Alabama Map Library; Sandra Boling White of the Georgia Archives; Sylvia E. Castaño, Assistant Director of the University of Houston Law Libraries; Marybelle W. Chase of Tulsa, Oklahoma; and Mary Katherine Earney of Marfa, Texas, for taking extra time and effort to share their knowledge and expertise. The two people to whom I am most indebted for countless hours of discussion, manuscript reading, and sharing of expertise are Robert T. Shelby of Bellaire, Texas, and Gay Carter, reference librarian at the University of Houston, Clear Lake Campus.

CHAPTER ONE

Cluster Genealogy

CLUSTER GENEALOGY—WHAT AND WHY?

Cluster genealogy has been called extended-family genealogy and whole-family genealogy. I prefer the concept of the cluster, for it implies the inclusion of neighbors as well as relatives. The concept means the widening of one's search to include not only a direct line of ancestors, but of brothers, sisters, aunts, uncles, cousins, spouses, children, and neighbors in *every* generation. The reasons and rewards are not always obvious, but they are very real.

First, by tracking brothers, sisters, and other relatives of an ancestor, you often find more information on that ancestor and the parents than by tracing only your direct line. One example is the search done for descendants of Emma and Charles Wesley Metcalf.

1. Emma's death certificate showed her parents' names as John Campbell and Emily Godwin.

2. Her sister Costella's death certificate gave the father's name as J.A.F. Campbell. This information made it so much easier to keep up with him in a region where John Campbell is a fairly common name. Other records showed that Costella's full name was Euphimia Costella.

3. Emily Godwin Campbell's tombstone gave her birthdate as 12 September 1825, making her 14 at the time of the 1840 census. She was married and living in Dale County, Alabama, by the time of the 1850 census.

4. To try to identify Emily's parents, we first searched for Godwins in Dale County in 1840. The three heads of household were Jonathan, Bennet, and Johnson, but only Johnson had females in Emily's age group, 10-15. (One had no young females at all, and the other had very young females.) Because county records from that period were destroyed in a courthouse fire, we had to rely heavily on census records to study this Johnson Godwin. Was he indeed Emily's father?

5. It was helpful that one of Emma's daughters re-membered that Euphimia Costella was named for an aunt Euphemia. (Spelling of this name varies greatly.)

6. The 1850 census showed *Effie* (age 23) as the oldest child in Johnson Godwin's household, and the J.A.F. Campbells were nearby.

7. In 1860, Johnson Godwin, the Campbells, and the Metcalfs were in Newton, in Dale County, Alabama, where Godwin and the Campbells also appeared in 1870. (The Metcalfs have not been found in the 1870 census.) We learned later that *Effa* and her husband, George Keahey, were then living in Erath County, Texas, where the 1870 census gave her name as *Euphemia* Keahey.

8. By 1880, the Campbells, Metcalfs, and other Dale County families had moved to Navarro County, Texas. (Families often moved in clusters.) Johnson Godwin did not appear on the Dale County census or the Texas Soundex. Family interviews sent the search for one Campbell son to Erath County, Texas. There we found not only young Campbell but Johnson Godwin. He lived with the Keaheys, as *father-in-law* of George Keahey, therefore father of *Euphimia* Keahey. (It turned out that one of the Keahey daughters had married that Campbell son.) The preponderance of evidence is, then, that Johnson Godwin was also the father of Emily Godwin Campbell. By studying the cluster of Godwins and Campbells, beginning with sisters Emma and Costella, we were able to find pieces of the genealogical puzzle that we could not have found by limiting the search to Emma and her mother, Emily.

As the Campbell-Godwin example shows, ancestors did not live in a vacuum. They often lived with or near relatives. Such was the case with the T.J. Robberson (Robertson) who lived with Calvin Croom and his family in Shreveport, Louisiana, in 1860. To a casual reader, T.J. would seem to be a clerk employed by the merchant Calvin, as may have been the case. However, this T(homas) J. was also my great-grandmother's brother and a step-brother to Calvin, as Calvin's father had married T.J.'s mother.

Another reason for studying the cluster of relatives is to confirm the accuracy of the information you find in any one document. Sometimes a given fact does not appear in more than one place, but a preponderance of evidence may appear from gathering whatever you can find.

In pursuing the cluster of relatives and neighbors, who sometimes turn out to be relatives, it is important to use as many primary and contemporary secondary sources as possible. Marriage records, deeds, wills, estate settlements, and court records are basic primary records, with the parties to a document directly involved in its creation. These records can contain mistakes, misspellings, and omissions, but they are first-hand sources of most of the information given and therefore are valuable to genealogists.

Manuscript sources that are contemporary with the people involved, such as diaries and letters, also contain much that is accurate and not available elsewhere. In studying a cluster of Coleman siblings of Cumberland County, Virginia, my cousin Thyrza McCollum was led by labels on photographs to Bolivar, Tennessee. Inquiring about Coleman descendants there, she was given my name by someone who knew that I had been there working on that family. When I went to visit Thyrza, she showed me a trunk of letters, some written by my great-great-grandmother to the Coleman in-laws. Among those was a letter that gave the death date of her father, Thomas Patton. Another gave information about a little girl in the family who lived and died between censuses. Without the letter being preserved, we would not have known of her at all. Because of Thyrza's concern for the Coleman cluster, I was the recipient of much valuable information and was able to share other information with her.

Birth records contain information possibly furnished by the parents but not always filed by them. That is why you can find a father's name given three different ways on birth records of his three children. At least those made at the time of the birth are closer to the source of information than death certificates. Obviously, family records and oral tradition play a vital role in the accuracy of death certificate and tombstone information. Thus, death certificates of siblings may contain slightly different information on the parents. These variations may cause confusion, as when a father's name is given as *John Calvin* and *Calvin S.* On the other hand, those which show *C.S.* and *Calvin S.* support each other, and are corroborated in other records.

Many census records and newspaper articles are contemporary with earlier generations of the family being studied. It cannot be known just who furnished the information and how accurate it was. The point remains that the searcher needs to consult as many sources as possible for the most complete information and to compare results to determine the accuracy of what is gathered. That is one effort of this book, to encourage you to branch out into many sources.

A third reason for studying genealogy in clusters is to gather family medical history. Much has been discovered in recent years about the hereditary tendencies in a number of medical and physical conditions, such as heart disease, diabetes, blindness or deafness, and, a relative newcomer, fragile X syndrome. In one family I know, the grandfather, Bill, died in 1910, at age 61, of a "tobacco heart." His son Mack died at 46 of a heart attack. Mack's son Terry died of a heart attack at age 43, and another son had successful quadruple by-pass surgery. Now Mack's grandsons are aware of this pattern in the family and know that they must monitor their physical conditions.

PUBLISHED FAMILY HISTORIES

Many people who have compiled clusters of family members publish their results. To the extent that the compiler has been careful and accurate and has documented the information, these books can be very useful. However, even if you find a book that includes your family, you would be well advised to use the information as clues for your own research rather than accept without reservation what is given.

The example below comes from one family history published in the early twentieth century, but similar problems appear even in recent books. This particular book contains many family groups in a cluster of related families spread over six or seven generations. It gives numerous vital statistics but not one shred of documentation. The author obviously was in contact with a number of his cousins and must have received information from them. However, this kind of discrepancy appears several times:

John Aaron, b 1825, m 1849, d 1851.
Wife Sarah, b 1829.
Son Aaron Hugh, b 1827, d 1904.
Daughter Elizabeth Miranda, b 1850.

However, according to the grandfather's estate settlement in the county records, John (no middle name) and Aaron Hugh were brothers, not father and son. John died young, leaving one daughter, Elizabeth Miranda. Now the dates make sense.

Most libraries with genealogy collections have a section of family histories. Large libraries, such as the Library of Congress and the Newberry Library of Chicago have hundreds of them listed in published catalogs. Some are well written and well documented, and some are not. The fact that they are in the library does not automatically make them reliable research sources. Of course, they may be very accurate on one part of the family and not on another. The genealogist, therefore, must be cautious in accepting what is given and should seek to verify it with other sources.

A reference that you may find helpful is *Genealogies Catalogued by the Library of Congress Since 1986: With a List of Established Forms of Family Names and a List of Genealogies Converted to Microfilm Since 1983* (Washington, DC: Library of Congress, 1992). The family histories published before 1900 and now on microfilm at the Library of Congress are available for purchase and for interlibrary loan. Check the catalog above for availability, and make your loan request through your local interlibrary loan specialist.

BIOGRAPHICAL DICTIONARIES

Many biographical dictionaries have been published in this country in the past century. They cover the famous and the not-so-famous throughout the country. Like published family histories, they can be great sources, or not so great. Much depends on the care with which each entry was produced. However, they can contain good clues. Finding entries on a member of your cluster of relatives can give you solid leads to pursue on your own ancestor.

Because these are not primary sources, they are not emphasized in this book. However, you can find the ones that your library reference section has by looking in the library catalog under *Biography—Dictionaries* or *United States—Biography—Dictionaries*. Many of them are multivolume sets. Some, such as *Appleton's Cyclopedia of American Biography* (New York: D. Appleton & Co., 1887) and the *Dictionary of American Biography* (New York: Charles Scribner's Sons, 1928-), cover a broad base of people. Others are more specialized, with sketches of governors and persons in Congress, the federal executive branch, the frontier, the Confederacy, various regions, and numerous professions. The *Biography and Genealogy Master Index*

(Detroit, MI: Gale Research, 1975-, now also available on CD-ROM) indexes over 450,000 biographical sketches in over ninety-five biographical dictionaries.

NAMING PATTERNS AS CLUSTER CLUES

Why do we have the names we have? Were you named for someone? What names in your extended family seem to be used generation after generation?

Perhaps the twentieth century has changed some of our naming practices with its unisex names such as Whitney, Taylor, Tyler, Jordan, Cody, and Morgan. However, families for centuries have used unisex names, sometimes without regard to spelling: Francis/Frances, Marion/Marian, Leslie, Charlie, Billie, Bobbie, Willie, Beverly. My own family used the name Fletcher for four generations, two males and two females.

Naming patterns are fascinating to study, and hopefully each genealogist is aware of the practices within his own family. After all, when you run into repeated given names in each generation and have to try to sort them out, you understand in a hurry how that practice affects the genealogist. Many families have such examples: *Evan* in the Shelby family for nearly three hundred years and *Major* in the Croom family for over two hundred years.

What about the habit of naming more than one child in the family the same name? Have you thought about Johann Christian Bach and his brother Johann Christoph Friedrich Bach, two of the surviving sons of Johann Sebastian Bach? Apart from baptismal names such as these, repetitions did happen when a child died and a succeeding child received the name. One Holmes family of Texas had three sons, all of whom died young: Alvie, Lester Leo, and Alvie Leo. These boys had an uncle Alvie of the same county. A friend of mine who is the fourth generation Joseph Tyra Wells tells that his grandfather was determined to have the name survive in the family and named all three of his sons Joseph. One Preuss family of Texas had a son Emil, a daughter Emilia, and a daughter Amalia, a German form of Emily. These siblings had a sister who named her daughters Emilie Hulda and Emma Emilie.

Sometimes the origins of names in the family are carried on. Unfortunately, many times they are not. Since I am the fourth Emily in my part of the Blalock family, I know the story of the name Emily. The first, born 150 years ago, died of consumption at age 37. When her husband remarried, he named the first daughter Emily after his first wife. My grandmother

Emily, for whom I was named, was a contemporary (and sister-in-law) of this second Emily and was named for the same lady, her father's sister.

Of course, popular heroes, presidents, friends, and prominent local citizens are honored with namesakes. At least four boys in Hardeman County, Tennessee, were named for local merchant Pitser Miller (1801-1881): Pitser Miller Chisum (1834), Pitser Miller Blalock (1848), William Mack Pitser Miller King (1851), and Pitser Miller Bishop (1880).

In these days of smaller families, parents will not have the opportunity to name children after all grandparents, favorite relatives, friends, or heroes. If they choose to use family names at all, they must be selective and careful. Instead of naming two sons for two grandfathers, they will often combine names from both sides of the family. That is how Thomas Blalock King (1972) got a name from each grandfather, and Laurence Samuel Hutchings (1984) got a name from a grandfather on one side and a great-grandfather on the other. Even in a family of twelve children, Mary Eliza Catherine Coleman (1848) received a name from each grandmother, Catherine Patton and Eliza Coleman. Susan William Ann Richardson (1811) was named for both parental grandparents, William and Ann Richardson.

Many public and family records identify a person by his or her given name and middle initial. However, genealogists know that middle names can be valuable clues and should be preserved. By studying middle names in the cluster of siblings and cousins, we find clues to relationships. It does not really matter whether the eldest son or the fourth son was named for the maternal grandfather. Examples abound all over the country for grandparents' and parents' names being used in every order among the children. What matters is that we record the source of the names, if indeed they have a reason for being used.

As for clues to origin, consider the middle name *Steele* as used in at least three generations of the Isaac McFadden family of South Carolina: Isaac's daughter, Elizabeth Steele McFadden (circa 1804); grandchildren Polly Steele McFadden, Elizabeth Steele McFadden, William Steele McFadden, and Isaac Steele Patton; and great-granddaughter Emma Steel Dunlop. The source of this middle name is Isaac's first wife, Elizabeth Steele (1763), daughter of James and Fanny (Lee) Steele. In these cases, the middle name is not only a clue to ancestry; it *is* ancestry. We know why it was used.

On the other hand, the name *Ewing* also appears in Isaac's family, with its origin obscured. Isaac and his first wife gave two children the same middle name: eldest son James Ewing McFadden (1784) and second daughter Catherine Ewing McFadden (1798). This daughter named her first son William Ewing Patton, and one of her granddaughters was named for her, Kate Ewing Coleman. Grandsons of Isaac included Samuel Ewing McFadden and Isaac Ewing McFadden. A lady thought to be Isaac's sister, Mary, and her husband, Samuel McKinney, had a son Ewin(g) McKinney and a grandson Ewin. Why did *Ewing* persist in several lines of the McFadden family? Because the name exists in the lines of Isaac and his supposed sister Mary, it is thought to have originated in the McFadden side of the family rather than his wife's Steele family. Perhaps we will never know for sure, but we do know there was a reason for using it. Only through the study of collateral lines and clusters of children in each generation are we even aware of the persistence of the name, which may someday lead to discovery of another ancestor's identity.

Many families use surnames as middle names that may or may not prove to be ancestral, but the genealogist must be aware of them and pursue them. Why did Nathan and Elizabeth (Garner) Brelsford name their second son Hiram *Hawkins* Brelsford (1802)? Why did Richard and Lucy Phillips name a son Peter *Talbot* Phillips (1769) and a daughter Elizabeth *Tolbert/Talbot* Phillips? Where did Henry *Brantley* Brown (circa 1800-1805) get his middle name? Is son *Yancey* Holmes' name a clue to the middle initial of his mother, Matilda Y. (nee Brown) Holmes?

It has often been said that American parents and their British Isles cousins have had a tendency to name eldest sons for paternal grandfathers, second sons for maternal grandfathers, and later sons for their father and uncles. I decided to test the hypothesis. My sampling was 750 eldest sons, born in the American colonies or United States between 1645 and my cut-off date of 1910. They were from mostly British Isles families, with some French and German backgrounds mixed in. Their birthplaces and residences ranged up and down the Atlantic seaboard from Massachusetts to South Carolina and inland across the lower South, through Kentucky and Tennessee, into the Ohio and Mississippi valleys, and into Iowa and Texas. For each eldest son, I had the name of his father and paternal grandfather.

I found that 27 percent (204 eldest sons) were given

either one or both names of the paternal grandfather. Just under 18 percent (132) carried one or both names of the father. These two categories overlap slightly when the eldest son is named for both father and grandfather or is the third to have the identical name. Few of the maternal grandfathers' names were identified in the sources, but nearly 6 percent of the eldest sons in the sample could be identified as having one or two names of the maternal grandfather, most often his surname. In many of the families, a son other than the eldest received the father's or paternal grandfa-ther's name. Of course, about half the eldest sons in the sampling were given neither a grandfather's nor the father's name.

These findings alert us to the *possibility* that the eldest son is named for the paternal grandfather but remind us that the practice was certainly not standardized. In searching for the father's father, the name of the eldest son *could be* a lead. In looking for the mother's maiden name or her father's name, the name of her eldest son *could be* a clue. In neither case is it assured.

CHAPTER TWO

Federal Census Records

Censuses can be taken for many reasons. In the case of the federal censuses, the primary motivation was, and is, counting the total population every ten years to determine representation in the House of Representatives. From the first census in 1790 to 1840, only heads of household were named, and family members were listed in age brackets. Beginning in 1850, every person in the house was listed by name, age, sex, race, birthplace, and occupation. If you have worked with these general population schedules, you already know that each succeeding census requested more detailed information from the populace. The particulars are listed in Appendix F.

This information makes the federal census one of the most useful and rewarding genealogical tools. In fact, after using family sources, many people turn to the census to begin their search of public records. In all years, the census contains valuable clues and information. A sizable portion of this data lies beyond the basic census in the supplemental schedules. Although some of these are not really genealogical, they are certainly historical and deserve attention.

To form the most complete picture of the family you are searching, it is advisable to look for family members in *each* census taken during their lifetimes. *Family* means the parents and children in a direct lineage as well as the collateral lines of brothers, sisters, and cousins in each generation, and even the families of spouses. The more you learn about this extended family, the more you are likely to learn about the direct lineage on which you are working. In cases where courthouse or archives fires have destroyed original records, the census data on a specific family may be the best or the only readily available source for a given time period. Of course, the genealogist must not only gather the information but must sort, thoroughly study, and carefully evaluate the findings before drawing conclusions. In many cases, corroborating evidence needs to be drawn from whatever other sources can be found.

Like nearly all sources, census records contain errors and omissions and therefore call for caution in their use. However, the benefits of using them far outweigh the drawbacks. The question for genealogists, then, is where to find and use these materials. This chapter makes an effort to answer the question by considering three areas: (1) where you can use the material in either original or printed form or on microfilm; (2) where you can purchase copies; and (3) from whom you can rent copies on interlibrary loan. This particular part of the chapter has been compiled with the assistance of the institutions listed.

CENSUS DAY

In each census year, one day was designated as census day. The information given to the census taker was to be correct as of that day, which was not necessarily the day that the enumeration was actually recorded at each house. Persons who died after census day were to be included because they were alive on census day. Babies born after census were to be omitted because they were not yet members of the household on census day. Of course, these instructions were not always followed to the letter, but we must be aware of them and begin our study of the information as if they were followed. We need not assume that an entry contains errors or omissions before we have studied it and compared it with data from other sources. However, it is helpful to note the date of the actual enumeration when it is given at the top of the page. It does show each family as residents of a given place on *that* day and may help you interpret the information furnished in the report.

How can you know whether a given family was observing the "census-day rule"? You perhaps cannot know for certain, but these reports on infants illustrate how the rule works. In 1870, census day was June 1.

In Milam County, Texas, enumerated in August, the Ben Duckworth family reported a son Benjamin F., Junior, age 1/12, or one month. Because this census asked for the month of birth if born within the year, we get the information that this baby was born in April. Thus, we realize that the family was following the census-day rule. The baby was not yet two months old on June 1. Likewise, in 1900 the Joseph M. Martin family of Smith County, Mississippi, reported son, Clifton Martin, age five months, and gave his birth as December 1899. We know that the baby had not yet reached six months of age by June 1. Because these families followed the census-day rule in part of their interview, one would hope that they reported the rest of their information with the same care and accuracy.

The searcher's curiosity, however, is naturally aroused in the case of the James Blakeney family of Tippah County, Mississippi, who talked to the enumerator on 26 October 1850 and reported the youngest member of the family, Nancy C., age 1/365. Was she born on October 25 or on May 31? The census alone does not answer the question but considerably narrows the choices.

Of course, it was likely the enumerators who had to explain the rules to the families. The St. Joseph County, Michigan, enumerator in 1830 was Elias Taylor, who seemed to take his job seriously. He wanted to include all those who fell within his jurisdiction but did not want to count anyone who might have been reported in a former place of residence. Thus, on the first page of his county census, he marked five families with an asterisk. On the last page he explained: "Those families marked thus * are such as were mooving (*sic*) on the 1st day of June and could not as they verily believed be taken [enumerated] else where."

Census Day 1790-1960

1790, 1800, 1810, 1820. First Monday in August
1830, 1840, 1850, 1860,
1870, 1880, 1890, 1900. June 1
1880 Indian Schedule.   October 1
1910.   April 15
1920.   January 1
1930, 1940, 1950, 1960. April 1

1790 FEDERAL CENSUS AND SUBSTITUTES

The original purpose of the federal census, of course, was to count the population to determine each state's representation in the House of Representatives. The first federal census in 1790 went only slightly beyond that scope to distinguish between males over and under 16, females, other free persons, and slaves, and to count dwellings, but the information gathered was not uniform in all states. Although some of those first schedules have been lost over the years, eleven of them are extant, published, and indexed: Connecticut, Maine (although Maine was then still part of Massachusetts), Maryland (except Allegany, Calvert, and Somerset counties), Massachusetts, New Hampshire, New York, North Carolina (except Caswell, Granville, and Orange counties), Pennsylvania, Rhode Island, South Carolina, and Vermont.

Much debate takes place over the definition of a census and the use of other kinds of records to create a substitute when an original is destroyed. Understandably, some argue that a census is a census and nothing else substitutes for it, for lists of heads of household cannot provide the missing information on family members and their ages that the original census may have given. Others acknowledge that a lost census cannot be actually duplicated from noncensus sources but try to identify as many as possible of the heads of household of a community at a given time. This information in itself can be valuable even if it is not complete. For myself, because I prefer to have a little information rather than none, I appreciate the substitutes that are available and will call them substitutes, not censuses. The Texas researcher Gifford E. White has provided a compromise in his book, *1830 Citizens of Texas* (Austin, TX: Eakin Press, 1983). He includes some actual census material as well as evidence from the other sources to create a body of information about who was in the area in that year, but he does not call it a *census*.

With the 1790 federal census, it may be a little easier to accept substitutes, since the original census provided little information about family members and reports varied somewhat from place to place. Indeed, substitute schedules have been compiled for some of the lost records.

North Carolina. Tax lists for Caswell, Granville, and Orange counties were published with the 1790 census schedules, which the Government Printing Office issued in 1908. Period tax lists for Caswell (1777, 1780, 1784) and Orange (1784-1793) have also been published by T.L.C. Genealogy Books of Miami, Florida. (See appendix for address.)

Maryland. Helping to offset the loss of its 1790 census, Somerset County, established in 1666, has a number of county records, including wills and estate records, land and marriage records, a 1783 tax list, and the 1778 oaths of fidelity to Maryland. These oaths were published by Richard S. Uhrbrock in the *National Genealogical Society Quarterly*, Vol. 59 (1971), p 103-104. Allegany County, created in 1789 from Washington County, has records from its early years, some beginning in 1791 or 1792. Washington County records may also aid in an Allegany County search. For Calvert County, which dates from 1654, only a few eighteenth-century records still exist, due to a courthouse fire in 1882. Records such as the partial 1783 tax list or the oaths of fidelity of 1778 may be the best substitute available.

Delaware. To compile *The Reconstructed Seventeen Ninety Census of Delaware* (Arlington, VA: National Genealogical Society, 1954), Leon De Valinger, Jr., used tax lists, although these show only property owners.

Georgia. *The Reconstructed 1790 Census of Georgia: Substitutes for Georgia's Lost 1790 Census*, by Marie DeLamar and Elisabeth Rothstein (Baltimore: Genealogical Publishing Company, 1989 reprint of 1976 edition) includes names from a number of sources, including wills, deeds, tax records, court minutes, voter lists, newspapers, and jury lists in an attempt to identify more people.

New Jersey. *New Jersey in 1793: An Abstract Index to the 1793 Militia Census of the State of New Jersey* (James S. Norton, abstracter, Salt Lake City: Institute of Family Research, 1973) serves as one substitute source for that state.

Tennessee. Tennessee was part of North Carolina until May 1790, when it was organized as the Southwest Territory. Although its 1790 census is lost, various sources are available to help searchers identify early Tennessee residents of the 1790 period:

1. *Index to Early Tennessee Tax Lists* (Byron and Barbara Sistler, compilers and publishers, Nashville, Tennessee). The tax lists included span the years from 1783 to 1825, but not all counties have existing lists from all those years.

2. *Early Tennessee Tax Lists* (Mary Barnett Curtis, compiler, Ft. Worth, Texas: Arrow Printing Co., 1964) contains tax lists for twenty-two East Tennessee counties for which no census exists before 1830. The lists are alphabetical by county, with no master index.

3. *Census of the Cumberland Settlements, 1770-1790: Davidson, Sumner, and Tennessee Counties* (Richard C. Fulcher, comp., Baltimore: Genealogical

Publishing Company, 1987). This record is compiled from deed and land records, court minutes, marriage records, wills and inventories, tax rolls, territorial papers, newspapers, and other sources from these early middle Tennessee counties.

4. *Territorial Papers of the United States*, Volume IV, pages 431-442, lists appointments by Governor Blount between October and December 1790, for militia officers, sheriffs and constables, justices of the peace, civil officers, and attorneys licensed to practice law in the territory. These and other such documents identify some of the heads of household in the territory during the census year.

5. *The Commission Book of Governor John Sevier, 1796-1801*, (Nashville: Tennessee Historical Commission, 1957). This includes civil and military appointments and licenses, with an index.

6. *Tennessee Marriages, Early to 1800* (Bountiful, UT: Precision Indexing, 1990) is alphabetical by brides and grooms and gives the marriage date and county in which it is recorded.

Kentucky. Kentucky was part of Virginia until July 1790, and the census enumeration began in August. Although Kentucky was not yet a state, it was a separate district from Virginia when the census was taken. *The First Census of Kentucky 1790*, a substitute compiled by Charles B. Heinemann (Baltimore: Genealogical Publishing Company, 1981 reprint), used tax lists of Kentucky counties existing at the time of the 1790 census: Bourbon, Fayette, Jefferson, Lincoln, Madison, Mason, Mercer, Nelson, and Woodford. However, these are not necessarily 1790 lists. Another Kentucky source is *The 1787 Census of Virginia* (Netti Schreiner-Yantis and Florene Speakman Love, compilers, Springfield, VA: Genealogical Books in Print, 1987, 3 vols.). Although made from tax lists, these volumes contain more information than some of the 1790 census returns because this particular tax enumeration was to name all free males over 21, not just heads of household. The 1787 Kentucky counties of Bourbon, Fayette, Lincoln, Madison, Nelson, and part of Mercer are included in these Virginia returns. To try to fill in the blanks left by the loss of the Jefferson and part of the Mercer County lists, the compilers added names from other Mercer County records and used 1789 tax lists from Mercer and Jefferson counties. (See further discussion below.)

Virginia and West Virginia. The Virginia substitute schedule published by the Census Bureau (Washington, D.C.: 1908) was compiled from state census enumerations of 1782-1785, housed in the state library. These records included thirty-nine counties:

Albemarle	Middlesex
Amelia	Monongalia (WV)
Amherst	Nansemond
Charlotte	New Kent
Chesterfield	Norfolk
Cumberland	Northumberland
Essex	Orange
Fairfax	Pittsylvania
Fluvanna	Powhatan
Frederick	Prince Edward
Gloucester	Princess Anne
Greenbrier (WV)	Richmond
Greensville	Rockingham
Halifax	Shenandoah
Hampshire (WV)	Stafford
Hanover	Surry
Harrison (WV)	Sussex
Isle of Wight	Warwick
Lancaster	Williamsburg town
Mecklenburg	

Forty counties were missing from this compilation. *Virginia Tax Payers, 1782-1787: Other Than Those Published by the United States Census Bureau* (Augusta B. Fothergill and John Mark Naugle, comp., Baltimore: Genealogical Publishing Company, 1978) makes up for many of those omissions, using personal property tax lists for the following counties:

Accomack	James City
Augusta	King George
Bedford	King and Queen
Berkeley (WV)	King William
Botetourt	Lincoln (KY)
Brunswick	Loudon
Buckingham	Louisa
Campbell	Lunenburg
Caroline	Montgomery
Charles City	Northampton
Culpepper	Prince George
Dinwiddie	Prince William
Elizabeth City	Rockbridge
Fauquier	Southampton
Fayette (KY)	Spotsylvania
Goochland	Washington
Hardy (WV)	Westmoreland
Henrico	York
Henry	

Franklin and Russell counties, formed in 1785, are not included in these lists, but searchers should consult the lists of the parent counties of Bedford-Henry-Patrick (for Franklin) and Washington (for Russell). Ohio county, in present West Virginia, was formed in 1776 and has early land and probate records, which may help make up for the loss of 1790 census information. The counties of Pendleton and Randolph, also now in West Virginia, were formed in 1787; lists for their parent counties may reveal many of their residents: Augusta, Hardy, and Rockingham for Pendleton County; and Harrison, for Randolph County. A number of these Virginia and West Virginia counties have early records of other kinds, which can help locate and identify ancestors.

These two books cover most of the states of Virginia and present West Virginia but concentrate on the earlier dates of 1782-1785. Since Kentucky and Virginia were focal points of migration in the years before and after the Revolutionary War, thousands of people moved to, from, and through those regions every year. *The 1787 Census of Virginia* (Netti Schreiner-Yantis and Florene Speakman Love, compilers, Springfield, VA: Genealogical Books in Print, 1987, 2 vols.), therefore, is a major source of information, if not a true census, from a very fluid population area. In one way, the tax lists that form these volumes are a better census than the 1790 census; they name not only heads of household but also other white men over 21.

For example, my ancestor Elliott Coleman of Cumberland County, Virginia, was listed just below William Coleman, to whom his tax was charged.[1] This William is likely his father, rather than his brother by the same name. Elliott was apparently still living at home; he did not marry until two years later. In addition, the report indicates no young men in William's household between 16 and 21. The study of other records has suggested that Elliott was 22 at this time. In some of the lists, white males between 16 and 21 were named, not just listed by number. Females are excluded from the lists unless they were heads of household, in which case they were not subject to taxes. The report indicates that William Coleman's taxable property included seven slaves over 16 years of age, eight slaves under 16, eight horses and/or mules, and twenty-eight head of cattle. Nearby were his brothers Parmenas and Julielmus (usually Gulielmus). A Henry Coleman was apparently living with Samuel Allen, to whom his tax was charged. In some cases, though probably not this one, a young man living with a family of a different surname could provide a clue to a son-in-law relationship, a young man married to one of the daughters of the household.

These two volumes of 1787 tax lists include all the counties and towns listed above, in addition to the following:

Alexandria	Nelson (KY)
Bourbon (KY)	Ohio (WV)
Franklin	Petersburg town
Fredericksburg town	Randolph (WV)
Jefferson (KY)	Richmond city
Madison (KY)	Winchester city
Mercer (KY)	

Northwest Territory. The Northwest Ordinance of July 1787 set in place the procedures for governing the territory north of the Ohio River and became the model for the creation of new states. The states of Ohio, Indiana, Illinois, Wisconsin, and Michigan eventually came from this Northwest Territory. In 1790 the area was sparsely settled, with most inhabitants in Washington, Marietta, and Hamilton (Cincinnati) counties, Point Garrison, and Ft. Harmar in Ohio territory; Kaskaskia, Prairie du Pont, and Cahokia in the Illinois territory; Petite Cote in Michigan; Knox County in Indiana territory. Volumes II and III of the *Territorial Papers of the United States* contain some census returns and other useful lists of early inhabitants. (See chapter three for more discussion of the *Territorial Papers*).

Volume II
p 252-253, a May 1790 petition from 46 inhabitants of the Illinois country.
p 253-257, lands claimed by 42 Kaskaskia inhabitants from governor's Feb. 1791 report.
p 257-258, Kaskaskia inhabitants before and after 1783.
p 259, census of Cahokia, 1790-91 (heads of household).
p 260-261, census of Prairie du Pont, 1790-91 (heads of household).
p 263ff, 100+ individuals with land claims in the District of Cahokia on or before 1783.
p 278-279, inhabitants of Prairie du Rocher, 1790.
p 281-282, inhabitants of Kaskaskia, Cahokia, and Prairie du Rocher, 1790.
p 285-287, heads of family of Post Vincennes in Knox County, 1783.

p 422, a petition of about 120 French inhabitants of Gallipolis, 1792.
p 470, a 1793 estimate of the numbers of people in the settlements of the whole Territory.

Volume III (See this volume for dates on either side of 1790.)
p 291-293, civil and militia appointments for Washington County (Ohio), December 1789.
p 295, civil and militia appointments for Hamilton County (Ohio), January 1790.
p 304-305, civil and militia appointments for St. Clair County (Illinois), April 1790.
p 333, militia orders, Hamilton and Washington counties, Ohio, September-December 1790.

Ancestral Genealogical Endexing Schedules (AGES) in Salt Lake City has published an index to some of these and other records, which constitutes a 1790 substitute census of the area. In addition, the *Territorial Papers* themselves are well indexed at the end of each volume.

The scattered residents of the Indian lands that became Alabama and Mississippi were not covered by the 1790 census. Some of the land was still claimed by Georgia but was not organized into counties of the state of Georgia. Therefore, any American residents in those Indian lands are probably not included in the substitute for the 1790 Georgia census. Land west of the Mississippi, as well as Florida, Spanish West Florida, and eastern Louisiana, were, of course, not yet parts of the United States; other sources have to be consulted for evidence of 1790 residents.

1820 AND 1832 CENSUSES OF MANUFACTURERS

In 1820 Congress authorized a census of manufacturers. Although it was meant to be a survey of those who made more than $500 a year, the reports actually include many smaller operations. The returns are microfilmed on National Archives series M279. They are not complete, but individuals making more than $500 annually are indexed.

The census asked for information on raw materials, employees, machinery, expenses, kinds of articles made and their market value. David Patton of Shelbyville, Bedford County, Tennessee, was a cabinet "workman," who used walnut, cherry, and poplar planks to make bureaus, "cabboards," and tables of all kinds with a set of cabinet tools that cost him about $100.

He cleared about $200 annually and remarked, "This is tolerable good business but sales is not fast." Hatter Jessy Evans of Shelbyville employed five men and paid out about $200 in wages annually. (Was he using some apprentice or slave labor?) His fur hats had a market value of up to $10, and wool ones, $2. He cleared about $670 annually, saying, "This has been a profitable business to me."

A census of manufactures was taken again in 1832 in an effort to determine the effects of foreign competition and tariffs on domestic industry. The returns were published under the title *Documents Relative to the Manufactures in the United States Collected and Transmitted to the House of Representatives in Compliance with a Resolution of January 19, 1832 by the Secretary of the Treasury.* They were originally published in 1833 as House Document 308 (in 2 volumes), of the twenty-second Congress, first session, Serial #222 and #223. (See chapter eight for the Serial Set.) The two volumes were reprinted in 1969 (New York: Burt Franklin, an affiliate of Lenox Hill Publishing and Distributing Corporation). The returns cover the following states, in the order listed:

Vol. I (Serial 222)—Maine, New Hampshire, Vermont, Rhode Island, Connecticut.

Vol. II (Serial 223)—New York, New Jersey, Pennsylvania, Delaware, and Ohio.

The text contains statistics and much information on individual manufacturers. For example, from Hamilton County, Ohio, tanner and currier Henry B. Funk reported that he employed ten men at an average wage of $22 per month. Using mostly domestic raw materials, he manufactured about $18,000 in articles during the year.

1840 REVOLUTIONARY PENSIONERS

The 1840 federal census form included a space to list "Pensioners for Revolutionary or Military Services" and their ages. The column appears on the second page of the schedule after the slave columns. Each of these persons was to be included in the foregoing tally of the household in which he lived, but not all were actually included. A number of these pensioners, such as James Browne (age 91) and John Walker (85) of Wake County, North Carolina, were still the heads of their own households, as one can see from reading the returns. One of these Wake County heads of household was pensioner Jesse Harris (80), a free black man. Other veterans were living with relatives of

the same name, such as William Wood (82) and John Green (88), also of Wake County, who were living with Marcum Wood and Samuel Green.

Still other pensioners were living in households of a different surname, and the genealogist usually hopes that this situation may lead to identifying a married daughter, a sister, or another relative. Examples from Wake County, North Carolina, include Thomas Holland (84), living with Lewis Barkers; Joseph Shaw (83), living with Drury King; and Richard Pipen (86), in the household of Willie Chambles. Each of these veterans was the oldest person listed in the family, and the head of household was considerably younger. The genealogist, therefore, needs to be aware that the head of household, as in these cases, was not always the oldest person in the family. In addition, although these three men do appear in a North Carolina 1840 index listed below, these examples alert the searcher to remember that pensioners who were not heads of household will probably not appear in indexes that cover heads of household only. To find them, the searcher may have to read the entire county where they were thought to be living. Furthermore, those pensioners who were heads of household are not indicated as pensioners in most indexes. As in all the censuses, this one can contain mistakes. In this listing, there may be men listed as pensioners who in fact were not, and other pensioners may be omitted.

Searchers using the 1840 pensioner lists must also remember that these pensioners were not limited to Revolutionary soldiers and sailors. It is clear that Thomas T. Doty (44) and Robert Rains (56) listed as pensioners in Madison County, Alabama, were not Revolutionary veterans. Both were born after the Revolution. Their military service came later. Perhaps their pensions were for disabilities.

In 1841, the government published this Census of Pensioners for Revolutionary and Military Service, which gives the names and ages of pensioners and the heads of household with whom they were living. The Norman Ross Publishing Company of New York City has issued a reprint of this two-hundred-page volume. The Genealogical Publishing Company of Baltimore in 1989 issued a two-in-one volume that includes the census of pensioners and an index. In addition, some indexes to the 1840 heads of household do include pensioners:

1. Alabama. (Betty Drake, comp., originally 1973, available from Reprint Company Publishers.)

For twelve counties formed from the Creek and Cherokee Cessions of the 1830s.

2. Iowa. (Bettylou Headlee, comp., Fullerton, California: Mrs. Beverly Stercula, 1968.) There were six pensioners in Iowa in 1840.
3. Michigan. (Estelle A. McGlynn, comp., ed., Detroit Society for Genealogical Research, Inc., 1977.)
4. Mississippi. (Thomas E. and Berniece D. Coyle, comp., Lewisville, Texas: Coyle Data Co., 1990.)
5. North Carolina. (Gerald M. Petty, comp. and publisher, Columbus, Ohio, 1974.)

SLAVE SCHEDULES

The slave schedules of 1850 and 1860 can be helpful but do not contain a great amount of genealogical information. As sometimes happens in the general population schedules, many pages are faded and difficult to read. The slave owners or their agents are listed, usually by full name, although in some cases women are listed simply as *Mrs.* or *Widow* and their surname. Slaves are listed individually by sex and age. Only in Bowie County, Texas, in 1850 have I seen the slaves listed by name. Infirmities such as blindness, deafness, or idiocy are identified. In Monroe County, Alabama, in 1850, at least seven sets of twins were labeled.

Slave schedules were made for Alabama, Arkansas, Delaware, District of Columbia, Florida, Georgia, Kentucky, Louisiana, Maryland, Mississippi, Missouri, North Carolina, New Jersey (1850 only), South Carolina, Tennessee, Texas, Virginia, and the Indian lands west of Arkansas (1860 only). The 1850 Delaware slave schedule is included at the end of the Sussex County returns, roll 55 of M432 of the National Archives microfilm. The 1850 District of Columbia slave schedule is likewise at the end of the Schedule No. 1 returns, on roll 57 of M432.

No 1850 census was taken for the unorganized territory that became Oklahoma. However, the 1860 general population census for Arkansas included white residents in "Indian lands west of Arkansas," i.e., the nations of the Five Civilized Tribes. The 1860 slave schedule for Arkansas also included slave owners and slaves in these western lands. In the Creek nation were 1,651 slaves, and in the Choctaw nation, 2,298. In the Chickasaw nation were 917 slaves, and in the Cherokee nation, 2,527. A total of 7,393 slaves were enumerated in the Indian nations. Slave owners included whites, Indians, and residents of mixed blood. In the

Creek nation one slave owner was named as "Hope a Negro."

It is interesting to note that in New Jersey in 1850, about 232 slaves were counted in the slave schedule. Only about 35 of those were under the age of 50. The other 197 ranged in age from 50 to 95. The greatest concentration of slaves younger than 50 was in Monmouth County. Throughout the state, most of the individuals above age 50 were the only slave within the household. Of course, free blacks lived throughout the country and are listed in the general population census for 1790 through 1860.

1850-1880 SUPPLEMENTAL SCHEDULES

The four federal enumerations between 1850 and 1880 contain supplemental schedules that provide the family historian with interesting information on agriculture, industry, and society. These are not genealogical in that they do not contain relationships and vital statistics of individuals. However, the schedules are important glimpses into the past that add to our knowledge of how our ancestors lived and of their society.

The **agriculture schedules** contain information for many genealogists since the majority of the population lived in rural areas and a large percentage of those people were farmers. In 1850, the schedule had forty-six columns of questions, including the name of the farm owner or agent; the number of acres both improved and unimproved; cash value of the farm and its implements; cash value and numbers of livestock; and amount and value of produce, crops, and homemade manufactures. The information was to cover the year preceding the enumeration, that is, 1 June 1849 (1859, 1869, 1879) to 1 June 1850 (1860, 1870, but 31 May 1880, as printed on the forms). In 1850, for instance, W.W. Chapman of Washington County, Oregon Territory, owned 2 horses, 45 milch (*sic*) cows, and 2 oxen. During the preceding year, he had grown 100 bushels of Irish potatoes and made 200 pounds of butter. C.A. Welch of the same county valued his 105 acres of improved land at $3,000 and his livestock at $1,300. His stock included 9 horses, 3 cows, 10 oxen, 4 other cattle, 24 sheep, and 15 swine. He reported that he had made 800 pounds of butter and 200 pounds of cheese.

The 1860 agriculture schedule was virtually the same as 1850. The 1870 added a few queries, such as the value of forest products, giving fifty-two columns of categorized information. The 1880 schedule increased to one hundred columns of requested information. Most of the categories remained the same but asked for more detail, including the first questions about poultry and the number of eggs produced in the preceding year. Not all pertinent blanks were always filled out.

The **industry schedules** asked for the same kind of information: name of company or individual; name and value of product made; quantities, kinds, and values of raw materials used; the kinds of motive power or machinery used; and the work force employed and their wages. One illustration from 1850 is William Williams of Polk County, Oregon Territory, who owned a sawmill valued at $1,200. He used water power to mill 2,880 logs valued at $3,500. He employed an average of four men, whose wages cost the owner $100 a month. In 1849, the mill produced 720,000 feet of lumber valued at $28,800. In 1869-1870 in Boise City, Idaho Territory, William Neily made 160 pairs of boots, and his neighbor Peter J. Pefly made 50 saddles.

The 1850 and 1860 schedules were the same. The 1870 form asked for the number of horsepower used, the number and kinds of machines, the number of children or youth employed, the number of months the business operated during that year, and annual wages of employees. The 1880 schedule had inquiries for special classes of manufacturing establishments: boot and shoe factories, cheese and butter factories, flouring and grist mills, salt works, lumber and saw mills, brick yards and tile works, paper mills, coal mines, quarries, and agriculture implement works. The questions asked for capital invested, number and daily wages of employees, length of operation or season, and specific information peculiar to each of the industries.

The 1880 manufacturing schedule shows W.J. Leatherwood of Baker County, Oregon, who had $3,000 in capital invested in a saw mill that worked eight months a year. He paid $2.50 a day wages for ordinary laborers (as opposed to skilled labor), who worked eight hours a day in winter and spring, ten hours a day in summer and fall. C.W. Bonham, a blacksmith of the same county, put in ten-hour days twelve months a year. When he had helpers, he paid $1.50 a day for ordinary labor and $3.50 for skilled.

The **social statistics schedules** from these same census years do not name individuals but give historically pertinent information about each town, township, ward, or parish in the counties. The statistics include the number and kinds of schools, number of pupils and faculty members, the number and kinds of libraries, the nature and circulation of newspapers and periodicals, the seating capacity of churches and other places of worship, the number of paupers of U.S. and foreign birth, and expenditures for their support, and information on wages. The 1850 statistics tell us that in Hillsborough County, Florida, the Indian corn crop that year was cut in half by drought. The Idaho 1870 statistics inform us that a carpenter in Ada County could make $6 a day without board, but at Rocky Bar in Alturas County, he could make $8 a day. Workers who received board from their employers usually earned $10 to $15 a week less than those paid without board.

These supplemental schedules are available for use in many state libraries, archives, and historical societies, or large public and university libraries with genealogy collections. For purchase contact the National Archives, Scholarly Resources, the American Genealogical Lending Library, or some state or university archives marked "P" on the chart at the end of this chapter. For interlibrary loan consult state libraries, archives, or societies marked "ILL" on the chart at the end of the chapter, the Family History Library in Salt Lake City (hereafter FHL), or the American Genealogical Lending Library (hereafter AGLL). Duke University (Durham, North Carolina) has copies for loan or purchase for a number of Southern states.

A *Report on the Social Statistics of Cities* (George E. Waring, Jr., comp.) was published by the Government Printing Office in 1886, with information gathered in the 1880 census. These descriptions of 222 cities give details about location, history, and climate; transportation, streets, and navigation; markets, commerce, manufacturing, institutions, parks and amusement places; burial and cemeteries, epidemics, pesthouses, and prevention and treatment of infectious diseases; street cleaning, police and fire departments, sewage and garbage departments, drinking water, and recording of births, disease, and deaths. Not all cities reported on all subjects, but researchers can gain valuable historical information on each city. The report can be found in libraries that have the U.S. Serial Set: House Miscellaneous Document 42, part 18 (47-2) serial 2148 (New England and Middle States — New York, New Jersey, Pennsylvania, and Delaware); House Miscellaneous Document 42, part 19 (47-2) serial 2149 (Southern and Western states and territories); each volume ends with an index. Most libraries that are government documents depositories have the Serial Set.

(See chapter eight for more discussion of the Serial Set.)

1850-1880 MORTALITY SCHEDULES

The mortality schedules provide genealogical information on persons who died between 1 June 1849 (1859, 1869, 1879) and 1 June 1850 (1860, 1870, but 31 May 1880) — or during the year preceding the census enumeration. The 1850 and 1860 schedules asked for name, age, sex, race/color, free or slave status, marital status, birthplace, month of death, occupation, cause of death, and the number of days the person was ill. Note that slaves were named in these schedules, but there is no surname, and the slave owner's name is not specified. If a slave owner reported a death in his own family and any deaths among his slaves at the same time, the deceased persons could be listed on consecutive lines of the schedule page. Thus, the name just before or perhaps just after a slave's name could be a clue to the identification of the farm or plantation where the slave lived.

The 1870 schedules also asked if the mother or father of the deceased were of foreign birth. In addition, the 1880 form asked how long the person had been a resident of the county, where the causal disease or condition was contracted, and the name of the attending physician. Of course, not all the blanks were always filled in, but each entry provides some information.

Persons on the mortality schedule were not to be included in the general population schedule, which was to include only *living* persons in the household on census day. However, this instruction must have been confusing to some enumerators or families. One example is the two sons of Napoleon and Laura (Myer) Shelby of Clarke County, Mississippi, who were listed in the 1880 census, then crossed out with *dead* written beside both names. The mortality schedule shows each of the children: three-year-old Charles who died in June (no year indicated) and one-year-old Verne who died in April (1880). Technically, Charles should have been listed on the mortality schedule only if he died in June 1879, and, in that case, not at all on the population schedule. Since he appears on both lists, it may be that he died in June 1880, between June 1 and the date of the enumerator's visit.

It is interesting to observe the various terms used to list cause of death, such as "congestion of the brain" or "softening of the brain." Consider the entry for Hamburg native Charles Quail, a married 32-year-old

Clarke County, Washington, saloon keeper who died in May 1860, after two and one-fourth months of illness. The cause of death was "mortification." The enumerator's remarks explain that his wounds received during the Indian wars were the final "mortifying cause" of death. In these years, common causes of death were consumption, pneumonia, diarrhea and related conditions, fevers of various kinds (typhoid, malaria, etc.), drowning and accidental wounds, childbirth, and various conditions thought to be related to the heart. Occasionally, the searcher can identify epidemics, such as occurred in McLennan County, Texas, in 1870 when 39 children and 11 adults died of measles. The enumerator in Jasper County, Mississippi, reported that most of the deaths in his county in 1850 resulted from scarlet fever.

Benjamin Thigpen was an assistant marshal who took his job of enumeration seriously. He added these remarks to the mortality schedule of Jasper County, Mississippi, in 1860:

> *The most Fatal and prevailing Diseases are Typhoid Fever and Pneumonia the former mostly in the autumn and fall the latter in winter and spring. The Typhoid fever seems to prevail mostly in the hill country rather than in the Pararie (sic) and swamp lands. It Generally attacks Adult persons between the ages of fifteen and forty-five years and in (sic) a good degree fatal. The diseases prevailing mostly among children are worms and measles . . . Causes of Typhoid Fever said to be Atmospheric and that of Pneumonia the sudden changes pertaining to the Climate. The Character of the water in the Pararie (sic) soil is lime and in the Hills freestone. The nature of the soil is principly (sic) lime and Lime is its only natural Fertilizer. Some portion however is Sandy. The Rocks are Flint Pebbles and some small Lime Rocks. The Natural Growth is Pine Oak Hickory Blackjack in the hill lands and in the swamps sweet and Black Gums Poplar Beech magnolia Ash &c &c. Springs late and cool. A Disease called Black Tonge (sic) prevailed among the cattle & deer to an alarming extent a part of the year ending June the 1st 1860 without any known Local or stensible cause.*

Enumerators also added remarks about crops and productions in their county and about particular cases, which they reported in the schedule. Erastus B. Johnson of Choctaw County, Mississippi, added a note to the 1870 report of the death of Bazel Willson, a 68-year-old farmer. The comment may indicate particular friendship with and respect for the deceased or may have been the request of the family member who gave the information: "He is not dead but sleeping in Jesus."

Many of the original mortality schedules are stored at the National Archives or in institutions of the state to which they pertain. Microfilm copies are available for use in many of the larger public and university libraries and special libraries, such as the Daughters of the American Revolution in Arlington, Virginia. Many of the state libraries, archives, or historical societies have these schedules for their own state and neighboring states; from some of these institutions, you can also purchase or rent microfilm copies. Microfilm for purchase is available from the National Archives, Scholarly Resources, and the AGLL. For interlibrary loan, contact the AGLL and the FHL (through its nationwide branches). A number of the schedules have been printed. Consult the chart at the end of this chapter for more specific information.

1880 DEFECTIVE, DEPENDENT, DELINQUENT SCHEDULES

In 1880, the census schedules included a special enumeration of people who were residents of various asylums, such as prisons or poorhouses, or who had various afflictions that made them dependent on others for support, such as deaf-mutes, homeless children, the indigent, the insane, or the blind. The purpose of this special schedule was to identify people in these categories and to learn more specifically about their situation. One William Douglas lived in Middleton in Ada County, Idaho. He was totally blind, yet partly self-supporting, and had lived for six years in an institution for the blind in Newton, Iowa, from which he was released in 1876. In Whiteville, Hardeman County, Tennessee, the names of Rufus Green and Calvin Hall were recorded on the schedule of "insane" persons. Before the schedules were sent off, Dr. A.P. Waddell, M.D., scratched out the names and wrote, "I have known Rufus Green and Cal Hall for many years—they are both colored and are both of sound mind." In the same county, Ben Oppenheimer of Bolivar had been deaf since the age of three, due to scarlet fever. He had lived for three years at the Kentucky State Mute Asylum, from which he was discharged in 1855. About

William Burnette, listed as insane, the enumerator J.R. Jones of Hardeman County wrote,

I cannot learn any thing in reference to the above named person only that he was of sound mind up to the Shiloh Battle in April 1862 but soon after said battle he became insane and has been so ever since. He is in good health and lives with his brother George L. Burnette. He is a married man but his wife left him after he became insane. No physician has ever examined him; it is believed that he was so frightened that he became insane.

These DDD schedules were made in most states. Even in the states where they were not made or no longer exist, some of the information is available in the regular population schedules, from which the DDD schedules were taken. Microfilm copies are available from many of the same places as the mortality and supplemental schedules. Consult the chart at the end of this chapter for more specific information on where you can use, purchase, or rent these schedules.

SOUNDEX

Beginning with the 1880 census, many census records have been indexed using the Soundex coding system, which sorts names by their sounds. Soundex is usually available as microfilm of the original card file, and its value is enormous. It gives not only the members of the household and their ages, but the family's location on the census (supervisor's district, enumeration district, sheet number, line number). This tool is especially valuable when you do not know where a particular family was living. The film is arranged by state, then alphabetically by the first letter of the surname, then numerically by Soundex code: A000, A100, A106, A235, A356, and so forth. Within each code, given names are alphabetical. If several people have the same name, they are listed in the alphabetical order of birthplace, i.e., state or country. The 1880 Soundex is incomplete in that it lists only people who had children under ten years of age in their household.

The Soundex code is based on the sound of the name, and letters with similar sounds are given the same code. Begin with the initial letter of the surname and set it aside as the first part of the code. Strike out all vowels (*a, e, i, o, u*) and *y, w,* and *h*. Change the remaining letters into numbers according to the chart below. Double letters, or two letters with the same code, are coded as only one digit. If you run out of key letters before you have a three-digit code, simply add zeros. If you complete a three-digit code before you have gone through the entire name, disregard the remaining letters.

Code Number	Key Letters
1	b, p, f, v
2	c, s, k, g, j, q, x, z
3	d, t
4	l
5	m, n
6	r

Examples of Soundex Coding

HUGHES
H 2   2   0
H220 is the code.

ADCOCK
A 3 2   2
A322 is the code.

SCHMIDT
S   5   3   0
S530 is the code.

MACKAY
M 2   0 0
M200 is the code.

WILLOUGHBY
W 4   2   1
W421 is the code.

LEA (or LEE)
L   000
L000 is the code.

Of course, names are sometimes spelled in different ways in public records or misread when being indexed. It may be necessary to search several Soundex codes before you find the family you want. One example is *Blakeney*, which is sometimes recorded as *Blakeley*, or even *Blakey*. If the code B425 (Blakeney) does not contain the family for whom you are searching, you may have to try B424 or B420. Closely related codes are sometimes mixed together on the microfilm, especially when each contains relatively few names.

Sometimes, prefixes to names, such as *van, de, de la, and le*, are omitted in coding. However, I have found the name DelHomme under D450 and have not had to search under *H*. Native American and Chinese names may be coded under the first word of the name or the name that appears last, even though it may not be the actual surname. To find these households, you may have to check various possibilities.

Those members of religious orders whose names begin with *Sister* or *Brother* will be indexed under S236 and B636, with *Sister* and *Brother* considered their surnames for indexing purposes. In the Soundex lists, these persons are not always in alphabetical order. For example, the 1900 Louisiana Soundex for S236 lists Sister Roserio first, before the names beginning with *A*. In addition, the top of this list includes three ladies whose names were not designated *Sister* but whose

relationship was given as Sister of Charity, Sacred Heart Convent, St. James Parish. Their names were given as A. Higgins, A. Schernaildre, and A. Stanard; yet they were coded under S236. Several professors at the St. Vincent Academy in Baton Rouge were listed separately under B636: *Brother* Adelard, *Brother* David, and *Brother* Justinian. However, Brother Jerome of Alexandria, Rapides Parish, was named as head of household with Brothers Humbert, Theodore, and Calestine living in the house. The latter three were *not* entered in the Soundex under their own names. The inconsistencies are clear, but the researcher seeking these people has basically one Soundex code with which to begin. Of course, members of religious orders do not normally retain the family surnames under which they were born; therefore, these names should not be expected in the census or Soundex. In cases where several members of the same religious house have the same given name, the searcher may be able to distinguish among them by the birthdates given in the census report.

The Soundex is available for 1880, 1900, and 1920 census schedules; however, the 1910 census is only partially Soundexed. Refer to the chart for Soundex availability for 1910. The 1910 Soundex also includes separate rolls of microfilm for certain cities: Alabama—Birmingham, Mobile, Montgomery; Georgia—Atlanta, Augusta, Macon, Savannah; Louisiana—(miracode) New Orleans, Shreveport; and Tennessee—Chattanooga, Knoxville, Memphis, Nashville. In addition, part of the 1880 Illinois Soundex was omitted in the filming. Those names in the "O200-O240" codes have been privately printed by Nancy G. Frederick of Evanston, Illinois.

To find availability and film numbers of specific census and Soundex rolls for military schedules and particular cities and counties in the general population schedules, refer to the booklets published by the National Archives Trust Fund Board. One covers 1790-1890. The 1900, 1910, and 1920 censuses each has its own booklet. These publications are available from the National Archives and can be found in most libraries with census collections.

1910 Soundex Availability

Soundex Available for

Alabama	South Carolina
Georgia	Tennessee
Louisiana	Texas
Mississippi	

(Soundex gives enumeration district and page number.)

Miracode Available for

Arkansas	Missouri
California	North Carolina
Florida	Ohio
Illinois	Oklahoma
Kansas	Pennsylvania
Kentucky	Virginia
Michigan	West Virginia

(Miracode gives enumeration district and family [visitation] number.) Miracode uses the same coding system as Soundex.

No Indexing Available For

Alaska	Nebraska
Arizona	Nevada
Colorado	New Hampshire
Connecticut	New Jersey
Delaware	New Mexico
District of Columbia	New York
Hawaii	North Dakota
Idaho	Oregon
Indiana	Puerto Rico
Iowa	Rhode Island
Maine	South Dakota
Maryland	Utah
Massachusetts	Vermont
Military Installations	Washington
Minnesota	Wisconsin
Montana	Wyoming

1885 CENSUS

In 1885 the federal government offered to help pay for a census for any state that wanted to take one between the decennial censuses. The states that accepted the offer were Colorado, the Dakotas (still one territory), Florida, Nebraska, and New Mexico Territory. These included population schedules very much like the 1880 enumerations, with agriculture, industry, and mortality schedules as well. Film of these may be purchased from the National Archives or Scholarly Resources. Film numbers are Colorado-M158, Florida-M845, Nebraska-M532, New Mexico Territory-M846. Schedules are available for use at the archives or historical society of each of these states. The North Dakota part of the territorial census is available on microfilm on interlibrary loan from the Historical Society in Bismarck. The South Dakota originals of the territorial census, with the agriculture and mortality schedules,

are at the state archives, from which microfilm copies are available on interlibrary loan. The AGLL rents or sells microfilm of at least the Colorado, Florida, and Nebraska schedules. The FHL also rents the microfilm for Colorado, Florida, Nebraska, New Mexico, and the partial South Dakota portion of the Dakota Territorial schedules.

1890 CENSUS

Most of the 1890 census was destroyed by fire. However, the surviving pages housed in the National Archives are indexed on two rolls of microfilm, National Archives code M496: roll 1 — surnames A-J and roll 2 — surnames K-Z. The fragments themselves use parts of three rolls of microfilm, National Archives code M407: roll 1 — Alabama, roll 2 — Washington, D.C., and roll 3 — the rest of the country. The extent of the records is summarized in the following chart. Apart from the records in the National Archives, the Georgia Archives has three rolls of microfilm, with a fourth in preparation, of the copy of the Washington County, Georgia, schedule, which that county purchased from the government before the fire. The film cannot be ordered on interlibrary loan from that repository, but may be purchased at $20 per roll. At this writing, the fourth volume is being indexed prior to filming. The first three rolls can be rented from the FHL.

1890 Census — Surviving Population Schedules

ALABAMA — Perry County, about three-fourths roll of microfilm, the largest unit surviving.

DISTRICT OF COLUMBIA — about one-half roll of microfilm.

GEORGIA — Columbus in Muscogee County: only the households of James C. Denton and Catherine Davis. Washington County 1890 census available at the Georgia Archives.

ILLINOIS — Mound Township including Grant Village, in McDonough County: about 240 households. Most of the entries are legible.

MINNESOTA — Rockford Township in Wright County: only the George Wolford family.

NEW JERSEY — Jersey City in Hudson County: only the three households of James Nelson, Samuel Cross, and Thomas Clooney.

NEW YORK — Eastchester in Westchester County: only the John Neormann (?) family. Brookhaven Township in Suffolk County: only the Joel H. Raynor family.

NORTH CAROLINA — South Point Township in

Gaston County: only the four households of George Martin, Miles J. Slanes (?), Christopher Buff, and Able Linbarger, with whom Edgar Love lived. River Bend Township in Gaston County: about 96 households. Township 2 in Cleveland County: six households.

OHIO — Cincinnati in Hamilton County: only the Alexander Hay family and a young black widow, Amand(a)? Williams, who lived alone. Wayne Township in Clinton County: the three households of Dempsey Sexton, Jeremiah Keith, and William W. Syferd.

SOUTH DAKOTA — Jefferson Township in Union County: only the James M. Lafferre family.

TEXAS — Justice Precinct 6 in Ellis County: about 43 families. Mountain Peak town in Ellis County: 14 families. Ovilla Precinct in Ellis County: only the households of Whitfield F. Bockett and Wilhering/Whithering W. Wood. Precinct 5 in Hood County: only the William Locklin/Lockley family (name spelled both ways on the same page). Justice Precinct 6 in Rusk County: only the Dallas Forman(?) family. Justice Precinct 7 in Rusk County: only the Joseph J. Wallace family. Trinity town in Trinity County: only the William T. Evans family. Precinct 2 of Trinity County: about 26 families. Kaufman town in Kaufman County: only Green S. Clark, Sr., and his wife. The place designation of this entry is illegible on the microfilm but must have been identified in some other way.

The 1890 census form itself was different from those used before and after 1890. The column headings ran down the left side of the page, and the information itself ran across it in five columns per page, making room for five people to a page. The given names in a household read across the top row, with the surnames below. Civil War veterans had a space in which to give their type of service. Below were the columns for relationship to head of household, age, race, marital status, length of marriage, birthplace, birthplace of parents, occupation, language, and education information.

1890 UNION VETERANS AND WIDOWS

A special 1890 census of Union veterans or their widows provides information about each man's service during the Civil War. It does not substitute for the lost 1890 population schedules because it provides different information and does not cover the entire population, but it contains very helpful data. Unfortunately, this census is not complete, but it does use 118 rolls of microfilm (M123). The reports are organized by state, then numerically by supervisor district, then alphabetically by county. Returns are available for the District of Columbia (Lincoln Post No. 3), fragments of states alphabetically from California through Kansas, part of Kentucky, states alphabetically from Louisiana through Wyoming, Oklahoma and Indian Territory, and veterans or widows on naval vessels and in naval yards. The California-Kansas fragments cover about 220 servicemen from these localities:

California: Alcatraz military post at San Francisco.
Connecticut: Ft. Trumbull at New London, the naval station at New London, Hartford County Hospital in Hartford.
Delaware: State Hospital for the Insane at New Castle.
Florida: Ft. Barrancas at Warrington in Escambia County, St. Francis Barracks in St. Johns County, part of Jefferson County.
Idaho: Boise Barracks in Ada County and Ft. Sherman in Kootenai County.
Illinois: part of Chicago in Cook County, and Henderson County.
Indiana: Boonville in Warrick County, and four from Reynolds, White County.
Kansas: Great Bend in Barton County.
New York: one soldier from a New York unit whose entry is mostly illegible and whose residence is not given.

Several examples will illustrate the value of this source. In Dillon, Beaverhead County, Montana, lived Eliza A. Black, widow of George Black, who had been a private in Company D of the Eighth Illinois Infantry, serving three years from 9 September 1861 to 9 September 1864. The widow in 1890 was in "destitute circumstance." In the same place lived Henry Wills, alias Charles Wright, who had been a private in Company B, First Kansas Infantry, for two and one-half years (no dates given) and who had received a gunshot wound in his left leg. Also in Dillon lived Eviton J. Conger, colonel from the First District of Columbia Cavalry (April 1861-September 1865), who had participated in the capture of the "assassin Booth." At Bannack, Montana, lived James R. Abrams, who had been chief engineer on the USS *Syren*, 1863-1864, one and one-half years. In Leesville, Gonzales County, Texas, were three men who had all served as privates in Company C, Ninth Kentucky Cavalry: Rufus Foster, Lawyer Franklin, and Charley Hill.

In addition to Union veterans, the census takers occasionally included a Confederate soldier. However, southerners also joined units recruited locally to fight on the Union side. The Limestone County, Texas, census includes men who had fought in the First Tennessee Cavalry and Second Florida Cavalry. Both were Union soldiers whose compiled service records match the information given in the census. Robertson County, Texas, includes at least one Union soldier from the First Alabama Cavalry, U.S.A., not C.S.A. Other names occasionally are marked out with *Conf.* written beside them. I have checked several of these in compiled service record indexes for C.S.A. and U.S.A. units and have found them in neither set of records. Of course, not all paperwork survived the war and storage over the years. Nevertheless, this census is another valuable source of information. In some cases, it may be the only available source of the particular information given.

1880-1920 INDEX TO INSTITUTIONS

This resource is a microfilm copy of a card index, organized by state and then alphabetically by the name of the institution. The entry gives the name of the institution; the city and/or county of location; the number of persons residing there; and the volume, enumeration district, and page number of its location on the census. The lists include such institutions as schools, universities, academies, college dormitories, hospitals, orphan homes, alms houses/poorhouses, jails, state penitentiaries, Masonic homes, homes for the aged, marine and army barracks, domestic military forts and posts, industrial schools and homes, homes for ladies, ships and tugs in port, naval vessels, hotels, railroad and timber camps, mines, other commercial operations at which employees lived, Indian reservations, fire stations, life-saving stations, religious houses, and Shaker communities.

For 1880, the institutions are found at the end of the last roll of the Soundex set for each state. Institution indexes were not included for California, or for Indian Territory (now Oklahoma), which has no census from this year.

The 1900 index (T1083) consists of eight rolls of microfilm that are alphabetical by state. In addition,

institutions in the Philippines, Alaska, Hawaii, and Indian Territory are included, as well as all the U.S. military and naval installations outside the continental U.S. and ships in port or at sea.

Included before or after the institutions for each state in the 1900 list are the Soundex cards for people whose surnames were not reported (and are marked *N.R.*) or were indecipherable, especially foreign and Indian names. In an attempt to help identify these persons, some of the *N.R.* cards indicate surnames of other members of the same household or surnames listed before and after that name on the actual schedule. This list helps to account for some of the people who do not appear on the regular Soundex.

The 1910 Institutions index is available only for Alabama, Louisiana, Mississippi, South Carolina, Tennessee, and Texas. The institutions are found at the end of the last Soundex roll for each of these states.

The 1920 Institutions index is also filmed at the end of the last roll of Soundex for each state or territory. Such indexes were made for all states and territories except Arizona, Florida, Georgia, Rhode Island, South Carolina, South Dakota, Tennessee, and Guam.

1900 AND 1910 ENUMERATION DISTRICT DESCRIPTIONS

These volumes are what their title suggests—descriptions of the boundaries of the enumeration districts used in taking the census. They are organized by state, then numerically by supervisor's district. Within each of these districts, the enumeration districts themselves are numerical, with the enumerator's name, the county or town where the enumerator district is located, and a brief description of the boundaries of that enumeration district. Actually, descriptions for 1830-1950 are available. The early volumes are called Accounts of Compensation to Assistant Marshalls and give census taker's name, rate of pay, and the geographic jurisdiction that he covered. They are part of the National Archives Record Group 29, Records of the Bureau of the Census. All but the 1900 descriptions are part of the T1224 set of National Archives microfilm.

Until I needed this source, I had not thought much about it, but it saved me much time. In looking for the John A. Iiams family in Harris County, Texas, in 1900, I first tried the Soundex for the code I520. I found adult relatives George and Frank but no John or Mary (his wife). Because the capital letter *I* in older handwriting often is confused with *J* or *S*, this name is often misspelled or misread. I considered the alternative

Soundex codes, with initial letters *J* or *S*. The most likely would have been J520, which also includes all the Joneses, about a roll and a half of film. I decided against that route. Reading the entire city also seemed an inefficient use of time and energy.

I knew that John and Mary had both died before 1910 and that John died first, by about 1902, leaving at least one son, named Claxton, born about 1900-1901. I did not know whether John would appear in the 1900 census at all, nor did I know the names of any other children. The 1900 Soundex had not answered those questions. The city directory entry for 1900 suggested that John was still living when the directory was put together and gave me an address for the family—1403 Johnson. I found the street on a current map and drew a little map of my own showing today's major thoroughfares (some of which were major streets then), railroad tracks, the nearest bayous, the cemetery in the area, cross streets, and parallel streets. I had already found relatives in Enumeration District 66 and felt it was probably in the same ward as the Johnson address. Thus, I expected to find Johnson Street in an Enumeration District numbered in the sixties and located in the same ward. Yet I still did not want to read all the enumeration districts on either side of E.D. 66.

That's when I tried the enumeration district descriptions. The information that threw me was that several of these districts used the city limits, as they existed then, instead of streets or bayous for the boundaries, and I could not tell exactly where these were. Learning that several of the districts went into the central business district or north of White Oak Bayou helped me narrow the choices to two or three. I chose Enumeration District 63 as the most likely and changed to the census microfilm. Once into that district, I turned page by page, reading the street names down the left side, streets I recognized as being near Johnson. Before long, Johnson appeared, with only three houses in the 1400 block. There at 1403 were John A. and Mary Iiams, married for seven years, with their son Frank, age 6, the only child born to the couple at that time. The entire process, once I had found the address on a city map, took less than an hour and was much more time-efficient than searching rolls of other Soundex codes. I still do not know, and do not care, whether this family was actually included in the Soundex under an alternate spelling.

Rural areas are also included in the enumeration district descriptions. They may be more difficult to plot on a map than city districts, but they read very much like many land deeds. The part of Clinton District, West Virginia, in Enumeration District 80 in 1900 is described this way: all of the district west of a line beginning where the county road crosses Marion County line, at or near Ross' Mill on White Day Creek, thence with said road to the Morgantown and Bridgeport turnpike at Corother's Tannery, and thence with said turnpike to Morgan district line.

The ten rolls of microfilm for 1900 (T1210) and thirteen for 1910 (T1224) are available for purchase from the National Archives or Scholarly Resources, for purchase or rent from the AGLL, for rent from FHL, and for use in many libraries with large census collections.

1910 CROSS INDEX TO SELECTED CITY STREETS

Another finding aid that is valuable, especially since the 1910 census is not fully indexed, is the street index for certain larger cities (M1283). The searcher would need to know the street address of the household in order to use the index. It contains no surnames, only addresses. For example, in Atlanta, Georgia, 202 Lake Avenue was in Enumeration District 113, but 282 Lake Avenue was in E.D. 112. Even knowing a street name without the number would save the researcher much time by narrowing down the districts in which to search. City directories for these communities can often supply the needed addresses. Refer to the chart for the cities available in this index, which can be purchased from the National Archives or Scholarly Resources, rented from the FHL or AGLL, or used in many libraries with large census collections.

Cities Available in 1910 Cross Index to City Streets

Alabama—Birmingham, Mobile, Montgomery
Arizona—Phoenix
California—Long Beach, Los Angeles, San Diego, San Francisco
Colorado—Denver and its institutions
District of Columbia
Florida—Tampa
Georgia—Atlanta, Augusta, Macon, Savannah
Illinois—Chicago, Peoria
Indiana—Fort Wayne, Gary, Indianapolis, South Bend
Kansas—Kansas City, Wichita
Maryland—Baltimore
Michigan—Detroit, Grand Rapids

Nebraska—Omaha
New Jersey—Elizabeth, Newark, Patterson
New York—New York City, Brooklyn, Bronx, Manhattan, Richmond
North Carolina—Charlotte
Ohio—Akron, Canton, Cleveland, Dayton, Youngstown
Oklahoma—Oklahoma City, Tulsa
Pennsylvania—Erie, Philadelphia, Reading
Texas—San Antonio
Virginia—Richmond
Washington—Seattle

1900-1920 MILITARY/NAVAL CENSUSES

The 1900 census of **military and naval installations outside the continental U.S.**, including ships, is part of the T623 census microfilm series. The personnel in these schedules are Soundexed (in T1081) apart from the general population since they are enumerated separately from the general population returns that are organized by state. Use this military/naval Soundex if you are looking for a specific person or family. The names of overseas installations themselves are included in the T1083 Index to Institutions under *Military and Naval Institutions*. Most of these installations were located in the Philippine Islands, Puerto Rico, or Cuba. Use the institutions index if you already know the name of the post, station, or ship you want to find.

Domestic military and naval installations and their personnel are included in the general 1900 population schedule for the county and state in which they were located. The individuals stationed at domestic installations are Soundexed with the general population, according to their usual Soundex code. The domestic installations themselves are indexed with other institutions in the state in which they were located.

The **1910 military/naval schedules** (part of T624) are microfilmed but have not been Soundexed. The only ones appearing in the institution indexes would be those located in the states that have such indexes (see Institution Index topic above). These schedules contain posts and stations in the Philippine Islands and Panama Canal Zone; ships stationed in U.S. ports or such other areas as Japan, Panama, Guam, and the Philippines; and the Naval Academy, military hospitals, and other such installations. Some of the pages, such as those from the USS *Louisiana* and the USS *Texas*, are typewritten! The forms used are the same as the regular population schedule forms, and they often report the specific assignment and rank of each serviceman.

The **1920 military/naval/consular service census** from overseas locations is Soundexed (M1600) and includes an institution index. As in the other census years, domestic military and naval installations are part of the general population census and Soundex.

One 1910 example illustrates the value of searching these records. At Camp Eldridge, Laguna, Philippine Islands, First Lt. John J. Fulmer (31, born in Pennsylvania) lived with his wife of one year, Viola J. (23, born in Louisiana). Living with them, or visiting, were Lena Brooks (46, born in Louisiana) and Helen Brooks (10, born in Michigan), John's mother-in-law and sister-in-law. Lena Brooks reported that she had been married for twenty-five years and that five of her six children were living. Somewhere, a genealogist may be scouring the countryside for these Brooks ladies, without realizing that Viola Brooks had married an army officer who was stationed in the Philippines in 1910.

1900-1920 CENSUS OF TERRITORIES

The U.S. acquired overseas possessions in 1898 as a result of the Spanish-American War and the annexation of Hawaii. At this time, of course, Alaska, Arizona, Oklahoma, and New Mexico were still territories as well.

Censuses were taken in 1900 and 1910 for the territories of Hawaii, Alaska, Arizona, New Mexico, and Oklahoma/Indian Territory (statehood, 1907). For 1910, a census without a Soundex exists for Puerto Rico. American personnel attached to military and naval installations in overseas possessions would be found in the military/naval schedules. These are Soundexed for 1900 and 1920.

Territories and possessions covered by the census and Soundex for 1920 include the Virgin Islands, Guam, American Samoa, Puerto Rico, Panama Canal Zone, Alaska, and Hawaii.

1920 CENSUS

The 1920 census (T625) was released in 1992 and is currently available, with Soundex, for all the states. This census includes the military and naval population living abroad. It does not include a separate Indian schedule as do 1900 and 1910.

CENSUSES AFTER 1920

The current law requires census records to be kept confidential for seventy-two years. Those who need to get information from their own family's closed census returns must contact the Census Bureau office in Jeffersonville, Indiana: Personal Census Search Unit, Data Preparation Division. Bureau of the Census, P.O. Box 1545, Jeffersonville IN 47131-0001; phone (812)285-5314. This office was in Pittsburg, Kansas, until 1991.

An individual may request his or her own record from the census of 1930 and after by furnishing full name, birthdate if known, birthplace, race, sex, and parents' names; complete address on April 1 of the census year, including street address, city, county, and state; and the names of the persons in the household, especially the head of household if other than a parent. Persons living in rural areas are asked to furnish a map that may help in finding the proper household. The fee for a search, as set in January 1993, is $40. This fee includes the search of one census year for one person and a transcript of the information, if found. The transcript is a typed report with an official seal certifying that the information is a correct copy of what is on the original. Included is the applicant's name, age, birthplace, citizenship, relationship to the head of the household, and name of the head of household. This report does not include any other family members' names or census information. The primary purpose of this report is proof of age, citizenship, or parentage.

For all other information on the one census entry, such as occupation, education, or language, the applicant must request a *full schedule*, i.e., complete entry, and pay an additional $10 fee. Full schedule searches are possible only for the censuses up to and including 1950.

A search for parents or other family members can be made for the same census year with proper authorization. The basic search will provide the name of each person for whom a $2 fee is paid. A full schedule can be released for those other persons in the household for $10 per person. The authorization required for release of information on any other person must come from that person or the legal guardian. If the person is deceased, the release must come from the spouse, a parent, child, sibling, estate administrator or executor, or legal beneficiary, along with a certified copy of the death certificate. In certain situations, legal evidence of the need for the information must be provided, for the records are considered confidential. The report will be sent only to the person to whom the information pertains or to the authorized representative in the immediate family, not to any collateral relatives, e.g., cousins, nephews, or aunts. The statement for release of information should be included with the application form and may read something like this: "I hereby authorize the Bureau of the Census to send a transcript of my census record to (name) Signed _____."

The necessary application form BC-600 may be obtained from the Jeffersonville office or regional Census Bureau offices located in Atlanta, Boston, Charlotte (North Carolina), Chicago, Dallas, Denver, Detroit, Kansas City, Los Angeles, New York, Philadelphia, or Seattle. The instructions and fee structure are explained on the application form. The search usually takes between two and four weeks.

FEDERAL POPULATION SCHEDULES FOR THE TERRITORIES

The states that spent some years as territories often do have population schedules for the period before statehood. The chart below lists the existing censuses, not substitutes, that were made for these states and, where applicable, the parent state or territory in whose census they were included. The date given with the state name is the date of statehood.

Alabama (1819) — Federal territorial censuses before statehood no longer exist.

Alaska (1959) — See above, 1900-1920 Census of Territories.

Arizona (1912) — 1850-60, enumerated as Arizona County in New Mexico. 1870-1910 as Arizona Territory. 1870-some residents may be included with Pah-Ute County, Nevada, and perhaps Washington County, Utah.

Arkansas (1836) — 1830 as Arkansas Territory.

Colorado (1876) — 1860, Arapahoe County included in Kansas Territory, northeast Colorado towns included with Nebraska. For south central area, try Taos or Mora counties, New Mexico Territory. 1870 as Colorado Territory.

Florida (1845) — 1830, 1840 as Florida Territory.

Hawaii (1959) — 1900 forward as Hawaii Territory. See above, 1900-1920 Census of Territories.

Idaho (1890) — 1860, included as parts of Utah and Washington. 1870-1880 as Idaho Territory.

Illinois (1818) — 1810 as Illinois Territory. Randolph

County schedule extant, covering much of southern Illinois. St. Clair County (then the northern two-thirds to three-fourths of state) is lost.

Indiana (1816)—1810 as Indiana Territory; Clark, Knox, Harrison, Dearborn counties extant.

Iowa (1846)—1840 as Iowa Territory, but part of Clayton County included with Minnesota.

Kansas (1861)—1860 as Kansas Territory.

Louisiana (1812)—1810 as Louisiana/Orleans Territory.

Michigan (1837)—1810 as Michigan Territory, but lost except part of Detroit and Michilimackinac. 1820-1830 as Michigan Territory.

Minnesota (1858)—1830 included in Michigan Territory as Chippewa and Crawford counties, 1840, northeastern part included with Wisconsin Territory, southern and western parts with Iowa Territory. 1850 as Minnesota Territory.

Mississippi (1817)—1810 territorial census exists for Amite, Baldwin, Claiborne, Franklin, Jefferson, Warren, Washington counties. See chapter three for details.

Missouri (1821)—1830 as state of Missouri. Missouri residents do not seem to be included in 1810 Louisiana/Orleans Territory census. (Missouri was then Louisiana Territory, separate from Orleans Territory, which became the state of Louisiana. No 1820 census for Missouri exists.

Montana (1889)—1860, eastern part included with unorganized part of Nebraska Territory; western part included in Washington Territory. Check also Dakota Territory. 1870-1880 as Montana Territory.

Nebraska (1867)—1860 as Nebraska Territory.

Nevada (1864)—1850 and 1860, most of present state included with Utah Territory.

New Mexico (1912)—1850-1910 as New Mexico Territory.

North Dakota (1889)—1850, Pembina County included as part of Minnesota. 1860, western part included with Nebraska Territory, eastern part as Dakota Territory.

Ohio (1803)—1800 census of Northwest Territory lost.

Oklahoma (1907)—1860 with Arkansas, as Indian lands west of Arkansas. Has also been published (Dorothy J. Tincup Mauldin, comp., Tulsa, Oklahoma: Oklahoma Yesterday Publishers, 1980s). Also published as *Indian Lands West of Arkansas (Oklahoma): Population Schedule of the*

U.S. Census (by Frances Woods, Ft. Worth, Texas: Arrow Printing Co., 1964). 1900, Oklahoma Territory and Indian Territory.

Oregon (1859)—1850 as Oregon Territory.

South Dakota (1889)—1860, western part included with Nebraska Territory, eastern part as Dakota Territory.

Utah (1896)—1850-1880 as Utah Territory.

Washington (1889)—1850, included as part of Oregon Territory. 1860-1880 as Washington Territory. 1860-1870 includes some people in San Juan Islands as part of Whatcom County.

Wisconsin (1848)—1820-1830 with Michigan Territory. 1840, as Wisconsin Territory.

Wyoming (1890)—1850, with Utah. 1860, with Nebraska Territory. 1870, 1880 as Wyoming Territory.

USING THE POPULATION SCHEDULES OF THE CENSUS

It is common knowledge that people were missed in every census. Even when other documents prove that a family was in a particular county in a particular census year, the family may not be enumerated in the census. Such omissions may be due to the loss of the original schedule or part of it, to mistakes in copying the pages that were sent to Washington, to isolation of the family in a hard-to-reach location, to absence of the family when the enumerator went to their house (and no neighbors to provide information), to accidental omission by the census taker, or to inclement weather, which prevented the census taker from reaching the family. If the family was on the road moving to a new home, they may have been missed in both old and new locations. (Occasionally, they were picked up by two enumerators and appear twice.)

The most troublesome census in my experience is 1870, but consider some of the factors that contributed to the omissions and mistakes. Everywhere immigration was increasing, and these newcomers were on the move to new homes. Many Civil War widows were now remarried and starting new families. Railroads all over the country were rebuilding or expanding, and people saw economic opportunity along the routes. Boom towns along the railroads thrived, some only momentarily; and every day saw new arrivals and departures, especially at the town at the end of the line. It is a wonder that in such areas any census was taken at all. Especially in the South, this was a period of depression and great transition. Older families were moving out in droves to new lives farther west, and new families were moving in from the North and Europe. The census of 1870 was the first after the Civil War, and some areas of the South were still under military rule. Perhaps bitter memories and feelings in these areas caused families to evade the enumerator's visit and simply "go fishing."

However, not all of the seemingly lost families were omitted.

"Lost Relatives" May Not Be Lost

Some "lost" individuals or families are actually listed and waiting to be found. If you do not find the family in the index or Soundex, consider these options:

1. Read the census for the *entire* county where you feel they were living in the summer and fall of that year. I have found a number of families this way.

2. Read the nearest neighboring county, surrounding counties, parent county, or counties along a travel route from a previous home.

3. Look for siblings, in-laws, or other relatives, the whole cluster of the extended family. Sometimes, children living with their mother and a stepfather are listed by the stepfather's surname, even when that was not their legal name. Cousins, nieces, nephews, aunts, uncles, grandparents, or other relatives may be living with a family with the same surname and may not be indexed separately. Even people with different surnames in a household are not always indexed under their own names.

Whether from haste, carelessness, or lack of information, some people were listed without a surname or without a given name. The 1920 census of Limestone County, Texas, contains one such puzzle. An Oldham man, age 63, was boarding with R. James Manning at Thornton. No given name was reported for him. Was he Lafayette Oldham? The age matches, and a son's death record shows that Lafayette was living in Thornton in 1914. No death record or cemetery record for him has yet been found. This census gave his birthplace as Texas, but 1880 and 1900 reported a Mississippi birthplace. However, if the person who left out Oldham's given name also gave his birthplace information to the census taker, one has reason to doubt its accuracy. It is certainly possible that the nameless man was indeed Lafayette, but a number of other sources must be checked, including census records for his surviving children or other relatives in the event that he was living with one of them. In the meantime, he remains one of those lost people.

4. If you have reason to believe that the microfilm copy you have been studying has pages or households missing, ask to see the original at the state archives or other repository that may have it. Not all originals still exist, but many do. For preservation reasons, these are not usually made accessible to the public when microfilm copies are available, except in special cases. Many of the copies that were sent to Washington and later filmed were as complete as the originals, which remained in the states, but it is possible that families were skipped in the copying process, that names were shortened to initials to save copying time, or that other differences occurred.

5. Practice writing the surname you are searching in alternative spellings. You can use these variations to search both the index and the census returns. How might a census taker or other official write the name upon hearing it, especially when spoken with the local or a foreign accent? That's how *Priscilla* became *Prisiller*, *Sarah* became *Sahry*, and *Arabella* became *R. Obella* in the records. That's how *Schmidt* became *Smith* and how *Shelby* was written as *Shealvy* and *Chelby*. Think of ways the name might have been shortened or altered unintentionally when the enumerator or other recorder was in a hurry, was unfamiliar with the name, or the family could not spell it for him. Consider these variant spellings of Crane: Krane, Crain, Crayne. A Soundex would catch all the C spellings of this name together, but a printed index would have them scattered through the alphabetical list. Because *n* and *u* are sometimes written so that they are virtually indistinguishable, the name could be read as *Kraus* or *Crow*, depending on the quality of the handwriting.

For literate people who also try to enunciate and listen carefully, it is sometimes difficult to understand the confusion that occurs with surnames in the records. When they find *Johnson* and *Johnston* used interchangeably, or *Garner* and *Gardner*, they can understand, but mixing *Pollock* and *Polk*, or *Powell* and *Poole*, is a little harder for them to accept. Pronunciation is the root of the problem, for in the English language especially, we do not always pronounce words and spell them with the same rules or customs. *Powell* and *Poole* are often pronounced the same way, as *pool*. *Gloucester* is pronounced *Gloster*, and *Cocke* is said as *Cook*. Three such names that have been confused and interchanged are *Barnett(e)*, *Bernard*, and *Barnard*. Each one can be heard pronounced with the accent on the first or second syllable—six different pronunciations, or maybe just one pronunciation. Add handwriting to the problem and the searcher has to contend with the mixing of these three with *Barrett* and *Bennett*. These are not just spelling variations of one name but are five distinct names; yet the searcher in any one of them must use them all as if they were spelling variations. The same confusion exists for *Thomas*, *Thompson*, and *Thomason*, also for *Robertson*, *Robberson*, *Robinson*, *Robison*, *Robson*, *Roberts*, *Robb*, and *Robbins*.

Perhaps pronunciation or perhaps haste on the part of the enumerator explains why one Holmes family was recorded as *Haynes* in the 1850 census, and how one Williamson family went into the record as *Willison* in the 1870 census and as *Williams* in one marriage record. Have you not heard people pronounce this name also as *Wilmson*? Speech patterns or illiteracy on the part of family members, or carelessness or lack of real acquaintance with the family on the part of the enumerator may account for the continual mix-up in names. The searcher must be alert to these realities. Keeping a written list of variations of your research names can help you make a more thorough search.

6. Remember that differing handwriting styles and unfamiliarity with names in a county may cause surnames to be indexed incorrectly, even by careful transcribers. After reading an entire county and finding a particular Shelby family in the 1820 census, I went back to the index and read the entire *S* listing to see whether it had actually been missed in the index or indexed under an alternate spelling that I had not thought of. I finally found the head of household, Evan, indexed under *Strelvy*. The indexer had simply misread the name. In this same family, I was also searching for the given name *Frank* in the 1870 census and was elated to find it in the index. However, my hopes were dashed when I realized that the indexer had recorded *Frank*, but the actual entry was a very poorly written *Isack*. It was easy to understand how the mistake had been made, but I knew from deed records that this resident was Dr. Isaac Shelby.

Problem-Solving With Census Records

Cluster genealogy is an effective method of working on family history, and census records are important tools in this effort. Being alert to the cluster of people around an ancestor provides valuable clues, suggestions, and answers. In the case of burned courthouses, especially in the South, census records are sometimes

the only evidence for, if not actual proof of, relationships and vital data. Below are a few of many possible situations in which census records of the cluster aid in solving some of the problems common to genealogical searches.

Case 1—Clues to Wife's Maiden Name. Have you ever read a census and been tempted to skip over persons of a different surname who were listed with your family? If you are tempted to do this, it is time to reform your habits. Sometimes, these people were employees or boarders, but often they were relatives of some kind. The presence of such persons may be clues to important information, such as the wife's maiden name. In counties where marriage records exist, it is relatively easy to determine the wife's maiden name, but in the case of burned counties, this kind of clue in the census may be vital to your search. The example used here is from a group of families that lived in four successive counties during a century of their history. All four counties suffered courthouse fires after the families moved farther west.

The counties are Chesterfield in South Carolina and Covington, Jasper, and Smith in Mississippi. The loss of most early records makes finding the maiden names of wives in these counties a real challenge. Evan Shelby moved his family from Chesterfield County to Jasper County about the time it was formed, after a brief stay in neighboring Covington County. Evan's son John P. Shelby married about 1842 (we do not know where) and appeared in the Smith County 1850 census with his wife, Matilda (28, South Carolina), and three young sons. Nearby were three Blakeney families. John's father Evan, brother Alfred, and their families lived just across the county line in Jasper County in a cluster of Blakeney and Shelby families. Both Blakeneys and Shelbys shared given names: William, John, Alfred, Alvin, Harriett, Louisa, and Matilda. Living with the John P. Shelby family in 1850 was Robert Blakeney (25, Mississippi). The first reaction was, "Ah-hah. Blakeney might be Matilda's maiden name. This Robert might be her younger brother."

We have found no Shelby family records to help in the search for Matilda's maiden name. However, one of John and Matilda's great-grandsons remembers asking his father about her name. The answer was a clear uncertainty. The older man thought it might have started with a *Bl*, but none of the names they could think of sounded familiar. They did not think about *Blakeney*.

Pursuing these two clues (census and vague recollection) involved following as many of the Blakeneys and Shelbys as possible and amassing many census records. In this effort, another clue became apparent—Evan Shelby was the only Shelby in the 1820 census of South Carolina and five Blakeney families lived in the same county, Chesterfield. These were the only Blakeneys in the state, according to the census, except for one cousin family in the nearest neighboring county. To learn about the proximity of these families to each other, we consulted the Mills Atlas of South Carolina. The Chesterfield map, prepared in 1819, showed only one Shelby residence. Its closest neighbor was a Blakeney, and several other Blakeneys were nearby.

By about 1827, when Evan Shelby moved to Mississippi, his son John P. was eight or nine years old, not of courting age. Matilda would have been only four or five at that time. Did her family move to Mississippi? The only Smith-Jasper area Blakeney couple of the age to be her parents had a Matilda in their family in the 1850 census. If her family stayed in South Carolina, how did she and John get together?

From the *Pre-1956 Imprints* of the *National Union Catalog*, we learned that a Blakeney had written a family history in 1928. Through interlibrary loan, we were able to borrow the book from the College of William and Mary in Williamsburg, Virginia, to whom we are most grateful. To our excitement, the book was about the Chesterfield County Blakeneys, by a John O. Blakeney, who had been born in Jasper County, Mississippi, in 1852.

Although the author did not document each piece of information he gave, he included many birth dates, as if from family Bibles, even when he had no marriage and death dates. In a cousin line to his own, we found John Blakeney of Chesterfield County, South Carolina, and his twenty (yes, twenty) children by three wives. Among the children of his first wife were James, who married Harriet Shelby, and Matilda, who married John Shelby. This James and Harriet we had found living next to John's brother Alfred Shelby and one house down from Evan Shelby in the 1850 census. (From the census, we figured that they had married about 1841 or 1842. Their seven-year-old son John was born in Mississippi.) Harriet may well be the daughter of Evan Shelby and a sister of John and Alfred. The 1830 and 1840 censuses of Evan's household have one young female of Harriet's age who had not been identified up to this point of the search. Since census records indicate that the father, John Blakeney, remained

in South Carolina, Matilda Blakeney and John Shelby must not have grown up together. They may have renewed childhood acquaintance through the marriage of James Blakeney and Harriet Shelby.

The problem with the Blakeney book was the note printed with Matilda's entry: "born Sept. 24, 1822, m John Shelby, Hill County, Texas." The birth date agreed with census information we had found, and the husband's name was definitely the one we had hoped to see. However, John and Matilda did not go to Hill County when they moved to Texas in 1868 or 1869. We have deed records and a legislative petition signature to show that John P. Shelby was in Robertson County in 1870 and thereafter. Since John P., Matilda, and family do not appear in the copy or original of the 1870 census in Robertson County (or in Mississippi or Louisiana along the route), we do not know whether Matilda made the trip to Texas. Family tradition suggests she may have died in Mississippi before the family moved.

Nevertheless, we had to check in Hill County to see whether any John and Matilda Shelby lived there. There seem to have been no Shelbys there before the 1870s. The J.T. and M.A. Shelbys in the 1880 census of Hill County were not born in South Carolina but in Arkansas and Georgia. Their ages were 36 and 34, not even close to the John (61) and Matilda (would have been 58) of this search, and the Hill County children had completely different names, ages, and birthplaces. This Hill County couple does not match the criteria necessary to be the daughter and son-in-law of John Blakeney. Although we have never found another John and Matilda Shelby in the South in that period, we continue to search for evidence that *this* Matilda was indeed the daughter of John Blakeney of Chesterfield. It is reassuring that we have found no evidence to suggest that she was *not*.

One additional piece of positive evidence is the 1875 will of this John Blakeney, which names his daughter Matilda Shelby. Of course, we do not know whether our Matilda lived until 1875. However, the will mentions the children of the first two wives only to say that they have already "been advanced out of my estate heretofore as much as I designed that they should have." Because of this, the old man made no statement to indicate whether any of them were deceased or had heirs. Therefore, we cannot interpret the will one way or another as a clue to Matilda's being alive or dead in 1875.

The fact remains that in these burned counties,

early records are scarce. Therefore, census records have consistently been the principal source of clues and evidence. The presence of Robert Blakeney in the household of John P. Shelby in 1850 was a red flag that demanded attention. From the Blakeney records we have gathered, it seems that Robert was not in fact Matilda's brother but a cousin whose exact relationship has not been determined. Still, the preponderance of evidence suggests that this Matilda Shelby really was a daughter of John Blakeney of Chesterfield, South Carolina.

Case 2—Finding a Family in a Previous State. Census records of 1850 and after, of course, show the birthplace of each individual. The birthplaces of children in a family may help you track the family through former residences. Following a couple and their children across state lines is certainly made easier with the availability of many census indexes and other such finding aids being developed in most states. However, this example involves a family with a common name. Even in indexes, such a name may cover columns or pages and involve a lengthy search. Further complicating the search was the fact that I had no name for the head of household, only the surname—Brown(e).

In working on W.F.M. Holmes of Gonzales County, Texas, I found his marriage record to Matilda Y. Browne in neighboring Wilson County, 31 January 1861. The 1860 census, then, was the place to begin looking for the family from which Matilda came. The Gonzales County census showed Matilda (19, born in Arkansas) with S.H. Brown (22) and Needham P. Brown (17), both also born in Arkansas. They lived in the household of a young planter, W.W. Sorrell, and his wife, their children, and five other persons of different surnames. No one else in the household was Arkansas-born. For the moment, I ruled out the possibility of Matilda being S.H. Browne's wife and attacked the problem by considering this a case of three Browne siblings living together as single young adults.

The census showed Matilda's soon-to-be-husband, W.F.M. Holmes, not far away and living in the household of A.S. Miller, his wife and children, two German immigrants, and a young stock raiser, J.H. Owens, his wife and three children. The Owens wife was Mary C. (24), born in Arkansas, as were the two older children, J.W. (6) and Martha (4). The baby Mary P. Owens, age 6 months, was born in Texas.

The Browne siblings did not appear in the Texas 1850 census, and I had no father's name to look for in Arkansas in 1850. I knew that, because families often moved in groups in that period, these young people had very likely traveled with another family. The Owens family came to Texas from Arkansas, after about 1856, according to the census reporting of the births of their children. Since Brown(e) families were likely to be numerous in Arkansas, I decided to narrow the search by first trying counties with both Owens *and* Brown(e) families in case they had come from the same county. Fifteen counties showed both surnames. After reading four or five of these counties, I found Matilda (8) and Needham (10) with Menisa (17, sister?) and mother Eliza (42, born in North Carolina) in the household of a young couple, Ewing and Emeline (23, North Carolina) McCracken in Madison County, Arkansas, with their 2-year-old son Henry. One possibility is that Emeline was another sister of Matilda. Single women, such as Eliza, and their children often lived with an older child who was already married, just as widowed daughters often moved home with their parents. Because county marriage and tax records were destroyed by a 1900 fire, it was not possible to determine Emeline's maiden name quickly, nor was that the focus of the search at that time.

Deed records in the county showed only one Eliza Brown prior to 1850, and she was the wife of H.B. Brown. An 1849 deed gave his full name as Henry Brantley Brown, who was also the county clerk from 1836 to 1848. Remember that Eliza Brown and Emeline McCracken were both born in North Carolina, Emeline in about 1827. A check of North Carolina marriage records showed Brantley Brown marrying Eliza Norris in November 1826, in Wake County, where county records show at least two men named *Needham* Norris. Adding evidence to the possibility that Emeline was a daughter of Eliza and Henry Brantley Brown is the name of Emeline's son—Henry.

The last record found for Henry Brantley Brown was a note signed on 17 November 1849. He does not appear in the 1850 census or the county mortality schedule for their county. To answer remaining questions, the family has much to pursue, including the marriage record of a Brantley Brown in Wake County, North Carolina, in 1854.

Nevertheless, the initial search for Matilda Browne Holmes's parents was done with census records and a cluster approach, which saved considerable time.

Case 3—Working with the 1880 Soundex. In working on the life and family of Stephen J. Ford, we learned from a record left by his second wife that he died in 1885. We found him in the 1850 and 1860 censuses and in Confederate service records, but not in the 1870 census. We wanted to find him in the 1880 census to fill in some of the gaps between his Civil War service and his death. From a family record that he wrote, we knew that in 1880, he was a widower with three young daughters. However, his record did not show where he and his family lived at that time. If you have worked with the 1880 Soundex, you will remember that it covers only households that include children under ten years of age. Stephen did not appear in the 1880 Soundex, even though we knew he had three small children. Rather than read a three- or four-parish area of Louisiana where he was thought to be living, I checked the Soundex for his children. Daughters Kate and Maggie were listed as boarders in the household of a William Armstrong. I knew from gathering information on the family of Stephen's sister Sarah, the only identified relative of his generation, that William Armstrong was Sarah's son. Neither the Soundex nor the reading of that parish located the third child, infant Sallie, but reading the entire parish did locate Stephen as a widower, living alone and in a different enumeration district. This explains why he did not appear in the Soundex. Apparently, after his first wife, Lucy, died, he felt that he could not support or care for the three little girls alone and arranged for them to live elsewhere until he remarried and brought the family back together, as he did the following year.

From this census record, we had a parish in which to focus a search for further records, including the 1881 marriage of Stephen and his second wife, Emily. This illustrates the limitations of the 1880 Soundex in trying to locate a head of household when we did not know that the family was not all together.

Case 4 — Extraneous People in a Household. In every census, families appear with additional people living in the household. These extra people range in age from infants a few months old to the very elderly. Sometimes they were employees of the head of household. For various reasons, families sometimes took in unrelated boarders — the need for extra income that boarders might pay, children and youth working away from home in a household of neighbors or relatives, or single young adults, such as school teachers, clerks, and lawyers who needed a place to live. Often, children and youth with a different surname were offspring of the mother by a former marriage. They may have been orphaned cousins, nieces or nephews, or grandchildren, or for some other reason may have been living with relatives other than their own parents.

Even in the censuses where relationship can be given, it is not always recorded or accurate. The point for the genealogist to consider is that there was a reason for these "extra" people being in the household. What was it? The following are examples from the 1850-1870 censuses, with age and birthplace given for each person. Each case has a proven kinship between the main family and the extra person(s). Test yourself. What are the most likely possibilities for a relationship? How would you search for the answer?

Example 1: 1860 San Augustine Co., Texas

A.	Huston	61	Pa (NY in 1850 census)
Elizabeth	"	55	Oh (Pa in 1850 census)
J.N.	"	18	Tx
Henry	"	15	Tx
Priscilla	"	14	Tx
Alla	"	10	Tx
Mary M.	Kyle	20	Tx
Ella	"	2	Tx

Example 2: 1850 Hardeman Co., Tennessee

Elliott G. Coleman		27	Va
Catherine	"	19	SC
Mary	"	2	Tn
Lucy	"	$^2/_{12}$	Tn
William	"	19	Va

Example 3: 1870 Cherokee Co., Texas

Moses Cummings		44	Tn
Cordelia	"	35	Tx (Pa-1850, Mi-1860)
James	"	20	Tn
Martha	"	16	Tn
John A.	"	14	Tx
Mary	"	12	Tx
Columbus	"	4	Tx
Ella	"	2	Tx
Elizabeth	Everett	16	Tx
Almanza	"	14	Tx

Example 4: 1860 Smith Co., Mississippi

Joseph	Martin	60	Ga
Nancy	"	54	Ga
Oquin C.	"	29	Ms
James T.	"	27	Ms
William S.	"	24	Ms
Nancy H.	"	17	Ms
Karen V.	"	14	Ms
Robert J.W.	"	12	Ms
Mary C.	"	9	Ms
William R.	"	4	Ms
Terra A.	"	3	Ms
Harriet A.	"	1	Ms

Answers to the identity of the extra person(s) in the household:

1. Married (and/or widowed or divorced) daughter and her child living with her parents and siblings.
2. Husband's younger brother living with the family.
3. Wife's two children by first husband. First four children are husband's by first wife. Two youngest are from current marriage.
4. Widower son and his three children living with his parents.

These examples illustrate common challenges in the use of census records. While there are many possible answers to the presence of people in a household other than the nuclear family, these people were often relatives. In example one above, Mary was listed as a 10-year-old with this same family in 1850, and county marriage records show her marriage in 1857 to Col. Absolom S. Kyle. Someone concentrating on that family would want to check probate and cemetery records to determine when Absolom Kyle died or look for a possible divorce record. Example two is proven by family letters, which talk about brother William being with the family. Example three is supported by previous census records showing the Cummings children with Moses and the Everett children with Cordelia. The county marriage record shows that Moses Cummings married Cordelia Everett on 13 March 1865.

Example four comes from a family that lived near the boundary of two burned counties, Smith and Jasper, Mississippi. Census records, therefore, play an important role in the study of this family and its neighbors. The 1850 census of the Joseph Martin household showed Joseph without a wife and Oquin (19) as the eldest child at home. The youngest child was Robert, age 2. They were living next to the John P. Shelby family. The area newspaper, the *Eastern Clarion*, printed a notice that on 20 Nov. 1858, Harriett Martin, wife of O.C. Martin, had died at their residence on Clear Creek, Smith County, leaving three small children. It stated that she was the daughter of Alfred and Demarius Shelby of Jasper County, where she was born and lived until her marriage on 4 January 1855.[2] Harriett indeed had appeared in the 1850 census with her parents and siblings, including younger sister Terry.

The 1860 census, then, showed that Oquin C. Martin was either still living in his father's household or had moved back there after his wife died. His father,

Joseph, had apparently remarried between censuses and had had one additional child, Mary C. Martin, now age 9. It is very unlikely that the three youngest children (ages 4, 3, 1) would be the children of his now 54-year-old wife. These three, William, *Terra*, and Harriet, were children of O.C. and Harriett, living with their father and grandparents. William (14) and *Terry* (13) appeared in 1870 with O.C., his new wife, Louisa, and their three children under the age of five. (The presence of three Bankster children ages 13, 12, and 10 suggests that Louisa's former husband was a Bankster.) Daughter Harriett Martin appeared with the Martin grandparents in both 1870 and 1880. In fact, by 1880 Joseph Martin had apparently died. Living with his widow, Nancy, were their *daughter* Mary C. (28) and *granddaughter* Harret (*sic*) A. (21), only one house away from the Oquin C. Martin family. Following this cluster of both Martins and Shelbys adds to the knowledge of both lines and accounts for the extra people in the Martin household. In addition, this cluster approach suggests another connection between these two families.

The Harriett Shelby who married O.C. Martin had a younger brother named William born about 1844-1845 in Mississippi. He appeared with his parents in the 1850 and 1860 censuses in Smith County. In 1870 in the same county, he lived with his wife, Nancy, (26, born in Mississippi) and their children, Louisa, Radford, and Nancy, *next to* Joseph and Nancy Martin. The 1880 census showed them with five additional children. This time, the wife's name was listed as Nancy H. (age 35, Mississippi), and her parents' birthplaces were given as Georgia and Mississippi. Notice in example four above that Joseph Martin was born in Georgia and had a daughter Nancy H. (17, Mississippi) in his household in 1860. (In the 1850 census, she was listed as eight years old.) It seems very possible that Nancy H. Shelby, wife of William, was the daughter of Joseph Martin.

The fact that the two families were already connected from one marrige and were neighbors adds to this reasoning. The ages given in the four census records for Nancy (if indeed one and the same person) were 8, 17, 26, and 35. This kind of discrepancy is not unusual and is not great enough to negate the argument. In the 1880 census, Joseph Martin's sons Oquin C., Robert J., and Matthew (listed with the family only in the 1850 census) gave both parents' birthplaces as Georgia. In all four cases, counting Nancy as a sibling, the father's birthplace is consistently Georgia and agrees with what Joseph Martin gave for himself in the three prior censuses. In seeking to explain the Mississippi birth given for Nancy Shelby's mother, one must ask whether Nancy may have had a different mother from the three boys. However, although Oquin and Matthew were older than their sister Nancy, Robert was younger. It is well known that siblings, or *whoever gave the census taker the information*, did not always know or agree on the birthplace of parents. Thus, this discrepancy too is not enough to disprove the suggestion that Nancy H. Martin married William Shelby, especially since the 1900 census showed both of Nancy H. Shelby's parents born in Georgia.

Case 5 — Working with Birthplaces. If you have worked with many censuses of 1850 and after, you have probably noticed that birthplaces given for any one person may vary. Cordelia Huston Everett Cummings, who spent most of her ninety-two years in east Texas, was listed in 1850 with a Pennsylvania birthplace; in 1860 with Michigan; 1870 and 1880 with Texas. We have no way of knowing who gave each census taker the information, but we can make an effort to discover which is actually correct. The family Bible record gives her birthdate as 11 February 1830. The *Handbook of Texas*[3] states that her father, Almanzon Huston, came to San Augustine, Texas, in 1824. However, an article in the San Augustine (Texas) *Rambler*, 1 June 1967, by a family member, reported that the parents married on 6 April 1819 in Erie County, Pennsylvania, and moved to Niles, Michigan, in May 1829. The *Territorial Papers of the United States* (Vol. XII, p 86) for Michigan show Almanzon signing a petition in St. Joseph County in October 1829. And he appears as head of the household in Niles Township, Berrien County, Michigan, in the 1830 census. The problem with the census is that the family had two daughters under the age of five by census day that year, but only one is listed in that age bracket in the census. In addition, an A. Huston was among Michigan territorial inhabitants who signed a petition in November 1831 (*Territorial Papers*, Vol XII, p 369). Huston's earliest deed in his Texas county of San Augustine was signed 22 September 1834 (Book C, p 140). These documents support the Michigan birthplace for daughter Cordelia and pretty well negate Texas as her birthplace. One possible explanation could be offered in support of the Pennsylvania birthplace. Three earlier siblings apparently were born in Pennsylvania. If the mother's family was still in Pennsylvania, it is conceivable that she returned home to have her baby. How-ever, that would have been a long journey of some three hundred miles, and it is not certain whether the mother's family was still there at that time.

From comparing birthplaces of all the children in a family, you can sometimes pick up clues to the family's migration. For example, Ben and Josephine Duckworth went to Texas from Jasper County, Mississippi, where she appeared in the 1850 and 1860 censuses with her parents, Alfred and Demarius Shelby. In 1870, the couple was in Milam County, Texas, with children Robert (4, Mississippi), May (2, Mississippi), and Benjamin F. Jr. (1/12, Texas). This census helps us estimate that the family moved to Texas in 1868 or 1869. In fact, Ben was a witness to a deed of his wife's uncle John P. Shelby in neighboring Robertson County, Texas, in March 1870. By 1880, the Duckworths had moved back to Mississippi. Among the children, the 1880 census shows son Eddie (7, Texas) and daughter Maude (5, Mississippi). This information helps the searcher with a range of dates for their moving: possibly late 1873 until early 1875. You could round off the choices by saying they moved about 1874 until you found more evidence for a particular time.

An illustration that requires a more involved search is the case of G.W. Harrison and family who were in Victoria, Texas, in 1850. The list of children shows that the four eldest were born in Virginia between 1832 and 1839. The nine-year-old was born in Florida. The six-year-old was born back in Virginia, and the three-year-old was born in Arkansas. The 1840 census apparently found them in Apalachicola, Franklin County, Florida, although one living son was left off the enumeration. The birth of the next child in Virginia could mean that the family moved back to Virginia or that the mother went back home to have the baby about 1843 or 1844. The birth of the last child in Arkansas took place in 1846 or early 1847. Then, both parents were in Victoria County, Texas, by July 1847, when they sold a slave named Ritter and bought land. The census record cannot help us determine where in Arkansas they lived, but it can help narrow the range of time in which to look for them there.

A different situation arises when the census taker gives us more information than we expected. Occasionally, for *birthplace*, the enumerator wrote down the exact town or county in which each person was born. Chatham County, Georgia, is one of several Georgia counties in the 1860 census to furnish this marvelous information, in beautiful handwriting as well. Patience R. Pleasants (56, a "lady of leisure") was born in Petersburg, Virginia. Living with her was apparently a daughter, Eloise (32), born in Richmond, Virginia. Eloise's husband, Alexander Campbell, a 32-year-old wharf clerk, was from Argyleshire, Scotland. What a boon to searchers to get this immigrant's birthplace, especially since Campbell is such a common name here and in Scotland.

Also in Chatham County, in the county jail, were I. Egbert Farnum (34, an adventurer) from Charleston, South Carolina, in jail for piracy; John Lawson (50, a merchant) from Sevier County, Tennessee, in jail for bank robbery; Louis W. Wells (45, a commission merchant) from Hartford County, Connecticut, locked up for swindling; and Betty C. McLean (30, a prostitute) from Kilkenny, Ireland, in jail for vagrancy.

Chatham County in 1860 had hundreds of immigrants, especially from Ireland and Germany. Although the parents' birthplaces in the following family were not very specific, notice that enumerator Charles J. White was meticulous about recording vital information for the children. The parents, John and Louisa Schwencke (both 39, both born in Prussia), had three children. The eldest son, John, was born in New York City and in June 1860 was 10 years and 10 months of age (written $10^{10}/_{12}$). The second son, Charles, was born in Philadelphia and was 7 years, 4 months of age. The youngest child was daughter Louisa, born in Savannah, age 3 years and 11 months.

If these parents gave accurate ages for their children, then we can figure birthdates fairly closely. John had already passed his tenth birthday by June 1 (census day) and completed ten months of his eleventh year. We could estimate his birthdate as July 1849. Charles had turned seven earlier in 1860 and had completed four months of his eighth year. We could therefore estimate his birthdate as January 1853. Louisa had completed eleven months of her fourth year by June 1, 1860. This suggests that she would turn four in June and implies a June 1856 birthdate. Not only do we get more precise birthdate possibilities from this census, we get more precise information on when and where to look for the family as they became established in their new country.

In 1850, Caldwell County, Kentucky, was one county that supplied more specific birthplaces on the census than was required. For inhabitants born in Kentucky, the enumerator listed the county of birth. The family of Abraham Crider can be more easily traced with this information. Abraham was 30 and born in Livingston County, Kentucky. His wife, Sarah (27) was

born in Caldwell County, as were the two older children, John H. (7) and Sarah A. (5). The third child, William (4), was born in Crittenden County, neighboring on the northwest, and Daniel M. (1) was born in Illinois, across the Ohio River from Crittenden and Livingston. Now, in 1850, the family was back in Caldwell. Next to this family was John Crider, Jr. (57) from Virginia, his wife, Elizabeth (49), from North Carolina, and another William (5), born in Caldwell County, Kentucky. One immediately wants to pursue the possibility that Abraham was the son of this John, Jr. Based on the census information, one could certainly focus a search in Caldwell and Crittenden and their parent county of Livingston. The practice of searching in parent and neighboring counties often pays off, but with this census information you would suspect that the family had actually lived in all three of these. This family had apparently moved several times but had stayed in the same general area. (Yes, there is always the possibility that only the wife was in each county giving birth to the child at some relative's house and that *her* relatives were the ones moving.)

WHERE TO FIND CENSUS SCHEDULES

1790-1920 Population Schedules, Slave Schedules, Soundex, etc.

It is one thing to know about a particular census schedule, but it is quite another to locate it so that you can use it. It may be great to know where the originals are for all these census volumes, but most of the originals are not available for the public to use. Fortunately, microfilm copies of the general population schedules are readily available. The National Archives and its twelve branches have extensive census collections. Each branch has all the regular population and Soundex schedules, the 1900 and 1910 enumeration district descriptions, and the 1910 cross index to selected city streets. Some of the branches have scattered supplemental and mortality schedules and the 1885 state-federal censuses. Inquire of the branch in your research area for specifics; the branches are listed in Appendix D. Many public and university libraries, historical societies, archives, and specialty libraries in each state have the population schedules for their state and often for surrounding states. Larger genealogy and public libraries have these census records for all or many states. These collections often include the slave schedules, Soundex, Union veterans and widows, and other related schedules discussed in this chapter.

It is not possible in this book to list all libraries that have census records. Call or write the libraries in your area for their holdings. Investigate rental through your local public library, a branch of the FHL or the AGLL. For interlibrary loan or purchase of microfilm copies, consult the list at the end of this chapter. Refer to the library/archives appendix for addresses of the repositories listed in that chart.

Many genealogical periodicals have published selected censuses. Periodical indexes are discussed in chapter eight. In addition, printed census schedules and indexes are available from various publishers including historical societies, genealogical societies, AGES, Genealogical Publishing Company, Heritage Books, Iowa Genealogical Society, the Reprint Publishers Company, and Byron Sistler and Associates. You will find their addresses in Appendix E.

The following chart deals with what I call the *AIMS Schedules* discussed in this chapter, but many of these same libraries and archives have the population schedules as well.

AIMS Schedules, 1850-1880

The chart below is given to help genealogists learn where they can go to use the records pertaining to their search area. The libraries listed generally have microfilm or printed copies available for patron use. They may have the originals, but for obvious reasons these often have limited access. The chart indicates the presence of the schedules for that state, for the years indicated, and reflects information supplied by these institutions. In addition are listed major research facilities that do not have these particular schedules. Naming them in no way intends or implies criticism of their collection, but hopes to save readers time in figuring out where to go and staff librarians time in dealing with researchers looking for the schedules. Of course, some of these institutions may acquire the schedules in the future, and other libraries, not listed here, may have the schedules for their own state. In addition, a number of the mortality schedules have been published. For these publications, inquire in your area libraries, or consult publishers' catalogs.

Addresses for the libraries and archives in this chart are listed in the appendix. Rental and purchase information is at the end of the chart.

A = Agricultural
I = Industry/Manufacturing
M = Mortality
S = Social Statistics
DDD = 1880 Defective, Dependent, Delinquent Schedule
50, 60, 70, 80 = Years available

Alabama Archives — A 50-80, I 50-70 (80 limited use of original), M 50-80, S 50-70, DDD.

Alabama, Birmingham Public Library — A 50-80, I 50-80, M 50-80.

Alaska — none taken.

Arizona State Library and Archives — M 50-80.

Arkansas Archives — A 50-80, I 50-80, M 50-80, S 50-70, DDD.

Arkansas, Southwest Arkansas Regional Archives, Washington — M 50-80.

Arkansas, University of Arkansas, Fayetteville — A 50-80, I 50-80, M 50-80, S 50-70, DDD.

California Archives — A 60, 80, I 60, 80, S 60, 80.

California State Library — A 50-80, I 50-80, M 50-80, S 50-80.

California, University of California at Berkeley, Bancroft Library — A 50-80, I 50-80, M 50-80, S 50-70, DDD.

Colorado Archives — AIM for the 1885 state census. See North Carolina — Duke University.

Colorado Historical Society — M 70.

Colorado, Denver Public Library — M 70-80.

Connecticut State Library — A 50-80, I 50-80, M 50-80, S 50-70, DDD.

Delaware Archives — A 50-80, I 50-80, M 50-80, S 50-80, DDD.

Delaware Historical Society — A 50-80, I 50-80, M 50-80, S 50-60, DDD.

District of Columbia Historical Society — none of these. See North Carolina — Duke University.

District of Columbia, National Archives — has most AIMS for GA, IL, IA, KS, LA, MA, MI, NE, OH, PA, TN, TX, VA, WA. Plus M for AZ, CO, DC, GA, KY, LA, TN. Inquire about others.

Florida Archives — A 50-80, I 50-80, M 50-80, S 50-80. May have DDD.

Florida State Library — A 50-80, I 50-80, M 50-80, S 50-80.

Florida State University Library — DDD.

Georgia Archives — A 50-80, I 60, 80, M 50-80, S 50-70, DDD.

Georgia Historical Society — A 50-60, M 50-60. See

North Carolina – Duke University.

Hawaii – not applicable, not part of US until 1898.

Idaho Historical Society, Genealogy Department – A 70-80, I 70-80, M 70-80, S 70, 80?

Idaho Historical Society, Library and Archives – M 80.

Idaho State Archives – A 70-80, I 70-80, M 70-80, S 70, DDD, plus M-80 for Dakota Terr. 1870 schedules do not include Alturas Co. 1880 schedules for Oneida-Washington Cos. only.

Illinois Archives – A 50-80, I 50-80 (70 A-L counties only), M 50-80, S 50-70, DDD.

Illinois State Historical Library – none of these.

Illinois, Newberry Library – A 50-80, I 50-80, M 50-80, S 50-80, plus AIM for many other states.

Indiana, Allen County Public Library – A 50-80, I 50-80, M 50-80. Has mortality schedules for nearly all other states.

Indiana Archives – A 50-80, I 50-80, S 50-80, DDD.

Indiana Historical Society – none of these.

Indiana State Library-Genealogy Section – M 50-80. Also M for AZ, CO, DC, GA, KY, LA, TN.

Iowa Genealogical Society – M 50-80, plus some M for IL, IN, KS.

Iowa Historical Society & Archives, Des Moines – A 50-80, I 50-80, M 50-80, S 50-80, DDD.

Iowa Historical Society & Archives, Iowa City – A 50-80, I 50-80, M 50-80, S 50-80, DDD.

Kansas Historical Society – A 60-80, I 60-80, M 60-80. Ask about DDD, National Archives Film T 1130.

Kentucky Archives – A 50-80, I 50-80, M 50-80, plus M for AZ, CO, DC, GA, LA, TN, 50-80.

Kentucky, Filson Club – M 50 (part)-80. See North Carolina – Duke University.

Louisiana, New Orleans Public Library, Louisiana Section – I 80, M 50-80. See North Carolina – Duke University.

Louisiana State Library, Louisiana Section – A 50-80, M 50-80, S 50-80, DDD.

Louisiana State University, Middleton Library – A 50-80, I 50-80, M 50-80, S 50-80, DDD.

Maine Archives – A 50-80, I 50-80, M 50-80, S 50-80. (M 60 also includes "miscellaneous.") DDD.

Maine Historical Society – M 70.

Maryland Archives – A 50-80, I 50-60, 80, M 50-80, S 50-70, DDD.

Maryland Historical Society – M 50-80.

Massachusetts Archives – A 50-80, I 50-80, M 50-80, S 50-80.

Massachusetts Historical Society – none of these.

Massachusetts, New England Historic Genealogical Society – none of these.

Massachusetts State Library – none of these.

Michigan Archives – A 50-80, I 50-80, M 50-80, S 50-80.

Michigan State Library – A 60-80, I 60-80, M 50-80, S 50-80, DDD.

Minnesota Historical Society – A 60-80, I 60-80, M 60-80, S 60-80, DDD.

Mississippi Archives – A 50-80, I 50-80, M 50-80, S 50-70, DDD.

Missouri Historical Society – A 50-80, I 50-80, M 50-80. Ask about DDD.

Montana Historical Society and Archives – A 70-80, I 70-80, M 70-80, S 70-80, DDD.

Nebraska Historical Society – A 50-80, I 50-80, M 50-80, DDD.

Nevada Archives – A 60-80, I 60-80, M 60-80, S 60-80, DDD. (each 1860 as part of UT)

Nevada Historical Society – A 70, I 70-80, M 70-80, S 70, DDD.

New Hampshire Archives – A 50-80, I 50-80, M 50-80.

New Hampshire Historical Society – none of these.

New Hampshire State Library – A 50-80, I 50-80, M 50-80, S 50-80, DDD.

New Jersey Archives – A 50-80, I 50-80, M 70-80, S 50-60.

New Jersey, Rutgers University, Alexander Library – A 50-80, I 50-80, M 50-80, S 50-80.

New Jersey State Library – A 50-80, I 50-80, M 50-80, S 50-80.

New Mexico, Albuquerque Public Library – none of these.

New Mexico Archives – A 50-70, M 50-70.

New York City Public Library – M 50-80.

New York Genealogical and Biographical Society – A 50-80, I 50-80, M 50-80, S 50-80, DDD.

New York Historical Society – none of these.

New York State Library – A 50-80, I 50-80 (70 for Essex-Yates counties), M 50-80, S 50-70 (60 for Monroe-Yates), DDD.

North Carolina Archives – A 50-80, I 50-80, M 50-80, S 50-80, DDD.

North Carolina, Duke University – has CO (A 70-80, I 70-80, S 70, DDD), DC (all A, I, S 50-70, DDD), GA (all A, I-80, S 50-70, DDD), KY (all A, I, S 50-70, DDD), LA (All A, I 80, S 50-70, DDD), MT (A, 80), NV (A 80), TN (all A, I 50, 80, parts 60-70, S

50-70, DDD), VA (Halifax Co., AIMS 60 plus Slave Schedule plus Population Schedule), WY (A 80).

North Carolina, University of North Carolina—A, I 50-80 for AL, AR, DE, FL, GA, KY, LA, MD, MS, NC, SC, TX, VA, WV.

North Dakota Historical Society—M 80 (See South Dakota). Also state M 85.

Ohio, Cincinnati Public Library—M 50-60, 80.

Ohio Historical Society—A 50-70, 80?, I-some, M 50-60, S-not sure, DDD.

Ohio State Library and Archives—A 50-80, I 50-80, M 50 (counties H-W), 60 all, 80 (counties A-Geauga), DDD.

Ohio, Western Reserve Historical Society—M 50-60, 80.

Oklahoma—Apparently none taken. The only census from these years is 1860.

Oregon Archives—A 50, 70-80, I 50-80, M 50-80, S 50-70, DDD.

Oregon State Library—A 50-80, I 50-80, M 50-80, S 50-80, DDD.

Pennsylvania Archives—none of these.

Pennsylvania State Library—A 50-80, I 50-80, M 70-80, S 60-80, DDD.

Rhode Island Archives—A 50-80, I 50-80, M 50-80, S 50-80.

Rhode Island Historical Society—A 50, 60-some, I 50-60, M 50-60, S 50.

South Carolina Archives—A 50-80, I 50-80, M 50-80, S 50-80, DDD.

South Carolina, University of South Carolina, South Caroliniana Library—M 50-60 indexes

South Dakota Archives & Historical Society—A 70-80, M 60-80, plus state 1885, DDD.

Tennessee Archives and State Library—A-50-80, I 50-80, M 50-60, 80, DDD. See North Carolina—Duke University.

Texas Archives—A 50-80, I 50-80, M 50-80, S 50-70, DDD.

Texas, Dallas Public Library—A 50-80, I 50-80, M 50-80, S 50-80, DDD.

Texas, Houston Public Library, Clayton Library—M 50-80. Plus M for about thirty other states, some A I S and DDD for FL, ID, OR, TN, WY.

Utah, Family History Library, Salt Lake City—A 50-80, I 60-70, M 50-80, S 50-70. Also has some schedules for most other states.

Vermont Archives—none of these.

Vermont Department of Libraries—A 50-80, I 50-80, M 70-80. Ask about M 50-60.

Vermont Historical Society—none of these.

Virginia Archives and State Library—A 50-80, I 50-80, M 50-80, S 50-80, DDD.

Virginia, DAR Library—M in books or on microfilm for a number of states.

Virginia Historical Society—A 60.

Washington Archives—A 60-80, I 60-80, M 60-80, S 60-80. Ask about DDD, National Archives Film A1154.

Washington, Seattle Public Library—M 60-70.

Washington D.C., see District of Columbia.

West Virginia Archives—A 50-80, I 50-80, M 50-80, S 50-80, DDD.

West Virginia, Marshall University Archives—M 50-80, plus M 50 for OH, 50-60 for KY.

West Virginia University, Morgantown—A 50-80, I 50-80, M 50-80, S 50-80.

Wisconsin Historical Society—A 50-80, I 50-80, M 50-80, S 50-80. Ask about DDD.

Wyoming Archives—A 70, I 80, M 70-80, S 70, DDD.

Interlibrary Loan and Purchase. Libraries that offer census or the AIMS and DDD schedules for interlibrary loan or purchase are listed below. This list does not imply that these are the only libraries with these services. You can write or call a library to inquire about the availability of a particular schedule. Interlibrary loan means rental, and fees vary. Usually the most economical way is to make the request through your local public or university library's Interlibrary Loan Department, but the best availability may be through the lending libraries, with whom you must deal directly.

ILL= Interlibrary Loan
P= Purchase of microfilm copies
AIMS, DDD= same as above
Census= Federal census schedules, sometimes Soundex, Slave, Union Vets and Widows for that state.

Arizona Archives—Census - ILL.

Arizona Historical Society—Census - P.

Arkansas, University of Arkansas, Fayetteville—AIMS, DDD - ILL, some P possible.

California State Library—AIMS - ILL to any U.S. Library.

Colorado Historical Society—Census, M - P.

Florida Archives—Census, AIMS - P.

Georgia—Some P.

Illinois Archives—Census - ILL or P. AIMS, DDD - P.

Iowa Historical Society, Des Moines and Iowa City—Census and Iowa M - ILL.

Kansas Historical Society—Census, AIM - ILL, some P. Write or call (913) 296-4776 for details.

Kentucky Archives—Census, AIM - P.

Louisiana State Library—Census, AS, DDD - ILL.

Minnesota Historical Society—AIMS, DDD - ILL, P.

Mississippi Archives—Census, AIMS, DDD - P.

New York Public Library—Census, M - P.

North Carolina Archives—Census, AIMS, DDD - P.

North Carolina, Duke University—AIMS, DDD - ILL. P through Newspapers/Microforms Dept.

North Carolina, University of North Carolina—AI - ILL (all), P (all except AR, DE, SC).

Oregon State Library—M - ILL. Inquire about the others.

South Carolina Archives—AIMS, DDD - P.

Utah, Family History Library—Census, AIMS - Loan through their Family History Centers.

Wyoming Archives—Census, AIMS, DDD - P.

Scholarly Resources—Authorized dealer for purchase of any National Archives microfilm copies.

National Archives—Purchase of census for all states, AIMS schedules for many (50-80 unless otherwise noted)—GA (Film no. T1137), IL (T1133), IA (T1156), KS (A1130), LA (T1136), MA (T1204), MI (T1164), MI (M 50 only, from OH State Library, T1163), NE (60-80, T1128), OH (T1159), PA (A 50-80, T1138) (I 50-80, T1157) (S 50-80, T597), TN (T1135), TX (T1134), VA (T1132), WA (60-80, A1154). Mortality schedules formerly in the custody of the DAR (T655)—AZ, CO, DC, GA, KY, LA, TN. Inquire about more recent acquisitions.

American Genealogical Lending Library—Loan to members only, purchase at discount to members, and full price to nonmembers. All available census and Soundex. Selected slave, Union vets, and other schedules. Various AIMS for IL, KS, MA, MT, NE, OR, TX, VA. Mortality schedules, same as National Archives, plus MS, NV, OR, WV. Inquire about more recent acquisitions.

National Archives Microfilm Rental Program—Loan of general population census schedules only.

Family History Library, Salt Lake City—Loan through their Family History Centers. Catalog available at those centers.

Footnotes are on page 175.

CHAPTER THREE

State Censuses and State Records

STATE CENSUSES

A census is a counting of people, begun on the federal level for the purposes of determining representation in the federal House of Representatives and used for state legislative representation as well. This kind of census needs to know the whole number of persons in a given area. The enumeration, therefore, has to include citizens and noncitizens, adults and children, males and females, and in earlier years, free and non-free. According to the process set out in the Northwest Ordinance of 1787, a territory could form a legislature when it had five thousand free white males age 21 or older and could become a state when it had a population of sixty thousand free persons. This process was a primary reason for frequent territorial censuses. On a smaller scale, a census was sometimes taken for the purpose of taxation or militia service, as when counting males over 21, or to identify school-age children.

The decennial federal census records are valuable and necessary records for genealogists, but they are not complete. To fill the gaps between federal enumerations and to help make up for the missing schedules, genealogists must rely on other sources. Censuses taken under the authority of the state or territorial governments can provide such assistance.

Not all states have taken state censuses, and many that were taken were statistical only, without names. Although some name only heads of household, others name each individual within the household as well. The purely statistical censuses do not provide genealogical information and, therefore, are not considered here.

How Can State Censuses Help?

State censuses help genealogists in exactly the same ways that federal censuses do. They present a picture of the family between decennial censuses, can indicate children born since the last census, or can suggest whether family members have died or moved away. If for some reason the family was missed in a federal census, the state enumeration may help fill the gap in information.

Especially useful state censuses, even the ones that name only heads of households, are those in states that have suffered the loss of courthouse records in fires. The 1866 Mississippi census for Jasper County is a good example. The 1860 federal census had shown John Moffitt (86, South Carolina) and wife, Elisabeth (82, Virginia). In the state census, dated 4 December 1865, both are shown still alive. John was listed in the 90-100 column, and his wife, in the 80-90 bracket. This information helps narrow down the range of possible death dates for this long-lived couple.

In neighboring Smith County, Mississippi, the John P. Shelby family appeared on the 1866 state census. From previous census and family records, both parents can be identified as the male and female in the 40-50 age bracket. From the same sources, names could be put with the two boys under 10 and the two boys between 10 and 20. The interesting statistics fall in the remaining two categories. John and his wife had two sons who should appear in the twenty to thirty group: George, who would be about 20-21, and William, about 22-23. Only one is marked in that column. We know from later census records, Confederate service record, and pension application that George lived and moved with the family to Texas by 1870. However, the last known record of William is the 1860 census. He does not appear in Civil War records or later censuses, and apparently is not with the family in this state census. Although this census did not solve the problem of his whereabouts, it did aid in identifying another family member.

In the same family, in the column for females under 10, the census indicates two little girls. The only one shown in the 1860 census was Mary, born between 1854 and 1858. (Records vary considerably on her birthdate.) Who was the second girl? The answer seems to be in the deed records of the Texas county to which the family moved. When the older brother, Irvin, died intestate in 1912, his heirs were listed in a deed record, selling his land. Because Irvin never married, had no direct descendants, and both his parents had died, his heirs were his brothers and sisters, or their heirs. All the brothers except William were listed, as was sister Mary, now a widow. However, five additional people were named as heirs. Census and marriage records showed that these five were Oldham children born to Lafayette and Anna/Annie M. (Shelby) Oldham. According to their marriage record in the Robertson County courthouse, this couple married in 1879 *at Mr. Shelby's*. The marriage record did not indicate whether Mr. Shelby was her father. Nevertheless, Annie was one of Irvin's heirs. In order for Annie's children to be heirs in 1912, she must have already died.

For whatever reason, this Shelby family does not show up in the 1870 census in this county although deed records and a legislative petition show they were there. Therefore, we cannot know whether Annie was living with the family in 1870. We do know she was a Shelby and she was a legal heir of Irvin. That gives two possible scenarios. Either she was a daughter of John P. and Matilda and therefore a sister to Irvin and the others, or she was the only heir of deceased brother William. If she was a daughter of William, she would have been born when William was about 17 or 18 years old, which was pretty young for a man to marry in those years. If she was a daughter of John P. and his wife, she would have been born in the five-year gap between two known siblings, when the mother was 39. Whatever the answer, the fact remains that the state census in 1866 seems to show her with the family as the other little girl under 10 years of age. She was five. This state census was the first indication that there might have been another child in the family.

Where Are State Censuses?

The list below concentrates only on state censuses that named heads of household or family members, not on substitutes or statistical censuses. The chart is organized to help searchers know where to <u>find and use</u> these sources. Alphabetical by state, it includes repositories that have originals or microfilm copies. Because other libraries in each state may well have this material, inquire within your research area. A number of state censuses have been published and may be <u>purchased</u> from state historical societies, libraries or ar-

chives as well as commercial publishers. Many of these censuses are available on <u>interlibrary loan</u> from the FHL or the AGLL. Contact these institutions for availability. The following abbreviations are used in the chart:

> *Date= year of the census. It assumes heads of household only, unless otherwise noted.*
> *ILL= Interlibrary loan of microfilm copies from this institution.*
> *P= Purchase of microfilm copies available from this institution.*

Alabama Archives—1855, not all counties, has printed index. 1866, not indexed. See also pre-1817 Mississippi schedules. Partial 1820 census (Baldwin, Conecuh, Dallas, Franklin, Limestone, St. Clair, Shelby, Wilcox counties) as published in *Alabama Historical Quarterly*, vol. 6 (1944), p 339-515.

Alaska State Library—Early Alaska censuses were lists of native inhabitants of individual towns or islands and can be found in the U.S. Serial Set. (See chapter eight for explanations.)

1870 Sitka census, H.exdoc. 5 (42-1) serial 1470, p 13-26. Family members with name, age, birthplace, occupation, relation to head, and remarks on conditions.

1880 Sitka census in *Report of Commander of Navy Ship Stationed at Sitka, 1879-1880, on Affairs in Alaska* (Captain L.A. Beardslee), S.exdoc. 71 (47-1, vol 4), serial 1989, p 34. April 1880, U.S. citizens by birth, names heads of household only. Naturalized citizens listed with birthplace.

1881 Sitka census, February 1881, H.exdoc. 81 (47-1) serial 2027, p 14-22. Family members with name, age, nationality, occupation. Page 23, Indian village at Sitka, heads only. In *Report of Naval Officers Cruising in Alaska Waters.*

1885 Cape Smyth, Pt. Barrow, H.exdoc. 44 (48-2) serial 2298. Page 49, Eskimo families. Page 50, individuals with age, height, weight.

1890-1895 St. George Island, H.exdoc. 92, pt. 1 (55-1) serial 3576. Family members with age, relationship to head. 1890-p 256. 1891-p 315. 1892-p 357. 1893-p 441. 1894-p 464, includes birth, marriage, death records. 1895-p 485.

1890-1895 St. Paul Island, same document as above. Family members with age, relationship to head. 1890-p 253, includes birthplace, occupation. 1892-p 354. 1894-p 462. 1895-p 481, includes birthplace.

1904—St. George (p 58) and St. Paul (p 43) islands, native population, S.doc. 98 (59-1) serial 4911. Family members with age, relationship to head. St. George gives birthdates, and lists government employees by name only. Page 50-St. Paul births and deaths from doctor during 1903-1904 year.

1905—St. George (p 113) and St. Paul (p 105) islands, serial 4911 (same as above). Family members with age, relationship to head. St. George gives birthdates.

1907—St. George (p 118) and St. Paul (p 101) islands, S.doc. 376 (60-1) serial 5242. Family members with age, relationship to head. St. George includes birthdates.

Arizona Archives—1864, 1866, 1872, 1876, 1882. All persons by town and county. Names only. Not available for all counties in each year.

Arizona Historical Society—1864.

Arkansas Archives—1823 (Arkansas County only), 1829 (incomplete) sheriff censuses.

Arkansas, Southwest Arkansas Regional Archives—1823, 1829 sheriff censuses (incomplete).

California Archives—1852.

California Bancroft Library, University of California, Berkeley—Typescripts of 1852, by DAR.

California State Library—1852. ILL. See also Historical Society of Southern California *Quarterly* for Spanish period censuses, 1790, 1816, 1836, 1844.

Colorado Archives—1885.

Colorado Historical Society—1885, family members included. P. Also available for purchase from National Archives (M158) or Scholarly Resources, for rent from AGLL or FHL.

Connecticut State Library—1669-1670, heads of household with numbers of family members and grain inventory. Part of the Wyllys papers in the Historical Society, vol 21. Other censuses are statistical only.

Delaware Archives—Delaware had no state censuses.

Florida Archives—Fragments exist for several early censuses: 1825 (Leon County), 1855 (Marion County), 1867 (Hernando, Madison, Orange, Santa Rosa counties), 1875 (Alachua County), 1885 (except Alachua, Clay, Nassau, and Columbia counties). 1935, 1945, both have missing pre-

cincts. 1885 also available for <u>purchase</u> from national Archives (M845) or Scholarly Resources, for <u>rent</u> from AGLL or FHL.

Georgia Archives—Georgia took septennial censuses, 1799, 1804—at least 1859. Fragments exist in Archives. Heads of household with number in household. For 1838 (Laurens, Newton, Tattnall) and 1845 (Dooly, Forsyth, Warren), see Brigid S. Townsend, comp., *Indexes to Seven State Census Reports for Counties in Georgia, 1838-1845* (Atlanta: R.J. Taylor, Jr., Foundation, 1975). For 1859 Columbia, see *Georgia Genealogical Society Quarterly*, Vol 13 (Winter 1977), 253 ff. For 1827 Taliaferro school census, 1838 Lumpkin, and 1845 Chatham, see *Censuses for Georgia Counties* (Atlanta, GA: R.J. Taylor, Jr., Foundation, 1979). Others in the Archives include these counties: 1800 Oglethorpe; 1852 Jasper, Chatham, and city of Augusta; 1859 Terrell.

Hawaii Archives—Fragments of 1866 (mostly Maui), 1878, 1890, 1896 (part of Honolulu only). Scattered districts on various islands. No complete coverage.

Idaho Historical Society Library and Archives—No state censuses.

Illinois Archives—1818, 1825 fragments, 1835 fragments, 1845 fragments, 1855, 1865. Some counties missing for 1855, 1865. ILL of 1855, 1865. P.

Illinois, Newberry Library—1855, 1865, 1825 (fragments), 1835, 1845. Also has the 1885 for CO, ND, SD, FL, NE, NM. Has NE 1875; WI 1905; NY 1855 (part), 1875 (part), 1905 (part), 1925; IA 1915 (part).

Illinois State Historical Library—1865, index for some counties.

Indiana, Allen County Public Library—1807.

Indiana Historical Society—1807, early territorial census, heads of household.

Indiana State Archives—No state censuses record names of households. They are enumerations of eligible voters. Some of these may be in county auditor's office or state library.

Iowa Genealogical Society—1856, 1915, part of 1925. Also Wisconsin 1855, 1875, part of 1895. Also Nebraska 1885. P of hard copy publications for some counties of 1849, 1852, 1856, 1863, 1869, 1885, 1895.

Iowa Historical Society, Des Moines—1836 (Dubuque and Des Moines, heads of household and numbers of family members in age categories).

1856, 1885, 1895, 1905 (incomplete and very difficult to read), 1915, 1925. (1856-1925 are whole family censuses.) ILL for 1856, 1885, 1915 from Historical Society, Iowa City. P for 1856, 1885-1925, and incomplete heads of household censuses from 1836-1897, available from Crest Information Technologies, P.O. Box 73700, 720 First Avenue NW, Cedar Rapids, IA 52407-3700, phone (800)366-0077. Besides 1836, these incomplete censuses include 1838, 1844, 1846, 1847, 1849, 1851, 1852, 1853, 1854 (many counties), 1859 (many counties), 1881, 1888, 1889, 1891-1893 (fragments), 1895, 1896, 1897. See *Hawkeye Heritage* for many that have been published.

Kansas Historical Society—1865, 1875, 1885, 1895, 1905, 1915, 1925. Contact Archives for list of available enumerations made for organization of new counties. ILL for 1865-1925, with appropriate call number. CAll (913)296-4776 for assistance with call numbers before placing request for ILL. ILL requests must go through system such as ALA or KIC (OCLC not available at this writing) from another library, not from an individual. See also Willard Heiss (comp.), *The Census of the Territory of Kansas, February, 1855* (Knightstown, IN: Eastern Indiana Publishing Co., 1968).

Kentucky Archives—No heads of household or family state censuses.

Louisiana State Library—No heads of household or family state censuses.

Maine Archives—1837 fragments (Bangor, Portland, and unincorporated towns).

Maine Historical Society—1837, town of Eliot. No statewide censuses.

Maryland—No statewide censuses taken.

Massachusetts Archives—1855, 1865, list family members. The only state censuses with names.

Massachusetts, New England Historic Genealogical Society—1855, 1865, list family members.

Michigan Archives—Only a few state census records survive. The Archives has partial enumerations for 1845, 1854, 1864, 1874, 1884, 1894. Also contact the historical library at the University of Michigan, 1150 Beal Avenue, Ann Arbor, MI 48109.

Michigan State Library—Some state censuses available. Check with county courthouses and local libraries.

Minnesota Historical Society—1849, 1857, 1865, 1875, 1885, 1895, 1905. ILL or P for all except 1849. 1857 also available from National Archives (T1175), Scholarly Resources.

Mississippi Archives—1792, 1801, 1805, 1808, 1810, 1813, 1816, 1822-1825, 1833, 1837, 1841, 1845, 1853, 1866. None are complete for entire state. Many of these are published in *Mississippi Genealogical Exchange*. Scattered town censuses. 1805 Wilkinson County in *Journal of Mississippi History* (Vol. 11, p 104-111). 1809 Madison County in *Territorial Papers of the U.S.* (Vol. 5, p 684-692). 1809 Washington County in *Territorial Papers of the U.S.* (Vol 5, p 693-696). 1810 censuses in *Journal of Mississippi History*: Amite (Vol. 10, p 150-171); Baldwin (Vol 11, p 207-213); Claiborne and Warren (Vol. 13, p 50-63); Franklin (Vol. 13, p 249-255); Jefferson (Vol. 15, p 34-46); Washington (Vol. 14, p 67-79). Originals of these 1805 and 1810 schedules are in the Archives, Territorial Archives, Series A, Vol. 10, 23, and 24.

Missouri Archives—State census for a few counties. 1876, the most complete. Check with individual counties. (1844 was another census year.)

Missouri Historical Society—1787-St. Louis and Ste. Genevieve. 1791-St. Louis area. 1803-New Madrid and Cape Girardeau. 1845-St. Louis.

Montana Historical Society—A state census was apparently voted on but never taken.

Nebraska Historical Society (and state archives)— 1854-1856, fifteen counties in eastern Nebraska. Also published in *Nebraska and Midwest Genealogical Record* (1932-1942). Also published by Evelyn M. Cox, Ellensburg, WA, 1973, and by Nebraksa Genealogical Society, 1922-1944. 1865 (Otoe, Cuming counties). 1869 (Stanton, Butler counties. 1885 statewide census, purchase from National Archives (M352) or Scholarly Resources, rent from FHL or AGLL.

Nevada State Archives—1861-1863 (ILL), with index for Storey and Ormsbee counties. This census varies from county to county because instructions were not clear. Some list male heads of household only; some are statistical only; some list all family members. It is one census, completed over a period of time. Counties available for 1862—Douglas, Storey, Washoe, Lyon, Humboldt, Ormsby. Available for 1863—Lander County. Other censuses called for by statute, but only 1875 was taken. 1875 indexed, ILL, P on fiche. Index-ILL.

Nevada Historical Society — 1862 (does not include all counties, apparently is an early filming of the 1861-1863), 1875.

Nevada, University of Nevada, Reno — 1861-1863, 1875 in Government Publications Dept.

New Hampshire Archives — No state censuses were taken.

New Jersey — New York City Public Library has NJ 1855, 1865, 1885, 1895, 1905, 1915.

New Jersey Archives — 1855 (incomplete), 1865 (incomplete), 1875 (Essex, Sussex only), 1885, 1895, 1905, 1915. Some do include family members, especially 1895-1915.

New Jersey State Library — 1855, 1865, 1875?, 1885, 1895, 1905, 1915.

New Mexico, Albuquerque Public Library — some early Spanish and Mexican censuses. Preterritorial censuses are incomplete.

New Mexico Archives — See Virginia L. Olmsted, *Spanish and Mexican Colonial Censuses of New Mexico, 1790, 1823, 1845* (Albuquerque: New Mexico Genealogical Society, 1975). A second volume from the Society covers the 1750, 1790 (part), and 1830 Spanish and Mexican Colonial Censuses. Contact the NM Genealogical Society, P.O. Box 8283, Albuquerque, NM 87198-8283. These include household members. 1885 territorial census is the only one since 1845. 1885, purchase from the New Mexico Archives, National Archives (M846), or Scholarly Resources, rent from FHL.

New York City Public Library — 1855, 1905, 1915, 1925, but not all counties. New York County (Manhattan) 1905, 1915, 1925 available at county clerk's office, 60 Centre Street, NY 10007. That county's 1890 Police census available at Division of Old Records, NY County Clerk, 31 Chambers Street, NY 10007. Kings County (Brooklyn) 1855, 1865, 1875, 1892, 1905, 1915, 1925 available at the county clerk's office, New Supreme Court Building, 308 Adams Street, Brooklyn, NY 11201. Bronx County 1915, 1925 at county clerk's office, 851 Grand Concourse, Bronx, NY 10451. Queens County 1892, 1915, 1925 at county clerk's office, 88-11 Sutphin Blvd., Jamaica, NY 11435. Staten Island 1915, 1925 at county clerk's office, County Court House, Staten Island, NY 10301. Try other county clerks to learn which ones they have.

New York Genealogical and Biographical Society — 1825-1875 (every ten years). Not all counties available.

New York State Library — 1825, 1835, 1845, 1855, 1865, 1875, 1892, 1905, 1915, 1925. (1855 especially helpful because it gives county of birth, length of residence in current location.) Consult county clerks and county historians for what they have.

North Carolina Archives — 1785-1787, incomplete. None after 1790.

North Dakota Historical Society — 1857 Pembina County. 1885, northern part of Dakota Territory. 1915, 1925. ILL for 1885, 1915, 1925. These give name and age of all family members. 1885 also gives occupation and birthplace and includes agricultural, industrial, mortality schedules and Civil War veterans. 1925 from AGLL — ILL or P.

Ohio Archives — Ohio did not maintain state census records.

Ohio Historical Society — 1803 census of Ohio, Northwest Territory, in preparation for statehood. Ohio had no state census as such.

Oklahoma Historical Society — 1890 First Territorial Census of Oklahoma (of unassigned lands, not Indian Territory), indexed, includes family members. P. For rent from AGLL and FHL.

Oregon Archives — 1842-1846 various counties. 1849, males over 21, territorial apportionment census (see also under Washington state). 1849 territorial census. 1850-1859 various counties. 1865, Benton, Columbia, Marion, Umatilla counties. 1870, 1875 Umatilla County. 1885 Linn, Umatilla counties. 1895, Linn, Morrow, Multnomah, Marion counties. 1905, Baker, Lane, Linn, Marion counties.

Oregon Historical Society — 1841-1849, indexes. 1842-1859 provisional, territorial censuses.

Oregon State Library — Some. ILL. P from State Archives.

Pennsylvania Historical Society and State Library — No real state censuses.

Rhode Island — AGLL lists *Census of the Inhabitants of the Colony of Rhode Island and Providence Plantations, 1774, taken by order of the General Assembly*, originally published 1858, arranged by John R. Bartlett with index by E.E. Brownell (Baltimore: Genealogical Publishing Company, 1969).

Rhode Island Archives—1865, 1875, 1885, 1915, 1925, 1935.

Rhode Island Historical Society—1865.

South Carolina Archives—1829-Fairfield, Laurens districts. 1839-Kershaw, Chesterfield districts. 1869-all counties except Clarendon, Oconee, Spartanburg. 1875-Clarendon, Newberry, Marlboro, and partial schedules for Abbeville, Beaufort, Fairfield, Lancaster, and Sumter counties.

South Dakota Historical Society and State Archives—1885, 1905, 1915, 1925, 1935, 1945. 1895 state census ILL, available for Beadle, Brule, Pratt/now Jones, Presho/now Lyman, Campbell, Charles Mix counties only. 1885 census, also ILL, available for these counties: Beadle, Butte, Charles Mix, Edmunds, Fall River, Faulk, Hand, Hanson, Hutchinson, Hyde, Lake, Lincoln, Marshall, McPherson, Moody, Roberts, Sanborn, Spink, Stanley, and Turner.

Tennessee State Library—No state censuses extant.

Texas—No state censuses. Mexican and Republic censuses: 1830-San Antonio and Nacogdoches, transcribed in Gifford E. White, *1830 Citizens of Texas* (Austin, TX: Eakin Press, 1983). 1829, 1834-1836 in *National Genealogical Society Quarterly*. Vol. 40-44; reprinted as *The First Census of Texas, 1829-1836*, by Marion Day Mullins (Washington, DC [now Arlington, VA]: NGS, 1976). Austin's Colony census 1819-1826 in *National Genealogical Society Quarterly*, Vol. 45 (1957); printed as a book, 1959.

Utah, Family History Library—1856 territorial census with every name index.

Vermont Historical Society—Vermont has never taken a state census.

Virginia—No state censuses.

Washington Archives—1856, 1857, 1858, 1860, 1871, 1873, 1874, 1875, 1877, 1878, 1879, 1880, 1881, 1883, 1885, 1887, 1889, 1891, 1892. Various counties each year. P.

Washington, in Oregon Archives and Historical Society—1849 territorial census.

Washington, Seattle Public Library—1871-1892 Auditor Census rolls from State Archives.

Washington State Library—Auditor Census Rolls, compiled by county assessors, 1871, 1873, 1877, 1881, 1883, 1885, 1887, 1889, 1892, various counties each year. Family members.

West Virginia—No state censuses.

Wisconsin Historical Society—1836, 1838, 1842, 1846, 1847, 1855, 1865 (fragments),1875, 1885, 1895, 1905 (families).

Wisconsin—*Milwaukee County, Wisconsin Censuses of 1846 and 1847*, indexed (Miami Beach, FL: TLC Genealogy Books, current).

Wisconsin, University of Wisconsin at Milwaukee—1865-Ozaukee, Sheboygan counties.

Wyoming Archives—1869, family members included.

Census Substitutes and Early Residents Lists

When a census record is lost and therefore no longer available for searching, genealogists and historians sometimes pull together information of a similar nature to help overcome the loss. This substitute census, then, is an effort to identify as many of the people as possible who may have appeared in the original record. Usually these substitutes include only heads of household because these are the people most often identified in the records that are used to compile the substitute. Married women and children were not likely to be found in tax records and were not eligible to vote, subject to military service, or called for jury duty. Thus they do not usually appear in census substitutes. Nor are most substitutes able to give numbers of family members. Nor can the substitutes give age and birthplace information for the men whom they list, unless the compilation is annotated and edited to include that kind of data. Nevertheless, they can be extremely useful for identifying a community of people at a given time.

Occasionally, lists of residents are called censuses, in the broadest sense of the term—an effort to identify a large group of people in a given place at a given time. One example is Jay Mac Holbrook's *Connecticut 1670 Census* (Oxford, Massachusetts: Holbrook Research Institute, 1977), which has amplified an existing head of household census made in Hartford, Wethersfield, and Windsor. Holbrook used tax, land, probate, church, and other records to identify over two thousand people, almost all men, in the colony in the period between 1667 and 1673. No attempt is made to identify relationships or family groups. Other examples are listed in chapter two in the discussion of the 1790 census.

Various sources that include large numbers of people are used as substitute censuses. Very useful examples are tax lists, voter lists, and legislative petitions. However, in a much more narrow sense, any source that identifies an individual and/or family in a given place at a given time becomes a substitute for a census record. In this sense, every record of an individual is like a census substitute and is sometimes more helpful than the best census. Whether the source places the individual among a large community group, a family group, an extended family cluster, or several friends who act as witnesses to a document, the genealogist can learn something more about the ancestor.

The following are some of the document groups that are used as census substitutes. For others, consult guides to research in your state(s) of interest, guides to the archives of these states, and the catalogs of the FHL and AGLL, under the name of the state, county, or city.

Alabama—1907-Confederate Soldiers in Alabama. *Deep South Genealogical Quarterly* of Mobile Genealogical Society, scattered eighteenth-century enumerations in Vol. 1-3, 5. *Alabama Genealogical Register* of Tuscaloosa, vol. 9, early Washington County enumerations and 1819 residents of northern Alabama.

Alaska—1903-1904 school list, St. Paul Island, S.doc. 98 (59-1), serial 4911, p 50. Forty pupils: name, age, attendance, and marks. 1871-Petition of St. George residents, p 25-26 of S.exdoc. 12 (44-1) serial 1664. 1876-Memorial of citizens of California, Oregon, Washington Territory, Alaska Territory, and British Columbia stationed at Ft. Wrangel, S.exdoc. 14 (44-2), serial 1718, p 4-5.

Arizona Archives—Great Registers of Voters, various years from 1866-1938. School superintendent censuses, various years from 1870-1963. Tax rolls from 1872-1958, coverage for each county varies in archives holdings.

California Archives—Mission and presidio residents lists, late eighteenth century. Some twentieth-century town and city enumerations.

Colorado Archives—1861 poll lists (voters only), 1866 enumeration of northeastern Colorado.

Connecticut—Salisbury, Litchfield County, taxpayers in 1746, 1756, 1760, in an article by Donna Valley Russell, *National Genealogical Society Quarterly*, Vol. 71 (1983) p 94-98.

Delaware—"Delaware Settlers, 1693," by Alice Reinders, *National Genealogical Society Quarterly*, Vol. 53 (1965), p 205-206. Various residents lists for seventeenth century, incomplete.

Florida Archives—1855 and 1866 children's census.

Georgia Archives—School censuses, some coun-

ties, about 1898-about 1938. Check also in individual counties for these.

Hawaii Archives—Various compiled materials, including school censuses.

Idaho Historical Society Library, Archives, and Genealogy Dept.—1863 poll list, men only.

Illinois—Military census, 1861-1863.

Indiana Archives and State Library—Voter enumerations (men over 21), every six years beginning 1853. Veterans' enrollments, 1886, 1890, 1894.

Iowa Genealogical Society—Iowa Old Age Assessment Rolls, 1934-1938, half the state.

Kansas Historical Society—Kansas Board of Agriculture enumerations 1873-1924, 1926-1979.

Kentucky—School censuses, late nineteenth and early twentieth century, ask local boards of education. *The 1795 Census of Kentucky* (Miami Beach: TLC Genealogy Books, current), state-wide tax list.

Louisiana—Early residents lists, *Louisiana Historical Society Quarterly* (Vols. 1-6). 1804 Free Persons of Color, in *Territorial Papers of the U.S.* (Vol. II, p 174-175). Other early lists have been published by Genealogical Publishing Company, Polyanthos Press, University of Southwestern Louisiana.

Maryland—1778 oaths of allegiance: St. Mary's County, *National Genealogical Society Quarterly*, Vol. 41 (1953), p 69-74, 119-124; Queen Anne County, *Daughters of the American Revolution Magazine*, Vol. 101 (1967), p 545-546. Eighteenth century residents lists in Calendar of Maryland State Papers and Maryland Archives, including a 1776 census.

Massachusetts—*The Pioneers of Massachusetts [1620-1650]*, compiled by Charles Henry Pope from contemporary documents (Baltimore: Genealogical Publishing Company, 1991, reprint of 1900 original). *List of Freemen of Massachusetts, 1630-1691*, by Lucius R. Paige (Baltimore: Genealogical Publishing Company, 1988 reprint of 1849 original).

Michigan—1888 enumeration of Civil War veterans. *National Genealogical Society Quarterly* and *Detroit Society for Genealogical Research Magazine* have published some early residents lists. One is "Detroit 1796 Census," by Donna Valley Stuart, *National Genealogical Society Quarterly*, Vol. 69 (1981), p 185-194.

Mississippi—1723 Natchez residents, *National Ge-*

nealogical Society Quarterly, Vol. 59 (1971), p 94-95. 1798-1799 oaths of allegiance, Natchez district, *National Genealogical Society Quarterly*, Vol. 52 (1964), p 108-116. Spanish censuses, 1792, 1797 in state Archives. 1907, 1925-1933 enumerations of Confederate soldiers and widows.

Missouri—*Anglo-Americans in Spanish Archives*, by Lawrence Feldman (Baltimore: Genealogical Publishing Company, 1991), includes settlers in upper Louisiana.

Montana Historical Society—1864 listing of eligible voters, names only. Publications of the Historical Society contain some early residents lists.

New Hampshire—*Genealogical Dictionary of Maine and New Hampshire*, compiled by Sybil Noyes, Charles T. Libby, and Walter G. Davis on families established before 1699 (Baltimore: Genealogical Publishing Company, 1991 reprint of 1928-1938 volumes). *New Hampshire 1732 Census*, by Jay Mack Holbrook (Oxford, Massachusetts: Holbrook Research Institute, 1981), compiled from tax lists, land ownership, church, and town records. *New Hampshire 1776 Census*, by Jay Mack Holbrook (Oxford, Massachusetts: Holbrook Research Institute, 1976), from New Hampshire Association Test of 1776, adult males only, but the most complete listing of that year.

New York—*Lists of Inhabitants of Colonial New York: Excerpted from The Documentary History of the State of New York*, by Edmund B. O'Callaghan (Baltimore: Genealogical Publishing Company, 1979 reprint of excerpts from 1849-1851 original). Various counties and towns, 1675-1799, called both censuses and lists of freeholders, indexed. *Early New York State Census Records, 1663-1772*, Carol M. Meyers, comp. (Gardena, California: RAM Publishers, 1965, 2nd ed.), indexed.

North Carolina—*North Carolina Taxpayers, 1701-1786* and *North Carolina Taxpayers, 1679-1790*, compiled by Clarence E. Ratcliff (Baltimore: Genealogical Publishing Company, 1989, 1990).

Ohio—*The 1812 Census of Ohio: A Statewide Index of Taxpayers* (Miami Beach: TLC Genealogy Books, current).

Ohio Historical Society—Quadrennial enumerations 1803-1911, which were white male inhabitants over 21 only. Beginning 1863, they included

black males. Various counties for various years. Some school children censuses.

Ohio Regional Research Centers—Quadrennial enumerations and other resources at University of Akron Library, Bowling Green State University Library, University of Cincinnati Library, Ohio University Library (Athens), and Wright State University Library (Dayton).

Ohio, Western Reserve Historical Society—Quadrennial "censuses" for several Ohio counties.

Oregon Historical Society—1893 school census, Jackson County. 1905 military census, Lane County.

Pennsylvania Historical Society and Pennsylvania State Library—1779-1863, septennial enumerations.

Rhode Island—*The Rhode Island 1777 Military Census*, transcribed by Mildred M. Chamberlain (Baltimore: Genealogical Publishing Company, 1985). *Rhode Island Freemen, 1747-1755: A Census of Registered Voters*, by Bruce C. MacGunnigle (Baltimore: Genealogical Publishing Company, 1982 reprint). *Rhode Island Census, 1782*, by Jay Mack Holbrook (Oxford, Massachusetts: Holbrook Institute, 1979).

South Carolina Archives—Incomplete agricultural censuses in 1868 and 1875.

South Dakota Historical Society and Archives—School census records, various counties. Special veterans census 1895, ILL.

Tennessee Archives—1891 incomplete census of males over 21.

Texas Archives—1828 *padron* or full census. See also *1840 Citizens of Texas*, by Gifford White (Austin, Texas: privately published, 1983-1988, 3 vols.) compiled from land grants and tax rolls. *The 1840 Census of the Republic of Texas*, by Gifford E. White (Austin, Texas: Pemberton Press, 1966), compiled from tax lists. *Republic of Texas: Poll Lists for 1846*, by Marion Day Mullins (Baltimore: Genealogical Publishing Company, 1982 reprint of 1974 original). 1854-1855 scholastic census of school-age children, for forty-seven counties (Ellis-Wharton counties). 1867-1870 voter registrations. School census records, 1920s forward, Robertson County, County Judge's office; inquire in other counties.

Utah, Family History Library—1851, 1852 church bishops' reports of residents.

Virginia—*Early Virginia Immigrants, 1623-1666*,

compiled from state records by George Cabell Greer (Baltimore: Genealogical Publishing Company, 1989 reprint of 1912 original). *Virginia in 1740: A Reconstructed Census*, compiled from many sources (Miami Beach: TLC Genealogy Books, current).

Washington, in Oregon Archives and Historical Society—Apportionment census of males over 21-Lewis, Tualatin, and Vancouver included in Oregon census.

TERRITORIAL PAPERS

Long lists of inhabitants are good genealogical tools because they identify many people in one place and can be checked rather quickly. These can help you determine the county in which your ancestor lived and give you a specific location in which to search. These lists can also help you pinpoint when your ancestor was there. One of the best sources for such lists, though not available for all states, is the *Territorial Papers of the United States*, originally published by the Government Printing Office for the State Department and the National Archives between 1934 and 1975. These are government documents from the territorial period of these particular states. They include letters dealing with many issues, some maps, postal schedules, militia muster rolls, appointments, petitions to Congress about specific concerns, voter lists, jury lists, and much more. Although they are technically federal documents, they are state and local history. Most of the matters handled in these documents would have been the jurisdiction of the state or county governments if the region had been a state. For this reason, they are discussed in this chapter.

One beauty of these comprehensively indexed books is that they cover the early period of each area when population was sometimes sparse and local records may no longer exist. They also cover life in the area before or between federal census records. The letters, petitions, memorials, recommendations, and protests present such concerns as the need for closer land offices, requests for roads, requests for clearing navigable streams of obstructions, advice on which men to appoint or not appoint to various offices, and views on the effects of Congressional decisions concerning boundaries, Indian affairs, and land distribution.

Occasionally, nongovernmental matters appear as well. In Volume 13, for the Louisiana-Missouri Territory, is printed a letter of James L. Donaldson of St. Louis, dated 5 July 1806, to his father-in-law, Dr. William Stewart of Baltimore. The letter reported on a number of events and sent loving greetings to Mrs. Stewart. In an era when death frequently came early and health was a concern expressed often in letters to family and friends, it is not surprising that Donaldson added this note about his wife (to her father): "Jane never was heartier in her life."

The *Territorial Papers* are available for use in many large public, university, and research libraries throughout the country. They are available for interlibrary loan on microfilm through the AGLL. Hard-copy volumes numbered one through twenty-six may be purchased individually from AMS Press. Microform copies may be purchased from the Law Library Microform Consortium, the National Archives (M721), or Scholarly Resources. (See appendix E for addresses.) If your public library is in one of these areas and does not own the volume(s) pertaining to your own territorial period, perhaps acquisition of the hard-copy edition would be a worthy project for local genealogists to pursue.

The reference list below is but a sampling of the contents of the *Territorial Papers* to encourage searchers in these areas to use these valuable sources. The page numbers given are for the actual lists of names, some of them chosen because of the large numbers of names included. The documents to which these names are attached precede them. In these petitions, as in any petition drive or public issue, not all people who could express their views did. Therefore, the lists do not represent all inhabitants of the area at that date. The specific references included here were chosen to represent the variety of documents in the *Papers* as well as their geographic diversity. Some areas had a parent territory, in whose *Papers* earlier material can be found. (See Appendix G on reading roman numerals.)

Alabama, Territory 1817-1819 (Vol. XVIII)
The first federal census available is 1830.

Volume V (Mississippi Territory): p 71, petition from inhabitants of Tombigbee and Tensaw, August 1799.

p 294-295, petition from inhabitants of the Alabama River, November 1803.

p 741-742, petition from inhabitants of Tombigbee, 1809.

Volume VI (Mississippi Territory): p 743, petition from merchants of St. Stephens, December 1816.

p 751, petition from inhabitants of Mobile and Baldwin counties, January 1817.

p 759-761, petition by settlers on public lands west of Tennessee River, January 1817.

Volume XVIII: p 195-200, petition of about 300 residents of Clarke, Monroe, Washington, Mobile, and Baldwin counties, fall 1817.

p 614-616, petition of inhabitants of Cherokee County, 1819.

p 517-525, letters remaining at the post offices at Huntsville and St. Stephens, January 1819. p 537-540, letters at the Claiborne post office, same date.

Arkansas, Territory 1819-1836
(Vol. XIX, XX, XXI)

The first federal census available is 1830.

Volume XIV (Louisiana-Missouri Territory): p 471-479, petition from inhabitants of Louisiana Territory, September 1811. Includes names from Arkansas District.

p 528, 545, petitions of inhabitants of Arkansas District, early 1812.

Volume XV (Louisiana-Missouri Territory): p 88, Arkansas Grand Jury, October 1815.

Volume XIX: p 12-14, petition of 144 inhabitants of Arkansas County, Missouri Territory, November 1818.

p 385-389, petition of inhabitants of Arkansas Territory, 1821.

p 596-598, jurors for the Superior Court at Little Rock, August and December 1822.

Volume XX: p 69-76, Arkansas militia commissions, 1820-1825.

p 139-142, petition of inhabitants of Miller County, 1825.

p 536, list of preemption rights granted at the land office at Batesville, September 1827.

Volume XXI: p 211-212, bills of review filed with the Superior Court for adjudication of Spanish land claims, April 1830.

p 544-551, muster roll of 110 mounted rangers, September 1832.

p 868-873, petition of inhabitants of the territory, December 1833.

Florida, Territory 1821-1845
(Vol. XXII, XXIII, XXIV, XXV, XXVI)

First available federal census is 1830.

Volume XXII: p 314-315, petition of Spanish citizens of West Florida, December 1821.

p 813-814, 816-817, petitions of citizens of East Florida, December 1823.

p 477-478, petition of inhabitants of St. Johns River, June 1822.

Volume XXIII: p 3-4, petition of citizens of Pensacola, West Florida, July 1824.

p 676-678, petit jurors for the Superior Court at St. Augustine, November 1826.

p 948-949, petition of citizens of Jackson County, December 1827.

Volume XXIV: p 575-576, petition of citizens of Jefferson County, fall 1831.

p 597-599, 601-605, petition of inhabitants of Alachua, St. Johns, and Duval counties, December 1831.

p 685, trustees of the Presbyterian Church, St. Augustine, March 1832.

p 998-999, petition of 147 inhabitants of St. Augustine, April 1834.

Volume XXV: p 77-79, stockholders of Tallahassee Railroad Company, December 1834.

p 572-583, petition of citizens of the territory, January 1839.

p 625-633, petition of citizens of East Florida, August 1839.

Volume XXVI: p 494-504, petition of residents of Leon, Gadsden, Jackson, and Calhoun counties, July 1842.

p 604-608, petition of inhabitants of East Florida, January 1843.

p 717-721, permits to applicants for land, with land descriptions in section, township, and range, August 1843.

Illinois, Territory 1809-1818 (Vol. XVI, XVII)

First federal census is 1810.

Volume III (Northwest Territory): (See chapter two for 1790 list).

p 12-13, petition of inhabitants of the Illinois Country, January 1799.

p 77-78, petition of inhabitants of the Illinois Country, February 1800.

Volume VII (Indiana Territory): p 230-231, petition of inhabitants of Kaskaskia, October 1803.

p 253-254, petition from inhabitants of Fort Massac, January 1805.

p 319-323, petition from inhabitants of Randolph and St. Clair counties, December 1805.

p 432, memorial from inhabitants of Peoria, February 1807.

p 549-550, petition from people of the Illinois Country, April 1808.

Volume XVI: p 64, petition of inhabitants of Shawneetown, November 1809.

p 207-208, petition of citizens of the territory in the land district of Kaskaskia, 1812.

p 226-227, 232-237, muster rolls of Illinois militia, June 1812.

Volume XVII: p 138-139, 106 volunteers for a company of rangers, March 1815.

p 459, petition of citizens of Shawneetown, Illinois Territory, December 1816.

p 568-570, men who were volunteers with George Rogers Clark from Illinois against the post of Vincennes, 1779, during the Revolution, list dated February 1818.

Indiana, Territory 1800-1816 (Vol. VII, VIII)

First federal census is 1820.

Volume II (Northwest Territory): p 621, petition from inhabitants of Knox County, August 1797, list includes seven widows.

p 636, petition from inhabitants of Vincennes, December 1797.

Volume III (Northwest Territory): p 106-108, petition from inhabitants of Wayne County, September 1800.

p 380-384, 411-414, territorial appointments, summer 1792 and October 1793, including Knox County.

p 448-449, 454, civil and militia appointments for Wayne County, August-September 1796.

Volume VII: p 309-311, petition of inhabitants of the territory, October 1805.

p 612-613, 620-621, 628-630, petitions from citizens of Knox County, fall 1808.

p 651-655, poll book of the election in Dearborn County, May 1809.

p 687-690, petition from citizens of Clark County, December 1809.

Volume VIII: p 143-147, petitions from citizens of the territory, December 1811.

p 245-250, recommendations from citizens of Dearborn County, 1813.

p 333-335, memorial from citizens of the territory, February 1815.

Iowa, Territory 1838-1846

First federal census is 1840.

Volume XII (Michigan Territory): p 1170-1171, 1174-1175, petitions of inhabitants of Dubuque

and Des Moines counties, April 1836.

Volume XXVII (Wisconsin Territory): p 936-938, petition from inhabitants of Lee and Van-Buren counties, with some from Ft. Madison, Des Moines, date unclear, but between December 1836 and March 1838.

p 978-982, petition from inhabitants of Dubuque County, April 1838.

Louisiana (Territory of Orleans), 1803-1812 (Vol. IX)

First federal census, 1810.

p 174-175, "free people of color" of Louisiana, January 1804.

p 326-327, petition of inhabitants of Pointe Coupee, November 1804.

p 1009-1012, memorial from inhabitants of Feliciana County (*sic*), March 1812.

Michigan, Territory 1805-1837 (Vol. X, XI, XII)

First federal census, 1820.

Volume VII (Indiana Territory): p 103-106, 119-122, petitions from inhabitants of Detroit, 1803.

p 230-231, memorial from citizens of Detroit, October 1804.

Volume X: p 119-122, petition from inhabitants of Detroit, July 1807.

p. 142-149, petition from inhabitants of the territory, October 1807.

p 393-395, list of land patents received from land office, July 1812.

p 678-680, petition from inhabitants of River Raisin (River aux Raisen), December 1816.

Volume XI: p 465-479, voters of Detroit and counties of Monroe, Oakland, Macomb, St. Clair, and Michillimackinac, September 1823. Over 1,200 names.

p 735-737, men discharged at Ft. Brady, Sault Ste. Marie, 1824-1825. Gives birthplace, place of enlistment, date of discharge.

p 787-806, tax rolls for Wayne and Washtenaw counties, with place of residence, 1825.

p 866-918, voters of Monroe, Lenawee, Wayne, Oakland, Macomb, St. Clair, and Michillimackinac counties and Detroit, 1825. Over 1,700 names.

Volume XII: p 643-654, petition of inhabitants of the territory, December 1833.

p 621-624, petition of inhabitants of St. Joseph County, November 1833.

p 1036-1052, petition of inhabitants of the territory and others, November 1835.

p 1156-1167, petition of citizens concerned over changes in the southern boundary with Ohio, March 1836.

Mississippi, Territory 1798-1817 (Vol. V, VI)
First federal census, 1820.

Volume V: p 9-12, memorial from citizens of Natchez, October 1797.

p 66-68, jury report and list from Pickering (now Jefferson) County, 1799.

p 110-117, memorial from citizens of the territory, December 1800.

p 684-692, census of Madison County, 1809. Heads of household plus age categories of family members.

p 734-737, petition of inhabitants east of the Pearl River, May 1809.

Volume VI: p 108-113, petition by intruders on Chickasaw Lands, September 1810 about 450 names.

p 308-315, report on aliens, August 1812.

p 495-498, petition by about 300 inhabitants of Marion and Lawrence counties, January 1815.

p 609-617, petition by inhabitants west of the Pearl River, December 1815.

Missouri (originally, Louisiana Territory), 1803-1821 (Vol. XIII, XIV, XV)
First federal census, 1830.

Volume XIII: p 139-144, petition from citizens of St. Genevieve District, June 1805.

p 330-349, petition from inhabitants of districts of St. Louis, St. Charles, and St. Genevieve, December 1805-January 1806.

p 468-486, memorial from citizens of the territory, 1806.

Volume XIV: p 358-362, petition from inhabitants of the territory, January 1810.

p 385-397, memorial from inhabitants of the territory, 1810.

p 560-562, muster rolls of Nathan Boone's company, June 1812.

Volume XV: p 353-354, petition from inhabitants of St. Ferdinand township, St. Louis County, February 1818.

p 558-561, petition of inhabitants of Howard Land District, December 1819.

p 571-573, petition of inhabitants of New Madrid and Cape Girardeau, December 1819.

Ohio (Territory Northwest of the Ohio River), 1787-1803 (Vol. II, III)
See chapter two for 1790 inhabitants. First federal census available, 1820.

Volume II: p 424-425, petition of French inhabitants of Gallipolis, December 1792.

p 598-601, petition of inhabitants of Gallipolis, April 1797.

p 640, petition from inhabitants of Scioto, February 1798.

Volume III: p 31-35, petition from inhabitants of Hamilton County, July 1799.

p 63-65, petition from inhabitants on east side of Scioto River, August 1799.

p 476-478, civil and militia appointments for Jefferson County, July 1797.

Tennessee (Territory South of the Ohio River), 1790-1796 (Vol. IV)
First federal census, 1810 (fragments only) and 1820. See chapter two for 1790 material.

p 73, memorial from civil and militia officers of Mero District, August 1791.

p 452-458, civil and militia appointments for 1793.

p 464-470, civil and militia appointments for 1795.

Vermont
Vermont was never a territory, but Volume XVII (Illinois Territory), p 321-324, contains a petition from many citizens of Vermont, March 1816.

Volume XVII (Illinois Territory): p 321-324, petition from many citizens of Vermont, March 1816.

Wisconsin, Territory 1836-1848 (Vol. XXVII, XXVIII)
First federal census, 1820 as part of Michigan Territory.

Volume XVII (Illinois Territory): p 518-519, petition of inhabitants of Green Bay, July 1817.

Volume XI (Michigan Territory): p 199, voter list from Green Bay and Brown counties, September 1821.

p 209-213, petition from inhabitants on Green Bay and Fox River, and of Prairie du Chien, December 1821.

p 480-482, voters of Green Bay, Prairie du Chien, Crawford County, September 1823.

p 896-897, 915-916, voters of Brown County, May, June 1825.

Volume XII (Michigan Territory): p 63, 70-71,

petitions from Brown and Crawford counties, 1829.

p 110-112, petition from inhabitants of Prairie du Chien, January 1830.

p 137, 205-206, petitions from Iowa County, 1830.

Volume XXVII: many pages of land patents, 1846-1848.

p 9-13, petition of citizens of Burlington, January 1836.

p 978-982, petition of citizens of Iowa County, April 1838.

p 1080-1086, Oneida Indians, October 1838.

Volume XXVIII: p 409-410, petition of inhabitants of western portion of Wisconsin, February 1842.

p 775-776, petition of 112 citizens of Fond du Lac County, January 1845.

p 1002-1013, petition of settlers on Rock River and Milwaukee Canal Tract, October 1846.

p 1141-1142, petition of 123 female residents at Rosendale, February 1848.

Additional territorial papers have been microfilmed by the National Archives in four sets:

Iowa (1838-1846), M325, 102 rolls of microfilm, with a printed descriptive pamphlet.

Minnesota (1849-1858), M1050, 11 rolls of microfilm.

Oregon (1848-1859), M1049, 12 rolls of microfilm.

Wisconsin (1836-1848), M236, 122 rolls of microfilm, a supplement of the volumes listed above, not indexed.

Territorial Papers of the United States Senate is another microfilm collection of similar materials from the National Archives (M200, 20 rolls). The dates given below are the range of the documents, not necessarily the dates of territorial existence. After 1873, territorial affairs were handled by the Department of the Interior. Be sure to consult the parent territory for any additional information, as in the chart above.

Alabama and Arkansas (1818-1836), roll 8.
Arizona and the Dakotas (1857-1873), roll 18.
Colorado and Nevada (1860-1868), roll 17.
Florida (1806-1845), rolls 9-11.
Idaho, Montana, Wyoming (1863-1871), roll 19.
Indiana (1792-1830), roll 4.
Kansas and Nebraska (1853-1867), roll 16.
Louisiana-Missouri (1804-1822), roll 7.
Louisiana (Territory of Orleans) (1803-1815), roll 5.
Michigan (1803-1847), roll 6.

Minnesota (1847-1868), roll 14.
Mississippi (1799-1818), roll 3.
New Mexico (1840-1854), roll 14.
Ohio (Territory Northwest of the Ohio River) (1791-1813), roll 1.
Oregon (1824-1871), roll 13.
Tennessee (Territory South of the Ohio River) (1789-1808), roll 2.
Utah and Washington (1849-1868), roll 15.
Wisconsin (1834-1849), roll 12.
Miscellaneous Papers (1806-1867), roll 20.

The western states for the most part were the last to be settled and the last to become states. Their territorial papers are found in the records of the State Department until 1873 and thereafter in the records of the Interior Department. They too have been microfilmed by the National Archives and are available for <u>purchase</u> from the Archives or Scholarly Resources.

State	State Dept. Coverage	Interior Dept. Coverage
Alaska	acquired 1868	1869-1913 M430
Arizona	1864-1872 M342	1868-1913 M429
Colorado	1859-1874 M3	1861-1888 M431
Dakotas	1861-1873 M309	1863-1889 M310
Florida	1777-1824 M116	statehood 1845
Idaho	1863-1872 M445	1864-1890 M191
Kansas	1854-1861 M218	statehood 1861
Missouri	1812-1820 M1134	statehood 1821
Montana	1864-1872 M356	1867-1889 M192
Nebraska	1854-1867 M228	statehood 1867
Nevada	1861-1864 M13	statehood 1864
New Mexico	1851-1872 T17	1851-1914 M364
Oklahoma	organized as territory 1890	1889-1912 M828
Oregon	1848-1858 M419	statehood 1859
Orleans Territory	1764-1823 T260	Louisiana statehood 1812
Northwest of Ohio R	1787-1801 M470	Ohio statehood 1803, Indiana Terr. 1800
Southwest of Ohio R	1790-1795 M471	Tennessee statehood 1796
Utah	1853-1873 M12	1850-1902 M428
Washington	1854-1872 M26	1854-1902 M189
Wyoming	1868-1873 M85	1870-1890 M204

INDEX OF ECONOMIC MATERIAL IN DOCUMENTS OF THE STATES OF THE UNITED STATES

Between 1907 and 1922, the Carnegie Institute in Washington, D.C., published a series of books (reprinted by Kraus Reprint) that were the project of Adelaide R. Hasse. These books are comprehensive indexes to printed reports of departments and legislatures within these states. The reports all relate in some way to the economy of the state and are indexed chronologically under such topics as agriculture, education, mining, public health, labor, industry, railroads, climate, imports and exports, and the state's defective, dependent, and delinquent populations. These documents contain much state history. While many of them are statistical summaries, others contain information about specific individuals, companies, institutions, and towns. Because of these specifics, they are potentially valuable for genealogists. Although the original plan was to cover all the states, the actual publications covered only thirteen:

> California 1849-1904
> Delaware 1789-1904
> Illinois 1809-1904
> Kentucky 1792-1904
> Maine 1820-1904
> Massachusetts 1789-1904
> New Hampshire 1789-1904
> New Jersey 1789-1904
> New York 1789-1904
> Ohio 1787-1904
> Pennsylvania 1790-1904
> Rhode Island 1789-1904
> Vermont 1789-1904

The Maine volume of the index, for example, lists a number of reports on Swedish settlements in the state in the late nineteenth century. If your ancestors were Swedish immigrants in Maine, you would want to read these. If your family were farmers, you would be particularly interested in several reports about the effect of climate on agriculture. An 1865 report of the Board of Agriculture mentioned the large exodus of New England farmers to Ohio in 1816 due to an unusually long cold season. Another report discussed the 1880 drought as one of the severest on record and the agricultural damage it caused in various parts of Maine. The index cites the agency, publication name, date, and page numbers for each entry.

The California volume includes many items that could be of specific genealogical value. The following is a sampling. (Specific references for locating these are in the California volume.)

1852-1865 — historical list of county superintendents of education.
1856 — a petition from the San Rafael Orphanage for Boys praying for state aid, with a list of the orphans.
1873-1900 — annual reports of the state superintendent of public instruction listing holders of state teachers' certificates.
1890 — "history of the horse life" of J.C. Simpson, California's most successful breeder.
1891 — directory of grape growers, wine makers, and distillers of California and principal grape growers and wine makers of the eastern states.

Appendixes to the State and Assembly Journals in the California Archives contain the lists of county superintendents and certified teachers. In Humboldt County, for example, Rev. W.L. Jones was superintendent from 1861-1868, and in Calaveras County, Robert Thompson served from 1858-1863. (2 [1866], p 293) Teachers with life diplomas in effect in 1873 included Miss Minnie F. Austin and Theodore Bradley, whose certificates were issued 27 December 1866. (I [1873-1874], p 285) The Senate Journal for 1856 (p 434) listed the 33 boys of the San Rafael Orphanage, including Thomas (14), John (9), and Daniel (8) McAuliff of Sacramento. The youngest was James Nugent (4) of Nevada.

These indexes can save a researcher time because they cover a massive number of state documents in one convenient place. Many public and university libraries have the set, and volumes are available for purchase individually from Kraus. Once you find an entry that affects your research, contact the state library or archives, or other state document depositories. In addition, the compiler gave credit to the New York Public Library and the Library of Congress for the use of their collections in locating the materials to index. Perhaps they and the National Archives could help locate materials cited.

STATE ARCHIVES

Archives are public records. They are kept by many institutions, organizations, and governments. At the state level, archives contain thousands of documents generated by departments and agencies of the government as well as correspondence from citizens to those agencies. Each state is organized in its own way. Some states have separate state library and state archives. In other states, these two are basically one institution. In other states, the state historical society houses the archives. Regardless of the location, each state archives has its own finding aids to help researchers know what is in their collection.

Many of the state archives include research materials that are not government documents. Newspapers published in the state, maps of the state, and private or business papers of citizens often are housed at the archives. These types of special collections are discussed in chapter seven. In addition, local and county histories, genealogical periodicals, cemetery transcriptions, church records, and county and city records may also form part of the archives or related library.

Much of what is kept in state archives has genealogical use. State censuses and census substitutes discussed earlier are good examples. Appellate court records and legislative memorials and petitions are others. (See chapter eight.) States in the eastern U.S. have colonial and Revolutionary War records in their archives. Included in the South are pension applications and other records arising from the years of the Confederacy.

Texas passed a Confederate pension law in May 1899, and some 58,000 veterans and widows filed applications. These included men and women who had spent the Civil War years in many places, for the original law stated they had to have been a resident of Texas since 1 January 1880. The law was amended in later years to relax the requirements. One Mississippi veteran who applied for and received a pension was John P. Shelby. He appeared before the county judge of Robertson County on 14 August 1899 to make application, accompanied by three "credible citizens," who under oath stated that he indeed enlisted in the service of the Confederacy and that he was now "unable to support himself by labor of any sort." These three witnesses were two sons, I.R. and J.A. Shelby, and daughter, Mrs. M.V. Liels (*sic*). (The application does not ask for or state the relationships.) The affidavit of Dr. G.M. Abney testified to the applicant's inability to support himself due to age (81). The application itself gave his name, age, and residence (Petteway, Texas) where he had lived for twenty-nine years. This information coincides with other evidence that he was in the county in early 1870, even though he does not appear in the census of that year. He further said he had served in Company B (Nixon's), Denny's Regi-

ment, Mississippi Cavalry for twelve months, owned no real or personal property, was in feeble health, suffering from diabetes and old age. The medical information was particularly interesting to his descendents since several of his grandchildren also developed diabetes.

Certain elected officials, as they took office, had to sign bonds that they would faithfully execute their offices or owe a penalty in the amount specified on the bond. A separate file of these bonds and oaths of office are in some state archives. When one J. Orville Shelby (not the Confederate general) was elected presiding justice of the police court of Liberty County, Texas, in December 1869, he and two friends as securities signed a bond that he would safely keep the records and faithfully discharge his duties or have to pay $500 penalty. In addition, because he was in the South after the Civil War, he also had to swear as part of his oath of office that he had never been an elected official swearing to support the Constitution of the United States and then "engaged in insurrection or rebellion against" the United States or "given aid or comfort to the enemies thereof." These papers are filed in the Texas State Archives, along with those of thousands of other elected officials.

Below is a sampling of holdings of various state archives, other than what is included elsewhere in this book. It is given to encourage searchers to use the archives of their research areas and to purchase the guide books available on their collections.

Alabama — Original Alabama land office ledgers, unpublished cemetery transcriptions.

Alaska — Territorial court records, extensive materials related to native population.

Arizona — District court records, auto license registrations 1912-1917.

Arkansas — County records, military service records of Arkansans, state land office records.

California — Military records 1850-1942, professional and vocational licenses.

Connecticut — State court records, town records, pictorial archives, compiled vital records.

Delaware — Card index to vital records.

Florida — Military records of Floridians, homestead applications, drivers' licenses, photographs.

Georgia — Reconstruction era oaths and voter registrations, county map file, photographs.

Hawaii — Manuscript, map, photograph collections.

Illinois — Name Index to Early Illinois Records, covering censuses, government records, etc.

Indiana — Military records of Indianians, state land office records, photographs.

Iowa — State land office records and plats, adjutant general's records on Iowa units before 1900.

Kansas — Military records of Kansans, school records, records of teaching certificates issued.

Kentucky — Military records of Kentuckians, scattered birth/death records 1852-1911.

Maryland — Birth, death, marriage records, wills and estate records, land and court records.

Massachusetts — State vital records 1841-1890, Massachusetts colonial court records index.

Michigan — Military records for Michigan veterans, photographs, naturalization records.

Mississippi — Death records 1912-1937, some funeral home records, voter registrations.

Missouri — Military records of Missourians, French/Spanish land grants, U.S./state land sales.

Montana — Vertical file, manuscripts and private papers.

Nebraska — Military rosters of Nebraskans, some state business directories 1879-1917 (ILL).

Nevada — Admittances to state orphans' home from 1870, auto license registrations from 1913.

New Jersey — Township minutes, tavern licenses, vital records. Has published guide to sources.

North Carolina — County records, apprentice bonds, information circular on early state courts.

North Dakota — Naturalization papers, oral history, photographs.

Ohio — Photographs, county histories, records of adjutant general and residential institutions.

Pennsylvania — Professional and occupational licenses and records.

South Carolina — Military and pension records, naturalizations, tax returns.

South Dakota — Naturalizations, veterans graves registration project (as in many states).

Tennessee — Military records of Tennesseans, naturalizations in county court records.

Texas — Confederate Home records, muster rolls, Republic of Texas records. Published guide.

Utah — Territorial militia records, local government records, court records, naturalizations.

Vermont — Manuscript Vermont State Papers (late eighteenth to mid-nineteenth century), indexed.

Virginia — Birth/death records 1853-1896, county and municipal records. Published guides.

Washington — Birth/death registers 1890-1907, professional licenses, territorial court files.

West Virginia — Family and business papers, Civil War records, maps, county court records.

Wyoming — District court records from many counties, territorial records.

OTHER RECORDS

State institutions such as prisons, residential institutions, and hospitals sometimes maintain their own records. Getting genealogical information from these may require a statement of why the information is needed and the relationship of the searcher to the person in the institution. One family discovered in the county probate files that a relative had been sent to the state "insane asylum" early in the century. The probate record contained an affidavit from the father that said that insanity was hereditary in the family. Somewhat concerned at this development, the searcher then requested information from the state hospital in an effort to find out more and was told that an uncle (unnamed) was the other person affected by insanity. Now the searcher is trying to determine the uncle's identity.

States and cities began registering vital statistics (births, deaths, marriages) at different times and in different ways. Because these records are most often generated in the county, they are discussed in chapter five, County Records. Birth and death records may be available in some states only through the state vital statistics or vital records office, but most marriage records are accessible at the county level (town in New England, independent towns and cities in Virginia).

State court systems, other than the appellate courts, usually do the bulk of their business at the county level. Each state has its own court structure. Chapter five discusses court records as genealogical tools. Chapter eight discusses appellate courts.

CHAPTER FOUR

Federal Records

Federal records of many kinds are essential sources for research in history and genealogy. Because many of these are published in books or on microform, they are more accessible than ever before to the public. Federal records discussed elsewhere in this book are these:

Federal census, including 1840 pensioners and 1890 Union veterans — chapter two.

Territorial Papers of the United States — chapter three. (These do not apply to states that were never territories: California, Kentucky, Maine, Texas, Vermont, West Virginia, and the original thirteen states.)

Maps published by the United States Geological Survey and other agencies — chapter seven.

Appellate courts, government documents, Serial Set, public statutes — chapter eight.

Records relating to American Indians — chapter ten.

Immigration and naturalization records — chapter eleven.

LIBRARY OF CONGRESS AND NATIONAL ARCHIVES

Researchers are fortunate to have available the massive records and resources in the two primary federal depositories, the Library of Congress and the National Archives. Because it is beyond the scope of this book to describe in detail the holdings of either institution, the reader is encouraged to study the published guides to the collections, especially before visiting.

The Library of Congress, often called the largest library in the world, contains extensive collections of published, manuscript, and microform works that would keep a genealogist busy for years. Numerous finding aids and subject bibliographies describe its holdings, and some of these, which are pertinent to history and genealogy, are listed throughout this book. Also, the library catalog is accessible online through INTERNET. Some maps, books, and other sources are available through the Photoduplication service. Contact the library for current fees and instructions. Other guides to the library include these:

A Guide to the Microfilm Collection of Early State Records, Lillian A. Hamrick, ed. (Washington, DC: Library of Congress, 1950). Supplement by William Sumner Jenkins, 1951.

The Library of Congress: A Guide to Historical and Genealogical Research, by James C. Neagles (Salt Lake City, UT: Ancestry, 1990). Very useful. A must before visiting.

Manuscripts on Microfilm: A Checklist of the Holdings in the Manuscript Division (Washington, DC: Library of Congress, 1973).

Special Collections in the Library of Congress, Annette Melville, comp. (Washington, DC: Library of Congress, 1980).

The National Archives contains primarily federal records, beginning with the American Revolution and Continental Congress. The Washington National Records Center in Suitland, Maryland, has been a second location where researchers could use certain record groups of Archives materials. However, the new Archives II building in College Park, Maryland, opened in the spring of 1994. By 1996, the Suitland, Maryland, center will no longer house National Archives materials. It will remain a federal records center, but not for the Archives. Moving millions of records also means the shifting of some record groups between the main Archives building (Archives I) in Washington, Archives II in College Park, and the regional Archives branches. Categories of records scheduled to remain in Archives I include genealogical materials and records of Congress and the Supreme Court, American Indians, pre–World War II Army and Navy, and World War I, Great Depression, and New Deal agencies. Archives II and the regional branches will hold other civilian and military record groups. At this writing, these transfers are scheduled to be completed in 1996. If you plan to visit any of the facilities, ask ahead of time about the location of the records you need to use, and contact regional branches about records added to their collections.

National Archives records are organized by department and function. To guide researchers through over 450 record groups, many publications, such as these, are available:

The Archives: A Guide to the National Archives Field Branches, Loretto Dennis Szucs and Sandra Hargreaves Luebking (Salt Lake City, UT: Ancestry, Inc., 1988). Most useful.

The following titles are all National Archives publications:

Black History: A Guide to Civilian Records in the National Archives, Debra L. Newman, comp. (1984). A helpful guide for any searcher.

Guide to Genealogical Research in the National Archives, revised edition (1985). Very useful, whether you are planning a visit or not.

Guide to National Archives of the United States (1988, reprint of 1974 edition).

Guide to Pre-Federal Records in the National Archives. Howard H. Wehmann, comp., revised by Benjamin L. DeWhitt (1989).

Guide to Records in the National Archives: _____ Region (each regional Archives branch) (1989). See Appendix D for list of regional branches.

National Archives Microfilm Resources for Research: A Comprehensive Catalog (revised 1990).

Our Family, Our Town: Essays on Family and Local History Sources in the National Archives, Timothy Walch, comp. (1987).

Using Records in the National Archives for Genealogical Research (Washington, DC: National Archives and Records Administration, 1986, revised). General Information Leaflet #5.

The following subject catalogs of microfilm available from the National Archives all have the subtitle *A Select List of National Archives Microfilm Publications*. They contain detailed descriptions of the records and roll-by-roll listings:

American Indians (1984)
Black Studies (1984)
Central States (1985)

Chesapeake/Mid-Atlantic States (1985)
Diplomatic Records (1986)
Federal Court Records (1987)
Genealogical and Biographical Research (1983)
Immigrant and Passenger Arrivals (1983)
Military Service Records (1985)
New England States (1985)
The South and Southwest (1985)
The West (1985)

Researchers may request copies of records in three areas of the Archives: ship passenger arrivals, census, and military service (including pension and bounty land warrant applications). Contact the Archives (Washington, DC 20408) for current fees and the necessary forms.

Searches of ship passenger arrival records must be requested on Form NATF 81, Order for Copies of Passenger Arrival Records. The request must contain the following information: (1) full name of the arriving passenger, (2) the port of arrival, (3) exact date of arrival or name of the ship. Additional information, such as names of accompanying passengers or passenger's age, can aid in the search.

Requests for census records must be submitted on Form NATF 82, Order for Copies of Census Records. The Archives staff does not research the census for patrons. If you want a copy of a particular record from a census that has been opened to the public (at this writing, 1790-1920), you must provide the county and state, the census year, the exact page number, and for 1880-1920 censuses, the enumeration district number. If you have access to the microfilm and a printer, it is easier, cheaper, and quicker to make such copies yourself. (See chapter two for copies of closed census records.)

Requests for military service records and veterans' benefits records (pension and bounty-land warrant applications) must be submitted on Form NATF 80, Order for Copies of Veterans Records, one form for each record requested. Information needed for this search includes (1) full name of soldier or widow, (2) the war in which he served or the dates of his service, (3) the state from which he served. For Civil War records, indicate Union or Confederate forces. (Confederate pensions are state records and not held at the National Archives.) Request Standard Form 180 to obtain more recent service records.

MILITARY RECORDS

Federal military records begin with the American Revolution. The eastern states have militia records from the colonial period, and many of these have been published. In the South, former Confederate States have pension records from Civil War service. Eastern states have some Revolutionary records as well, due to the fact that units in the Revolution were organized both by states and by the Continental Congress. Most of the records of genealogical interest fall into two groups: compiled service records and veterans' benefits. Thousands of envelopes containing original records and abstracts for individual veterans are at the National Archives.

Compiled Service Records and Other Evidence of Service

The National Archives has microfilmed numerous compiled service records and other evidence of service on volunteer soldiers, navy personnel, and marines who served between 1775 and the early twentieth century. These records are abstracts compiled from muster rolls, pay lists, hospital and prison records, and other sources. Most records give little more than the serviceman's name, rank, unit, and dates of muster rolls or rosters. Some show age, birthplace, physical description, and residence, as well as any imprisonment or medical information. These abstracts are arranged by war or time period, then by state and unit, with surnames alphabetical in each unit. Indexes and other records can help determine the regiment in which the solider served.

A typical example of a service record is that of Confederate Private S.D. Williamson of Company E, 38th Alabama Regiment. His record contains two abstracts: (1) He appeared on a roll of prisoners of war captured at Blakely, Alabama, on 9 April 1865 and received at Ship Island, Mississippi, 15 April 1865. (2) He appeared on a roll of prisoners of war transferred from Ship Island to Vicksburg, Mississippi, 1 May 1865.

Revolutionary service records are in the Archives Record Group 93. Records from later periods are primarily in Record Groups 94 and 407, and Confederate records, in Record Group 109. The Archives has many records that have not been microfilmed. However, the following list of microfilmed records represents the records most readily accessible to searchers, for <u>use</u> in research libraries, for <u>purchase</u> from the National Archives or Scholarly Resources, and for <u>rent</u> from the AGLL or FHL. Each item refers to compiled service records or their indexes, unless otherwise described. (The M and T numbers are the Archives publication numbers.)

1. **Records of Revolutionary War Soldiers, 1775-1783.**
   a. General index (M860). Units from the 13 colonies, Continental troops, some sailors, and civilian employees. Compiled service records of this group (M881).
   b. Index, Connecticut soldiers not identified with a particular unit (M920).
   c. Index, Georgia units (M1051), North Carolina units (M257).
   d. Revolutionary War rolls, 1775-1783 (M246). Muster rolls, payrolls, etc., arranged by state and unit.
   e. Index to records, American naval personnel (M879 and T516). About 1,000 sailors and civilian employees. (Duplicated in M860).
   f. Records of American naval personnel and . . . departments of Quartermaster General and Commissary General (M880).
   g. Personnel returns (with physical descriptions) of some Massachusetts units (M913).
   h. Central treasury records (M1015). Roll 6, certificates of indebtedness issued to Continental soldiers 1783-1786. Roll 7, pension payments to Pennsylvanians 1785-1804.
   i. Special index to numbered records, War Dept. collection of Revolutionary War records (M847). The documents themselves, called The Manuscript File, are in M859, pertaining to pay, procurement, personnel records, enlistment papers, etc.
   j. Numbered record books, War Dept. collection (M853), Roll 1, index. Includes oaths of allegiance, oaths of office, commissions, pay, and settlement of accounts.
   k. War Dept. correspondence, 1791-1797 (M1062). Indian affairs, pensions, etc.

2. **Records of volunteer soldiers who served from 1784 until 1811 (M905). Index (M694).**

3. **Records of volunteer soldiers who served in the War of 1812 (and concurrent Indian Wars).**
   a. Index (M602). Index to Louisiana units (M229), North Carolina units (M250), South Carolina units (M652).

b. Records, soldiers from the Territory of Mississippi (M678).

c. Muster rolls, payrolls, militia and regular army, Battle of Tippecanoe, 1811 (T1085).

4. **Records of volunteer soldiers who served during Indian Wars and disturbances, 1815-1858.**

   a. Index (M629).

   b. Cherokee disturbances and removal, index, units from Alabama (M243), Georgia (M907), North Carolina (M256), Tennessee and the field and staff of the Army of the Cherokee Nation (M908). No microfilmed service records for these groups.

   c. Creek War, index to Alabama units (M244). Records, Florida militia (M1086).

   d. Florida War (Second Seminole War 1836-1843), index, Alabama units (M245), Louisiana units (M239).

   e. Florida Indian Wars, 1835-1858, records, Florida units (M1086).

   f. War of 1837-1838, index, Louisiana units (M241).

5. **Records of volunteer soldiers who served during the Patriot War, 1838-1839.**

   Index, Michigan units (M630) and New York units (M631). No microfilmed records.

6. **Records of volunteer soldiers who served during the Mexican War, 1846-1848.**

   a. Index (M616).

   b. Records, units from Mississippi (M863), Pennsylvania (M1028), Tennessee (M638), Texas (M278), Mormon units (M351).

7. **Records of volunteer Union soldiers who served during the Civil War, 1861-1865.**

   a. U.S. Colored Troops, index (M589). Veterans Reserve Corps, index (M636).

   b. U.S. Volunteers, 1st-6th regiments, records (M1017) (former Confederate POWs).

   c. Indexes, volunteer Union soldiers in organizations not raised by states or territories (M1290). Includes Veteran Volunteers, Confederate POWs who enlisted in U.S. Army, Indian Home Guards, U.S. Sharp Shooters, etc.

   d. Units by state (Film numbers: index and records). One number indicates index only.

   Alabama, M263, M276   Arizona, M532

Arkansas, M383, M399
California, M533
Colorado Territory, M534
Connecticut, M535
Dakota Territory, M536
Delaware, M537
District of Columbia, M538
Florida, M264, M400
Georgia, M385, M403
Idaho — see Washington
Illinois, M539
Indiana, M540
Iowa, M541
Kansas, M542
Kentucky, M386, M397
Louisiana, M387, M396
Maine, M543
Maryland, M388, M384
Massachusetts, M544
Michigan, M545
Minnesota, M546
Mississippi, M389, M404
Missouri, M390, M405
Montana — see Wash-
ington Territory
Nebraska Territory, M547
Nevada, M548
New Hampshire, M549
New Jersey, M550
New Mexico Territory, M242, M427
New York, M551
North Carolina, M391, M401
Ohio, M552
Oregon, M553
Pennsylvania, M554
Rhode Island, M555
South Carolina, none
Tennessee, M392, M395
Texas, M393, M402
Utah Territory, M556, M692
Vermont, M557
Virginia, M394, M398
Washington Territory, M558
West Virginia, M507, M508
Wisconsin, M559
Wyoming — see Washington Territory

8. **Records of movements and activities of volunteer Union organizations. (Compiled service histories of units, merges, disbandment, dates of service, etc.) (M594, by state.)**

9. **Records of Confederate soldiers who served during the Civil War, 1861-1865.**

   Many of the Confederate records were lost in the final days of the war. The service records in the Archives are compiled from the surviving Confederate and state records, Union prison and parole records.

   a. Consolidated index to compiled service records of Confederate soldiers (M253).

   b. Organizations raised by the Confederate government, index (M818), records (M258).

   c. General and staff officers and nonregimental enlisted men, including military judges, chaplains, agents, drillmasters, and aides-de-camp. Index (M818), records (M331).

   d. Unfiled papers belonging to Confederate service records (M347). Alphabetical.

e. Records of Confederate naval and marine personnel (M260).

f. Selected records of Confederate prisoners of war (M598), general and by prison.

g. Register of Confederates who died in federal prisons and military hospitals (M918).

h. Records of Virginia forces, 1861 (M998), primarily correspondence.

i. Confederate Army casualty lists and reports (M836), by state and unit.

j. Case files, applications of former Confederates for Presidential pardons (M1003).

k. Reference files relating to Confederate medical officers (T456).

l. Units by state, index, and records film numbers.

Alabama, M374, M311	Mississippi, M232, M269
Arizona Territory, M375, M318	Missouri, M380, M322
Arkansas, M376, M317	North Carolina, M230, M270
Florida, M225, M251	South Carolina, M381, M267
Georgia, M226, M266	
Kentucky, M377, M319	Tennessee, M231, M268
Louisiana, M378, M320	Texas, M227, M323
Maryland, M379, M321	Virginia, M382, M324

10. **Records of Confederate movements and activities (M861). Compiled unit histories, by state.**

11. **Records of volunteer soldiers who served during the war with Spain, 1898.**
    a. Index (M871), index to Louisiana units (M240), to North Carolina units (M413).
    b. Records, Florida infantry (M1087).

12. **Records of volunteer soldiers who served during the Philippine Insurrection, 1899-1903. Index (M872).**

13. **Registers of Enlistments, U.S. regular army, 1798-1914 (M233).**

14. **Returns from military posts, 1800-1916 (M617).**

15. **Returns, regular army, infantry regiments, 1821-1916 (M665), cavalry regiments, 1833-1916 (M744), artillery regiments, 1821-1901 (M727), field artillery, 1901-1916 (M728), Coast Artillery Corps, 1901-1916 (M691), Corps of Engineers 1832-1916 (M851), engineer battalions, 1846-1916 (M690).**

16. **Index to navy rendezvous reports (enlistments): 1846-1861, 1865-1884 (T1098). Civil War years, 1861-1865 (T1099). Armed Guard personnel 1917-1920 (T1101). Naval Auxiliary Service, 1917-1918 (T1100).**

17. **Abstracts of service records, naval officers, 1798-1893 (M330).**

18. **Records, navy courts-martial and Courts of Inquiry, 1799-1867 (M273). Rolls 1-2, index.**

19. **Muster Rolls, U.S. Marine Corps, 1789-1892 (T1118).**

20. **United States Military Academy cadet application papers, 1805-1866 (M688). Roll 1, index.**

21. **United States Naval Academy registers of delinquencies, 1846-1850 and 1853-1882, and academic and conduct records, 1881-1908 (M991).**

22. **Selected documents relating to blacks nominated for appointment to the U.S. Military Academy, 1870-1887 (M1002).**

23. **Documents relating to the military and naval service of blacks awarded the Congressional Medal of Honor from the Civil War to the Spanish-American War (M929).**

NOTE: See chapter nine for other military records relating to African-American servicemen.

Pension and Bounty Land Warrant Applications

The records of veterans' benefits are the pension applications and bounty land warrants arising out of military service. Pension records based on Revolutionary War service cover the entire nineteenth century. Applications prior to 1800 were burned in a War Department fire in November 1800. Until 1818, a Revolutionary pension application had to be a needy and disabled (invalid) veteran or the indigent heir of a deceased veteran. In 1818, Congress authorized the first service pensions, based on service without disability as a requirement, but need was still a prerequisite. In 1828 and 1832, Congress liberalized this program so that need was no longer a consideration.

Applications for such pensions often contain supporting evidence that is valuable for genealogists. An example is the file of John Blakeney, and later his widow, Nancy, which gives a detailed service history and the following genealogical information:

John served as a private foot soldier, called out in 1776 by South Carolina. After several times being called up, he went to North Carolina to visit relatives and was drafted there. Army discharge papers "got burnt in my House many years past." Home was and is Chesterfield District, SC. Lives 1/2 mile from North Carolina line and 27 miles from his own courthouse. Thus, he applied for pension in North Carolina because of convenience. Born in Bute County, NC, 14 January 1758. Moved to Rowan County near Salisbury, then to South Carolina. Married Nancy May in 1785 or 1786, Anson County, NC. Daughter Nancy born 8 August 1786. Daughter Jane born 6 February 1788. Daughter Susannah born 12 September 1789. Son John born 9 August 1791. Son James born 6 February 1794. Daughter Elizabeth born 22 May 1797. John died at their residence. Two death dates given for John: 30 March 1848 (accepted for the beginning of the widow's pension) and 31 March 1849 (in later document). In October 1851, Nancy gave her age as 81. In August 1855, her age given as 90. Nancy signed her application with her mark.

The bounty land warrants were certificates for free public land. The promise of free land was an effort to encourage enlistments and was a reward for service after the war. Unlike the early pensions, bounty land warrants did not have a requirement of indigency. One reason that so many veterans sold their warrants was that until 1830, the warrants could be used for land only in the U.S. Military District in Ohio. Gradually that restriction was relaxed, and by 1842 they could be redeemed at any federal land office.

National Archives microfilm relating to pension and bounty land warrant applications and files include the following:

1. Selected records from Revolutionary War pension and bounty land warrant application files, 1800-1900 (M805). (Not complete files, but selected for genealogical interest.)
2. Revolutionary War pension and bounty land warrant application files, 1800-1900 (M804). (Complete files of some 80,000 applications.) Published index by National Genealogical Soci-

ety in bibliography on page 60. Rolls are arranged alphabetically.

3. U.S. Revolutionary War bounty land warrants used in the Military District of Ohio (M829). Roll 1 contains indexes.
4. Register of Revolutionary War land warrants, Act of 1788 Military District of Ohio, 1799-1805 (T1008).
5. Virginia Half Pay and other related Revolutionary War pension application files (M910).
6. Index to War of 1812 pension application files (M313).
7. War of 1812 military bounty land warrants, 1815-1858 (M848).
8. Old War index to pension files, 1815-1926 (T316). (Old Wars—Revolution to 1861.)
9. Ledgers of payments to pensioners, 1818-1872 (T718).
10. Index to Mexican War pension files, 1887-1926 (T317).
11. Selected pension application files, Mormon Battalion, Mexican War (T1196).
12. Index to Indian Wars pension files, 1892-1926 (T318).
13. General index to pension files, 1861-1934 (T288). (Civil War and later service.)
14. Organization index to pension files of veterans who served between 1861 and 1900 (T289). Same material as number 13 above, but by unit instead of alphabetical.
15. Veterans Administration Pension Payment Cards, 1870-1933 (M850) (except WWI).
16. Index to General Correspondence of Record and Pension Office, 1889-1920 (M686).

Private Relief Acts

Most of the veterans who qualified for pensions met the requirements set down in laws of Congress. However, other veterans or heirs had special circumstances needing individual attention beyond or in exception to the public statutes. Congress dealt with these cases through private relief acts. These private acts appear in the *Congressional Record* and journals as well as the Serial Set. Those that occurred between 1789 and 1845 appear also in Volume 6 of the *Public Statutes of the United States*. Later cases appear in the *Statutes* volume for each session of Congress. The Serial Set is the source for the documents relating to each case. (See chapter eight for further discussion.)

Draft Registration Cards

Draft registration cards for World War I are located at the National Archives branch in East Point, Georgia. The law required registration of all men between eighteen and forty-five years of age, which covered birth years from 1873 to 1900. With the form furnished by the archives branch, you can request a search. You must be able to furnish the full name and address at the time of registration. (Street address is necessary for men living in large cities.) The information on the registration varies but may include name, age, sometimes birthdate and birthplace, citizenship status, occupation, nearest relative (relationship not always specified), physical description, and signature. A small fee is charged for a copy of the record, if found. The project to microfilm these records is scheduled for completion about 1995.

Military Discharge Papers

Military discharge papers are often filed in county courthouses and can provide interesting information for the genealogist. The World War I honorable discharge of William Taylor Oldham, filed in Robertson County, Texas, gives the following information about the serviceman:

Served as Private First Class, Laundry Company 307. Inducted 15 June 1918 at Franklin, TX. Member of the American Expeditionary Force (AEF) 2 September 1918 to 8 July 1919. Assigned to 351 Butcher Company, 5 September 1918; to 307 Laundry Company, 25 January 1919; to Cas. Det. Demot. Group, 14-19 July 1919. Discharged 21 July 1919 at Camp Pike, Arkansas. Entitled to travel pay to Bremond, TX. Paid in full $128.21, including $60 bonus pay. His first service. Born at Bremond, TX. Farmer, age 27, single. Fair complexion. 5 feet 7½ inches tall. Not qualified as marksman or gunner. Not mounted. Received immunizations 21 June 1918. Not wounded. Good physical condition at time of discharge. Excellent character, no AWOL, no absence.

Twentieth-Century Records

Although the National Archives has the early records of most of the services, existing records of more recent veterans are at the National Personnel Records Center (MPRC), 9700 Page Avenue, St. Louis MO 63132-5100. Their release of information form states, "Although the Privacy Act (1974) does not apply to the records of deceased individuals, Department of Defense instructions indicate that we must have the written consent of the next of kin if the individual is deceased. For the purposes of the release authorization, the next of kin is defined as any of the following: unremarried widow or widower, son, daughter, father, mother, brother, or sister." A fire at this facility on 12 July 1973 destroyed many of the records of twentieth-century military personnel, including these: (1) Army officers separated from the service between 30 June 1917 and 1959 (about 80 percent loss), (2) Army enlisted personnel separated from the service between 30 October 1912 and 1959 (about 80 percent loss), (3) Air Force and Army Air Corps officers and enlisted personnel separated between 1947 and 1963, especially Air Force servicemen whose surnames begin with *I* through *Z*. Records remaining at the Center include Army and Air Force personnel separated after 1956, Navy enlisted men separated after 1885, Navy officers separated after 1902, Marine Corps officers separated after 1895, Marine Corps enlisted personnel separated after 1904, Coast Guard officers separated after 1928, Coast Guard enlisted men separated after 1914, and civilian employees of the Coast Guard predecessor agencies (Revenue Cutter, Life-Saving, and Lighthouse Services), 1864-1919.[4] You can request a search on their Standard Form 180 available from their office, the National Archives, and other federal centers.

A computerized file on CD-ROM available at Family History Centers and other research libraries is the index to U.S. Military Personnel Who Died in Korea or Vietnam, 1950-1975. The file in 1993 contained only Korean War deaths. The information given on each individual includes birth date and place, death date and place, rank and service number, race, and type of service.

Records of the Merchant Marine from 1937 forward are housed at the office of the Commandant of the Coast Guard. These records give birth date, service information, and sometimes death date, if the family notified the office of the death. Information can be obtained with a signed release by a living mariner, a court order in case of litigation, or a copy of the death certificate for records of a deceased mariner. The office is required to keep the records for sixty years. Thus, records more than sixty years old are likely to be destroyed. The National Archives has a few records prior to 1937 but is not given records as they pass that sixty-year requirement. The address for Merchant

Marine records since 1937 is Commandant (G-MVP-1), U.S. Coast Guard, 2100 Second Street SW, Washington, DC 20593-0001. This same office keeps Coast Guard military records only six months before sending them on to the National Personnel Records Center in St. Louis, Missouri.

An interesting and valuable source that came about because of Civil War service is *The Tennessee Civil War Veterans Questionnaires*, Gustavus W. Dyer and John Trotwood Moore, comp. (Easley [now Greenville], South Carolina: Southern Historical Press, 1985, 5 vols.). Questionnaires were sent to all known living Civil War Veterans (Union and Confederate) in Tennessee in 1914, 1915, and 1920. Some 1,650 were completed and returned and are housed at the Tennessee State Library and Archives. The responses concern family history as well as military service.

Bibliography—Other Than Civil War

The bibliographies given here are in no way exhaustive but contain some basic reference materials and examples of resources available other than general histories. Works on loyalists during the Revolutionary period are included here as well. In addition, numerous periodicals exist that may help you in your search for military and naval ancestors. Through interlibrary loan and university and research libraries, you have access to hundreds of published and manuscript materials, from both the government and the private sector. (See chapter eight for use of government documents. See also bibliographies in chapters seven and eight.)

Abstracts of Graves of Revolutionary Patriots, by Patricia Law Hatcher (Dallas, TX: Pioneer Heritage Press, 1988). Alphabetical list. 4 vols.

American Loyalist Claims, abstracted from the Public Record Office, London, Audit Office, Series 13, bundles 1-35, 37, by Peter Wilson Coldham (Washington, DC [now Arlington, VA]: National Genealogical Society, 1980). Indexed.

American Loyalist Claims, 1730-1835, microfilmed records from Public Record Office, London, available from Family History Library.

American Military Cemeteries: A Comprehensive Illustrated Guide to the Hallowed Grounds of the United States Including Cemeteries Overseas, by Dean W. Holt (Jefferson, NC: McFarland and Co., 1992).

A Bibliography of Loyalist Source Material in the United States, Canada, and Great Britain, Gregory Palmer, ed. (Westport, CT: Meckler Publishing Co., 1982).

Blacks in the American Armed Forces, 1776-1983: A Bibliography, by Lenwood G. Davis and George Hill (Westport, CT: Greenwood Press, 1985).

Fighters for Independence: A Guide to Sources of Biographical Information on Soldiers and Sailors of the American Revolution, by J. Todd White (Chicago: University of Chicago Press, 1977).

General Abstracts of Revolutionary War Pension Files, Virgil D. White, abstracter (Waynesboro, TN: National Historical Publishing Company, 1990).

German-American Troops in the American Revolution: J.R. Rosengarten's Survey of German Archives and Sources, Don Heinrich Tolzmann, ed. (Bowie, MD: Heritage Books, 1993).

The German-American Troops in the North American War of Independence, 1776-1783, by Max Von Eelking, trans. and abridged by J.D. Rosengarten, 1983 (Bowie, MD: Heritage Books, reprint).

The German Regiment of Maryland and Pennsylvania in the Continental Army, 1776-1781, by Henry J. Retzer (Westminster, MD: Family Line Publications, 1991).

Historical Register of Officers of the Continental Army During the War of the Revolution, 1775-1783, by Francis B. Heitman (Washington, DC: 1914, reprint 1932; reprint 1982, Genealogical Publishing Company, Baltimore).

Index of Revolutionary War Pension Applications, Max E. Hoyt, Frank Johnson Metcalf, et al. (Washington, DC [now Arlington, VA]: National Genealogical Society, 1966, revised and enlarged, 1976).

Index to Maps of the American Revolution in Books and Periodicals, by David Sanders Clark (Washington, DC: the author, 1969).

An Index to Mexican War Pension Applications, Barbara Schull Wolfe, transcriber (Indianapolis: Heritage House, 1985).

Index to Mexican War Pension Files, Virgil D. White, transcriber (Waynesboro, TN: National Historical Publishing Company, 1989).

Index to Series I of American Loyalist Claims and *Index to Series II of American Loyalist Claims*, by Clifford S. Dwyer, from Public Record Office,

Audit Office, London (DeFuniak Springs, FL: RAM Publishing, 1985, 1986).

Index to U.S. Invalid Pension Records, 1801-1815, Murtie June Clark, author (Baltimore: Genealogical Publishing Company, 1991).

Index to Volunteer Soldiers, 1784-1811, Virgil D. White, transcriber (Waynesboro, TN: National Historical Publishing Company, 1987).

Index to the War of 1812 Pension Files, Virgil D. White, transcriber (Waynesboro, TN: National Historical Publishing Company, 1989).

The King's Mountain Men, by Katherine Keogh White (Baltimore: Genealogical Publishing Company, 1966). Biographical sketches.

Known Military Dead During the Spanish-American War and the Philippines Insurrection, 1898-1901, Clarence Stewart Peterson, comp. (Baltimore: the author, 1958). Others by same author: (1) *Known Military Dead During the Mexican War, 1846-1848* (1957). (2) *Known Military and Civilian Dead in the Minnesota Sioux Indian Massacre in 1862* (1958). (3) *Known Military Dead During the War of 1812* (1955).

List of Log Books of U.S. Navy Ships, Stations, and Miscellaneous Units, 1801-1947, Claudia Bradley et al, comp. (Washington, DC: National Archives and Records Service, 1978).

List of Pensioners on the Roll January 1, 1883 (Washington, DC: U.S. Pension Bureau, as part of the Serial Set, S.Exdoc.84 (47-2) 2078-2082. Reprint, 1970, Genealogical Publishing Company, Baltimore), 5 vols.

Loyalists in the Southern Campaign of the Revolutionary War: Officer Rolls of Loyalists, by Murtie June Clark (Baltimore: Genealogical Publishing Company, 1981). 3 vols.

Major Index to the Pension List of the War of 1812, by Annie Walker Burns (Washington, DC: the author, n.d.), 6 vols. Alphabetical abstracts.

Mariners of the American Revolution, Marion and Jack Kaminkow, comp. (Baltimore: Magna Carta Book Co., 1967).

Naval Historical Foundation Manuscript Collection: A Catalog (Washington, DC: Library of Congress, 1974).

Naval Records of the American Revolution, 1775-1788, by Charles Henry Lincoln (Washington, DC: Government Printing Office, 1906; reprint by Heritage Books, Bowie, MD, 1992). A calendar, from originals in the Library of Congress.

The New Loyalist Index, by Paul J. Bunnell (Bowie, MD: Heritage Books, 1989).

Official Army Register (Washington, DC: Office of the Secretary of War, annual, 1875-1978).

The Old United Empire Loyalists List, by United Empire Loyalist Centennial Committee, Toronto (Baltimore: Genealogical Publishing Company, 1985).

The Pension List of 1792-1795: With Other Revolutionary War Pension Records, Murtie June Clark, comp. (Baltimore: Genealogical Publishing Company, 1991). Indexed. Includes the claims reports from the *American State Papers: Claims* and abstracts of acts of Congress, 1789-1815, invalid pension claims.

Pension List of 1820 (War Department document originally published 1820 by Gales and Seaton, Washington, DC; reprint 1991, Genealogical Publishing Company, Baltimore).

Pension Roll of 1835 (Originally published 1835 as part of the Serial Set, S.doc.514 (23-1) serial 249-251. Reprint 1992, Genealogical Publishing Company, Baltimore). 4 vols, with index. Names and records of 60,700 soldiers.

Pensioners of the Revolutionary War Struck Off the Roll. (War Department report to the House of Representatives, originally published 1836 as part of the Serial Set, H.doc.127 (24-1) serial 289. Reprint 1969, Genealogical Publishing Company, Baltimore).

Pierce's Register: Register of the Certificates issued by John Pierce, Esquire, Paymaster General and Commissioner of Army Accounts for the U.S., to Officers and Soldiers of the Continental Army Under Act of July 4, 1783 (War Department document, originally published 1915, reprint 1987, Genealogical Publishing Company, Baltimore).

Preliminary Guide to the Manuscript Collection of the U.S. Military Academy Library, by J. Thomas Russell (West Point, NY: Military Academy, 1968).

Records of the Revolutionary War, by W.T.R. Saffell (Baltimore: 1894; reprint by J.T. McAllister, 1913 with index to Saffell's list of Virginia soldiers in the Revolution; reprint 1969 by Genealogical Publishing Company, Baltimore; reprint 1991, Genealogical Publishing Company for Clearfield Company Reprints.) Lots of lists, including officers with bounty land warrants issued before end of 1784.

Register of the Army of the United States (Washington, DC: Adjutant and Inspector General's Office, 1813).

Register of the Army and Navy of the United States (Washington, DC: Peter Force, 1830).

Research Guide to Loyalist Ancestors: Archives, Manuscripts, and Published Sources, by Paul J. Bunnell (Bowie, MD: Heritage Books, 1990).

Revolutionary Pensioners: A Transcript of the Pension List of the United States for 1813 (Baltimore: Southern Book Company, 1953, reprint of 1813 original).

U.S. Naval History Sources in the United States, Dean C. Allard et al., comp. (Washington, DC: Government Printing Office, 1979). Department of the Navy, History Division.

National Archives publications:

Records of the Adjutant General's Office, Lucille H. Pendell and Elizabeth Bethel, comp., 1949, Preliminary Inventory number 17.

Records of the United States Marine Corps, Maizie Johnson, comp., 1970, Inventory number 2.

Records of the United States Military Academy, Stanley P. Tozeski, comp., 1976, Preliminary Inventory number 185.

Records of the United States Naval Academy, Geraldine N. Phillips and Aloha South, comp. 1975, Inventory number 11.

War Department Collection of Revolutionary War Records, Mabel E. Deutrich, comp., revised by Howard H. Wehmann, 1970, Preliminary Inventory number 144.

Bibliography—Civil War

The Appomattox Roster: A List of Paroles of the Army of Northern Virginia Issued at Appomattox Courthouse on April 9, 1865 (New York: Antiquarian Press, Ltd, 1962, reprint of 1887 original). Indexed.

Black Union Soldiers in the Civil War, by Hondon B. Hargrove (Jefferson, NC: McFarland and Company, Inc., 1988).

Civil War Claims in the South: An Index of Civil War Damage Claims Filed Before the Southern Claims Commission, 1871-1880, by Gary B. Mills (Laguna Hills, CA: Aegean Park Press, 1980). See records on National Archives microfilm publication M87.

Compendium of the Confederate Armies, by Stewart Sifakis (New York: Facts on File, 1992), volumes by state. Companion to Frederick H. Dyer's *Compendium of the War of the Rebellion* (Union), 1909, 3 vols.

The Confederacy; A Guide to the Archives of the Confederate States of America, by Henry Putney Beers (Washington, DC: National Archives and Records Administration, 1986).

Confederate POW's: Soldiers and Sailors Who Died in Federal Prisons and Military Hospitals in the North (Nacogdoches, TX: Carolyn Ericson and Frances Ingmire, 1984 reprint of 1912 War Department original). Gives name, prison, cemetery, rank and unit, death date.

Confederate Research Sources: A Guide to Archives Collections, by James C. Neagles (Salt Lake City, UT: Ancestry, 1986).

Confederate Soldiers, Sailors, and Civilians Who Died as Prisoners of War at Camp Douglas, Illinois, 1862-1865. (Kalamazoo, MI: Edgar Gray Publications, n.d.) By same publisher: *Confederate Soldiers and Sailors Who Died as Prisoners of War at Camp Butler, Illinois, 1862-1865*, Alexis A. Praus, comp., n.d.

Confederate Staff Officers, 1861-1865, by James H. Crute, Jr.(Powhatan, VA: Derwent Books, 1982).

Era of the Civil War, 1820-1876, by Louise Arnold and Richard Sommers, Army Military History Institute (Washington, DC: Government Printing Office, 1982). Bibliography of the institute's collection on the Civil War.

The Gettysburg Death Roster: The Confederate Dead at Gettysburg, Robert K. Krick, comp. (Dayton, OH: The Press of Morningside Bookshop, 1985, revised edition) (1985 address: 260 Oak Street, Dayton, OH 45410.) Alphabetical list with unit name and rank. Compiler estimates the list is at least 85 percent complete, with about 4,000 names.

A Guide to Civil War Maps in the National Archives (Washington, DC: National Archives, revised edition, 1986).

The History of the Confederate States Marine Corps and Service Records of Confederate Enlisted Marines, by Ralph W. Donnelly (Washington, North Carolina: the author, 1976, 1979).

Lee's Colonels: A Biographical Register of the Field Officers of the Army of Northern Virginia, by Robert K. Krick (Dayton, OH: Morningside Bookshop Press, 1979).

Libby Prison Autograph Book, January-February 1864, James B. Casey, ed. (Salt Lake City: Utah Genealogical Association, Monograph Series No. 1, 1984). Information from Alexander A. Taylor's autograph book kept while he was a prisoner at Libby Prison, Richmond, VA.

Military Bibliography of the Civil War, C.E. Dornbusch, comp. (New York: New York Public Library, 1961-1987). Revision and supplement to *Bibliography of State Participation in the Civil War*, by War Department Library, 1913 (3rd edition). Volume I—Regimental Publications and Personal Narratives, Northern States (1961, reprint 1971). Volume II—Regimental Publications and Personal Narratives, Southern, Border, and Western States and Territories; Federal Troops, Union and Confederate Biographies (1967). Volume III—General References; Armed Forces; Campaigns and Battles (1972). Volume IV—Regimental Publications and Personal Narratives; Union and Confederate Biographies, General References, Armed Forces, Campaigns and Battles (1987).

Military Operations of the Civil War: A Guide-Index to the Official Records of the Union and Confederate Armies, 1861-1865, Dallas Irvine, comp. (Washington, DC: National Archives, 1966-1980), 5 vols.

Official Army Register of the Volunteer Forces of the United States Army for 1861-1865 (Washington, DC: Adjutant General's Office, 1865; reprint 1987, Gaithersburg, MD: Ron R. Van Sickle Military Books). Each volume indexed. Part I—New England States. Part II—New York, New Jersey. Part III—Pennsylvania, Delaware, Maryland, District of Columbia. Part IV—Confederate States plus West Virginia, Kentucky. Part V—Ohio, Michigan. Part VI— Indiana, Illinois. Part VII—Missouri, Wisconsin, Iowa, Minnesota, California, Kansas, Oregon, Nevada. Part VIII—Territorial Troops (Washington, Utah, New Mexico, Nebraska, Colorado, Indian Territory, Dakotas, Arizona, Idaho, Montana), U.S. Troops—Veteran Reserve Corps, First Army Corps (Veterans), Colored Troops, and Miscellaneous. Lists by unit within each state or territory.

Personnel of the Civil War, William Frayne Amann, ed. (New York: Thomas Yoseloff, 1961). Volume I—Confederate, Volume II—Union. Popular names and official names of units. Volume II includes troops from the Indian nations and U.S. Colored Troops.

Point Lookout Prison Camp for Confederates, by Edwin W. Beitzell (Abell, MD: the author, 1972). Letters, diary, roster of deaths.

Register of Officers of the Confederate States Navy, 1861-1865 (Washington, DC: Department of the Navy, 1898, reprint 1931, reprint Mattituck, NY: J.M. Carroll and Co., 1983). Reprints by same company: (1) *List of Staff Officers of the Confederate States Army, 1861-1865* (1983 reprint of original published 1891, Government Printing Office, General Marcus J. Wright, compiler). (2) *General Officers of the Confederate Army, 1861-1865* (1983 reprint of 1911 original compiled by General Wright). (3) *List of Field Officers, Regiments, and Battalions in the Confederate States Army, 1861-1865* (reprint 1983).

Service Records of Confederate Enlisted Marines, by Ralph W. Donnelly (Washington, DC: the author, 1979). Alphabetical abstracts.

The Union: A Guide to Federal Archives Relating to the Civil War, by Kenneth W. Munden and Henry Putney Beers (Washington, DC: National Archives, 1986).

United States Navy: Official Records of the Union and Confederate Navies in the War of the Rebellion (Washington, DC: Government Printing Office, 1927, reprint New York: Antiquarian Press, Ltd., 1961). 30 volumes plus index volume.

The War of the Rebellion: A Compilation of the Official Records of the Union and Confederate Armies (Washington, DC: Government Printing Office, 1893). Series I (53 volumes), Reports and Operations. Series II (8 volumes), Prisoners of War, etc. Series III (5 volumes), Union Correspondence, etc. Series IV (3 volumes), Confederate Correspondence, etc. In addition to an index in each volume, there is a general index. Letters, reports, other documents.

National Archives publications:

Records Relating to Civil War Claims, United States and Great Britain, George S. Ulibarri and Daniel T. Goggin, comp., 1962, Preliminary Inventory number 135.

The Southeast During the Civil War: Selected War Department Records in the National Archives of the United States, Dale E. Floyd, comp., 1973, Reference Information Paper number 71.

AMERICAN STATE PAPERS

The *American State Papers* is a compilation of legislative and executive department documents, organized and published in topical units. They were published originally by Gales and Seaton in Washington, DC, 1832-1861. Many university and research libraries own sets of the originals. Microform copies are available as part of the Serial Set. (See chapter eight.)

Class I	Foreign Relations, 1789-1828	6 volumes
Class II	Indian Affairs, 1789-1827	2 volumes
Class III	Finance, 1789-1828	5 volumes
Class IV	Commerce and Navigation, 1789-1823	2 volumes
Class V	Military Affairs, 1789-1838	7 volumes
Class VI	Naval Affairs, 1794-1836	4 volumes
Class VII	Post Office Department, 1790-1833	1 volume
Class VIII	Public Lands, 1789-1837	8 volumes
Class IX	Claims, 1789-1823	1 volume
Class X	Miscellaneous, 1789-1823	2 volumes

In the Class IX volume are claims against the government for work done, compensation for losses during the Revolution, and pensions for Revolutionary War military service. Several reports beteen 1792 and 1795 list disabled Revolutionary pensioners. These reports are especially important now because all pension applications submitted before November 1800, were destroyed in a War Department fire that month. The reports do not duplicate the lost applications but identify a sizable number of veterans approved for pensions. Typical of the invalid pensioners in a 1792 report was Joshua Gilman of New Hampshire, who had been a private in Col. Hubbard's Regiment and was wounded in the left arm on 16 August 1777 at the Battle of Bennington. He was supposed to receive a monthly pension of $1.11, but the government was $20 in arrears on his payments (Class IX, p 58).

Class VIII contains reports, with occasional maps, of hundreds of public land grants and claims. A chart of Land Claims in Mississippi Territory, abstract for December 1806, shows Alexander Armstrong with a certificate dated 17 December 1806, for one hundred acres on the Bayou Pierre (I, 1902). Volume III con-

tains a "supplementary list of actual settlers" in Louisiana east of the Mississippi River and west of the Pearl River. Volume VII contains a statement in the amount of military land scrip issued to officers and soldiers of the Virginia Continental Line under an act of relief, 15 November 1834. The same volume contains long lists of "Indians owning farms in the Choctaw Nation 1831."

Each book has an index, but a more complete index for the Gales and Seaton Class VIII and IX volumes is *Grassroots of America: A Computerized Index to the American State Papers Land Grants and Claims (1789-1837)*, with other aids to research, Philip W. McMullin, ed. (Salt Lake City: Gendex Corp., 1972). One helpful reference in *Grassroots* is a map of the seventy-seven federal land offices opened to 1840, although not all of them were open *in* 1840. Not only can the searcher identify land offices in the central states, but we get a picture of why so many public-land settlers complained of the distant and difficulty of travel to the nearest office.

The New American State Papers, 1789-1860, Thomas C. Cochran, ed. (Wilmington, DE: Scholarly Resources, 1972-1981) is another series from manuscript collections at the National Archives and Library of Congress, with some of the documents from the Gales and Seaton volumes and the Serial Set. These volumes are facsimile reproductions of the original manuscript and published documents. They follow a similar topical arrangement to the older *American State Papers*, but are subdivided into subject headings within each set. These books are not indexed.

Agriculture, 1789-1860	19 volumes
Commerce and Navigation, 1789-1860	47 volumes
Indian Affairs, 1789-1860	13 volumes
Military Affairs, 1789-1860	19 volumes
Naval Affairs, 1789-1860	10 volumes
Public Finance, 1789-1860	32 volumes
Public Lands, 1789-1860	8 volumes

PUBLIC LANDS

Colonial land grants are not federal records. They are state records usually found in the archives of the original states, and many of these records have been published. Sales and other distribution of the state lands, such as the Georgia land lotteries or the Texas head-right (to Republic settlers) and pre-emption (home-stead) grants, are also state records found at state land offices, surveyor general offices, and archives. Abstracts of many such records are published.

As the original states ceded their western land claims to the Confederation government in the 1780s, Congress had to decide not only on a government for the new lands and a policy for the native peoples still living on much of that land, but also on a system of surveying and selling the land. This public domain was a vast area, still east of the Mississippi River, but soon to expand into the Louisiana Purchase and on to the Pacific Ocean. Debating the New England system of presurveyed townships and the Southern system of indiscriminate and irregular tracts, Congress adopted the Ordinance of 1785, which established the basis for public land organization and policy. Only the public land states are affected by this policy. They include all states west of the Mississippi River, except Texas and Hawaii, and these states east of the river: Wisconsin, Michigan, Illinois, Indiana, Ohio, Mississippi, Alabama, and Florida. Louisiana and Minnesota, split by the river, are public land states considered part of the first tier west of the river.

Under the Ordinance of 1785, all federal lands would be surveyed into vertical strips called ranges, each six miles wide, and horizontal strips of townships, each six miles wide. Like the longitude lines they are based on, ranges are numbered east or west of a principle meridian, e.g., Range 14 West (R14W). Like latitude lines, township strips are numbered north or south of base lines, e.g., Township 10 North (T10N). Range and township strips intersect to form blocks of land (townships), each six miles square. Within each block, six miles by six miles, are 36 sections, each one mile square, e.g., S1, S2, to S36. Each section contains 640 acres. Sections can be broken into quarter-sections: Northeast ¼, Northwest ¼, Southeast ¼, and Southwest ¼, each containing 160 acres. If the southwest quarter, for example, is further divided into quarters (NE, NW, SE, SW) of 40 acres each, the legal description would read SE¼ of SW¼, or NE¼ of SW¼, or N½ of SW¼ (80 acres). In this way, such tracts can be subdivided down into one-acre or smaller lots.

One forty-acre tract owned by Isaac Croom of Caddo Parish, Louisiana, was described in several deed records as SE¼ of NW¼ S32 T20(W) R15(N). Because we did not find a deed showing Isaac's purchase of this tract from another individual, we consulted the tract book of the Natchitoches District, in which Caddo Parish fell. Tract books from the Louisiana land offices are at the State Land Office in Baton Rouge (North at Fourth Street). The tract book is the record of the first transfer of each piece of public domain from the federal government to an individual citizen or company. The Natchitoches Tract Book showed that Isaac Croom was the first private owner of the land in question. He paid seventy-five cents an acre for it on 16 April 1859.

One reason for investigating each tract of land owned by this ancestor is to try to find clues on his second wife. The tract book itself does not show such genealogical information, but it allows the searcher in this case to learn that Isaac was the original private owner. He did not buy the land from a relative of his wife, nor did she inherit it from her father or first husband. Subsequent sales would be recorded in the county deed records.

Since the tract books and related township plats (maps) are set up by range, township, and section, they can also help the searcher identify neighbors, especially in an area where many tracts were purchased within the same time frame. In this way, tract books also act as an index to original purchasers (patentees) in an area. Additionally, if you know an ancestor owned land but do not have a legal description from deeds or an original patent, the tract book is the place to look for that description. These federal records are especially useful in counties that have lost deed records in courthouse fires.

Two sets of tract books were kept. The national version of the tract books continued the history of a piece of land, if it reverted back to the government. The local books from the individual land offices are often found at state land offices, historical societies, or archives, or at the National Archives regional branch that serves the state in question. The Fort Worth branch, for example, has Oklahoma tract books. Los Angeles (Laguna Niguel), San Francisco (San Bruno), and Denver have some tract books and plats for their regions. Contact other branches with public land states for their holdings. The National Archives at this writing has some tract books and patents for western states. The Cartographic Branch of the Archives has some township plats. (Contact Archives II for information.) Tract books and plats for eastern public-land states (east of the Mississippi River and the first tier of states on the west bank of the river) are located at the Bureau of Land Management Eastern States Office, now at 7450 Boston Boulevard, Springfield VA 22153 (formerly in Alexandria, VA.). For a fee, the staff can search tract books and plats if you provide the patentee's name and legal description or location of the land. Some tract books are available on microfilm at the Eastern States Office and from the FHL.

The individual case file for each land entry is the source of potentially valuable information for genealogists, especially in the case of settlers under the Homestead Act of 1862. According to this law, 160 acres of unclaimed land was available to any citizen (or alien who had legally declared his intention to become a citizen) for a small fee, with five years residence on and improvement of the land. In the case of immigrants, the case file typically includes naturalization papers. The National Archives has land-entry case files of the General Land Office dating from 1796 (Bureau of Land Management, RG49). At this writing, they are at the National Records Center in Suitland, Maryland, whose mailing address is Suitland Reference Branch (NNRR), c/o National Archives, Washington, DC 20409. (Other mail to the National Archives uses the zip code 20408.) These records are scheduled to be transferred to Archives I by 1996. When requesting copies of case files, you need to provide the state, land office name, legal description, name of patentee, and type of entry. Name indexes exist for files after 1908 for all public-land states and before 1908 for some.

When surveying and selling public lands, the federal government had to consider private claims on land granted by foreign governments (Britain, France, and Spain) when they owned the land. Evidence of these claims and the determinations made on their validity can be found in the *American State Papers*, the Serial Set, court records, possibly state archives, and, for Texas (state land, not federal), the General Land Office in Austin. One such report in the Serial Set is *Reports of the Committees on Private Land Claims of the Senate and House of Representatives*, from 19th Congress, 2d Session to 44th Congress, 1st Session, Senate Misc. Doc 81 (45-3) serial 1836. Many of the case files for such private claims are in the National Archives. Consult the *Guide to Genealogical Research in the National Archives* for more specific information.

Bibliography—A Sampling

Early Land Records of Wayne County, OH, Richard G. Smith, comp. (Wooster, OH: Wayne County Genealogical Society, 1988). U.S. patents, deeds, tax lists, school land sales, etc.

Federal Land Grants in the Territory of Orleans, the Delta Purchases, adapted from the *American State Papers: Public Lands*, Volume II, and arranged by counties as they existed in 1812, by Charles R. Madwell, Jr. (New Orleans: Polyanthos Press, 1975).

Federal Land Series: A Calendar of Archival Materials on the Land Patents Issued by the U.S. Government with Subject, Tract, and Name Indexes, by Clifford Neal Smith (Chicago: American Library Association, 1972-1986), 4 vols. Volume I—1788-1810. Volume II—Federal Bounty Land Warrants of the American Revolution, 1799-1835. Volume III—1810-1814 (continuation of Volume I). Volume IV—Grants in the Virginia Military District of Ohio.

Florida Land: Records of the Tallahassee and Newmansville General Land Office, 1825-1892, by Alvie L. Davidson (Bowie, MD: Heritage Books, 1989).

History of the Rectangular Survey System, Bureau of Land Management (Washington, DC: Government Printing Office, 1991).

Indiana Land Entries, by Margaret Ruth Waters (Originally published 1948, reprint Knightstown, IN: Bookmark, 1977). Volume 1—Cincinnati District, 1801-1840. Volume 2—Vincennes District, 1807-1877.

"Land and Tax Records," by William Thorndale, in *The Source: A Guidebook of American Genealogy*, Arlene Eakle and Johni Cerny, eds. (Salt Lake City: Ancestry, 1984), p 216-253.

Land Claims, Vincennes District: A Report and Documents from the Commissioner of the General Land Office in Relation to Land Claims in the Vincennes Land District in the State of Indiana, 1835, H.doc. 198 (23-2) serial 275, vol. 5. (Indianapolis: Indiana Historical Society, 1983).

The Land Office Business: The Settlement and Administration of American Public Lands, 1789-1837, by Malcolm J. Rohrbough (New York: Oxford University Press, 1968).

The Land Records of America and Their Genealogical Value, by E.K. Kirkham (Salt Lake City: Deseret, 1964).

Land Title Origins: A Tale of Force and Fraud, by Alfred N. Chandler (New York: Robert Schalkenbach Foundation, 1945). Chapters on regions. Bibliography.

Opportunity and Challenge: The Story of the Bureau of Land Management, Bureau of Land Management (Washington, DC: Government Printing Office, 1988).

Preliminary Inventory of the Land-Entry Papers of the General Land Office, Harry P. Yoshpe and Philip P. Brower (Washington, DC: National Archives, 1949, 1981), Preliminary Inventory number 22. Inventory of National Archives holdings. Inquire about any changes due to redistribution of records and completion of Archives II.

BUREAU OF REFUGEES, FREEDMEN, AND ABANDONED LANDS

Popularly called the Freedmen's Bureau, this agency of the federal government was organized under the War Department at the close of the Civil War to assist freed slaves in dealing with the many changes they faced as a result of emancipation. The bureau was involved in many varied activities, including surveying, seizing, leasing, and restoring to their owners "abandoned" lands in the former Confederate states. The microfilmed records describing these abandoned lands contain information on both black and white ancestors. A prime example comes from Nashville, Tennessee, where Mrs. Luzinca C. Brown owned and "abandoned" at least five pieces of property, of which the first was this house.[5]

> *One large 2 Story Brick Dwelling house on Cedar Street Nashville fronting the Capitol with Lot Extending from High Street to Vine & from Cedar to the Alley, & also has stable & outbuildings attached. This building was occupied by Gov Johnson as a residence upon his arrival here & up to Dec 17 1864 is still so occupied & no rent has been paid on the same. This Mrs. Brown left here at or about the time of the Stampede of the Confederates & went South, but where she is at this Date Dec 17 1864 is not known, having been reported to be in Europe &c, &c, &c (Undated note added in margin: "restored.")*

Also in Nashville were three brick dwellings owned by George Leascher, who "left here in Feb 1862 as a Capt in the Confederate Army & is at date *viz* Dec 17 1864 a prisoner of war at some point north of the Ohio River." One of his dwellings, on Jefferson Street, lot 49 on the map, was occupied by "Mrs. L." without rent. The government was using the other two to house laborers. (Although the owner's wife lived there, the government considered it abandoned.)

On the same roll of microfilm, in Part 3, *Lists, Reports, and Correspondence Pertaining to Land and Property, 1864-1868*, is information about George W. Holden of Bedford County, Tennessee. His farm, in the Ninth Civil District, was 112 acres, of which twenty were tillable. The property was seized on 22 March 1865, with the owner in the "Confederacy & reported in rebel service." A year later, in April 1866, a note was added to the entry, "Is in possession & has taken the Amnesty Oath."

Certainly not all Southern lands were considered abandoned, but the records are worth reading if you had families in these states. (See chapter nine for further discussion.)

The Freedmen's Bureau records also contain letters sent and received between the populace and the bureau offices as well as indentures and contracts made with former slaves. These are potential sources for identifying activities of ancestors, male and female, between censuses and in a very tumultuous period of Southern history. (See also Preliminary Inventory No. 174, *Records of the Bureau of Refugees, Freedmen, and Abandoned Lands, Washington Headquarters*, Elaine Everly, comp. [Washington, DC: National Archives, 1973]).

FEDERAL COURTS

The majority of court cases in the United States originate in state court systems. Therefore, their records are likely to have pertinent information for more genealogists than do federal courts. However, many federal cases do contain genealogical material.

The federal court system that Congress created in 1789 remained virtually the same until 1891. The lower level is still the district courts, of which ninety-four now exist, at least one in each state or territory and the District of Columbia. These are the federal trial courts, with original jurisdiction. Until 1891, the circuit courts were circuit-riding judges who had both appellate and original jurisdiction. Congress created the federal courts of appeals in 1891 as an intermediate appellate level and took away the appellate jurisdiction of the circuit courts, and in 1911, discontinued the circuit courts. The high court remains the Supreme Court.

Certain special courts exist outside this ladder, notably the Court of Claims, begun in 1855 to hear cases against the United States based on any federal law, regulation, or government contract. Later called the U.S. Claims Court, since 1992 this body has been called the U.S. Court of Federal Claims. Many cases grew out of the Civil War, especially from property seizures by the Army. Claims Court records are at the National Archives (RG123), as are Supreme Court records (RG267). Appeals of claims cases used to go to the Supreme Court but since 1982 have gone to the Court of Appeals for the Federal Circuit, which also replaced the U.S. Court of Customs and Patent Appeals.

If you know of a federal case involving an ancestor or other family member, try to determine the court and the approximate date before making a search. Most of the federal district and circuit court records, including case files, are arranged chronologically by court. Such records are kept at the court for only twenty-five to thirty years before being sent to the National Archives regional branch that serves the state where the court is located. (See Appendix D for archives branches and states they serve.) One exception is that most Minnesota federal court records are in the Kansas City branch; only the Duluth area records are in Chicago. The kinds of judicial records available vary from court to court but may include minute and docket books, record and final record books, case files, and some indexes. Cases deal with such issues as bankruptcy, naturalization, patent, and copyright infringement, land disputes, water and fishing rights, civil rights, Indian rights, draft and income tax evasion, admiralty cases, mail theft, counterfeiting, and prohibition violations (1920s). Several examples of genealogical material in federal cases are presented in chapter eight under Appellate Courts. Those branches whose states were once territories also have some territorial court records. Fort Worth and Atlanta (East Point) branches also have some Confederate court records for their states. Some of the branches have a few colonial and state court records.

Records from the federal courts of appeals are also spread among the regional Archives, the records from each circuit housed in the branch serving the city where the court usually sits, as outlined in the following table.

Circuit	States Within This Circuit	Regional Archives Branch Holding Appeals Court Records From This Circuit
First Circuit	ME, MA, NH, RI	Boston
Second Circuit	CT, NY, VT	New York City
Third Circuit	DE, NJ, PA	Philadelphia
Fourth Circuit	MD, NC, SC, VA, WV	Philadelphia
Fifth Circuit	LA, MS, TX	Ft. Worth
Sixth Circuit	KY, MI, OH, TN	Chicago
Seventh Circuit	IL, IN, WI	Chicago
Eighth Circuit	AR, IA, MN, MO, NE, ND, SD	Kansas City
Ninth Circuit	AK, AZ, CA, HI, ID, MT, NV, WA	San Francisco
Tenth Circuit	CO, KS, NM, OK, OR, UT, WY	Denver
Eleventh Circuit	AL, FL, GA (began 1980)	Records not yet in archives
D.C. Circuit	District of Columbia	In 1993, records still held by the court.

Over the years, changes have been made in the state groups within each circuit. Before 1980, for example, states now in the Eleventh Circuit were in the Fifth. Before 1929, states in the Tenth Circuit were in the Eighth. *The Archives: A Guide to the National Archives Field Branches* and each regional *Guide to Records in the National Archives* (both cited earlier in this chapter) can help you identify the location of specific records. (After these publications were issued, many of the Alaska records were transferred to the new Anchorage branch.)

A SAMPLING OF OTHER FEDERAL RECORDS

• During the Civil War, Congress authorized a direct tax in an effort to pay for the war. As Southern states surrendered, they too were affected by the tax, which covered luxury items such as carriages, yachts, billiard tables, pianofortes, and gold watches; annual incomes over $600; and certain licensed occupations. These Internal Revenue Assessment Lists have been microfilmed, with each territory or state and the District of Columbia having its own publication (M or T) number. The Union states are generally covered on the microfilm from 1862 to 1866, although some lists continue to 1872 or 1874. Lists for former Confederate states cover usually 1865 and 1866. Especially in the South, many people did not qualify by the end of the war; therefore, they will not be listed on the rolls. The primary genealogical value of these rolls is further evidence of an ancestor being in a given place at a specific time, especially between decennial censuses. Microfilm numbers for each state are listed in *National Archives Microfilm Resources for Research: A Comprehensive Catalog* (cited earlier).

• Records of retired or former civil service (civilian) employees of the government are kept at the National Personnel Records Center (CPR), 111 Winnebago Street, St. Louis, MO 63118. Information on file usually includes birth date, employment data, and death date if the person died while still employed. Records do extend back into the nineteenth century. To obtain copies, you need to provide the ancestor's name, birth date, place and years of employment, Social Security number if applicable, and proof of death, such as death certificate or newspaper obituary.

• Passports were not required for U.S. citizens traveling abroad until the early twentieth century, nor was the issuing process standardized. However, in the records of the State Department (RG59 and 84), the National Archives has applications for passports issued from about 1789 forward. In late 1993, the Archives had passports issued between 1789 and 1905, and the Washington National Records Center in Suitland, Maryland, had those issued between 1906 and 1925. Because of records shifting between 1993 and 1996, it is advisable to write or call in advance to determine the location of the records you need to study. In order to make a search, you need the name of the individual receiving the passport and the approximate date of departure or issue. Indexes (M1371) are arranged by date and therein, loosely by alphabet. The applications themselves have been filmed, and in late 1993 the microfilm was being prepared for sending to the branch Archives. Information on applications varies but can include age, birthplace, citizenship, residence, physical description, occupation, affidavits of character, and family data.

• The United States Social Security Death Index (about 1935 forward) is available on CD-ROM in the Family History Centers and other research libraries. By entering the name of the deceased person, a searcher can learn birth and death date, place where the Social Security card was issued, Social Security number, and residence of the person at the time of death. The index, though extensive, is not complete.

Getting this same kind of information directly from the Social Security Administration (SSA) takes more effort, but records are more complete. The application for a Social Security number contains such information as full name, birth date and place, and sometimes parents' names, spouse's name, and employment information. Death date may be included if the number was issued in order to process survivor benefits. (This situation occurs especially in the early years of the system.) Claims filed may also contain death and survivor information. Because the form was usually completed by the applicant, parent, or spouse, it can be a reliable source for research. It may be the only available source of birth information, especially for persons born before their states or communities required birth registrations.

Many stories circulate about how genealogists can obtain this information from the application of a deceased ancestor. In talking with SSA representatives via the toll-free number (at this writing, 1-800-772-1213), I received conflicting instructions that also differed from what I had seen in genealogical publications and on electronic mail. Finally, a helpful and patient lady in my local office explained what apparently is the most current procedure. She urged genealogists not to write to the central SSA office in Baltimore but to visit their nearest branch office. She explained that applications filed before 1978 were microfilmed and destroyed. The microfilm is in storage and is very time-consuming to find. The Baltimore staff has a heavy workload dealing with current business and therefore prefers not to handle purely genealogical requests.

The good news is that the files are now computerized. Local branch offices can access the nationwide information quickly. Although some local offices may agree to handle genealogical requests by mail, others require that you appear in person. The documentation necessary for them to release information is your ID, the ancestor's Social Security number, and whatever it takes to prove your relationship to that person, such as a series of birth certificates showing your descent from that ancestor. If the person whose record you seek is living, he or she must sign a release authorizing you to obtain the information.

The Social Security representatives often invoke the Privacy Act in their conversations, just as we genealogists often cite the Freedom of Information Act. Most of those with whom I spoke do not understand why we want (much less, need) this information, which they consider confidential. The representatives also express concern that releasing information which may later be used fraudulently could cost them their jobs. Therefore, they are perhaps overly cautious in dealing with requests for information.

However, many genealogists have success by writing to Baltimore for a copy of the Social Security application (SS-5) of their ancestor: Social Security Administration, Freedom of Information Office, 4-H-8 Annex, 6401 Security Boulevard, Baltimore, MD 21235. Enclose the name of the deceased person whose application you need, death date (we also sent a copy of his death certificate), residence, Social Security number (often found on a death certificate), and any other pertinent information which may help them identify the right person. In our own letter, we stated our relation to the applicant, enclosed $7.00 for the copy, and gave the reason for the request: family history and trying to find the correct birth information for the applicant. We received our answer in about eight weeks. With the SS-5, we confirmed our grandfather's employer, his street address in 1936 when he filed his application, and his parents' names. We got our only copy of his signature and were able to settle a great confusion in birth information. Other sources had shown different birth years and two different cities as his birth place.

Since our search for answers in his own handwriting had been fruitless, we sought contemporary records for which he himself had furnished the information. When the signed Social Security application matched the Masonic record (for which the Mason himself must give the information) and agreed with either birth date or birth place on several more secondary documents, we felt we had settled the issue.

- Additional federal sources include the following:

Guide to the Smithsonian Archives (Washington, DC: Smithsonian Institution, 1978).

Index: Journals of the Continental Congress, 1774-1789, Kenneth E. Harris and Steven D. Tilley, comp. (Washington, DC: National Archives, 1976).

Index: Papers of the Continental Congress, 1774-1789, John P. Butler, comp. (Washington, DC: National Archives, 1978), 5 vols.

Sessional Indexes to the Annals of the United States Congress (Washington, DC: Gales and Seaton, 1851, reprint by United States Historical Documents Institute, 1970). Covers Congress 1789-1919, indexes proceedings and acts, including individual's names.

Records of the City of Georgetown, District of Columbia, 1800-1879, National Archives Microfilm publication M605, with descriptive guide available.

Records of the Government of District of Columbia, Dorothy S. Provine, comp. (Washington, DC: National Archives, 1976, Preliminary Inventory number 186).

United States Direct Tax of 1798: Tax Lists for Pennsylvania (National Archives, M372).

Footnotes are on page 175.

CHAPTER FIVE

County and Courthouse Records

Each state has its own county organization, but there are similarities that allow a general discussion of county (and independent city) records. Some states collect older county records into the state archives. Others leave old records in the counties. In still others, you will find county records at both the state archives or historical society and at the county courthouse. In any case, county records provide a gold mine of information for historians and genealogists.

One of my favorite activities in genealogical research is visiting county courthouses. Yet, some of the experiences in them are more "favorite" than others. After visiting one particular courthouse that we placed at the head of our "pitiful" list, a friend and I developed this set of equipment (beyond the basic pencil and paper) for the intrepid genealogist who frequents these places. If you have done much courthouse research, you will understand why each item is listed. If you have not, consider yourself forewarned.

1. Washable, dark, comfortable clothes and comfortable shoes. Carry a small clothes brush if you will be handling very old record books. The brush is for your clothes, not the books.
2. Work gloves to protect your hands when moving stuff piled in front of basement shelves that may hold the exact book you need, if you could get to it.
3. For basement work, hard hat, flashlight, dust mask, dust rag, perhaps flyswatter.
4. Magnifying glass.
5. Quarters or other change for copy machines, snack machines, parking meters.
6. One-dollar bills for parking lots and sometimes for copies of records.
7. Sandwich and beverage. (Most of us don't work carefully or thoroughly when we're tired and hungry. Of course, it is not advisable to eat inside the rooms with the records, although

some employees do. Take a break for fresh air and snack. The records will wait if you can.)
8. Your best smile, tact and patience. Take your vitamins before you go.
9. Your list of what you want to do at that courthouse, made out ahead of time, legibly, and put where you can get to it easily. Refer to it.

County records can be arbitrarily divided into groups for discussion purposes. They are not catalogued or stored in these divisions. In fact, different counties may keep them in different offices. If you cannot find out ahead of time where particular records are kept, ask when you arrive. Most courthouse employees are pleasant and helpful. However, we must take up a minimum of their time, for they have their own work to do. Some courthouses get so many visits and inquiries from genealogists that they are trying to limit accessibility and do not answer mail.

The following categories help group records and can act as a checklist for a search.

1. Vital records—birth, marriage, death records. Divorce records are discussed under courts since they are generated as court records. In addition to the actual record of these events, the courthouse may have related records, such as intent to marry or marriage affidavits of minors. These affidavits or permission from parent or guardian may also be filed with the returned license or in the marriage record book itself.

2. Records dealing with property, even if that is not the primary reason for the record's creation—property taxes, marks and brands, land records, wills and inventories, estate sales and settlements, and slave records, since slaves were considered property. (See chapter nine for slave records.)

3. Court records—civil, criminal, justice of the peace, probate, and others. Records can include dockets, minutes, and case files. Cases of particular interest

to genealogists are divorces and naturalizations. (See chapter eleven for naturalizations.)

4. Administrative records—minutes of county commissioners (known in some places as county supervisors or police jury), sheriff and jail records, professional licenses, business registrations or incorporation papers, drivers' licenses, car registration, voter registration, election returns, elected official bond books and records, county employee records, roads and bridges, any other taxes or registrations, and miscellaneous records.

VITAL RECORDS

Birth and death records have been kept in many forms. States began keeping these records at different times, with varying consistency, and with varying degrees of completeness. In many cases, the more recent the record, the more detailed is the information provided. Bare basics are all that appear in this birth record: born at Alto, Cherokee County, Texas, 22 January 1912, male, live birth, to A. and Mrs. Cummings. In many records, the mother's maiden name is requested, but it is not always given. Some certificates still ask for nationality or birthplace, race, and age of the parents; length of residence in the county or the local area; the specific street address of the family if in town; the baby's full name, time of birth, and birth order within the family; and the doctor's name.

As discussed in chapter one, birth or death records within one set of siblings may give different information on parents' names. Sometimes omissions or mistakes are due to haste in filing the record, lack of knowledge on the part of the doctor or other informant, or lack of concern or understanding of how important this information can be for descendants. Because of the discrepancies that often exist, the researcher is well advised to collect these records for all the siblings.

Delayed birth certificates are sometimes filed years after the event to clarify information, to add the baby's name, or to create a record that was not filed at the time of birth. Documents allowed as evidence of the birth may vary from state to state, but basically they must give age and parentage. They can include affidavits from parents, relatives, or friends who were old enough to remember the birth of this particular child to these particular parents, a census record that states a person's age at a given date and parents' names, a school record that gives the birth date and/or parentage, an old voter registration card, or other such rec-

ords. When these delayed certificates are processed at the state level, the county of birth receives a copy for their files. Sometimes the delayed records are indexed; sometimes they are not. County clerks tell me that the documents are returned to the sender and are not sent to the county. Additionally, in some areas, delayed birth registrations begin in the country probate court. Contact your particular research area for their practices.

Like birth records, death certificates can be sparse or full of details. The family in this case has records that identify this person, but the public record does not. *Mrs.* Shelby died on 13 November 1904 at Calvert (Robertson County, Texas) of typhoid fever. Her doctor was W.S. Parker of the same town. She was a white female, age 35, an American citizen, born in America, and a resident of Calvert. The form asked for no informant, next of kin, survivors, or parents' names.

On the other hand, the 1934 death certificate of Maggie Kane Wells of Houston, Texas, gave many facts. She was a white female, age 76 years, 10 months, and 20 days, born on 7 February 1858 in Cincinnati, Ohio, who had lived for 60 years in the city of Houston. She was the widow of J.T. Wells, but her parents' names were unknown to the informant, her daughter, Mrs. A.T. King of the same street address. She died at 1:07 P.M. on 27 December 1934 of congestive heart failure complicated by bronchitis, as attested by her physician J. Peyton Barnes, whose offices were at 308 Second National Bank, Houston. The undertaker was Settegast-Kopf Company on Milam Street, Houston, and burial was at the Glenwood Cemetery on December 28. This more detailed form gave clues for further searching, such as a visit to the funeral home, whose files yielded more information.

Death records, of course, can provide valuable data but are secondhand sources of birth information. You as the researcher, therefore, must be alert to the possibility that birthdate, birthplace, or parents' names and birthplaces may be incorrect and that you should corroborate this information with other sources. Comparing death certificates of siblings may, or may not, clear up discrepancies or omissions in information about *parents*. However, other sources will have to be used to provide comparative information on the *birth* of the deceased. Two cases illustrate the process.

First, the death certificate of Alfred Thomas King of Harris County, Texas, was filled out by his only son and gave Austin, Texas, as his birthplace on 20 June 1885. Actually the *5* is a correction written over a *6*.

However, two pieces of evidence point to different information. (1) The Houston city directories for 1880-1881 and 1884-1894 show the family in Houston, along with most of the mother's family. If the mother went to her mother's to have the baby, she had only a few blocks to travel. (2) Alfred's confirmation record at Houston's Episcopal Church of the Good Shepherd in 1930 says he was born in Houston in 1886. At the time of his confirmation and the recording of the information in the church register, his son was only five years old and would not have given this information. His wife could have been the informant, but it seems more likely that the minister asked Alfred directly. Indeed, Alfred and his widowed mother were living together in Austin at the same time of the 1900 census (which gave his birth as June 1885) but returned to Houston in time for Alfred to appear in the 1902 city directory. Records in Austin so far have not turned up any evidence for an Austin birth, and census information is not consistent on birthdate. Thus, the search goes on.

The second example is from a family living in a rural area where church records are sparse to nonexistent. A son was the informant for the death certificate for Mrs. Mary (Shelby) Liles and showed her birthdate as 2 February 1863. At her death in January 1929, one week before her next birthday, she was said to be 67 years and 11 months old. This points out one discrepancy on the certificate itself. If the age given was correct and she would have turned 68 the next week, her birth year would have been 1861. If the birthdate given was correct, she would have actually been 65 years and 11 months old when she died. However, the larger discrepancy is the fact that she appears with her parents and siblings in the 1860 census as a five-year-old! This indicates an 1855 birth year if the age and the February date are correct. The family has not been found in the 1870 census. The 1880 census gives her age as 21, which suggests an 1859 birth year and conflicts with the more consistently documented 1859 birthdate of her brother John. She and her family have not yet been located in the 1900 census, but the 1910 census reports her age as 53, which would indicate an 1857 birth year. Thus, the death certificate only complicated an already confused situation, which suggests birthdates from 1855 to 1863. Based on the 1860 census and data about her siblings, an 1854-1858 date seems most likely, but the jury is still out. The point remains that death certificates can be, but are not always, accurate and helpful. Information in them should be corroborated with data from other sources.

Birth and death records, especially from the nineteenth century, are sometimes available for searchers at county courthouses or city halls. Some cities initiated birth and death registration before their states did and maintain their own records. In a number of cities, births and deaths that occur within city limits are registered with the city rather than the county. In most states, these records are also centralized at the state level in the bureau or division of vital records, vital statistics, or health. Each state is organized slightly differently, and each has its own privacy law, which affects accessibility. References to help you find the records you need include these books:

Vital Records Handbook, by Thomas J. Kemp (Baltimore: Genealogical Publishing Company, 1989). Includes state by state listing of agency and address, cost, limitations or restrictions, and the necessary forms that may be photocopied. *International Vital Records Handbook* (same compiler and publisher, 1994) is an expanded edition covering sixty-seven countries and territories, including the United States.

Where To Write For Vital Records: Births, Deaths, Marriages, and Divorces, (Hyattsville, MD: U.S. Department of Health and Human Services, Public Health Service, 1993 or later edition). In libraries, or for sale at government bookstores or the Government Printing Office in Washington, DC. Gives agency, address, and availability of records for states and territories as well as records of citizens born "on the high seas" or in foreign countries.

MARRIAGE RECORDS

Marriage records too are vital records, usually found in county courthouses, with copies often in the state library, archives, or historical society. In some states, the records are also being centralized in the state vital statistics or vital records office, but the county (town in New England or independent incorporated towns and cities in Virginia) is the place where the license is issued and the record generated. The particular office in the county courthouse where the records are kept varies from county clerk to probate clerk or circuit court clerk. The vital statistics guides listed above and research guides to your state(s) of interest can give you the specific information you need to find marriage records.

Marriage records come in many varieties, some more complete than others. Almost until the twentieth century in many areas, grooms had to place themselves under bond before the wedding. Below are two examples of marriage bonds from Cumberland County, Virginia.

One example used a printed form: "We Elliott Coleman and William Daniel acknowledge ourselves indebted to Beverley Randolph, Esquire, Governour of Virginia, in the sum of fifty pounds current money, to be paid to the said Governour or his successors: Yet if there be no lawful cause to obstruct a marriage intended between Elliot (sic) Coleman and Elizabeth Daniel then this obligation to be void, else to remain in full force and virtue. Given under our hands & seals the 23 day of Nov. one thousand seven hundred and 89. Witness—"

Another example is a handwritten document. "Know all men by these presents that we Ferdinand G. Coleman and Peter T. Phillips are held and firmly bound unto Thomas M. Randolph Governor of Virginia in the just and full sum of $150 good and lawfull (sic) money of Virginia to be paid to the said governor or his successors upon these conditions that if there be no lawfull cause to obstruct a marriage intended to be had and solemnised [between] the said Coleman and Eliza Phillips of this county then the above obligations to be void or else to remain in full force and virtue given under our hand & seals—this 31st day of December 1821. Wit: T.C. Woodson Jr."

In both these cases, the surety on the bond was the bride's father. Sometimes it was a brother, other relative, or a friend.

Caldwell County, Kentucky, marriage bonds contain much more information than the names of the bride and groom and the dates of the bond and/or the wedding. For example, a typical bond gives the following information. The groom was Hiram H. Brelsford (Jr.), a 27-year-old merchant of the town of Princeton in that county. He was a native of the county, as was his mother. His father was born in Christian County, Kentucky. His bride was Emma Owen, age 21, also a native of Caldwell County. Her parents were born in Kentucky. This was the first marriage for both bride and groom, and they were married at the home of E.N. Owen on 25 May 1864. The surety on the bond was W.H. Kevil.

Marriage licenses are the other, more recent form of marriage record found in county courthouses. The following Texas license shows one standard form for this kind of instrument:

To any ordained Minister of the Gospel, Judge or Justice of the Peace—Greeting: You, or either of you, are hereby authorized to solemnize the Rites of Matrimony between Thomas M. Metcalfe and Miss Mattie E. Harrison and make due return of this License to my office within sixty days, certified according to law. Given under my hand and seal of this County, at office in the town of Georgetown, this 14th day of October 1884. J.W. Hodges, Clerk County Court, Williamson County, per (signed) C.R. Faubion, Deputy.

The lower part of this license gives the minister or judge a place to certify the solemnization of the marriage:

I, J.S. Tunnell, a Minister, hereby certify that I solemnized the Rites of Matrimony between Thos. M. Metcalf and Miss Mattie E. Harrison on the 16th day of October 1884. (signed) J.S. Tunnell.

The last part of the license reports its return to the clerk's office and its filing in the county record:

Returned, this 17th day of October 1884. A true copy of the original recorded this the _____ day of _____ 188 _____ (signed) J.W. Hodges, Clerk of County Court, Williamson County.

The outside of this license indicates that it was registered on 8 December 1884 on page 502 of the marriage volume currently being filled.

The part of the bond or license that tells about the marriage ceremony itself sometimes includes other helpful details. For example, when I.N. Turley of Crittendon County, Kentucky, married Julia A.C. Hamby on 12 January 1860, the minister's return added that he was an *M. of M.E.*, minister of the Methodist Episcopal Church, and had married the couple at S.P. Hamby's. Since young ladies often married at home, this information may be a clue to the bride's father's name, as well as to the church the family attended.

PROPERTY AND PROBATE RECORDS

Records that give information about property make up a sizable portion of any courthouse collection. People record evidence of their property, pay taxes on property, give away property, buy and sell property, and fight over property. Much of this property is land and the buildings on it but may also include livestock and, before 1865, slaves. The importance of these records for genealogists cannot be overestimated, for they are much more than just evidence of property and residence. They often contain information on clusters of relatives living in the area and valuable proof of relationships.

Marks and brands on livestock may not give much more genealogical information than the residence of a particular ancestor at a given time, but they are interesting. They may be found in various places, usually court minutes or separate books reserved for such registration. In the court minutes of Davidson County, Tennessee, on "Wensday," 7 January 1784, James Shaw recorded his stock ear marks and his brand *IS*, created from his initials. In the separate Revised Mark and Brand book in Robertson County, Texas, on 5 June 1879, John P. Shelby registered his *BA* brand, placed on the animal's hip. His mark was a cross in the left ear and a notch in the tip of the right ear. The form also furnished the information that he lived two miles east of Bremond. Since his brand had nothing to do with his name or residence, it is thought that perhaps he bought the cattle already branded and was simply registering their existing brand.

Annual property taxes are sometimes combined with poll taxes (head taxes) in county records, and many counties no longer keep their tax records beyond a certain number of years. When I have asked to see old tax records in various counties, I have been taken to the books for the 1940s or 1950s, which are the oldest they still have. In some cases the older records have been microfilmed and placed at the state archives or historical society. Other counties have stashed their nineteenth century tax books in old jails and basement storage areas impossible to reach. They obviously do not recognize the value of these records in the history of the county.

Of course, not all residents of the county own taxable property; therefore, not all residents of the county are listed on the property tax rolls. However, these assessment lists give a good, if not complete, picture of residents and their taxable wealth. They also are valuable in helping to identify when a family moved in or out of the county, or at least when they were present. Although many tax lists are recorded more or less alphabetically, some are written down in the order that the assessor visited the families. This kind of record can be very useful in determining place of residence,

neighbors, and, sometimes, relationships. An interesting article by Ruth Land Hatten in the *National Genealogical Society Quarterly* (Volume 81, Number 1 [March 1993], p 46-50) compares census and tax records of a given year to identify a "missing" ancestor. An example of relationships found in tax records comes from Hawkins County, Tennessee, in 1809, where John Armstrong "Son to James" is taxed for three hundred acres, one white poll and two black polls.[6]

An illustration from Caldwell County, Kentucky, shows the growth of John Turley's estate beginning in 1835:

1835	260 acres of land on Skinframe Creek, 6 horses, 1 stud or jack.	$1,011 value
1837	260 acres, $3/acre value, 6 horses, 3 slaves (1 over 16 years).	$1,720 value
1838	260 acres (value $780), 7 horses ($400), 3 slaves (1 over 16) ($700), other property ($100).	$1,980 value
1839	260 acres ($800), 6 horses ($300), 4 slaves (2 over 16) ($1,400).	$2,500 value
1840	260 acres ($1,000), 6 horses, 4 slaves (2 over 16), 16 cattle ($50).	$3,000 value
1841	260 acres ($1,500), 103 acres on Donaldson Creek ($300), 6 horses ($300), 5 slaves (2 over 16) ($2,000), 17 cattle ($50).	$4,150 value
1842	260 + 107 acres ($1,400), 7 horses ($200), 7 slaves (2 over 16) ($2,000).	$3,600 value
1843	260 + 109 acres ($2,050), 5 horses ($150), 1 mule ($75), 15 cattle ($75), 7 slaves (3 over 16) ($1,000).	$4,250 value
1844	260 ($2,080) + 115 acres ($450), 5 horses ($200), 18 cattle ($75), 9 slaves (4 over 16) ($2,700).	$5,455 value
1845	Margaret Turley—260 acres, 0 men over 21 in household, 6 horses, 9 slaves (4 over 16), 15 cattle.	$5,005 value

The tombstone in Hill Cemetery of Caldwell County shows that John W. Turley died on 28 September 1844, survived fifteen years by his wife, Margaret. The tax record reflects John's death, and Margaret appears thereafter as the head of the household.

Deed Records

Deed records as a class are one of the most valuable sources for genealogists. Deeds of trust, deeds of gift, warranty deeds, powers of attorney, and prenuptial agreements are not the only kinds of property records found in deed books but are among the most common and most useful for genealogists. Regardless of the kind of instrument you find, you can learn about relationships, dates, marriages, former residences, new residences, and other pertinent details of family history. To gain the most from the deed records in a county for your time period:

1. Look in both direct and reverse (indirect) indexes where both exist. Direct indexes are arranged by grantor or seller; reverse indexes, by grantee or buyer. Indexes vary in style and rarely are strictly alphabetical. Most are alphabetical by initial letter of the surname; sometimes, by given name within each surname section. Take time to familiarize yourself with each index style. Be aware that recording, and therefore indexing, sometimes took place years after the executing of the original instrument.

2. Note all entries under your surname(s), whether you recognize the given names or not.

3. Look for generations of the surname before and after your particular ancestor.

4. Write down the source of your information so that you or someone else could find it again. Copy or abstract all information given in each deed, including dates, witnesses, residences, conditions and considerations, property descriptions, whether parties signed their names or signed by mark. (Signatures and marks in deed books are usually not the actual signatures of the parties.)

5. Be alert for relationships mentioned or implied. Witnesses were often relatives.

6. Look at deeds recorded at the same time, within a few pages before or after your ancestor's deeds, to see if family members appear as witnesses to other instruments.

7. Allow yourself time to do a thorough job the first time, perhaps with some study time overnight and a return visit to catch what might have been overlooked the day before.

The deed of trust is an instrument made to secure payment of debt by transferring title to property to one or more trustees. Especially after the Civil War in the South, many of these deeds were executed. Everyone was in debt, and few had money with which to pay those debts. When my ancestor E.G. Coleman had to write his deed of trust in June 1867, he listed among his property a number of notes due him for several thousand dollars. He also owed money, which he was having trouble paying. This deed of trust gave him one year to pay the debts he owed or face the sale of his property at public auction. Thus, he turned over to George Wood and brother A.A. Coleman his livestock, his home, wagons and buggy, all his farming utensils, the pianoforte, his growing crops of cotton, corn, and fodder, and "all interest I have in real and personal estate of my late father Ferdinand G. Coleman dec'd late of Cumberland County, Virginia." This one statement was the key that unlocked the door to previous generations. (Hardeman County, Tennessee Deed Bk U, p 56)

Deeds of gift were often used to distribute property among one's children. That is the way Jesse Croom, Sr. of Wayne County, North Carolina, gave his son Charles 150 acres on 17 January 1787. The key wording is "for and in consideration of the Natural Love and Affection he hath and bears unto the said Charles Croom his son, . . . (Jesse) hath given, granted, and confirmed . . . unto the said Charles Croom a certain Plantation . . ." containing 150 acres, originally granted to Jesse Croom on 27 April 1767. (Deed Bk 3, p 424)

Warranty deeds, called by the shorter term *deed*, transferred property with the guarantee of a good title. In the public land states, property conveyed in these deeds was identified by the section or fraction of section, township and range in which it lay. In the other states, the metes and bounds system of surveying property was used, with trees and rock piles as typical corners of property lines. The following description is an example of the use of metes and bounds. W.L. Harrison in 1861 bought land in Williamson County, Texas, which lay on both sides of the South San Gabriel River, on a portion of the headright of Benjamin S. Mudd and described as follows:

Beginning at the northwest corner of Mrs. Martha Ward's land, at a stone for a corner, then west 19° south to the South San Gabriel River, then down the river with its meanderings

346 yards to a pile of stones on the north bank, then south 19° east to the south boundary of Norman Miller, then east with said line to Martha Ward's west boundary, then north 19° west with Ward's line to the place of beginning, containing 80 acres, more or less. (Deed Bk 8, p 377)

Another valuable feature of deeds is the naming of the seller's wife. In some areas, the wife signed the deed with her husband. In other areas, the wife was taken aside by appointees of the court to acknowledge the sale and relinquish her dower rights in the property. In such states, the wife acquired by marriage a legal right to part of her husband's estate for her use during her lifetime if she survived him. Therefore, when a husband sold property while his wife was living, the buyer usually made certain that the wife relinquished her rights in the property and could not come to claim a share of the property after her husband's death. The relinquishment usually follows the recording of the deed in the deed book. Its primary value for genealogists is the identification of the wife and the knowledge that she was living at that particular time. Sometimes, it is the only record of the wife's name, as with Thomas Coleman's wife, Elizabeth, (1769) in Cumberland County, Virginia, and William Harrison's first wife, Lucy, (1780s) in Petersburg, Virginia. The dates of multiple relinquishments may also help determine which children of the family were born of which wife.

A person can grant power of attorney to a relative, friend, or attorney to handle business in his behalf. Documents of this nature are also found in deed books, as in the case of William Harrison, clerk of the town of Petersburg, naming Edward Pegram, Esquire, his attorney, to sue for and recover all money due him, on 6 February 1786. (Petersburg Deed Book 1, p 292)

Between February 1786 and March 1789, Harrison's wife, Lucy, apparently died, and Harrison made plans to remarry. On 26 March 1789, he executed a document according to the agreements made with his bride-to-be prior to the marriage. (Petersburg Deed Book 1, p 492) Whereas they promised to marry each other, William, for love of Nancy, gave her his mansion house called Porter Hill where he then resided, four lots, the house and lot called Lark Hall, one hundred acres in Dinwiddie County, £500, and two slaves. "I further oblige myself to enable Nancy to give her brother Spencer £50 when he goes to Great Britain to finish his studies." Both William and Nancy signed the document, witnessed by her father David Vaughan and two others. This particular agreement was made between a young woman and a much older man who seems to have had no living children at the time. This may have been an agreement to guarantee her certain property and rights in the event of his death. Such a prenuptial agreement was often made when each party had separate property coming into the marriage and/or had children by a former marriage whose interests they wanted to protect.

Deeds were often made between relatives, but relationships are not always expressed. The following case is an example. In 1871, Thomas J. Robertson of Lafayette County, Arkansas, sold to John H. Harris of Caddo Parish, Louisiana, his undivided interest in land held in common with other heirs of his deceased mother Elizabeth C. Croom and stepfather Isaac Croom. (Caddo Parish Deed Book S, p 855) Especially when property is described in this way, the genealogist must look for a relationship. In this case, Robertson was selling to his brother-in-law. Harris and his wife owned their own one-sixth interest in the property, bought Robertson's one-sixth, and bought the father's undivided one-half. Several years later, they sold their five-sixths interest to C.S. Croom, the half-brother of Harris' wife. The documents themselves mentioned none of the relationships between the buyers and sellers, but buying and selling, especially of inherited property, was often done among relatives. Being alert to such possibilities may help you find relationships you were not aware of. The Robertson deed above also gave the first positive identification and whereabouts of this brother since the 1860 census.

An instrument of great genealogical value sometimes found in deed books is affidavits. The example given is one of several made within the same family because of intestate deaths. John F. Oldham of Robertson County, Texas, in 1909 made an affidavit saying that he was the son of B.F. Oldham and grandson of J.N. Oldham, who died in June 1879 or 1880. (Because he appeared in the 1880 census, the death must have occurred in 1880.) His wife, Mary, died in 1886. The only heirs at law of the said J.N. and Mary were J.C.L. and B.F. Oldham, sons of J.N. and Mary; M.A. McDaniel, wife of J.H. McDaniel; A.S. Jelks, wife of R.L. Jelks; and V.A. Hightower, wife of J.Q. Hightower, the last three being daughters of J.N. and Mary. Both grandparents died intestate and land inherited by their heirs (and described in the document) was sold to J.M. Oldham in 1887. (Deed Book 67, p 334) Other deeds and marriage records supplied most of the given names for the initials in the affidavit.

Contracts sometimes appear in deed books. An example is the agreement between E.G. Coleman and D.L. Kokernot, made 1 April 1876 in Gonzales County, Texas. By the instrument, Coleman bound himself to complete within thirty days the following job:

> Coleman will *"in a good and workmanlike manner well and substantially build a two-story house 20×30 feet on a tract of 1 acre of land on the water of Peach Creek it being a portion of the Hill League and donated by William E. Jones for the purpose of erecting said building thereon to be used as a school house and such other purposes as the school trustees may agree, with such lumber and other materials as the said Kokernot may furnish."* (Deed Book W, p 225)

Upon completion, Coleman was to receive $200. If either party defaulted on their part of the agreement, the penalty would be $250. On May 15, Coleman received $210 in payment for the job and extra work required.

In deed books are recorded a number of other documents dealing with property, its transfer and division. Many of the records are self-explanatory when you read the contents. In addition to deed books, documents concerning property may be found in various other record books, depending on the county. Examples include Small Estates Record, Wills Filed for Safekeeping, and Probate Court records, dockets, and minutes.

In the thirty public-land states, copies of tract books and township plats may be available in the county. They are usually at the state Land Office and/or at a Bureau of Land Management office. Many have been microfilmed and are available at research libraries or for rent from the FHL. (See chapter four for further discussion.)

Two books that shed light on the subject of property are these:

Inheritance in America From Colonial Times to the Present, Carol Shammas et al., (New Brunswick, NJ: Rutgers University Press, 1987).

Women and the Law of Property in Early America, by Marylynn Salmon (Chapel Hill, NC: The University of North Carolina Press, 1986).

Probate Records

Another set of documents dealing with property and found in county courthouses are probate records: wills, inventories, and estate settlements, in addition to records of guardianship of minors and insanity cases. For genealogists, these records can be especially valuable for the relationships, residences, and marriages that they contain.

Of course, wills are written that leave everything to "my beloved wife and children," all unnamed. And at the other end of the spectrum are those like the will of William Coleman, Senior, of Cumberland County, Virginia, dated 23 May 1810. This will names the heirs in the way we wish all wills would: his son William and William's wife, Parmelia; grandson Spilsby, son of his son William; his son Henry; grandsons Henry and William D., sons of his son Henry; his son Elliott; grandson Ferdinand G., son of his son Elliott; his daughter Sarah, wife of Wyatt Coleman. (Will Book 4, p 43)

When a person dies, the probate court appoints someone to inventory and estimate the value of the deceased person's estate before a settlement and division of property can be made. The inventory lists provide fascinating reading because they give a picture of the home and farm or business. The following are a few of the items listed in William Coleman's estate, inventoried on 20 June 1811 in Cumberland County, Virginia. (Will Book 4, p 69)

Item	Value in Pounds.Shillings.Pence.
1 yoke spotted steers	13.10.00
1 cow with the bell on	4.10.00
1 sorrel mare and colt	30.00.00
8 tobacco hogsheads	2.08.00
1 cask w/ vinegar, 40 gallons	.12.00
4 spinning wheels	1.16.00
1 lot of coopers and carpenters tools	2.14.00
1 pare (*sic*) flat irons	.06.00
5 grubbing hoes	1.04.00
1 skillet and dutch oven	.06.00
1 loom	1.04.00
1 saddle, bridle	5.02.00
1 dozen pewter plates, 2 dishes, 5 spoons	1.10.00
half dozen knives and forks	.06.00
9 bee hives	4.01.00

1 set of books	1.10.00
1 corner cupboard	3.12.00
1 desk	3.12.00
13 chairs and 1 slate	1.04.09
2 beds and furniture	20.00.00
1 case of razors	.07.06
1 looking glass	.07.06
1 chest	.18.00
15 sheep and a house lamb	9.12.00
3 sows and 13 pigs	4.10.00

Besides the inventory, other accounting of income and expenses of the estate become part of the settlement record. Apart from an estate sale, cash receipts in this Coleman estate included sales of butter, lard, bacon, vinegar, corn, (goose) feathers, brandy, honey, fodder, wheat, tobacco, a skillet, and a cow. Expenses included such items as repairing the small chimney, weaving and cutting out cloth for Negro clothing, paying the executor's wife for "her attendance two days about cleaning up the house & attending to the cooking of the dinner at the funeral sermon of William Coleman," paying the minister for preaching the funeral sermon, and paying John Hudgins for "crying" the auction at the estate sale less items he purchased at the sale. When the various reports were accepted by the court in March 1814, the four heirs each received in slaves and cash an amount equal to 470 pounds, 5 shillings, 10½ pence. The final accounting two years later gave each heir another £10.8.3. (Will Book 4, p 307-313, Book 5, p 199) In some settlements, the entire estate sale is reproduced in the record book, with who bought what and for how much.

Many people, for whatever reasons, did not (and do not) write wills. The court and family or friends still must settle these intestate estates, especially when property division or settlement is involved. When Elliott Coleman died intestate in 1892 in Hays County, Texas, the court appointed Ed. A. Vaughan administrator. The twenty-one documents in the case file indicate that Coleman had a very small estate, was owed money, and had some outstanding bills himself. According to one letter in the file, his wife and two minor sons, Zeke and Turner, were by June residing in Mills County, Texas. Another document named some of the other children who were grown and living elsewhere. Thus, the administrator and a family friend, H.C. Wallace, took on the job of paying the creditors and settling the estate. After collecting money due the estate

and paying expenses, $18.38 remained to be apportioned out to the six creditors who had been only partially paid. Neither the death date nor the cemetery are named in the documents. However, a note dated 17 February 1892 listed funeral expenses. The doctor's bill included treatments prescribed until February 3. These papers suggest that the death occurred between February 3 and 16.

COURT RECORDS

Because each state sets up its own court system, researchers need to ask or read about the particular names and jurisdictions of courts in their research area at the time the ancestors lived there. Some of this information can be found in (1) the many books on research in each state, (2) some of the Martindale-Hubbell legal directories, (3) some encyclopedias, especially ones in the legal field, and (4) state almanacs. However, most states have a multilevel court system. At the lower level are courts of limited jurisdiction, such as justice of the peace, municipal, family, traffic, small claims, juvenile, and some county courts. These records are usually found in or near the county courthouse in the offices of the court. For various reasons, the early records of some of these courts no longer exist.

The second level of courts are those of general and original jurisdiction, such as district, circuit, and superior courts, courts of common pleas, some county courts, and, in New York, supreme courts. These courts handle both criminal and civil cases, often including divorce and probate. (Probate is sometimes a jurisdiction of the county court.) Offices and records of these courts are often in county courthouses or courthouse complexes.

Most states have intermediate appeals courts, called district or circuit courts of appeals or superior courts. The highest level court in most states is a supreme court with appellate jurisdiction. Appeals cases at both state and federal levels are illustrated in chapter eight.

County courts, by whatever name the state gives them, usually have jurisdiction over small civil claims and lesser crimes. In some areas, these courts can also sit as probate courts, dealing with wills, estate settlements, guardianship, and insanity cases. In the early years in Tennessee and North Carolina, the court of pleas and quarter sessions was a kind of county court, made up of justices of the peace. Two representative cases illustrate the kinds of issues brought before this court. In July 1784, James Shaw of Davidson County sued John Montgomery for settlement of a debt of £15.9. When the defendant did not show up in court and Shaw presented his evidence, the court instructed the sheriff to sell the attached property, including one dwelling house and one loom house and loom, to satisfy the debt. In October 1787, Shaw sued William Hopkins who had borrowed a horse and failed to return it. Shaw asked for damages of £30. The jury found in favor of the plaintiff, awarded Shaw £22.13.4 in damages, and charged Hopkins with the court costs.

County court minutes, especially older ones, reflect many activities of the court and community. These examples are representative of the business before the court in Davidson County, Tennessee, 1783-1792:

1. James Shaw was a witness in a trial in April 1783, and testified that he heard William Joiner agree to "pitch and corky" a boat (make it watertight) and give Jonathan Boyd $15 for the hire thereof.

2. James Shaw served on the grand jury for the July term, 1784, and the trial jury in April 1786, October 1787, and numerous other terms.

3. In July 1784, James Shaw was authorized to "keep a Ferry at the place afforesaid [Nashville] with good and sufficient boats and well attended for the purpose of passage of such as are desirous of crossing the said river [Cumberland]" at the following fees: 1 shilling for man and horse; 1 shilling for every pack horse and pack; 8 pence for a lead horse without a pack; 6 pence for every footman, 6 pence for every head of horned cattle, and 4 pence for every head of sheep and hogs.

4. The case of the *State vs. John Boyd*, charging the defendant with butchering a beef on the Sabbath Day, came to trial on 8 April 1788. Upon hearing the circumstances, the court acquitted Boyd.

5. James Shaw served on the jury on 8 April 1788, which found Samuel Martin not guilty of stealing a bull from James Bosley.

6. On 8 July 1788, the court appointed one man in each militia company to take a list of taxables (people and their taxable property).

7. On 9 July 1788, James Shaw and others were appointed to lay a road from the Isaac Thomas Ferry [at his residence] to Nashville, with Captain Bosley as overseer.

8. On 5 January 1789, Andrew Jackson, Esquire, produced his license to practice law in Tennessee and took the oath of an attorney.

9. On 9 January 1789, the court ordered Colonel Thomas Green to have a tavern license to keep an ordinary in Nashville where "he now is." The next day, the court resolved that the selling price of a quart of whiskey would be one dollar, and in proportion for amounts more or less than a quart.

10. On 10 October 1789, again on 12 July 1790, and again on 13 January 1791, Sampson Williams, sheriff, entered his protest against the sufficiency of the county jail.

11. On 13 July 1790, the court exempted Thomas Brown from jury duty because of his being "upon the scout after the Indians."

12. On 13 January 1791, the court established the following rates for tavernkeepers: 1 shilling for breakfast; 2 shillings for dinner [main mid-day meal]; 1 shilling for supper; 6 pence for a half pint of whiskey; 1 shilling for a half pint of rum or good brandy; 1 shilling for stabling a horse for twenty-four hours with hay or fodder; and 2 pence per man for a good bed for one night.

13. On 15 July 1791, William Black took the oath to serve as a deputy sheriff.

14. On 11 January 1792, James Shaw acknowledged the validity of a deed of Robert Wilson to Samuel Shannon, prior to its being recorded in the deed book.

The Rutherford County, North Carolina, Court of Pleas and Quarter Sessions handled the same types of cases and business, with the addition of this example of great interest to descendants. On Friday, 16 October 1801, William Metcalf was "brought before the court and charged by some of the members of Bills Creek Congregation for disorderly behavior at the place of worship and prays that said Metcalf be bound for his good behavior. [It is] ordered therefore that the said Metcalf be bound for 12 months and day in the sum of £100 with 2 securities in [the amount of] £50 each. Accordingly came the said Metcalf and was bound [for] £100. Thomas Dalton and Benjamin Williams security in £50 each."

State district courts or circuit courts may have both civil and criminal jurisdiction, with civil jurisdiction over suits involving large amounts of money, divorce, and others matters of law. Of course, many of these cases contain genealogical material, as illustrated in chapter eight. However, of special interest to genealogists are the divorce cases, often indexed and recorded separately from other cases. The record book itself usually gives only the fact that a divorce was granted to the two people named. The case file contains the petition from the plaintiff stating the grounds for the divorce and other pertinent documents. Depending on the laws of each state, either spouse could file for divorce.

The case of *Dave Perkins vs. Hulda Perkins* in Leon County, Texas, is an example of the husband asking for the divorce. The petition in the case file states that the two were married on 14 December 1882 in Leon County and lived happily together for the first six or eight years. Then the wife began using abusive language and cursing her husband, saying she cared nothing for him and had never loved him. After about 1890, she had refused to care for the household in such matters as cooking and washing for her husband and children. He said he could not afford to hire a servant to do those things for the family. Finally, on 10 January 1896, Hulda abandoned his bed and board, and Dave filed for the divorce, which was granted on 16 November 1896.

In the District Court Minutes are also recorded such items as grand jury and trial jury lists, bills of indictment in criminal matters, and civil cases pending before the court. In October 1846, the grand jury of Leon County, Texas, returned bills against Simeon Loyd, William Hightower, William Evans, Daniel McIver, George Floyd, and John McKay for playing at cards and against John McKay for offering a challenge to fight a duel. In this particular county, many of the case files of early trials were lost in a courthouse fire, but scattered ones do exist.

An early case that does contain genealogical information and whose file does exist is the *Heirs of Felix A. Richardson, deceased, vs. the State of Texas,* filed 30 June 1847. The petition names (1) the minor heirs, Ann, Marian, Elizabeth, and Felix A. Richardson, Jr., (2) their "next friend," Spruce M. Baird, (3) wife and relict of the deceased, Ann Reynolds, and (4) her new husband, Meredith S. Reynolds. In August 1861, these same minor heirs were back in court as adults, then living in Kentucky. Named as plaintiffs were Felix A. Richardson, Jr., B.K. McQuann and his wife, Marian; J.L. Smith and his wife, E.A.; and E. Porter and his wife, Elizabeth. Their concern was two large tracts of land in Leon County, Texas, of which William Kinginn (?) had taken possession with force and arms, from which he had cut and carried off timber valued at $10,000, and which he refused to vacate.

Other records found in court clerks' offices can include such things as dockets of cases, witness and jury pay lists, civil court fee books, and other records dealing with the day-to-day operation of the courts. An example is the Jeff Davis County, Texas, jury certificates book showing the 5 July 1907 payment of $.50 to petit jurors, including one searcher's ancestor, J.M. Nash.

The genealogist needs to be aware that older court records may be stored in basements, attics, and other hard-to-get-to areas. In one Tennessee county, when I wanted to find a court case pertinent to the settlement of an estate, I was told that the court records from the period I needed were stored in the old jail. The only person who had a key was in the hospital for surgery and would be out of the office at least two weeks! Some court docket and minute books have been microfilmed or abstracted for publication, but the case files, which contain the real meat of the case, are rarely found outside of the courthouse itself.

ADMINISTRATIVE RECORDS

Election returns and polling lists are interesting additions to any family history. They are found in various places. In Caldwell County, Kentucky, they are bundled neatly on a basement shelf. (It is not the kind of basement that required hard hat, work gloves, and flashlight.) They revealed that in Princeton on Monday morning, 7 November 1836, Ira Brelsford and Samuel Black had both cast their votes for Martin Van Buren for President. (Van Buren won that election.) Samuel Black remained a Democrat, supporting Van Buren in 1840, Polk in 1844, and Cass in 1848. Ira Brelsford, on the other hand, became a Whig, then supported Fillmore and the American Party in 1856, and Bell's Constitutional Union Party in 1860.

Some early polling lists for Cumberland County, Virginia, can be found in the county deed books. In Book 10 (p 15), for example, is the evidence that in April 1805, Peter T. Phillips and Elliott Coleman voted for John Randolph for Congress and John Hatcher and German Baker for the Assembly.

Other administrative records listed earlier in the chapter vary from county to county and in their usefulness for genealogists. Most of them can place an ancestor in a given county on a given date and show that he or she was living. Professional licenses, such as those for physicians and nurses, can show age, address, birthplace, and education information. The searcher can ask for availability of specific records and sometimes can browse among the records and find nice surprises, as I did in discovering the election returns in Kentucky. In that case, the employees were not aware that those records existed.

The following books are useful resources for county searching:

The American Counties, by Joseph Nathan Kane (Metuchen, NJ: The Scarecrow Press, Inc., 1983, 4th edition). Includes independent cities and boroughs.

Ancestry's Red Book: American State, County, and Town Sources, by Alice Eichholz (Salt Lake City: Ancestry, 1992).

County Courthouse Book, by Elizabeth Petty Bentley (Baltimore: Genealogical Publishing Company, 1990).

United States Local Histories in the Library of Congress: A Bibliography, Marion J. Kaminkow, ed. (Washington, DC: Library of Congress, 1975). 5 vols. Reprinted by Magna Carta Books, Baltimore.

WPA, Historical Records Survey, Inventories of County Archives, variously published. See also *Bibliography of Research Projects Reports: A Checklist of Historical Records Survey Publications* (Washington, DC: WPA, 1943).

Investigate the availability of publications on the counties of your research area.

COUNTY HISTORIES

Published county histories, like published family histories, can run the gamut of quality and reliability. Many of them include biographical sketches of individuals or families, and these too vary greatly in accuracy. However, these works are worth reading, for they often give good historical background on the local area, as well as capsuled histories of towns, churches, schools, and organizations in the county.

In the 1880s, several companies published county and local histories that included not only information on the first settlers, first officers, and first institutions, but also on the current residents and activities. The Goodspeed Publishing Company of Chicago published such histories of various states, county by county, including autobiographical sketches of citizens who chose to participate. The town sketches identified the trustees of the local academy, elders of the local churches, and officers of the lodges. Some of the Goodspeed's histories have been reprinted to include only the biographical sketches; others have been reissued in their entirety.

These reference books may be helpful in finding county histories:

A Bibliography of American County Histories, by P. William Filby (Baltimore: Genealogocial Publishing Company, 1985).

Consolidated Bibliography of County Histories in Fifty States in 1961: Consolidated 1935-1961, by Clarence Stewart Peterson, comp. (Baltimore: Genealogical Publishing Company, 1961)

Footnotes are on page 175.

CHAPTER SIX

Local Sources

Local sources can be extremely valuable for genealogists. In the local area, whether rural or urban, are cemeteries, churches, and schools. In towns and cities genealogists may find a variety of records related to residents, businesses and professions, organizations, and local government. Not all local areas will have every kind of record, but many areas will have something of value.

CEMETERIES

It is possible in the eastern part of this country to find cemeteries and readable tombstones dating back into the seventeenth century. Of course, thousands of our ancestors have unmarked graves, and in spite of laws to the contrary, many cemeteries have been bulldozed in the name of progress and profit. Nonetheless, when you are lucky enough to locate family tombstones, you can often glean valuable information. Use of published transcriptions and reading of the original inscriptions require caution on the part of the searcher.

If you know the cemetery in which certain ancestors were buried, you have half the task done and can plan a visit or arrange for someone to photograph tombstones for you. If you do not know a particular cemetery in which to look, you have several options.

1. Newspaper obituaries, death certificates, family Bibles and other records, older family members, county and local histories, church registers, some organization or lodge records, and funeral home files may supply the name of the cemetery.

2. Transcribed cemetery records arranged by county or state, especially when they are indexed, are relatively easy to investigate. Some repositories have card indexes to cemeteries. Many transcriptions have been published. Some may be rented from FHL and AGLL.

3. If you know the county in which the person lived at the time of death, you can begin by focusing on the cemeteries in that county. If no transcriptions exist for that county, you can get a map that shows the known cemeteries and begin visiting them. (See chapter seven for discussion of such maps.) Some cemeteries have associations or commercial offices that keep the records and take care of the grounds. They often have maps that identify the burials in each plot. These plot maps may indicate where and when a person was buried even if there is no stone to mark the spot.

You probably will not find tombstones for all your ancestors. Purchasing grave stones is expensive, but family groups still pool their resources to honor and remember ancestors by erecting markers.

The information found on tombstones runs the gamut. How many times have you seen small stones marked "Our Baby" or "Little Bennie, age 5"? Some, of course, give only the years instead of complete dates of a person's life: John A. Shelby, 1859-1931 (Petteway Cemetery, Robertson County, Texas). Some give only initials instead of given names: W.L. Harrison, b 29 October 1830, d 30 May 1866 (Liberty Hill, Williamson County, Texas). Others provide considerably more information:

Mary A. Blackwell
formerly widow of
   Edward Philpot
nee Miss Mary A. Taylor
b 6 May 1809
d 21 July 1886
(Crowder Cemetery,
   Hardeman County,
   Tennessee)

Susan Richardson Logan
wife of Rev. F.A. Mood
b Bloomhill, SC 5 Aug
   1843
d 13 Nov 1916
(Georgetown Cemetery,
   Williamson County,
   Texas)

The genealogist must be alert to the fact that family members are often buried in groups. These groups may represent several generations and different surnames. Having some background in the extended family is helpful before visiting cemeteries, but copying tombstones around an ancestor's grave can add much new information. For this reason, I prefer printed transcriptions of cemeteries that group names as they appear in the cemetery and not in alphabetical order.

Visiting the cemetery rather than relying on an alphabetical transcription gave the King family a surprise and a new avenue for searching. The great-grandparents, Thomas and Emilia King, share a small obelisk monument in Houston's Washington Cemetery. On the third side is engraved "William A. Rock, 13 May 187L (*sic*) — 2 April 1910." Who was this? In the course of gathering basic vital statistics, the family had found a local marriage record of a Thomas King to *Miss Amelia Rock* in December 1880, but the death record of Emilia King's son Alfred gave Emilia's maiden name as *Preuss*. Thus, the family had thought this marriage record was not for the same couple. Now, with the tombstone information, the obvious step was another try at the 1880 federal census, using the surname Rock instead of King or Preuss, which had revealed nothing of this family. The result was positive, showing Amelia Rock, "widowed or divorced," and her *son*, William Rock (age 7), and *daughters*, Emily and Mary (4 and 3). A search of the 1870 census showed Amelia Preuss and William Rock in Travis County, Texas, where their marriage was recorded in August 1872. The tombstone was the key to solving several mysteries, but the mystery of the *187L* date remains. The L is not an upside-down 7 but may be an incomplete *4*. The 1880 census suggests an 1873 birthdate for William, but his 1900 census entry, questionable in several other aspects, gives November 1876. Of course, William died before the 1910 census was taken. (And of course, the marriage record contained an error, she was *Mrs.* Amelia Rock.)

As wonderful as cemetery transcriptions can be, they can contain errors. One such error was an understandable mistake in reading the original stones. A transcription of Samuel and Keturah Black's tombstones in Caldwell County, Kentucky, actually contained six errors. It gave Samuel's dates as 11 October 1779 — 9 October 1859 "in 81rst year of his life" and Keturah's as 13 November 1779 — 19 August 1859 "in 79th year of age." The first problem is in the inscription itself. According to the transcription, Samuel would have turned 80 years of age had he lived two more days; thus, he was in his *80th* year when he died. In addition, since Keturah had already turned 79 on her last birthday, she was in her *80th* year when she died, if the transcribed dates were correct. If the tran-

scribed ages were correct, then birth or death dates could be wrong.

Two further discrepancies appeared in public records. One was that the 1850 census gave their ages as 77 and 70, which agreed with the tombstone birthdate for Keturah but suggested a 1772 birth year for Samuel. County records show Samuel signing a deed of gift on 30 August 1852, and the inventory of his estate, following his death, was made on 25 November 1852. The problem was solved by obtaining good photographs of the actual tombstones. The errors had occurred in the number 9s. Every 9 except in Keturah's birthdate was actually a 2 in the photograph. These were strange 2s with a large loop at the top. Perhaps the engraver had used a 9 and extended a line at the bottom to create a 2. Nevertheless the photographs were clear. The correct dates for Samuel were 11 October 177<u>2</u>-<u>26</u> October 185<u>2</u> and for Keturah, 13 November 1779-1<u>2</u> August 185<u>2</u>. Samuel had just turned 80 when he died and was indeed in his *81rst year*. Keturah was already 72 when she died. Perhaps that was the meaning of the inscription on her tombstone: *in 72nd year of age*.

CHURCH RECORDS

Church records of the greatest genealogical value are usually those of baptism, confirmation, marriage, and burial, but records such as minutes, officers lists, and membership lists can contain interesting and pertinent historical information on ancestors. Many churches have some records, but unfortunately not all churches that our ancestors attended are still in existence or have records extending beyond more recent years. Often the older records no longer exist, but transcriptions may. Sometimes the extant records are stored at a member's house or a parsonage rather than at the church itself. Fortunately, historical societies, archives, and libraries are gradually gathering old records for safekeeping.

Like courthouses, churches do suffer fires as the offices of my own church did on Palm Sunday night, 1979. Yes, we lost our baptism, marriage, and death records but were able to reconstruct the membership list. When my mother was gathering documents for a delayed birth certificate, she went to the church where she had been baptized to get a copy of the baptism record. She was told that those records had been stored in the parsonage for years, but a minister's wife, tired of the old books taking up closet space, had burned them! What does it take for people to understand the value of such records?

Content of Church Records

Church records can give very valuable information on the lives of its members, especially baptisms, confirmations or membership, funerals or burials, and marriages. Baptisms are one kind of record that churches have kept for centuries. (Sometimes baptism records and church newspapers give birthdates as well.) We Crooms hope that we have found our immigrant ancestor, Daniel Croom, in the Bishops Transcripts of Stone Parish, Gloucestershire in England, where a baptism record shows Daniell Croom, son of Henry Croom, baptized on 19 September 1680. A more recent baptism record contains even more helpful information.

> *Alfred Thomas King, residence 6004 Sherman, Houston, born 14 May 1925, son of Alfred Thomas King and Annie E. King, baptized 14 June 1925, by Rev. Thomas J. Windham, Clemens Memorial (Episcopal) Chapel, Houston, Texas. Sponsors: Louis Edward DelHomme and Emma Louise DelHomme.*

In the case of these sponsors, who were aunt and uncle of the baby, the church record gave us their full names, which we had not yet found in other sources.

In this same family, the parents were confirmed as adults. Annie E. King was confirmed on Palm Sunday, 20 March 1921, and her husband, on Easter Sunday, 20 April 1930. His confirmation record gave the additional information that he had been born in 1886 in Houston and was baptized in the Lutheran church. (His mother's relatives were German Lutherans in the city.) Another adult confirmation record gave the lady's maiden name. Elsie Mae Williamson Shelby, born 4 May 1914 in Hineston, Louisiana, was baptized in May 1927, in a Baptist church in Louisiana and was confirmed by Rev. Skardon D'Aubert on 6 December 1956. By this time the church was called the Church of the Good Shepherd.

The same church records reflect the burial of Annie King's father, Joseph T. Wells, age 67, who died on 9 December 1912 and was buried in Houston's Glenwood Cemetery on 10 December, with Rev. Thomas J. Windham officiating. It was helpful to find the death date in the church record since Mr. Wells has no death certificate and no tombstone.

The marriage records of the early years do not offer much besides the most basic facts: Jewell Black married Oscar T. Hausard at the rectory on 6 June 1928. Later marriage certificates give full names, ages, parentage, and family addresses of the bride and groom as well as full names of two witnesses. In this particular set of record books, Rev. Windham recorded weddings that he performed at the church, at the rectory, at the bride's home, and one at James Furniture Store. Although this particular church closed in the mid-1980s, its records are housed at another Episcopal church in the area.

Records of the Presbyterian Church in Bolivar, Tennessee, were transcribed by Mrs. Louise J. McAnulty in 1969. They reflect the same events in the lives of the members: baptism, membership, marriage, death. In addition, they give information on the leadership of the congregation. E.G. Coleman, for example, was admitted to membership by examination on 4 September 1854, two years after his wife and brothers joined. He was ordained a deacon on 19 June 1858 and dismissed on 9 January 1872, with his wife, Catherine, when they moved to Texas. General Rufus P. Neely joined the church on 9 February 1870 by profession of faith. James Fentress, installed an elder on 26 April 1868, was dismissed 7 March 1881, going to First Church, New Orleans.

The colonial Anglican (now Episcopal) churches kept, besides church registers, record books on the business operations of the individual parish by the committee called the vestry. For each meeting of the vestry, the report lists the names of members present and items of business handled, including the rector's salary, tithes assessed within the parish, and monies spent on indigents, repairs, and supplies. The Bristol Parish vestry, at Petersburg, Virginia, voted to receive my ancestor Rev. William Harrison as rector on 22 November 1762. On 13 February 1763, they recorded the spending of nine shillings on two bottles of "clarrot" for communion and on 27 September 1763, a little more than £4 on 11¼ yards of Irish linen and one ounce of thread for "suples" (surplices). In June 1752, when they expanded the south side of the church, they set down in the vestry book the specifications for the addition, including dimensions, thickness of the brick walls, kind of windows, size of floor planks, style of pews, and kind of roof, to be covered with "good cypress heart shingles." In 1765, it was reported that due to "an uncommon winter and the long and continued severity of it," nine bottles of "clarrett" stored for Communion had turned "sow (sour) and useless."

These details in themselves are not genealogical, but if your ancestors were part of the vestry or even part of the congregation, you would want to study this most interesting kind of historical source. An amazing number of vestry books and similar records survive. Many have been published or microfilmed.

Finding Church Records

If you know the church that certain ancestors attended, try to locate and inspect the records. Where are such records kept? Many individual churches keep their own records. Begin there. Some of these records have been microfilmed and placed in various collections in the state, or are available for rent from the FHL or AGLL. The church office or members can often tell you where the records are available for use. They can also tell you about denominational universities or archives. Some churches, especially those that no longer exist, may have given their records to such denominational archives, collections in denominational universities in the state or region, local or state historical societies or archives, other local churches of the same denomination, or local or regional public libraries with this kind of collection. Occasionally, local DAR chapters or historical/genealogical societies know where local church records are kept. Some church records have been published in historical and genealogical peridocials. Check the indexes and contents of the state's periodicals, as well as compiled periodical indexes, such as those discussed in chapter eight. Some church registers have been transcribed and published. Consult library catalogs or catalog databases to try to locate published or manuscript records. The *National Union Catalog of Manuscript Collections* (see chapter eight), the *Guide to Archives and Manuscripts in the United States*, Philip M. Hamer, ed. (New Haven, CT: Yale University Press, 1961), and the *Directory of Archives and Manuscript Repositories in the United States* (Phoenix, AZ; Oryx Press, 1988, 2nd edition) may also help you locate manuscript records.

If you know the family's denomination but not the individual church, try to identify the church from information in other sources pertaining to the whole cluster of relatives. These sources may include newspaper articles, obituaries, or wedding announcements of family members, especially the females; funeral home files; family Bibles, printed funeral notices, letters, scrapbooks, traditions, or older relatives; county or local histories; older members of the community in which the family lived; or county marriage or death records. If you can determine a minister who married and/or buried several family members, you probably should investigate the records of the church of which he was minister. Even if the family did not actually belong to the church, their names may appear in the records. You may need to survey several churches in the immediate area where the family lived.

If you are not sure of the family's denomination, some of these same sources may give you clues or answers. In addition, learning some history of the community and talking with old-timers, both in the family and in the community, can help you make an intelligent guess and get you started. You may want to consult Peter G. Mode's *Source Book and Bibliographical Guide for American Church History* (Boston: J.S. Canner and Company, 1964 reprint of 1921 original) and the *Handbook of American Denominations in the United States*, by Frank Mead (Nashville: Abingdon Press, 1970).

No complete union list of church records has been made, or probably can be made. The Works Progess Administration (WPA) during the 1930s made inventories of church records in many areas. Examples of other finding aids are the following:

Directory of Maryland Church Records, Edna A. Kanely, comp. (Silver Springs, MD: Family Line Publications, 1987), organized by county and including some Washington, DC, churches.

A Guide to Episcopal Records in Virginia, by Edith F. Axelson (Athens, GA: Iberian Publishing Co., 1988). Includes history of county formation as well as location of existing church records.

Preliminary Guide to Church Records Repositories, by August R. Suelflow (St. Louis [now Chicago]: Society of American Archivists, 1969).

A Survey of American Church Records, by E. Kay Kirkham (Logan, UT: Everton Publishers, 4th ed., 1978).

Besides local churches, public libraries, and historical societies, the following records depositories report collections of church history, which may include minutes, records, and publications. In the case of universities, seminaries, and associations, contact their libraries. Sometimes they have a collection within the main library, or they can direct you to the church history center. These may be able to suggest additional repositories in your research area. To locate church archives, libraries, and historical societies and their addresses, or identify other depositories with church record collections, consult the following references:

American Library Directory (New York: R.R. Bowker, latest edition).

Directory of Archives and Manuscript Repositories in the United States (Phoenix: Oryx Press, 1988, 2nd ed., or later edition).

Directory of Historical Organizations in the United States and Canada (Nashville: American Association for State and Local History, latest edition).

Encyclopedia of Associations: A Guide to National and International Organizations and *Encyclopedia of Associations: Regional, State, and Local Organizations* (Detroit: Gale Research, latest editions).

Guide to Archives and Manuscripts in the United States, Philip M. Hamer, ed. (New Haven, CT: Yale University Press, 1961, for National Historical Publications Commission).

National Union Catalog of Manuscript Collections (Washington, DC: Library of Congress, 1990, p xl under Religion, lists reporting repositories 1975-1990).

Yearbook of American and Canadian Churches (Nashville: Abingdon Press, latest edition).

Church Record Depositories and Historical Collections

Alabama Archives — All denominations. Also contact Samford University in Birmingham (Baptist).

Arkansas History Commission Archives — Mostly Baptist.

Arkansas, Southwest Regional Archives — Baptist and Presbyterian mostly.

Arkansas, University of Arkansas, Little Rock — Several denominations.

California — Contact Western Jewish History Center in Berkeley, Hebrew Union College Library in Los Angeles, Jewish Federation Council of Greater Los Angeles, Archdiocese of San Francisco in Colma (Catholic), Santa Barbara Mission Archives (Catholic), School of Theology at Claremont (Methodist and Protestant Episcopal), United Methodist Church Research Library at the University of the Pacific in Stockton, Center for Mennonite Brethren Studies in Fresno, Whittier College Library (Quaker), Pacific School of Religion at Berkeley (Methodist), Registrar of the Greek Orthodox Diocese of San Francisco (records after 1979 for AK, AZ, CA, HI, NV, OR, WA).

Colorado Historical Society — Some records, denominations not specified. Contact also Iliff School of Theology in Denver (Methodist), Registrar of Greek Orthodox Diocese of Denver (records after 1979 for CO, ID, KS, LA, MO, MT, NE, NM, ND, OK, SD, TX, UT, WY).

Connecticut State Library — Hundreds of Connecticut churches, partial name index, most on microfilm. Also contact Divinity Library at Yale University in New Haven (Congregational), Hartford Theological Seminary in Hartford (Congregational).

Delaware Archives — Not comprehensive, but some.

Delaware Historical Society — Many copies, some originals.

District of Columbia — Archives Department of Catholic University of America in Washington.

Florida Archives — Some Catholic records from St. Augustine, Tallahassee, Pensacola. Methodist and Baptist records from various counties.

Georgia Archives — Church and synagogue records. Contact also Emory University in Atlanta (Methodist), Columbia Theological Seminary in Decatur (Presbyterian), Shorter College in Rome (Baptist), Thomas College in Thomasville (church histories), Registrar of the Greek Orthodox Diocese of Atlanta (records after 1979 for AL, FL, GA, LA, MS, NC, SC, TN), Georgia Baptist Historical Collection at Mercer University in Macon.

Georgia Historical Society — Savannah churches.

Hawaii Archives — Episcopal church in Hawaii records.

Hawaii Mission Children's Society — Archives of Congregational Church in the Pacific.

Hawaii Roman Catholic Diocese, Honolulu — Some parish and diocesan records.

Illinois — Central Illinois Conference at Bloomington (Methodist), Jesuit-Krauss-McCormick Library in Chicago (Catholic, Lutheran, Presbyterian), Spertus College of Judaica in Chicago (Jewish), Church of the Brethren General Board in Elgin, Eureka College in Elmwood Park (Disciples of Christ), Archives of the Lutheran Church in America in Chicago, Garrett Evangelical Theological Seminary in Evanston (United Methodist and Evangelical United Brethren), American Theological Library Association in Evanston (has published church history and records, address in appendix), Registrar of the Greek Orthodox

Diocese of Chicago (records after 1979 for IL, IN (part), IA, MN, MO, WI).

Indiana, Allen County Public Library—Includes church records.

Indiana Historical Society—Various denominations, various locations, many Quaker records.

Indiana State Library—Many Roman Catholic diocesan records, church histories from many denominations. Contact also College of Indiana in Franklin (Baptist), Diocese of Gary (Catholic), DePauw University in Greencastle (Methodist), Hanover College in Hanover (Presbyterian), Christian Theological Seminary in Indianapolis (Disciples of Christ), Mennonite Historical Library and Archives in Goshen, Earlham College in Richmond (Quaker), Historical Center of the Free Methodist Church in Winona Lake, Archives of the University of Notre Dame in South Bend (Catholic, including early New Orleans).

Iowa Genealogical Society—Some Lutheran records for Des Moines. Also contact Episcopal Diocese in Des Moines, Westmar College in LeMars (Methodist), William Penn College in Oskaloosa (Quaker), and Catholic Diocese of Sioux City.

Iowa Historical Society, Des Moines and Iowa City—A few church records.

Kansas Historical Society—Church histories, original and microfilmed church records. Contact also Catholic Archdiocese of Kansas City, Bethel College in North Newton (Mennonite and Anabaptist), Friends University in Wichita (Quaker), Church of the Brethren Archives at McPherson College in McPherson.

Kentucky, Filson Club—Catholic, Evangelical, and United Church of Christ records from Louisville area.

Kentucky Department for Libraries and Archives—A few church records, arranged by county. Also contact Lexington Theological Seminary (Disciples of Christ), Louisville Presbyterian Theological Seminary, Kentucky Wesleyan College (Methodist), Southern Baptist Theological Seminary in Louisville, and Midway College in Midway (Disciples of Christ).

Louisiana State Library—Some Catholic and Baptist records, also available ILL on microfilm.

Maine Historical Society—Congregational, Quaker, Unitarian, and others. Contact also Shaker Library in New Gloucester (Quaker collection).

Maryland Archives—Good collection. Contact also

Jewish Historical Society of Maryland in Baltimore, Ner Israel Rabbinical College, Archdiocese of Baltimore (Catholic), Saint Mary's Seminary and University in Baltimore (Catholic), United Methodist Historical Society at Lovely Lane United Methodist Church in Baltimore, Mount Saint Mary's College and Seminary in Emmitsburg (Catholic), Maryland Baptist Historical Society in Lutherville, Lutheran Church in America in Baltimore, Johns Hopkins University in Baltimore (various).

Maryland Historical Society—Has a good collection of church records, including Maryland Diocese Archives (Episcopal).

Massachusetts, New England Historical Genealogical Society—Boston area. See their *Genealogist's Handbook for New England Research* for locations of others. Contact American Congregational Association in Boston, Episcopal Diocese Archives in Boston, New England Conference Depository at Boston University School of Theology Library (Methodist), Diocese of Boston (Catholic), Andover Newton Theological School in Newton Centre (Baptist), American Jewish Historical Society Library in Waltham, Archives of the Unitarian-Universalist Association in Boston, Harvard University Divinity School in Cambridge (Unitarian, Congregational), Registrar of Greek Orthodox Diocese of Boston (records after 1979 for CT, MA, ME, NH, RI, VT).

Michigan State Library—WPA inventories of church records. Also contact Albion College in Albion (Methodist), Western Theological Seminary in Holland (Reformed Church in America), Finnish-American Historical Archives in Hancock (ethnic Lutheran affiliations), Kalamazoo College in Kalamazoo (Baptist), Calvin College and Seminary in Grand Rapids (Christian Reformed-Dutch), Registrar of the Greek Orthodox Diocese of Detroit (records after 1979 for AR, IN [part], KY, MI, NY, OH [part], TN).

Minnesota Historical Society—Originals and copies. Contact also Bethel Theological Seminary in Arden Hills (Baptist), United Methodist Church Archives in Minneapolis, Catholic Historical Society of St. Paul at the College of St. Thomas in St. Paul, and Luther Northwestern Seminary in St. Paul (Lutheran).

Mississippi Archives—Originals and copies. See Donna Pannell's *Church Records in the Missis-*

sippi Department of Archives and History. Contact also Mississippi College in Clinton (Baptist), Mississippi Baptist Convention Board in Clinton, Reformed Theological Seminary in Jackson (Presbyterian), and Mississippi State University Library in State College (Baptist records).

Missouri Archives, Jefferson City, and Historical Society, St. Louis—Various denominations and locations. Also contact Culver-Stockton College in Canton (Disciples of Christ), Conception Abbey and Seminary in Conception (Catholic), Central Methodist College in Fayette, Missouri Baptist Historical Society at William Jewell College in Liberty, Missouri Valley College in Marshall (Cumberland Presbyterian), Christian Board of Publication in St. Louis (Disciples of Christ), Concordia Historical Institute of the Missouri Synod in St. Louis (Lutheran), Episcopal Diocese of Missouri in St. Louis, Eden Archives in Webster Grove (Evangelical and Reformed Churches).

Nebraska Historical Society—Ask for reference guide *Nebraska Church Records at the Nebraska State Historical Society*. Also contact Historical Center of the United Methodist Church at Nebraska Wesleyan University in Lincoln.

Nevada Historical Society—Archives of Episcopal Church in Nevada from 1862, includes records of Indian reservation missions.

New Hampshire Historical Society—Mainly Congregational and Baptist.

New Hampshire State Library—Some. Also contact Dartmouth College in Hanover (Congregational).

New Jersey State Library—Inquire for specifics. Also contact New Brunswick Theological Seminary (Reformed Church in America), United Methodist Archives Center at Drew University in Madison, Seventh Day Baptist Building in Plainfield, Princeton Theological Seminary in Princeton (Presbyterian), Registrar of the Greek Orthodox Diocese of New Jersey (8 East 79th St, New York, NY 10021) (records after 1979 for DC, MD, NJ, PA [part], VA; archdiocese office at the same address, nationwide records before 1979).

New Mexico, Albuquerque Public Library—Some Catholic records, Santa Fe Archdiocese.

New Mexico Archives—Catholic Church records.

New York Genealogical and Biographical Society—A major collection, mostly Protestant denominations, especially for Manhattan.

New York Public Library, Genealogy Section—Church records from all over the state.

New York State Library—Good collection, includes Shaker collection. Also contact World Jewish Genealogy Organization in Brooklyn, American Federation of Jews from Central Europe in New York City, Military Ordinariate in New York City (vital records sent in by military Catholic chaplains worldwide), Society of Friends New York Yearly Meeting in New York City (Quaker), Huguenot Historical Society in New Palta, American Baptist Historical Society in Rochester, Holland Society in New York City (Reformed Church), Greek Orthodox Archdiocese of North and South America (See under NJ, records prior to 1979, after 1979 kept by diocese registrars).

North Carolina Archives—All denominations, statewide. Permission from the church is needed in order to duplicate. There are no known surviving Church of England parish registers for colonial North Carolina. Also contact Duke University (Methodist), Elon College in Elon (United Church of Christ), Guilford College in Greensboro (Quaker collection), Historical Foundation of the Presbyterian and Reformed Churches at Montreat, Southeastern Baptist Theological Seminary and Wake Forest University at Wake Forest, and Southern Provinces Archives of the Moravian Church in America at Winston-Salem.

North Dakota Historical Society—Various churches, all holdings on the OCLC database.

Ohio Historical Society—A few, often DAR compilations.

Ohio State Library—Scattered records, varies from county to county.

Ohio, Western Reserve Historical Society—Holdings include Jewish History Archives and Shaker manuscripts. Also contact Mennonite Historical Library at Bluffton College in Bluffton (Mennonite and Amish), Malone College in Canton (Quaker), Ohio Wesleyan University and Methodist Theological Seminary in Delaware (Methodist), American Jewish Archives in Cincinnati, Wilmington College in Wilmington (Quaker), Evangelical United Brethren Historical Society in Dayton.

Oklahoma—Oklahoma Baptist University in Shawnee.

Oregon State Library—Catholic Church records, Pacific Northwest. Also contact Northwest Christian College in Eugene (Disciples of Christ), George Fox College in Newburg (Quaker), Western Conservative Baptist Seminary in Portland, and Willamette University in Salem (Methodist).

Pennsylvania Historical Society—All denominations, concentrating in Delaware Valley (PA-NJ). Also contact Friends Historical Association at Haverford College in Haverford (Quaker), Historical Commission of the United Church of Christ and Franklin and Marshall College in Lancaster (Evangelical and Reformed Churches and United Church of Christ), Lancaster Mennonite Historical Society (Mennonite, Amish), Mennonite Library and Archives in Lansdale, Moravian Historical Society in Nazareth, Reformed Presbyterian Theological Seminary, Friends Historical Library of Swarthmore College in Swarthmore (Quaker), Lutheran Theological Seminary in Gettysburg, Archives of the Moravian Church in Bethlehem, Registrar of the Greek Orthodox Diocese of Pittsburgh (records after 1979 for most of PA, OH, WV), Archives of the Roman Catholic Diocese of Harrisburg.

Pennsylvania, Philadelphia—American Catholic Historical Society of Philadelphia, Balch Institute for Ethnic Studies (Jewish archives), Lutheran Theological Seminary and Lutheran Archives Center, United Presbyterian Church in the USA Historical Society, Methodist Historical Center.

Pennsylvania State Library—Has some. Does not answer mail inquiries.

Rhode Island Historical Society—Mostly Baptist, Congregational, Unitarian, Quaker, and others. Also contact University of Rhode Island in Kingston (records of Rhode Island Episcopal Diocese), and Rhode Island Jewish Historical Association in Providence.

South Carolina Archives—Some published denominational and church histories; small collection of individual church records. Also contact Furman University in Greenville (Baptist), Charleston Diocese (Catholic), Charleston Library Society (South Carolina Jewish collection), Huguenot Society of South Carolina in Charleston, Lutheran Southern Seminary in Columbia, and Wofford College in Spartanburg (Methodist).

South Carolina Library—Does have some church records. Specifics in Stokes' *Guide to the Manuscripts Collection of the South Caroliniana Library*.

South Dakota Historical Society—Scattered small collections. Also contact Center for Western Studies at Augustana College in Sioux Falls (church records collection, especially Episcopal, Lutheran, United Church of Christ) and North American Baptist Seminary in Sioux Falls.

Tennessee State Library and Archives—Originals and microfilm copies. Also contact Emmanuel School of Religion in Johnson City (Church of Christ and Disciples of Christ), Memphis Theological Seminary in Memphis (Cumberland Presbyterian), Southern Baptist Convention Historical Library in Nashville, Disciples of Christ Historical Society in Nashville, Archives of the Jewish Federation of Nashville, Methodist Publishing House Library in Nashville, and University of the South in Sewanee (Protestant Episcopal, Southern Diocese).

Texas—Contact Baylor University in Waco (Baptist), Bridwell Library at Southern Methodist University in Dallas, Texas Catholic Historical Society in Austin, Episcopal Church Historical Society in Austin, Bishop College in Dallas (Black Baptist archives), Southwestern Baptist Theological Seminary in Fort Worth, Texas Christian University in Forth Worth (Disciples of Christ), Episcopal Diocese of West Texas in San Antonio, University of Texas in Austin (copies of early Protestant Episcopal records), Dallas Jewish Historical Society, Roman Catholic Archives in San Antonio.

Utah—Consult FHL and Catholic Diocese in Salt Lake City.

Vermont Historical Society—Scattered church records. Contact Special Collections at the Library of the University of Vermont, Burlington.

Virginia Historical Society and University of Virginia—Both have church records.

Virginia State Library—See *A Guide to Church Records in the Archives Branch of the Virginia State Library*, Jewell T. Clark and Elizabeth Terry Long (Richmond, VA: State Library, 1981). Also contact Randolph Macon College in Ashland (Methodist), Eastern Mennonite College and Seminary in Harrisonburg (Anabaptist and Mennonite), University of Richmond (Baptist), St. Paul's College in Laurenceville (Episcopal). Most vestry books for colonial Virginia Episcopal parishes have been published by the Virginia Historical Society.

West Virginia Archives—A few church records. Also

contact Bethany College in Bethany (Disciples of Christ), West Virginia Wesleyan College in Buckhannon (Methodist).

Wisconsin, University of Wisconsin, Milwaukee — Milwaukee Urban Archives, churches from Milwaukee, Ozaukee, Sheboygan, Washington, and Waukesha counties, microfilm. Detailed finding aid available at this Archives. Also contact Seventh Day Baptist Historical Society in Janesville, Historical Institute at the Wisconsin Evangelical Lutheran Seminary in Mequon.

SCHOOLS AND UNIVERSITIES

Public and private schools and universities sometimes are good sources of information about ancestors. However, many school records no longer exist. Records kept by schools or public school districts usually fall into two categories: those that answer the demands of the county or state government and those that deal with students and faculty. In the first group, school census records taken at the local or county level can provide names and ages of school children in the district at a given time. If such records are not in the school district office, they may exist in local or state archives and historical societies. I have also seen a few in county courthouses. Some school district tax offices have records that show taxes paid by heads of household within their jurisdiction, but these records are not often kept more than about twenty years.

In the second group, all kinds of schools and academies have enrollment records and transcripts that document a student's attendance, classes, and grades. These can be vital in an effort to prove age or perhaps parentage, residence, or citzenship, depending on the information provided on the record. Otherwise, they are merely interesting for the historical information they provide. One example is the college transcript of my great-grandmother Mattie Harrison from the class of 1882-1883 at Sam Houston Normal Institute (now University) in Huntsville, Texas. The record shows that she finished eighth in her class. (The page containing her record does not tell the exact number in the class but does indicate at least seventy-four.) Her classes included not only standard geography, math, science, grammar, literature, history, and government courses, but also various teacher training classes, penmanship, drawing, music, calisthenics, and a graduating essay.

From the next generation, my grandfather Hunter Metcalfe's transcript from Southwestern University in Georgetown, Texas, shows not only his classes and grades for each year but gives his date of birth (in this case a year off), patron's name (his father), the family's address, the high school from which he graduated, the date of entrance to the university, the degree he sought, and his graduation date of 1909.

Because of privacy laws, many schools and universities will no longer release transcripts or will make the process very involved. The laws and their interpretation vary considerably from state to state and institution to institution. You usually have to have the permission of the person whose record you are requesting, or the legal executor or guardian, especially if the record is less than fifty years old. If you request a record older than seventy-five years, you can explain that it is for family history and identify your relationship to the person whose transcript you seek, and you may not have any problem at all.

Lists or directories of former students and alumni may be more readily available than transcripts. For older colleges and universities, a number of these lists have been published, either in book form or in historical and genealogical periodicals. Alumni associations and university archives may also maintain some of these lists. Other records such as yearbooks, graduation programs, literary publications, alumni publications, newspapers, catalogs, and scrapbooks may be available at a school archives or within a special collection in the library.

Nationally affiliated organizations, such as Greek letter sororities and fraternities, honor societies, and service organizations, may maintain chapter history on the campus or may give you the address for the national office. From the headquarters you may learn membership dates, and perhaps birth or death date, for your ancestor. Chapter histories may reflect offices the ancestor held, but school yearbooks often provide this information. One source of information on some of these organizations is *Baird's Manual of American College Fraternities* (Menasha, WI: Baird's Manual Foundation, Inc., 1991, 20th ed., or later edition).

Many of these national organizations have periodicals dating back to the nineteenth and early twentieth centuries. These publications often report marriages and deaths of members and even the births of their children. The example, *The Adelphean* of Alpha Delta Pi Sorority (Vol. 8, No. 1, December 1914) announced the marriage of Grace Patrick, of the chapter in Georgetown, Texas, to Gilbert Gresham on September 16. The same issue reported that Ruth Bell was teaching German in Bartlett, Texas, and Lulu Talley was teaching history in Ozona, Texas.

Faculty lists may also be available in the school or university archives, publications, and yearbooks, but life history on faculty and employees may not be available. Personnel records would be subject to the same legal restrictions as students records or may not be kept at all beyond a certain year. Each school district or university is different.

Especially for small town and rural public schools, early records may simply not exist. Yearbooks and school publications may be found in the local public library or in the possession of families who have lived in the area for years. Other materials may be in the possession of descendants of teacher and principals. Some research libraries and archives do have school records collections. One example is the Milwaukee Urban Archives at the University of Wisconsin at Milwaukee.

Aids for finding school records include the *National Union Catalog of Manuscript Collections* (NUCMC, see chapter eight), the computerized catalog databases of the subscription services such as OCLC and RLIN, *Guide to Archives and Manuscripts in the United States*, Philip M. Hamer, ed. (New Haven, CT: Yale University Press, 1961), and *The Directory of Archives and Manuscript Repositories in the United States* (Phoenix: Oryx Press, 1988, 2nd eds.). These sources sometimes identify school records that have been given to archives or other manuscript collections. Consult the catalogs of the FHL and AGLL for the records they have.

In the absence of school records, try local newspapers. The Bolivar (Tennessee) *Bulletin* of 5 January 1867 announced that the excellent Bolivar Select School would begin the spring term on January 21 and printed the list of tuition and fees. On 15 June, the *Bulletin* covered the closing exercises. The faculty were Mrs. M.J. Thompson, principal and math teacher; Miss Anna C. Safford, English, Latin, and French; Rev. W.H. Thompson (Presbyterian minister), mental and moral science; and Miss Maggie Q. Wilkerson, vocal and instrumental music. For the ceremony, the Presbyterian church was decorated with "rare flowers and foliage green," and the forty to fifty young ladies of the student body, including my great-grandmother, were dressed in white with wreaths of flowers. The vocal class sang a "joyous gushing Welcome Song," and, after a prayer, "the celebrated Echo Song." Among the festivities were the giving of prizes and certificates for "unexceptional scholarship and honorable exertion." The next fall, the *Bulletin* announced a new faculty for the school, as the Thompsons were moving to Columbus, Kentucky, and Miss Safford, to Georgia. The new principal would be Mrs. William E. Glover, a native of North Carolina, educated in Virginia.

CITY DIRECTORIES

City directories as we know them date back to the 1780s for the cities of Philadelphia, Charleston, and New York, with other cities following throughout the nineteenth century. These began basically as business directories but have long included residents, with or without occupation being specified.

The Stockton, California, directory for 1856 gives helpful information about occupation, residence, and former residence. For example, Thomas Blair, cook at the Eagle Hotel, came from Scotland, and Charles R. Bowen, grocer on Hunter Street near Levee, was from Massachusetts. The Baltimore broadside that is considered one of the first directory-like compilations was called "list of families and other persons residing in the town of Baltimore, was taken in the year 1752, by a lady of respectability, and who was well acquainted with the place at the time, and is believed to be correct." It too gave information about the persons listed. Mrs. Hughes was the "only midwife among the English families," and Bill Adams was the "barber, the only one."

City directories and sometimes telephone directories can help genealogists in several important ways. First, knowing the address of the family in or near a census year can help find them in the census. An illustration of this process is in chapter two, under "1900 and 1910 Enumeration District Descriptions."

Second, city directories can give clues to the death or removal of family members. In working on the John A. and Mary Iiams family, we found John A. listed as a truck operator with the Texas and New Orleans Railroad in the 1897-1898 Houston city directory. Although he was missing from the next directory, he appeared in the 1900-1901 edition as a moulder with the Houston and Texas Central Railroad and in the 1900 census. The 1902-1903 city directory lists Mary Iiams, widow of John A. The directory was probably compiled during 1901 or early 1902, and the census indicates that John was still living on 1 June 1900. Thus, we have mid-1900 to mid-1902 as a narrowed range in which to look for a cemetery or probate record for John. No death record for him exists because Texas did not begin keeping these records until 1903.

An interesting result of the early death of parents in this family is that several of the children appear in the city directory at a young age. Mary Iiams, then as Miss Mary Rock, candymaker, and her brother, William Rock, (no occupation given) appeared in the 1892-1893 directory under their own names, living at the home of their mother, Amelia King. They were teenagers about 15 and 17 at the time. (Their step-father Thomas King had died in 1891.) Mary Iiam's half brother, Alfred King, was first listed in the 1902-1903 directory at about age 16, giving Mary's address as his residence. Then Mary's son Claxton Iiams (orphaned by 1910) appeared in the 1913 city directory at about age 11. His residence was his uncle Alfred King's home.

Another feature of some directories is an indication of the number of people living in the household. The 1902-1903 Houston directory shows widow Mary Iiams with three other people in her household. One of these was her brother, Alfred King, as shown in his own entry in the directory. Identifying the other two presents a problem. Their mother, Amelia King, was still living, and Mary had at least two sons, Claxton who was about one year old, and Frank, born about 1893-1894. Was son Frank still living? Was Amelia living elsewhere? If so, where? The directory report at least makes the genealogist ask the questions and search for answers.

City directories can also give an idea of when a family moved in or out of town, but a single omission from a directory does not necessarily mean they were gone. They may have chosen not to pay for a listing, in cases where payment was necessary, or may have been away when the directory representative came to their home. Although telephone directories may help identify families not in the city directories or changes of address, not everyone had a telephone, especially from the late 1870s to the 1940s.

City directories (original or in microform) are available for use in many local public and university libraries, state libraries and archives, and historical societies. Large collections are housed at the Library of Congress, the American Antiquarian Society, The New England Historic Genealogical Society, Cornell University, the New York Public Library, and New York Historical Society. Microform copies may be rented from the AGLL or the FHL.

Directories on microfilm and microfiche may be purchased from Research Publications. The early collection availble from the publisher is based on *Bibliography of American Directories Through 1860* by Dorothea N. Spear (Worchester, MA: American Antiquarian Society, 1961), which will help you identify which cities and dates are represented in the pre-1860 segment. The publisher also has guides to the collection: *City Directories of the United States 1860-1901: Reel Guide to the Microfilm Collection* and temporary reel guides to the 1902-1935 segment. (New directories in this segment are continually being added.) If your public library does not have copies of its own city directories, acquiring them would make a worthwhile project for local genealogists and historians. The following chart lists the cities available in late 1993.

Alabama—Greene County, Mobile, Birmingham.

Arizona—Phoenix, Tucson.

Arkansas—Little Rock.

California—Bakersfield, Fresno, Los Angeles, Marysville, Nevada City, Oakland, Sacramento, San Diego, San Francisco, Stockton, Tuolumne County.

Colorado—Colorado Springs, Denver.

Connecticut—Bridgeport, Connecticut Regional, Hartford, New Haven, New London, Norwich

Delaware—Delaware State, Wilmington.

District of Columbia.

Florida—Jacksonville, Miami, Tampa.

Georgia—Atlanta, Augusta, Columbus, Georgia Regional, Savannah.

Hawaii—Honolulu.

Idaho—Boise.

Illinois—Alton, Belleville, Bureau County, Chicago, Galena, Illinois Regional, Joliet, Kane County, Moline, Peoria, Quincy, Randolph County, Rockford, Rock Island, Springfield, Will County.

Indiana—Evansville, Fort Wayne, Indiana Regional, Indianapolis, Jefferson County, Lafayette, Lawrenceburg, Logansport, Madison, New Albany, Richmond, Shelbyville, Terre Haute.

Iowa—Burlington, Davenport, Des Moines, Dubuque, Henry County, Iowa Regional, Iowa City, Keokuk, Muscatine, State of Iowa (twentieth century).

Kansas—Atchison, Leavenworth, Topeka.

Kentucky—Covington, Kentucky Regional, Lexington, Louisville.

Louisiana—New Orleans.

Maine—Bangor, Biddeford, Maine Regional, Portland, Saco.

Maryland—Baltimore, Frederick.

Massachusetts—Boston, Brighton, Cambridge, Charlestown, Chelsea, Clinton, Dorchester, East Boston, Fall River, Fitchburg, Gloucester, Haverhill, Lawrence, Lowell, Lunenberg, Lynn, Massachusetts Regional, Medford, Milford, New Bedford, Newburyport, Pittsfield, Plymouth, Roxbury, Salem, Somerville, South Boston, Southbridge, Springfield, Taunton, Worcester.

Michigan—Ann Arbor, Battle Creek, Detroit, Grand Rapids, Kalamazoo, Michigan Regional.

Minnesota—Minneapolis, St. Anthony, St. Paul.

Mississippi—Jackson, Mississippi Valley, Vicksburg.

Missouri—Kansas City, Missouri Regional, St. Louis.

Montana—Great Falls, Montana Territory.

Nebraska—Omaha.

Nevada—Nevada Territory.

New Hampshire—Concord, Dover, Great Falls, Keene, Manchester, Nashua, New Hampshire Regional, New Ipswich, Peterborough, Portsmouth.

New Jersey—Camden, Essex County, Jersey City, Newark, New Brunswick, New Jersey Regional, Paterson, Trenton.

New Mexico—Albuquerque.

New York—Albany, Auburn, Binghamton, Brooklyn, Buffalo, Elmira, Geneva, Greenpoint, Hudson, Kingston, Middletown, Mirrisania, Newburgh, New York State Regional, New York City, Ogdensburg, Oswego, Poughkeepsie, Rochester, Rome, Schenectady, Syracuse, Troy, Utica, Watertown, Westchester County, Williamsburg, Yonkers.

North Carolina—Raleigh.

North Dakota—Fargo.

Ohio—Akron, Chillicothe, Cincinnati, Circleville, Cleveland, Columbus, Dayton, Delaware, Hamilton, Mansfield, Marietta, Mt. Vernon, Ohio Regional, Portsmouth, Sandusky, Springfield, Steubenville, Toledo, Zanesville.

Oklahoma—Oklahoma City, Tulsa.

Oregon—Portland.

Pennsylvania—Chester, Erie, Erie County, Harrisburg, Lancaster, Lancaster County, Monongahela Valley, Norristown, Pennsylvania Regional, Philadelphia, Pittsburgh, Reading, Scranton, West Chester.

Rhode Island—Newport, Pawtucket, Providence, Rhode Island Regional.

South Carolina—Camden, Charleston, Columbia.

Tennessee—Chattanooga, Clarksville, Knoxville, Memphis, Nashville, Tennessee Regional.

Texas—Amarillo, Austin, Dallas, Fort Worth, Galveston, Houston, San Antonio.

Utah—Salt Lake City.

Vermont—Barre, Burlington, Vermont Regional.

Virginia—Norfolk, Petersburg, Richmond, Virginia Regional, Wythe County.

Washington—Bellingham, Seattle.

West Virginia—Wheeling.

Wisconsin—Appleton, Beloit, Fond du Lac, Janesville, Kenosha, Madison, Milwaukee, Mineral Point, Oshkosh, Racine, Rock County, Waukesha, Whitewater, Wisconsin Regional.

FIRE INSURANCE MAPS

Maps produced for various fire insurance companies, primarily by the Sanborn Company, can be helpful in pinpointing homes or businesses of ancestors. The maps supply information on the size, shape, and construction material of buildings in many towns and cities, as well as street names, block and house numbers. One of the earliest known maps of this kind is Edmund Petrie's 1790 map of Charleston, South Carolina, made for the Phoenix Fire Insurance Company of London. Only a few such maps exist for years between 1790 and 1867. Since 1867, the Sanborn Company has produced thousands of maps, covering some twelve thousand large and small towns.

The largest collection of these is in the Library of Congress, from which you can request photocopies or microfilm copies. Maps less than seventy-five years old may still be under copyright, and you will need permission from the copyright owner before requesting the copies. The Sanborn Map Company can be reached at 629-T Fifth Avenue, Pelham, NY 10803.

The Library of Congress Photoduplication Service requires a deposit before a search can be made. In contacting this department, specify the city and state of the map you want, the date and street location. (Maps of larger towns fill a number of sheets.) You can find the necessary map numbers, available cities and dates in *Fire Insurance Maps in the Library of Congress: Plans of North American Cities and Towns Produced by the Sanborn Map Company* (Washington, DC: Library of Congress, 1981). The book is indexed but is also arranged alphabetically by state and city. It can be found in many government documents depositories in libraries.

In addition to the Library of Congress, a number

of other repositories have Sanborn map collections. University libraries often include maps as one of their special collections or as part of their state or regional history collection. The chart below shows some of the libraries whose collections include Sanborn maps.

University of Alabama	University of Missouri
Alaska Historical Library	Montana Historical Society
University of Arizona	University of Nebraska
University of Arkansas, Fayetteville	University of Nevada, Reno
Arkansas History Commission Archives	New Hampshire, Dartmouth College
California State University, Northridge	New Jersey, Princeton University
University of Colorado	University of New Mexico
Historical Society of Delaware	New York Public Library
University of Florida	University of North Carolina
University of Georgia	University of North Dakota
University of Hawaii	Ohio, Kent State University
University of Idaho	University of Oklahoma
University of Illinois, Urbana	Oregon State University
Indiana University, Bloomington	Pennsylvania State Library
State Historical Society of Iowa, Des Moines	Pennsylvania State University
State Historical Society of Iowa, Iowa City	Rhode Island, Brown University
University of Kansas	South Carolina Library
University of Kentucky	South Dakota, History Resource Center, Pierre
Louisiana State Library	
Louisiana State University	University of Tennessee
University of Maine	University of Texas, Barker Library
University of Maryland	University of Utah
Massachusetts, Harvard University	Utah State Historical Society
Library of Michigan	University of Vermont
Michigan, Detroit Public Library	Virginia State Library
Minnesota Historical Society	University of Washington
	Washington, Tacoma Public Library
Mississippi Archives	West Virginia University
Mississippi State University	

Wisconsin State Historical Society

University of Wyoming, Laramie

LOCAL BUSINESSES

Contemporary newspapers, city and business directories, and telephone directories all carried advertisements and notices about local businesses, their merchandise and services, and their proprietors or agents. For descendants of these owners, these publications are interesting, add spice to a family history, and are further evidence of an ancestor's presence in a particular place at a given time. Occasionally, such advertisements went a step further and listed the entire board of directors or trustees, especially of banks, insurance companies, and private schools.

For many businesses and professional offices, the only records we have are those advertisements. For others, journals, ledgers, and other records still exist, some even into the colonial period, in library and archives manuscript collections and in museums. The Texas Archives, for example, holds papers of at least two early Texas physicians, Alexander Ewing and James R. Kerr. Such papers and books often tell about customer or client accounts, who spent how much for what and sometimes whether they paid their bills on time. Like the advertisements, these records at least place ancestors in a given place on a given date.

One account book of an unnamed business in Jasper County, Mississippi, survived a destructive courthouse fire and is in the county courthouse labeled *Claim Docket and Chancery Court Minutes, Second District, Paulding.* Apparently, Henry M. Round became justice of the peace and after 14 April 1840 used the book for county records. Was he also the merchant who kept the ledger? Nevertheless, the business record identifies its customers. For example, listed under *Sundries D* is an entry that on 23 February 1838, Alfred Shelby "paid $128 on account—cotton." Then 11 August, A. Shelby, bought a shirt for $3.50 and a pair of pants for $5. Last, in August 1839, is the note "A. Shelby, amount to grocery ticket, $1.25." Although two land grant records exist for this Shelby in 1836 and 1837 in that county, the business records tell us that he was actually living and farming there and add a human quality to the facts available on him. Some such records contain more substantial genealogical information, such as death dates.

Although mercantile records are interesting and revealing, the business I have found most useful and most accessible for genealogical purposes is funeral homes. More and more of these records are being given to libraries and archives, but some companies allow searchers to look at the files in their offices. If we genealogists do not abuse this privilege, we may reap the benefit for years to come. (However, companies are not in business to search for ancestors for us and cannot have their work time taken up by searchers who do not know what they are looking for or do not have some specific search in mind and specific facts to work with.)

A good illustration of the value of funeral home records comes in the file of Mrs. Maggie Kane Wells of Houston, Texas, who died in 1934. Her death certificate on file at the state bureau of vital statistics gave her birth and death dates and places, cause of death, and the names of the funeral home and cemetery. With a specific funeral home to visit, I made an appointment with the secretary, and she pulled the file ahead of time. The contents were enlightening. We learned that the lady was 5 feet, 1 inch tall and weighed about 130 pounds. She had blue eyes, grey hair, and false teeth. She died on December 27, and the weather was cloudy and warm, not unusual for Houston. The obituaries from all three city newspapers were in the file. They named the thirty-one pallbearers and honorary pallbearers as well as her children, but not her twelve grandchildren or nine great-grandchildren. The published notices also mention "four nieces and nephews all of Cincinnati, Ohio." However, the funeral home folder had the original copy for the obituaries, and it said "four nieces and two nephews of Cincinnati." The slight error in publication could make a difference in trying to identify those Ohio relatives. Furthermore, the death certificate named the cemetery where she was buried, but the funeral home file contained a map that showed exactly where in the family plot she was buried and who was already buried in the same plot. Since she has no tombstone, her descendants still can know the location of her grave.

When Mrs. Wells's son-in-law died in 1941, the same funeral home was called in. That folder contained completely new information for the family record: an order of service for the funeral, the exact location in the cemetery where he was buried, the name of his surviving step-sister and her residence, and the name of his church and Masonic lodge.

Insurance company records also can contain pertinent genealogical information, such as birthdate and place, spouse and children or other beneficiaries, residence, occupation, death date and cause of death. If you know a specific insurance company that handled an ancestor's insurance needs, contact them for the particular information you need and have not found elsewhere. Usually family records and interviews with older relatives are the best sources for determining an insurance company to contact. Some beneficial societies existed, and still exist, primarily as insurance societies. Many are listed in the *Encyclopedia of Associations*. Also consult the catalog of the FHL for microfilmed records. One example in the FHL catalog is *Record of Benefits, 1883-1924* of the Bavarian Beneficial Society of Cincinnati; the original records are at Wright State University, Dayton, Ohio.

Funeral home, insurance, doctors', and lawyers' records and, to some extent, other business records can aid in genealogical searches. Ask in the local area for the location of such records, especially in public and university libraries and museums. Consult the catalog of the FHL under the name of your research locality. If a business that is still in operation seems likely to have information pertinent to a search, then make the contact and try to find the information. (Again, I would urge discretion. Taking up employee time, especially talking about family history, is not good public relations for the genealogy community, however polite and interested the employee might act. It is those who abuse the privilege of access who cause records to be closed to the rest of us.)

Getting information about or from records of defunct businesses can be a challenge. Many such records do not exist, but some do. Try to determine locally whether the business was sold, who purchased it, and whether the new owners retained the records. (Sometimes, the seller kept the records.) In this effort, you can talk with other businesses of a similar nature, the chamber of commerce, or a trade association. Local newspapers or city directories may give you clues to when a business ceased operation or who took it over. In addition, local public libraries, museums, universities, or state historical societies, libraries, and archives may have such business records. You can survey the sources mentioned earlier in this chapter to determine what records particular libraries and archives have.

Another side of the question is getting information about the businessmen themselves. Many professional and trade associations publish directories of members from time to time. Legal, medical, and dental organizations are well known, but such organizations exist for engineers, dairymen, morticians, architects, teachers, bankers, and many others. Their directories vary in genealogical usefulness. Most contain at least members' names and business addresses. Others give birth year, school, and graduation year. These journals and transactions often contain obituaries and the more extensive biographical information that the genealogist wants. (See chapter eight for discussion of legal directories.)

An early trade association, the Carpenters' Company of Philadelphia, published its rules of work in 1786 and included names of over 130 members, some by then deceased. This little volume was reprinted in a facsimile edition in 1971 (*The Rules of Work of the Carpenters' Company of the City and County of Philadelphia*, Charles E. Peterson, annotator, (n.p.): Bell Publishing, a division of Crown Publishers, Inc., for the Carpenters' Company, 1971).

Directories and records pertaining to clergy are usually in the various denominational archives. Law, medical, and dental schools usually have collections of their particular professional directories. Although legal directories have been published since 1868, the American Medical Association directory began in 1906. If you had an ancestor in such a profession or trade, inquire also about biographical dictionaries and compiled obituaries.

Medical Obituaries: American Physicians' Biographical Notices in Selected Medical Journals Before 1907, by Lisabeth M. Holloway (New York: Garland Publishing, 1981) is an extensive work compiled from society journals and other sources, with each entry documented. Physicians are listed alphabetically with birth and death dates, education, and professional information as found in the listed sources. In the work I learned that my ancestor George Logan (1778-1861) graduated from the University of Pennsylvania medical school in 1802, served in the United States Navy, 1810-1829, practiced in Charleston, South Carolina, and died in New Orleans. His son and my ancestor Thomas Muldrup Logan was incorrectly listed as Charles in his own biographical sketch. This source and others give Thomas's birthdate as 31 July 1808, but a family Bible gives 31 January. However, the published sketches and this family Bible are secondary sources. The Bible was kept by his daughter and son-in-law, probably with input from his wife or another family record. Nevertheless, these discrepancies illustrate the warning that even though the compiler of *Medical Obituaries* was thorough and careful, previously published information or family sources may contain mistakes. The gene-

alogist, therefore, must seek to verify the information with other records.

In related fields, several biographical dictionaries are available. At least two in the dental profession were compiled from questionnaires sent to American Dental Association member: *America's Dental Leaders: A National Biographic Volume of the Dental Profession* (Chicago: Distinction Press, Inc., 1953) and *Who's Who in American Dentistry*, Alvin J. DeBre (Los Angeles: Dale Dental Publishing Co., 1963). These two volumes overlap somewhat, but together they represent a significant portion of the profession between 1900 and 1963. Generations were well represented, with participating dentists giving birth dates at least back to 1874. The information included address, birth date and place, parents' names, spouse and children, education and professional involvement, publications, military service, hobbies, and extra-professional activities.

A more recent addition to the field of biographical dictionaries is *Who's Who in Health Care* (Rockville, MD: Aspen Systems Corporation, 1981, 2nd ed.). The entries give birth date, spouse and children, education, professional positions, memberships, publications and address.

Histories, both books and articles, written on professions and occupations can help provide information on ancestors. One example is *The History of Dentistry in the Republic of Texas, 1836-1945*, by Ernest Beerstecher, Jr. (Houston: Dental Branch, The University of Texas Health Science Center at Houston, 1975). This book includes a documented biographical directory of dental practitioners in the republic, compiled from many of the same sources that genealogists would use: city directories, newspapers, professional journals, and manuscript sources. A more general history is *The New England Merchants in the Seventeenth Century*, by Bernard Bailyn (New York: Harper and Row, 1955, reprint from original by Harvard University, 1955). See chapter eight for discussion of various periodical indexes that could help you find articles about ancestors or occupations.

Employee records are another aspect of business records. Larger companies and labor unions may be the best sources of information on employees. Family records, obituaries, city directories, and census records are standard sources of identifying an occupation and employer's name or company. Then the searcher can look for records of that business, as discussed earlier.

Two classes of employees in the early years of the

country were indentured servants and apprentices. Thousands of immigrants came in the seventeenth and eighteenth centuries as indentured servants, or re-demptioners, bound to an employer for a specified number of years (usually two to seven) to pay for their passage, to work off other debts, or to serve out a criminal sentence. They worked on farms, especially in Maryland, Virginia, and the Carolinas, and in towns, especially in Pennsylvania. Apprentices were usually minors, often orphans, who were bound to an employer, usually until the age of twenty-one, to learn the skills of a craft or trade. Some records of indentures and apprenticeships survive. A few have been published, primarily in periodicals. Others can sometimes be found in archives and manuscript collections. To identify such collections, consult the sources discussed earlier in this chapter. In addition, a number of indentures from the Philadelphia City Archives are available on microfilm rental from the FHL. These cover a period roughly from 1751 to 1888 and include children and redemptioner indentures and some apprentice records.

ORGANIZATIONS

Ancestors joined civic and fraternal organizations just as they joined churches and professional groups. Local newspapers, family papers, tombstones, obituaries, and local histories can help you determine which organizations your ancestors belonged to. Notices of meetings, special functions, and election of officers were regular parts of some community newspapers.

For example, the Bolivar (Tennessee) *Bulletin* noted on 24 February 1866 that the IOOF (Independent Order of Odd Fellows) Lodge 27 met each Tuesday night and that A.S. Coleman was an officer. By 13 June 1868, this same Coleman was an officer in the Sons of Temperance, Magnolia Division number 96, which met each Saturday night at the Odd Fellows Hall. In October 1874, he was senior warden of the Worth Encampment number 16 of the IOOF, which met two Wednesday nights a month. Where can you look for more information?

If a local chapter of an ancestor's organization still exists, contact the chapter for any information they might share. If the local chapter no longer functions but the national or state headquarters exists, ask there about records from defunct chapters. Also ask where you might find old copies of the organization's periodical, for many organizations publish one. The *Encyclopedia of Associations*, either the national organization volumes or the regional, state, and local organization volumes (cited earlier in this chapter), can give you addresses for many organizations. The *Greenwood Encyclopedia of American Institutions* (Westport, CT: Greenwood Press) is a series of books that helps identify organizations and gives background on them: *Fraternal Organizations*, by Alvin J. Schmidt (1980): *Social Service Organizations*, Peter Romanofsky, ed. (1978); *Farmers' Organizations*, by Lowell K. Dyson (1986); and *Labor Unions*, Gary M. Fink, ed. (1977). Other sources for fraternal organizations include these:

> *Cyclopedia of Fraternities*, by Albert C. Stevens (New York: E.B. Treat, 1907, 2d ed., reprint by Gale Research, 1966).
>
> A *Dictionary of Secret and Other Societies*, by Arthur Preuss (St. Louis: B. Herder Book Company, 1924, reprint by Gale Research, 1966).
>
> *Handbook of Secret Organizations*, by William J. Whalen (Milwaukee: Bruce Publishing Company, 1966).

Whether the organization exists or not, records may have been given to libraries, archives, or museums on the local or state level. The *National Union Catalog of Manuscript Collections*, the *Guide to Archives and Manuscripts in the United States*, and the *Directory of Archives and Manuscript Repositories in the United States* cited earlier in the chapter can help locate organizational records housed in these institutions.

One organization that often has information on its members is the Masons. Because the organization is more than two hundred years old in this country, some records reach back into the eighteenth century. Much depends on the individual lodge or state grand lodge. The information varies considerably in its completeness, especially for early records. In addition, most Masonic records deal with membership, not biographical data. Sometimes they include a death date.

The emblem on the tombstone of Rev. William Harrison told us that he was a Mason. The Grand Lodge of Virginia graciously provided the following information. Their earliest record of him was on the 1755 by-laws of the Blandford Lodge number 3 at Petersburg. The other records showed that he did not appear on the lodge roster for 1792, served as mayor of the city 1799-1800, served as lodge chaplain 1800-1804, and was listed under *deaths* from the lodge in 1813. No exact death date was sent in, but his tombstone gives the month and day. This information comes from lodge rosters, a lodge history, and grand lodge proceedings.

Other records of that lodge were lost in a fire before 1850. The librarian also mentioned that petitions for membership from the nineteenth century and before had little personal information, and few of these have survived in Virginia.[7]

LOCAL GOVERNMENT RECORDS

Town and city governments sometimes have records useful to genealogists. These may be minutes of the governing body, tax rolls, municipal court records, vital records, and perhaps personnel records, but each town or city has its own priorities and state regulations on what to keep and for how long. Contact your particular city of interest for specific holdings, and ask whether they have a city archives. In addition, consult the catalogs of the FHL and AGLL for microfilmed records.

The minutes of the city commission in Marfa, Texas, for example, show that on 18 January 1938, W.D. DeVolin was appointed to fill an unexpired term on the commission and was given the oath of office by H.O. Metcalfe. Salaries and other payments by the city are also included in this kind of record. The minutes of the Marfa tax board for 20 June 1928 show payment of $7 for legal services to the law firm of Mead and Metcalfe. Records of this kind are usually not indexed, but can provide evidence of ancestral activity.

The town of Calvert, Texas, suffered a city hall fire in the early twentieth century but has some of the city tax rolls back to 1905. In tracking the residences of John P. Shelby, we discovered that he was living in town at least from 1905 to 1908. His city tax of $2.20 in 1906 was based on the value of his lot, valued at $160, one vehicle, and a horse. By 1908, he had acquired three cows. It is an interesting sidenote that this lot, designated with block and lot number in the tax books and deed records, does not appear on the city map for that period, nor has the abstract company yet determined its exact location.

Some towns and cities maintain vital records for births and deaths that occurred within the city limits. This practice may also vary from county to county. If you do not know whether an ancestor might be recorded in town or county records, contact the state vital statistics office.

You would need to contact the particular town in which an ancestral family lived to learn what town records they have and for what time period. My most successful inquiries have been by telephone rather than by mail. Once you know the extent of existing records, you will be able to determine whether you need to visit city hall. In addition, some early town records, mostly from New England, have been published or microfilmed. Check with the AGLL, the FHL, and the New England Historic Genealogical Society for rental availability.

Footnotes are on page 175.

CHAPTER SEVEN

Special Collections

Of great interest to genealogists, outside of local and regional history and government documents, are newspapers, maps, and manuscripts. One or more of these special collections can be found at almost any university or research library. The information they hold is important for enhancing a genealogical project.

NEWSPAPERS

How Can Newspapers Help You in Genealogical Research?

Newspapers can be wonderful sources of information for local history and genealogy. Although some newspapers exist from the eighteenth century, they are, in most places, a tool for nineteenth and twentieth century research. The most significant information one might expect to find is notices or articles about marriages and deaths, but it can be very rewarding to read multiple issues of a given paper to glean other tidbits about ancestors and their community.

Marriage Notices. Simple marriage notices, as in the following example, may contain little more than the names of the bride and groom and the wedding date, but sometimes can provide clues to other information. On 4 December 1869 the Bolivar (Tennessee) *Bulletin* reported: Married on November 30 at the residence of the bride's father (unnamed) by Rev. F.P. Mullally, Pitser Blalock and Mary C. Coleman. This simple announcement in the New York *Tribune*, 29 April 1868, gives a little more information (italics added for illustration): Married "on *Monday*, April 27, *at Hartford*, by the Rev. Mr. Fisher, Wm. F. Geisse to Ella D., *only daughter of D.B. Coe, esq., of Brooklyn.*" More elaborate notices, of course, may include names of other relatives and attendants and descriptions of the celebration. Also, the ministers' names may be clues to church affiliation.

Death Notices. Often deaths were reported as simple notices, giving vital information but leaving the reader with unanswered questions. The Shreveport (Louisiana) *South-Western* reported on 11 June 1856 that on June 9, Thomas Robinson, carpenter, had died, at about 42 years of age. Where did he live? Did he have family? Where was he buried? At least the searcher gets a death date, occupation, and age, from which to figure an approximate birth date.

The Albany (New York) *Daily Albany Argus* on Tuesday morning, 9 February 1830, reported that "WILLIS, the famous bugleman and leader of the West Point band, died at that post on Monday and was buried with the honors of war." Did he have only one Name? On which Monday did he die? Yesterday? Was he buried at West Point? Did he leave family?

The 2 November 1900 Calvert (Texas) *Chronicle* reported: Died four miles east of Calvert last Saturday, of malarial fever, Mrs. J.M. Oldham, who leaves a husband and a large number of children; burial was at Mt. Vernon with twenty to thirty members of the W.O.W. (Sterling Camp), of which her husband is a member, attending. From what is given, the searcher can calculate her death date: The paper was printed on Friday; the previous Saturday was October 27. The reader learns which cemetery to visit to search for additional family information, gets clues to the family's residence, and finds another possible source of information about the husband. Unanswered, of course, are the questions of her given name, the number and names of her surviving children, her age, and, in an area with many Oldhams, her husband's given name.

Even elaborate obituaries do not answer all questions, but they can furnish many details. A lengthy obituary for Rev. Henry Metcalf, printed 6 September 1887, gave his birth date in Georgia, the name of the Alabama town where he grew up, his wedding date and wife's maiden name, his conversion date, the date he was licensed as a Methodist preacher, the dates of his ordination as deacon and elder, information about his preaching and his last sermon, the dates of his death and burial, and the cemetery near Corsicana, Texas, where he was laid to rest. One piece of information not included in the obituary, which would be useful to genealogists, is the names of the "many relatives" who mourned his death. Fortunately, the family kept this valuable clipping (although no one recorded the name of the newspaper from which it came), because it contains much information not available elsewhere. For example, the couple married in 1845, probably in Dale County, Alabama, whose marriage records were lost in a courthouse fire in 1884.

The genealogical information in this announcement from the New York *Tribune*, Wednesday, 29 April 1868 is the kind searchers hope to find: Died "at Chatham Four Corners, on Sunday evening last, Mrs. Mary C. Woodbridge, wife of W.A. Woodbridge and daughter of the late Joshua Wingate of Hallowell, Maine." As sad as the circumstances are, the following notice can give the genealogist answers that may not surface elsewhere: "The three days' old infant of J.G. Newton was buried yesterday, the mother having preceded the little one to the grave but two days." (Houston, Texas *Daily Post*, 20 October 1897)

Other Information. Advertisements, legal and personal notices, editorials, and local news abound in interesting and telling information. The Bolivar (Tennessee) *Palladium*, on 24 June 1831, advertised that William G. Steele was selling his tan-yard at Bolivar along with the forty acres adjoining it and the twenty-three acres with a dwelling and an apple and peach orchard. Why was he selling out? He said, "I am entirely unacquainted with the business."

Advertisements make up a considerable portion of early newspapers. Although they often are not abstracted and published, they can provide information for the genealogist. One example from the Albany (New York) *Daily Albany Argus* of 9 February 1830 reads: "TO LET, from the first of May next, that elegant three story brick dwelling house and lot No. 28 Montgomery st. (*sic*) occupied by G.W. Stanton. Also that commodious three story brick dwelling house and lot No. 33 Columbia st. occupied by B.G. Staats. Apply to C.W. Groesbeck & Co." Descendants of these families could find here the location and description of family residences, indication of a move, and the possibility that these families rented rather than owned their homes. In the 24 columns (four pages) of this issue of this newspaper, 12½ columns, just over half the issue, are filled with advertisements; 4½ columns concern debtors; the other 1½ columns of that page are other

legal notices; 4½ columns report news of the New York legislature; and the remaining column reports general news.

Legal notices in this *Daily Albany Argus* issue give good genealogical information. Besides notices about the many debtors in and out of jail, the paper printed an announcment that Charlotte Selby, of New York City, widow and devisee of Skeffington Selby, deceased, was applying to the legislature for an act releasing to her title to lot number 620 on the easterly side of Broadway in the city's Ninth Ward, extending from Broadway to Crosby Street. Was this the family residence? Do deed records give further information about this property?

Notices about individuals appear in newspapers as well. This one appears in the Houston (Texas) *Daily Post*, 20 October 1897. Wouldn't you love to know why he left, where he went, and whether he returned to the home?

> *Corsicana, Texas, October 18. — John Holyby, a boy about 12 years of age, light hair and grey eyes, has left the State Orphans' Home. Any information that will lead to his discovery will be very much appreciated. Parties will please correspond with the undersigned. All papers in the state are requested to copy this notice. Jink Evans, president of board of trustees, Corsicana, Texas.*

Editorial comments give readers an insight into local politics and circumstances. With the state still under military rule after the Civil War, the Bremond (Texas) *Central Texan* editor commented in his paper's second issue (4 June 1870) that the military still patrol the streets of Calvert, and they could better serve the country by patrolling the frontier.

Local news included illnesses, merchants with new buildings or new merchandise, fund-raising efforts, voter lists, school and social events, church and lodge functions, political meetings, reports on the local economy, and area farm and crop news. The Houston (Texas) *Daily Post* announced proudly on 20 October 1897:

> *The last of the patients pronounced by Dr. Guiteras as having yellow fever, made his appearance upon the street yesterday, Officer Henry Lee. He is still feeble from the effects of his long illness, but expects to be able to resume work today or tomorrow. This clears up all Dr.*

*Guiteras' yellow fever patients in Houston, each
having recovered with not a single death and
no contagion with the period of incubation
long since passed. These facts speak for themselves even more potently than health bulletins.*

The big fund-raising project reported in the Bolivar
(Tennessee) *Bulletin* during the summer and fall of
1866 was a Grand Tournament to be held at the local
fairgrounds. The proceeds from the contests and food
sales would be used for a monument to the Confederate dead. Long lists of names appeared in the newspaper as committees, entrants, and judges were announced. The "Grand Gala Day" was actually two days
of tilting contests, a "grand concert" by the ladies, and
a "grand Masquerade." Miss Irene McNeal was
crowned Queen of Love and Beauty by the winning
Knight of the White Plume, N.B. Cross. The masquerade prize went to "the man on the mule."

Where to Find Newspapers

It is still possible to find original issues of newspapers
that you may use. These may be available at county
courthouses, public and university libraries, historical
societies, and state archives or libraries. However,
many newspapers have been microfilmed, and these
copies are sometimes available on interlibrary loan
from these same institutions. Newspaper abstracts often appear in genealogical periodicals, and many have
been published. Publishers of newspaper abstracts include Boyd Publishing Company, Brent Holcomb, Byron Sistler and Associates, Reprint Company Publishers, Heritage Books, the Iowa Genealogical Society,
Southern Historical Press, and Genealogical Publishing Company. (See publishers in Appendix E for addresses.)

One way to determine which newspapers still exist
for your research area and where you can use them is
to consult union catalogs. Such union lists identify
which libraries or other institutions have which editions of which newspapers. (See chapter eight for further discussion.)

1. *American Newspapers, 1821-1936: A Union List
of Files Available in the United States and Canada*,
Winifred Gregory, ed. (New York: H.W. Wilson, 1937,
reprint by Kraus Reprint Corporation, New York,
1967). Still in the Kraus catalog. I have found this book
in libraries under the Library of Congress call number
Z6945.A53 and under Dewey Decimal number

16.071.A512. If not in the main stacks, it may be in the
Reference Section.

2. *Newspapers in Microform, United States, 1948-
1983* (Washington, DC: Library of Congress, 1984, 2
vol.). I have found this reference under Library of Congress call number Z6951.U469 and Dewey call number
011.35N558.

These catalogs are organized alphabetically by state,
within each state by town or city, and then by newspaper title. Each entry gives the dates of publication of
the newspaper, other titles it may have had, and the
depositories with holdings. The depositories are listed
as abbreviations, which are translated at the front of
volume into names. According to *Newspapers in Microform*, for example, the African-American newspaper *National Era* was published between 1847 and
1860 in Washington, D.C. By 1983, twenty different
institutions had complete or nearly complete microfilm sets. These included the Library of Congress,
Howard University, and American University, all in
Washington, D.C., as well as Sam Houston State University in Texas and the University of Hawaii. Remember that the *Newspapers in Microform* volumes list
only holdings on microfilm or other microcopy forms,
not originals or reprinted copies. This particular newspaper was reprinted by Negro Universities Press in
bound volumes and is found in that form in a number
of other locations.

The United States Newspaper Program is an attempt to update and concentrate this kind of information on the OCLC database. This project is a major
effort by hundreds of depositories to locate and pre-
serve all extant newspapers in the country. Finding a
listing on the database does not mean that the newspaper is available on interlibrary loan, but many libraries
do lend microfilm copies. Your local interlibaray loan
specialist can find out what is available. In addition,
consult the catalogs of the AGLL and the FHL for the
newspapers they have available for rental on microfilm.

Many states have printed bibliographies or union
catalogs on newsapers within that state, such as the
Guide to Wyoming Newspapers, 1867-1967, by Lola
Homsher (Cheyenne, WY: Wyoming State Library,
1971). Under the city of Cheyenne is listed, among
others, the *Daily Hornet* published between March
10 and April 11, 1878, with the information that the
Wyoming Archives has all issues, and the University of
Wyoming at Laramie has one edition. In libraries using
the Library of Congress call number system, these

guides for various states may be found under Z6952-6953. Libraries using the Dewey Decimal system would catalog these under 011.35, bibliographies on newspapers.

A bibliography of early newspapers is *A Checklist of American Eighteenth Century Newspapers in the Library of Congress*, compiled by John Van Ness Ingram (Washington, DC: Government Printing Office, 1912). This volume is organized by state, city, and title and is indexed.

The following list is an attempt to help searchers find, in each state, newspaper collections of that state's papers. A comprehensive listing is certainly beyond the scope of this book, but these institutions often can tell you which other libraries or archives in their state also have newspaper collections. The information given was supplied by the institutions. Several state archives, such as California, Florida, Massachusetts, and Washington reported that to date they do not have newspaper collections.

The following abbreviations are used:

1 = Pre-Civil War papers
2 = newspapers 1865-1900
3 = twentieth century papers
ILL = microfilm copies available from this institution on interlibrary loan

Alabama Archives — 1, 2, 3. ILL.
Alaska Archives and Records Management Services — 2 (a few), 3.
Alaska Historical Library — 3. ILL.
Arizona Historical Society Library — 2, 3.
Arizona State Library, Archives, and Public Records, Genealogy Section — 2, 3. ILL. Largest collection in the state. Consult also Phoenix Public Library and University of Arizona Library.
Arkansas History Commission Archives — 1, 2, 3. Significant collection.
Arkansas, Southwest Arkansas Regional Archives — 1, 2, 3.
Arkansas, University of Arkansas, Fayetteville — 1, 2, 3. Generally single or rare issues.
California, Bancroft Library, University of California at Berkeley — 1, 2, extensive collection, covering statewide newspapers. Includes African-American papers. Newspaper and Microcopy Dept. of the Library has twentieth-century papers.
California, San Diego Historical Society — City's newspapers on microfilm.

California State Library — 1. Plus indexes to San Francisco papers, 1894-1980.
California, Sutro Library — 1, 2. San Francisco papers.
Colorado Historical Society — 1, 2, 3. Microfilm copies may be purchased.
Connecticut Historical Society — Yes, including Hartford *Courant* from its beginning in 1764, with index to 1820. Scrapbooks of obituaries and clippings.
Connecticut State Library — 1, 2, 3. Extensive collection. Files of abstracts and clippings as well.
Delaware Historical Society — 1, 2, 3. Mainly from Wilmington.
Delaware State Archives — 1, 2, 3. Very few.
Delaware, University of Delaware Library — Yes. Has union list of Delaware newspapers.
Delaware, Wilmington Public Library — 1, 2, 3. *Delaware State Journal* 1838-1840, Wilmington *News Journal*, complete (began 1880).
District of Columbia Historical Society — 1, 2. *National Intelligencer*.
Florida State Library, Florida Collection — 1, 2, 3. Extensive collection. The Florida Collection is part of the state library and has papers dating back to 1829. The reference room of the state library also has late nineteenth-century and twentieth-century papers.
Florida State University Library — 1, 2, 3. Especially Tallahassee and Apalachicola newspapers.
Florida, University of Florida Library — 1, 2, 3. Extensive collection.
Georgia Archives — 1, 2, 3.
Georgia, Emory University — Yes.
Georgia Historical Society — 1, 2, 3. Primarily Savannah papers. Index for Savannah papers.
Georgia, University of Georgia, Athens — 1, 2, 3. Largest collection of newspapers in the state. Some indexes.
Georgia — University of Rochester, Rochester, New York, has collection of Southern newspapers, mostly Savannah.
Hawaii State Archives — Yes, includes nineteenth century.
Hawaii State Library — Comprehensive collection.
Hawaii Historical Society — 1, 2, 3. Early newspapers date from 1834. Indexes to marriages and birth notices, 1850-1950. Index to obituaries, 1836-1950.
Hawaii, Hamilton Library, University of Hawaii at

Manoa—Comprehensive collection.

Hawaii Public Library, Bishop Museum Library, and Hawaiian Mission Children's Society Library also have newspapers.

Hawaii, Maui Historical Society—Newspapers clippings of Maui history.

Idaho, Boise State University—2, 3. Idaho *Statesman* from 1864.

Idaho Historical Society, Genealogy Department—2, 3. Earliest is 1863. Extensive Idaho collection. ILL.

Idaho Historical Society, Library and Archives—2, 3. A few pre-1865. ILL to Idaho public libraries only.

Illinois, Chicago, Center for Research Libraries—U.S. Ethnic Newspaper Collection (foreign language newspapers printed in the U.S.).

Illinois, Chicago Historical Society—1, 2, 3. Mostly Chicago newspapers.

Illinois, Newberry Library—1, 2, 3.

Illinois State Historical Library—1, 2, 3. Extensive Illinois collection.

Illinois, University of Illinois-Urbana—Yes.

Indiana, Allen County Public Library—1, 2, 3 from Ft. Wayne and Indianapolis mostly. A number of local and county public libraries have their local papers.

Indiana Historical Society—1, 2, 3. Select issues, very limited.

Indiana State Library—1, 2, 3. ILL. Largest collection in state.

Iowa Department of Archives and History—Yes.

Iowa, State Historical Society, Des Moines—1, 2, 3. Has an Iowa newspaper bibliography. ILL.

Iowa, State Historical Society, Iowa City—1, 2, 3. Plus clippings file of Iowa biographies.

Kansas State Historical Society—1, 2, 3. ILL. Excellent, extensive collection. Also some Missouri and New York City papers and Kansas biographical clippings files.

Kentucky Archives—1, 2, 3. Small collection, primarily nineteenth century. Has state union list.

Kentucky, Filson Club—1, 2, 3. Second largest collection of periodicals in state, especially good collection of pre-Civil War newspapers.

Kentucky Historical Society—Yes.

Kentucky, University of Kentucky, Lexington—1, 2, 3. Largest collection in the state. ILL.

Louisiana, New Orleans Pulbic Library—Yes.

Louisiana State Library—1, 2, 3. Some ILL.

Louisiana State University, Hill Memorial Library—1, 2, 3.

Louisiana, Tulane University, Special Collections, Manuscripts and Rare Books Dept.—1, 2, 3.

Maine Historical Society—1, 2, 3.

Maine State Library—1, 2, 3.

Maine, University of Maine—1, 2, 3. Largest collection in the state.

Maryland Archives—1, 2, 3. Largest collection in the state.

Maryland, Enoch Pratt Free Library—1, 2, 3. Extensive collection.

Maryland Historical Society—1, 2. Plus index of all marriage and death notices in Baltimore newspapers, 1773-1840.

Maryland State Law Library—Comprehensive collection of *Maryland Gazette* (began 1729).

Maryland, University of Maryland McKeldin Library—1, 2, 3. ILL.

Massachusetts, American Antiquarian Society—Yes. Good collection, 1821-1865. Smaller post-Civil War collection.

Massachusetts, Boston Public Library—1, 2, 3. Massachusetts and New England.

Massachusetts, New England Historic Genealogical Society—1.

Michigan State Library—1, 2, 3. ILL within Michigan only. Extensive collection.

Minnesota Historical Society and State Archives—1, 2, 3. Largest collection in the state. Earliest paper published in state was 1849. ILL.

Mississippi Archives—1, 2, 3.

Missouri Historical Society, St. Louis—1, 2, 3. ILL. Includes virtually complete collection of Missouri *Republican*, which began in 1808, and Missouri *Gazette*, which published until 1919.

Missouri, State Historical Society in Columbia—1, 2, 3. Largest collection in the state.

Montana Historical Society—Yes. ILL. The strongest collection in the state. Has most of the newspapers ever published in Montana.

Nebraska Historical Society—1, 2, 3. ILL. Microfilm purchase. Largest collection in state.

Nevada Archives—2, 3. ILL. Has a number of indexes as well.

Nevada Historical Society—1, 2, 3. Index to *Territorial Enterprise*, 1859-1880s; plans to index to 1900.

Nevada, University of Nevada, Las Vegas—1, 2, 3.

Nevada, University of Nevada, Reno—1, 2, 3. ILL.

See *The Newspapers of Nevada: A History and Bibliography, 1854-1979*, by Richard E. Lingenfelter and Karen Rix Gash (Reno: University of Nevada Press, 1984).

New Hampshire Historical Society—1, 2. ILL.

New Jersey Archives—1, 2, 3. A major collection.

New Jersey Historical Society—Yes.

New Jersey, Rutgers University Library—1, 2, 3. A major collection.

New Jersey State Library—Yes. Many local libraries also have local newspapers.

New Mexico, Albuquerque Public Library—2, 3 (to 1912). Collects territorial papers only.

New Mexico Archives (Santa Fe), University of New Mexico (Albuquerque), and New Mexico State University (Las Cruces)—the largest collections in the state.

New York City Public Library—1, 2, 3.

New York Genealogical and Biographical Society—Pre-1900 abstracts of deaths, marriages.

New York Historical Society—Yes. One of the largest collections of eighteenth-century newspapers in the country.

New York State Library—1, 2, 3.

North Carolina Archives—1, 2, 3. Available for purchase.

North Carolina, Duke University—Yes.

North Carolina, University of North Carolina, Chapel Hill—Yes.

North Dakota Historical Society—1, 2, 3. The newspaper depository for the state. ILL. State newspaper inventory available, $25.

Ohio Historical Society—1, 2, 3. The Ohio newspaper depository, largest Ohio collection.

Ohio, Western Reserve Historical Society—1, 2, 3. Extensive collection.

Oklahoma Historical Society, Newspaper Archives—1, 2, 3. Has about 90 percent of all Oklahoma newspapers ever published, including Indian papers. Working on getting the rest.

Oklahoma Rudisill Library, Tulsa—2, 3. Tulsa newspapers.

Oklahoma, University of Oklahoma, Western History Collection—2, 3.

Oregon Archives—1, 2, 3. ILL from University of Oregon library.

Oregon Historical Society—1, 2, 3. Comprehensive collection of major Oregon newspapers. ILL in Oregon only. Vertical file of newspaper clippings as well.

Pennsylvania Historical Society—1, 2, 3. Extensive collection.

Pennsylvania State Library—1, 2, 3. "Largest in existence."

Pennsylvania, Western Pennsylvania Historical Society—Yes, western Pennsylvania newspapers.

Rhode Island Historical Society—1, 2, 3. Official repository of state newspapers. Contains almost every state newspaper known from 1732 to present, including a nearly complete file of Providence *Gazette* (1762-1825).

South Carolina Archives—1. South Carolina *Gazette*, 1732-1782 only. Plus Georgia *Gazette*.

South Carolina, Charleston Library Society—1, 2, 3.

South Caroliniana Library—1, 2, 3. South Carolina newspaper bibliography available ILL.

South Dakota Historical Society and Archives—2, 3. ILL. Extensive collection of most of the state's newspapers.

Tennessee Archives—1, 2, 3.

Texas Archives—1, 2, 3.

Texas, Barker Library, Austin—1, 2, 3. Extensive collection.

Texas, Houston Public Library—Texas Room, 1, 2 (Mostly Houston area). 3—Bibliographic Information Center.

Utah Historical Society—2, 3. Large collection. Plus biographical clippings file.

Utah, Family History Library—Yes. See catalog at Family History Centers nationwide.

Utah, Marriott Library, University of Utah—Yes.

Vermont State Library—Yes. Some ILL.

Virginia, College of William and Mary—1, 2, 3.

Virginia Historical Society, 1, 2, 3. Has card index to newspapers by year.

Virginia State Library—1, 2, 3. Index to Virginia newspapers on microfilm. Card index to articles. Some ILL; inquire for specific papers available.

Virginia, University of Virginia Library—Has card index to newspapers in Rare Book Department. Special Collections has large collection.

Washington, Seattle Public Library—2, 3. Only for Seattle

Washington State Library—1, 2, 3. ILL. State union list available.

Washington, University of Washington, Seattle—Pacific Northwest newspapers.

West Virginia Archives and History Library—1, 2, 3.

West Virginia, Marshall University—Some newspapers.

West Virginia, University of West Virginia, Morgan-town—1, 2, 3.

Wisconsin Historical Society—1, 2, 3. The major Wisconsin newspaper collection. Plus extensive collection of early trans-Appalachian newspapers, labor, black, Native American, ethnic, women's, U.S. Army Camp newspapers, and nineteenth-century religious newspapers.

Wisconsin, University of Wisconsin at Milwaukee Library—Very extensive collection.

Wyoming Archives, Historical Research Division—2, 3. Some ILL.

Wyoming, University of Wyoming—2, 3.

Indexes

One of the time-consuming aspects of newspaper research is that most papers are not indexed. If your newspaper of interest exists only in a few issues during the time period you need, you really have no problem. Even if you have a death date and want to search for an obituary in a small community newspaper, you will not spend very much time checking the several issues of the paper that appeared after the death occurred. However, working without specific dates or with larger newspapers requires much more research time.

Fortunately, more and more indexes are being prepared. Historical and genealogical societies are providing many of these, some as separate publications, some in the periodicals of the societies. One source for locating indexes is *Newspaper Indexes: A Location and Subject Guide For Researchers*, Anita Cheek Milner (Metuchen, NJ: Scarecrow Press, 1977-1982, 3 vols.). In addition, several commercial publishers have indexes available for major city newspapers. Some of these indexes began in the 1970s.

One of the most comprehensive indexes for a United States newspaper is *The New York Times Index: A Book of Record*. The index began in 1851. From 1913 to 1929, it was issued quarterly. Thus, in the January-March 1914 volume appears the entry *Novak, Rev. Alexis—death, Mar 6, 1:7*. This is the reference for the death notice of Rev. Novak, which was printed in the March 6 issue, the first page, column 7.

Another helpful resource for this newspaper is the *Personal Names Index to "The New York Times Index." 1851-1974*, a 22-volume set. (Byron A. and Valerie R. Falk, comp., Succasunna, NJ: Roxbury Data Interface, 1976.) These books are truly an index to an index. With each name is a citation to help find the item in the larger index. It certainly beats looking through 123 years of books! For the years 1913-1929, the citations give the year the name appeared and the quarterly index (I, II, III, or IV) you will find it in. For example, the entry *George Craig Severance—d 1922, I, 472* means that his death notice reference appears in the January-March index for 1922, page 472. For items that appeared in the other years, the citation gives the year and the page number of that year's index. The searcher then looks in that index to find the issue date and page reference. With such a specific reference, it is sometimes possible to obtain a photocopy of the item directly from an institution that has a collection of the newspapers, especially if they are on microfilm. Another source for searching the *Times* is the *New York Times Obituaries Index, 1858-1968* and *1969-1978* (New York: New York Times, 1970, 1980, 2 vols.). Check a library reference section for these books.

Bell and Howell and its subsidiary University Microfilms (UMI) publish on-going indexes, mostly dating from the 1970s, for the following newspapers. (These indexes may not help many genealogists now, but they will be useful in years to come.) These books contain a personal name index at the back and do include obituaries, listed under *deaths*, with abstracts and references for the issue date, section, page number, and column number.

Atlanta Constitution and *Journal Constitution*	(from 1962) *New Orleans Times-Picayune*
Baltimore Sun and *Evening Sun* (1819-1951, microfilm)	*The New York Times* (from 1851) *New York Times Tribune*
Barron's	(1875-1906,
Black Newspaper Index	microfilm)
Boston Globe	*St. Louis Post-Dispatch*
Chicago Sun Times	*San Francisco Chronicle*
Chicago Tribune	*USA Today* and its Asian
Christian Science Monitor (from 1945)	edition *Wall Street Journal* (from
Denver Post	1955)
Detroit News	*Washington Post*
Houston Post	*Washington Times*
Los Angeles Times	*Washington Star News*
Minneapolis Star and Tribune	(1894-1973, microfilm)
National Observer	

MAPS

Maps are essential tools for the study of history and genealogy. Every genealogist needs a road map or atlas of the state(s) and counties of research interest. In addition, historical atlases provide much interesting information about each region and its social, economic, religious, political, and military history. Most research libraries have map collections. Many government map publications can be found in libraries that are government documents depositories, and many maps can be purchased. What kinds of maps are available, and how can they aid in a genealogical search?

Maps, of course, help locate places. This is their primary function in genealogy: to locate cemeteries where ancestors might be buried and to learn where ancestors lived, worked, or worshipped. Finding such places is often the key to discovering further information: learning where to look for records, locating a tombstone, meeting old-timers who may know something about the family, finding an actual house where ancestors lived.

Finding and Using Maps

Some of the most useful maps are the general highway maps of each county, published by state highway or transportation departments in cooperation with the United States Department of Transportation, Federal Highway Administration. Although their comprehensiveness varies from state to state, they often show roads, waterways, communities, rural churches, and cemeteries. (They are extremely useful when one is cemetery hunting.) Rural maps sometimes identify the location of buildings, including residences, but do not name landowners. To buy these maps for the states you search, you can locate the proper agency in each state through a guide such as *The National Directory of State Agencies* (Gaithersburg, MD: Cambridge Information Group Directories, Inc., 1989 or later edition) available in library reference sections.

Government Maps

Other helpful maps for locating cemeteries and sites of ancestral residences, as well as for understanding how geography might have affected ancestors' lives, are topographic maps, made from aerial photographs by the United States Geological Survey (USGS). These maps show longitude and latitude designations, waterways, roads and trails, cemeteries, elevations, some vegetation, communities, and the location of buildings at the time the map was made. Like the general high-

way maps, these do not name individual residences or land owners.

The topographic maps may be used at the government documents depositories that receive the published maps of the USGS. The maps may be purchased from the USGS Map Distribution, P.O. Box 25286, Federal Center, Building 810, Denver, CO 80225 or from the many commercial map sellers around the country. Map depository libraries and map retailers in each state are listed in the *Catalog of Topographic and Other Published Maps* for each state. These catalogs are free on request from the USGS.

The topographic maps are only one kind of map that can be located through the *Monthly Catalog of Government Publications*. (See chapter eight.) By looking for a place name, such as a river or county, in this index, you can sometimes find maps issued by various government agencies, such as the USGS, the Corps of Engineers, the Forest Service, the Soil Conservation Service, or the National Oceanic and Atmospheric Administation (NOAA). Maps published by these agencies often show landmarks, cemeteries, schools, and the location, not names, of individual residences.

One genealogical use of such maps is illustrated by Texas genealogist Gay Carter. Her plotting of references from land records on a grid map of Jackson County, Alabama, suggested that the ancestral Glasscock property near Bridgeport was in the Tennessee River. Many maps indicate an island in that location, and some do not. Gay used the *Monthly Catalog* to find a U.S. Corps of Engineers navigation chart of the Tennessee River and identify Long Island (now Bridgeport Island) as the ancestral residence, mostly in Alabama with a tip in Tennessee. Such navigation charts have been published for other rivers including the Cumberland, Allegheny, Ohio, and Mississippi.

It is sometimes possible to find individual family residences or property identified on maps. Especially in the North and Midwest, the late nineteenth and early twentieth centuries saw the publication of comprehensive county atlases. These often show private land ownership, sometimes with boundary lines. *Railroad Maps of North America: The First Hundred Years*, by Andrew M. Modelski (Washington, DC: Library of Congress, 1984) contains many kinds of maps. Like county atlases, some of these maps are dotted with towns and villages. Some picture boundaries of individual tracts of land, and some name individual family residences. An excellent example in this book (page 9) is the Winchester-Potomac area of Virginia in 1832. The map shows many family homes as well as taverns, stores, churches, and other landmarks.

Such maps, made at the time the family lived in that location, can help determine if they lived near other relatives or who their nearest neighbors were. A very valuable research tool of this kind for early South Carolina is *Mills' Atlas*. The surveys for the atlas were made largely in 1819 and 1820 with some additions before publication in 1825. Each county map shows creeks and rivers, roads, churches, mills, stores, fords, ferries, and family residences in the rural areas at the time the map was made. The Chesterfield County map aided in the search for a wife's maiden name by identifying nearest neighboring families. (See chapter two.) The atlas has been printed several times, including the edition by Robert Pearce Wilkins and John D. Keels, Jr., Columbia, South Carolina, 1965. It is available at many research libraries.

Another good source for finding family residences, again in limited locations and time frame, is *The Official Atlas of the Civil War*.[8] The very helpful index to the atlas is *Civil War Maps: A Graphic Index to the Atlas to Accompany the Official Records of the Union and Confederate Armies*, Noel S. O'Reilly *et al.*, comp. (Chicago: Newberry Library, 1987.) This book is arranged alphabetically by state but with maps showing each area of the state that is covered by the plates in the atlas. Many of the maps cover small enough areas that individual family residences are labeled, as well as ferries, fords, and other landmarks that often carry the owner's name.

The *Territorial Papers* and *American State Papers: Public Lands* contain scattered maps. An early Missouri map, about 1816, appears in Volume XV (p 118). Although it does not specify individual residences, it too shows some ferries, villages, and courthouses, whose names may be the same as the families who established them.

Land ownership maps can be very helpful in searching for ancestral residences if such a map exists for the area and time you need. Consult abstract companies in your research area for availability of such maps in their files. General land offices in the various states may be another source of these maps, and most research libraries and archives have map collections. Another source is *Land Ownership Maps: A Checklist of Nineteenth Century United States County Maps in the Library of Congress*, by Richard W. Stephenson, comp. (Washington, DC: Library of Congress, 1967).

The book lists about 1,450 county land ownership maps, mostly in the Northeast and Midwest, along with good coverage of Virginia, California, and Texas. Copies of these maps may be ordered from the Photoduplication Service at the Library of Congress, specifying the county name, date and map entry number from Stephenson's book.

Most maps, of course, do not show family residences, but you can use standard sources for clues and identify the locations on current maps. For ancestors who lived in public land states where land was surveyed and sold in ranges, townships, and sections, you can obtain maps with these divisions already on them. Using deeds and other land records, you can plot fairly accurately where the family property was. If you can find such a map that also shows roads, you can more easily visit the site. However, you may have to make combined use of several maps to find the correct place. When deed records show rural property descriptions by metes and bounds, locating the site may be a little harder. With county atlases, abstract company maps, topographic and other maps, it is possible to pinpoint an ancestral home site. Texas researcher Gay Carter used family tradition, deed records, and a NOAA nautical map to locate the actual house where her Glas(s)cock ancestors had lived on Virginia's Northern Neck.

For ancestors who lived in a town or city, you can also plot on a city map information gained from other sources, such as deeds and city directories. When a deed record describes a piece of city property with block and lot number, you can often find maps in the courthouse, city hall, or abstract company files to show you the exact location and allow you to visit the site. Perhaps you can see the very house in which the family lived or the buildings where they worked. Even if the residence or workplace no longer stands, a Sanborn fire insurance map (see chapter six) may show you characteristics of the original building or changes made over the years. These may also give you an understanding of the immediate neighborhood, which you cannot get any other way. Remember that city streets sometimes have name changes. You may have to consult period maps as well as current maps to find a particular street address.

Finding a family residence on a county or city map can also help narrow the search for cemeteries in which family members may be buried or churches and schools they might have attended. The reverse could also prove helpful. If you know a cemetery in which family members are buried or a church the family attended, chances are they lived nearby at one time.

The use of city maps in conjunction with city directories can help find families in urban censuses. (See example in chapter two.) The same principle could be applied to a rural area if the searcher knows the name of a community near the family and can use township or county maps to narrow the area of the census in which to search.

Combining knowledge of a family's residence with the history of county boundary changes can tell you whether the family moved from one county to another or whether the family stayed in one place but became part of a newly created county. Knowing which counties surround an ancestor's residence gives you additional courthouses in which to look for deeds, marriage records, and the like, and in which to look for other relatives. A family who lived near a county line or state line often had relatives or records in that neighboring county or state or sometimes appeared in the newspaper of the neighboring area. Standard road maps and atlases can give you current county boundaries. Abstract companies in your research area may have the most specific records of boundary changes. Published references that can help you with historical county boundaries, boundary and name changes, and parent counties include these:

Atlas of Historical County Boundaries: Mississippi, John H. Long; ed. (New York: Simon and Schuster, Academic Reference Division, 1993). Volumes also available for New York; New Hampshire and Vermont; and Maine, Massachusetts, Connecticut, and Rhode Island. Volumes planned for the forty-eight contiguous states and Hawaii. Contact the publisher at (212)373-7353.

The Handy Book for Genealogists, George B. Everton, Sr., ed. (Logan, UT: The Everton Publishers, Inc., latest edition. 7th ed., 1981). County map of each state, list of county formation dates and parent counties.

Historical Atlas and Chronology of County Boundaries, 1788-1980, John H. Long, ed. (Boston, MA: G.K. Hall, 1984), 5 vols. covering the states of Delaware, Illinois, Indiana, Iowa, Maryland, Missouri, Minnesota, Michigan, New Jersey, North Dakota, Ohio, Pennsylvania, South Dakota, Wisconsin.

Historical U.S. County Outline Map Collection,

1840-1980 (Baltimore: University of Maryland Department of Geography).

Map Guide to the United States Federal Censuses, 1790-1920, by William Thorndale and William Dollarhide (Baltimore: Genealogical Publishing Company, 1987). An excellent guide to boundary changes and how they affected the census.

A Series of County Outline Maps of the Southeastern United States for the Period 1790-1980 (Chapel Hill, NC: University of North Carolina Department of Geography, 1973).

Maps often show roads and railroads in addition to waterways and mountain ranges. All of these features can help you determine ancestors' possible migration routes or nearest market towns. In addition, maps dealing with migrations, frontiers, and territorial development can be found in many history books and historical atlases. Additional sources that can aid in one's understanding of migration routes and frontiers are these:

Atlas of Early American History: The Revolutionary Era, 1760-1790, Lester J. Cappon et al., ed. (Princeton, NJ: Princeton University Press, for Newberry Library, 1976). Maps showing towns, Indian villages, counties in 1790, churches, Masonic lodges, taverns, ferries, schools and other aspects of economic and cultural life; some city maps as well.

The Development of Early Emigrant Trails in the United States East of the Mississippi River, by Marcus W. Lewis (Washington, DC [now Arlington, VA]: National Genealogical Society, 1933).

Maps Showing Explorers' Routes, Trails, and Early Roads in the United States: An Annotated List, Richard S. Ladd, comp. (Washington, DC: Library of Congress, 1962). Indexed.

Maps can sometimes help determine name changes of towns and villages. Historical atlases, historical travelers' maps and guidebooks, county maps, and others can indicate, for example, that Martinsville, Missouri, became Platte City, and Arkapolis, Arkansas, became Little Rock.

Part of the challenge for genealogists is finding the location of ancestral communities that no longer appear on road maps or county maps. How does one find Sunflower, New Hope, or Hard Times, Louisiana, supposedly in Franklin Parish, where an ancestor lived in the 1870s? (1) Searching contemporary maps and gazetteers wherever you can find them. (2) Talking to old-timers in the county or parish. (3) Comparing census and other information on families in the community with deed and plat book records, and plotting this data on a grid map of the county. (4) Reading local and county histories. (5) Searching postal directories, mail routes, postal route maps. (Some communities, of course, did not have post offices.) (6) Consulting the Geographic Names Information System (GNIS) and related databases. (See below.)

The Post Office Department Reports of Site Locations, 1837-1950 (National Archives microfilm series M1126) are forms, diagrams, and homemade maps sent to the department when a post office was established or moved. They were meant to identify the location of that post office, whether by township, range, and section or in relation to other landmarks, such as stores or houses. Most of the reports are post-Civil War, and some are for communities that no longer exist.

The GNIS of the USGS provides a service to the public to help locate place names and geographic features. A twenty-five year project began in 1976 to find such places on maps of all kinds, old and new, and to create a huge database. The information that you can gain from this database includes the name, former names, and the location of every kind of feature except roads and commercial establishments. One exception to the noncommercial rule is the inclusion of ferries, fords, stores, mills, boat landings, and the like on old maps. If you are having trouble finding a particular cemetery, church, or landmark in an ancestral area, or if you are trying to locate a community or other feature that no longer exists, contact the GNIS for assistance. Remember that the project is not yet complete but is well underway. A small fee could provide a more extensive search, such as complete listings for cemeteries or churches in a given county. You can reach the GNIS by mail at US Geological Survey, Branch of Geographic Names, 523 National Center, Reston, VA 22092, and by telephone at (703) 648-4544.

A research facility heavily involved in developing the GNIS database is the Map Library at the University of Alabama (P.O. Box 870322, Tuscaloosa, AL 35487). Their map collection is, of course, open to searchers, but they have recently abstracted database information that has not yet been entered into the GNIS in Reston. The search for Sunflower, New Hope, and Hard Times has received a considerable boost through their database. They were able to identify on topographic maps of Franklin Parish, Louisiana, and give us exact latitude and longitude locations for a Sunflower Cemetery and

New Hope Church in this mostly rural parish. These do not seem to appear on the highway department map and are not named there. Of course, cemeteries and churches on a map are often remnants of a community that once was in the same location. No place called Hard Times has yet shown up in Franklin Parish. However, on both a topographic map and some antique maps, a Hard Times Bend appears on the Mississippi River in neighboring Tensas Parish. It may well be that the ancestor in question did move for a short period to the neighboring parish, or that the community he called Hard Times in Franklin Parish simply has not been identified yet. Nevertheless, the search can now continue around the other two localities.

Another source for identifying defunct communities, double names, or possible name changes is Bullinger's Postal and Shippers Guides, published since 1871. This Westwood, New Jersey, company issued a centennial reprint of *The Monitor Guide to Post Offices and Railroad Stations in the United States and Canada-1876* in 1976. (Copies were still available in 1993.) This guide lists alphabetically hundreds of communities and towns that were post offices and/or railroad stations, with their county and state locations. Thus, communities that had neither post office nor railroad station are not included. The guide also distinguishes between post offices and railroad stations in the same place if their names are different. For example, Youngsville in Franklin County, North Carolina, is listed with a double name. Youngsville, as it is called today, was the railroad station name in 1876. At that time, its post office was called Pacific. In Prince George's County, Maryland, today's Oak Grove was then the post office name, with Brick Church as its railroad station. Spelling variations are not a new problem. This guide cautions, "If you do not find the place for which you are looking, try some other way of spelling the name, and look again."

Bibliography—A Sampling

The following additional publications may help you find maps in the Library of Congress and other collections. Some of the Library of Congress maps are available from the photoduplication service.

Alaska and the Northwest Part of North America, 1588-1898: Maps in the Library of Congress, P. Lee Phillips, comp. (Washington, DC: Government Printing Office, 1898).

Atlas of the American Revolution (Chicago: Rand

McNally, 1974). Has some city maps and a few that show family residences.

Checklist of Printed Maps of the Middle West to 1900, Robert W. Karrow, Jr., ed. (Chicago: Newberry Library, 1981-1983), 14 vols.

Civil War Maps: An Annotated List of Maps and Atlases in the Library of Congress, Richard W. Stephenson, ed. (Washington, DC: Library of Congress, 1989, 2nd ed.). Indexed.

Civil War Maps in the National Archives, Charlotte M. Ashby, et al., comp. (Washington, DC: National Archives, 1986, revised ed.).

Detroit and Vicinity Before 1900: An Annotated List of Maps, Alberta G.A. Koerner, comp. (Washington, DC: Library of Congress, 1968). Arranged chronologically.

A Genealogical and Historical Atlas of the U.S.A., by E.K. Kirkham (Salt Lake City: E.K. Kirkham, 1976).

Geography and Map Division: A Guide to its Collections and Services (Washington, DC: Library of Congress, 1975, revised edition). Includes fire insurance, railroad, county maps, etc.

Guide to U.S. Map Resources (Chicago: American Library Association, 1990).

A Handy Guide to Record Searching in the Larger Cities of the United States, by E.K. Kirkham (Logan, UT: Everton Publishers, 1974). Includes city maps with ward boundaries.

The Historical Atlas of United States Congressional Districts, 1789-1983, Kenneth C. Martin, ed. (New York: The Free Press, division of Macmillan, 1982).

A List of Geographical Atlases in the Library of Congress, Philip Lee Phillips et al., comp. (Washington, DC: Government Printing Office, 1909-1992), 9 vols., Annotated, indexed.

A List of Maps of America in the Library of Congress, P. Lee Phillips, comp. (Washington, DC: Government Printing Office, 1901). Includes states, counties, cities. Alphabetical by place name.

A List of Nineteenth Century Maps of the State of Alabama, Sara Elizabeth Mason (Birmingham, AL: Birmingham Public Library, 1973).

The Map Catalog (New York: Vantage Press, division of Random House, 1990).

Map Collections in the United States and Canada: A Directory (New York: Special Libraries Association, 1984, 4th edition).

Maps Relating to Virginia in the Virginia State Library and Other Depositories of the Commonwealth, Earl G. Swem, ed. (Richmond, VA: Virginia State Library, 1914).

The National Gazetteer: A Geographical Dictionary of the United States, by L. De Colange (London: Hamilton, Adams and Company, 1884).

Panoramic Maps of Anglo-American Cities: A Checklist of Maps in the Collections of the Library of Congress, Geography and Map Division. John R. Hebert, comp. (Washington, DC: Library of Congress, 1974).

Township Atlas of the United States, John L. Androit, comp. (McLean, VA: Androit Associates, 1977). Shows villages in townships.

Ward Maps of United States Cities: A Selective Checklist of Pre-1900 Maps in the Library of Congress, Michael H. Shelley, comp. (Washington, DC: Library of Congress, 1975). Covers thirty-five cities.

The West Point Atlas of American Wars, Volume I, 1689-1900, Vincent J. Esposito, ed. (New York: Praeger Publishers, 1959). Some of the Civil War maps show family residences.

A useful reference guide is *Maps Can Help You Trace Your Family Tree: How to Use Maps in Genealogy*, published by the USGS (updated 1991), free upon request from the USGS, and available at many government documents depositories.

MANUSCRIPT COLLECTIONS

Manuscript means *handwritten*, and this is often the content of many special collections. Manuscript collections frequently contain a great variety of items in small and large groupings, especially family, business, and organization papers. Larger groupings may have special catalogs to help searchers identify and access their contents. Many libraries and archives have some form of manuscript collection that pertains to their geographical area.

Locating the Collections

Identifying a manuscript collection to visit can be done in several ways. One is to consult the *National Union Catalog of Manuscript Collections,* discussed in chapter eight. As a follow-up to this source, you can write to the individual library for a more specific catalog of a particular collection. Sometimes the holding library will send copies of manuscripts for a small fee.

A handy source for surveying manuscript collections in your state of interest is the *Guide to Archives and Manuscripts in the United States*, Philip M. Hamer, ed. (New Haven, CT: Yale University Press, 1961, for the National Historical Publications Commission). This volume is arranged alphabetically by state and city and is indexed. It is a description of holdings for over one thousand institutions, including state archives and historical societies, research and public libraries, and museums. A revised and updated version, covering over forty-five hundred repositories is *The Directory of Archives and Manuscript Repositories in the United States* (Phoenix: Oryx Press, 1988, 2nd edition).

If you have access to online search through Online Computer Library Center (OCLC) or Research Libraries Information Network (RLIN), you may be able to identify a collection that contains material pertinent to your search. Many libraries are members of OCLC, which has in its database all kinds of books and materials on many subjects. OCLC (Dublin, Ohio) has published *A Guide to Special Collections in the OCLC Database*, by Philip Schieber, et al., comp. (Dublin, OH: OCLC, 1988).

RLIN is available to members of Research Library Group (Mountain View, California) and to members of CLASS (Cooperative Library Agency for Systems and Services, San Jose, California). Searches can be made by subject, author, title, or type of document, such as *diary*.

The National Inventory of Documentary Sources (NIDS) is a product of Chadwyck-Healey Company (Alexandria, Virginia) and includes actual catalogs, indexes, and other finding aids to help searchers learn more about particular collections, including those in federal depositories. NIDS is available to members on microfiche and CD-ROM.

Of course, you can contact libraries in your research area to find out what manuscript collections they have. The advantage of the computerized databases is that they can help you find materials pertinent to your search in many parts of the country where you might not think to look. The disadvantage of the computerized databases is that they are not accessible to each of us. The following is a sampling of bibliographies on manuscript collections:

Civil War Manuscripts: A Guide to Collections in the Manuscript Division of the Library of Congress, John R. Sellers, comp. (Washington, DC: Library of Congress, 1986).

A Guide to Major Manuscript Collections Acces-

sioned and Processed by the Library of the Western Reserve Historical Society Since 1970, by Kermit J. Pike (Cleveland: Western Reserve Historical Society, 1987).

A Guide to the Manuscripts and Archives of the Western Reserve Historical Society, by Kermit J. Pike (Cleveland: Western Reserve Historical Society, 1972).

Manuscript Sources in the Library of Congress for Research on the American Revolution, John R. Sellers et al. comp. (Washington, DC: Library of Congress, 1975).

Manuscripts on Microfilm: A Checklist of the Holdings in the Manuscript Division (Washington, DC: Library of Congress, 1973).

Members of Congress: A Checklist of Their Papers in the Manuscript Division (Washington, DC: Library of Congress, 1980).

Preliminary Listing of the San Francisco Manuscript Collections in the Library of the California Historical Society, by Diana Lachatnere (San Francisco: California Historical Society, 1980).

The University of Texas Archives: A Guide to the Historical Manuscript Collections in the University of Texas Library, Chester V. Kielman, ed./comp. (Austin, TX: University of Texas Press 1967). Indexed.

What is in Manuscript Collections?

What then are you looking for in a manuscript collection? Probably the most useful type of collection for genealogists is family papers, the same types of records that many families keep themselves: diaries, letters, family Bibles, scrapbooks, photographs, deeds, documents, and much more. An example of such a record is the Confederate passport of my ancestor Francis Asbury Mood. I had no idea he had a passport, but the original is in the collection of the Mood-Heritage Museum at Southwestern University in Georgetown, Texas, where this ancestor served as first president. The text of the document is basic:

> *I, the undersigned, Secretary of State of the Confederate States of America, hereby request all whom it may concern, to permit safely and freely to pass F.A. Mood, a Citizen of the Confederate States, and in case of need, to give him all lawful Aid and Protection. Given under my hand . . . this 11th day of January A.D. 1865.*

The fascinating part is Mood's signature and physical description: age 34, 5 feet 8 inches in height, with high forehead, hazel eyes, Roman nose, small mouth, round chin, brown hair, fair complexion, and oval face.

Another source in manuscript collections is diaries, many of which have been published. Bibliographies of these works include the following:

American Diaries, Laura Arksey, et al. comp. (Detroit: Gale Research Company, 1983-1986). Volume 1—diaries written 1492-1844. Volume 2—diaries written 1845-1980. The books include subject, name and geographic indexes.

American Diaries: An Annotated Bibliography of American Diaries Written Prior to the Year 1861, William Matthews, comp. (Berkeley, CA: University of California Press, 1945).

And So to Bed: A Bibliography of Diaries Published in English, by Patricia Pate-Havlice (Metuchen, NJ: Scarecrow Press, 1987). Indexed by name, subject, place. Includes an index to Matthews's work.

In manuscript collections, one can find business papers, which may include ledgers, journals, receipts, employee records, and various files. Lawyers' or doctors' or funeral home records are often good sources of information on other people in the town or area. School and organization papers may include enrollment and membership lists, publications, proceedings of various kinds, memorabilia, and newspaper clippings.

One of the most extensive manuscript collections for early American history is the Draper Manuscripts housed at the State Historical Society of Wisconsin.

These are largely letters, documents, and notes collected by Lyman Copeland Draper throughout the nineteenth century on the South and trans-Allegheny West. The collection has been divided into fifty series, representing such topics as Frontier Wars, Kentucky, King's Mountain, Revolutionary Pension Statements, North Carolina, Virginia, Tennessee, and South Carolina, and papers of Daniel Boone, George Rogers Clark, Thomas Sumter, Potter family, and others. A *Guide to the Draper Manuscripts* by Josephine L. Harper (Madison, WI, 1983) is available from the Wisconsin Historical Society.

Calendars of manuscript collections list the documents with brief descriptions. At least nine calendars, some with indexes, are available for portions of the Draper Manuscripts. McDowell Publications has hardbound copies. Chadwyck-Healey carries them in microfiche as well as microfilm copies of the collection. (See Appendix E for addresses.) Many university and research libraries around the country have complete sets of the microfilm copies. In addition, public libraries who own sets include Birmingham and Huntsville (Alabama); Carlsbad (California); Denver; Fort Wayne-Allen County (Indiana); New York City; Charlotte (North Carolina); Cincinnati-Hamilton County (Ohio); Memphis-Shelby County and Knox County (Tennessee); and Dallas and Houston-Clayton.

The nature of manuscript collections means that they vary both in content and in usefulness to a given search. However, they are well worth investigating, both for the social history and fascinating reading they contain and for the potential of genealogical clues and information.

Footnotes are on page 175.

CHAPTER EIGHT

Libraries

PART I — PUBLIC, PRIVATE, AND UNIVERSITY LIBRARIES

Public, private, and university libraries often own research materials that are valuable for genealogists. These collections may include books and periodicals on historical or genealogical subjects, local history collections, vertical files of genealogical information, and reference materials that aid the searcher in finding information. Many of these libraries also have local or regional manuscript, map, and newspaper collections and documents from federal or state governments. Regardless of the size of their collections, libraries are worth a visit. The major libraries have enough material to keep researchers busy for weeks or months. They make wonderful excuses for extended vacations.

In addition to local public and university libraries, genealogists are fortunate to have available the huge national public library, the Library of Congress, and a number of private (not government-funded) libraries that have large historical and genealogical collections. Some of the private institutions that are major research facilities are the Library of the Daughters of the American Revolution (Arlington, Virginia), the Newberry Library (Chicago), the Filson Club Library (Louisville, Kentucky), the New England Historic Genealogical Society (Boston), the American Antiquarian Society (Worcester, Massachusetts), the Confederate Research Center (Hillsboro, Texas), and the Family History Library of the Church of Jesus Christ of Latter-day Saints (Salt Lake City, Utah).

To find out about libraries in your own area or your research area, consult William P. Filby's *Directory of American Libraries with Genealogy and Local History Collections* (Wilmington, DE: Scholarly Resources, 1988). The *American Library Directory* (New Providence, NJ: R.R. Bowker, division of Reed Publishing, latest edition, 2 vols.) is organized by state and city and mentions collections such as genealogy or local

history that those libraries reported. This directory does not always include archives.

When visiting libraries, genealogists want to find books and periodicals with abstracts or marriage records, deeds, wills, and newspaper articles; family and county histories; and census and cemetery records. These sources are most often found in genealogy libraries, but many libraries have such materials. In fact, these are not the only sources that contain genealogical information and the historical studies that place ancestors in the perspective of their time and place.

History is a large category in many libraries, and each state, region, and territorial possession of the United States has its own section of shelves with books and scholarly journals pertaining to its history. For instance, one rather typical university library, far from Pennsylvania, contains several sections of shelving that are dedicated to books on historical topics in Pennsylvania, including books of letters, personal papers, diaries, biographies, town and state histories, and passenger lists. The ethnic and social histories include a wide range of subject matter of interest to genealogists working on Pennsylvania ancestors, such as the Irish, Jews, and African-Americans in Philadelphia, Slovak Catholics and Lutherans in Pittsburgh, the Moravian town of Bethlehem, and the Scots-Irish of Colonial Pennsylvania.

Many libraries have local or regional history collections that contain genealogical materials. Such a collection may also include a vertical file that contains folders on families of the area. These folders can hold letters, documents, scrapbooks, photographs, Bible records, family group charts, newspaper articles, obituaries, and other information on family members. Such a file may help you take your family back several generations, may help you find living family members who can share information, and is certainly a way for you to share with other searchers what you have collected and documented. Even if you cannot leave materials for the vertical file while you are visiting a library, you can send information at any time and ask that it be placed in the vertical file under the family name.

If your local public library does not have a genealogical vertical file, perhaps you can help form one. After all, family records make a valuable complement to public records, and the public library is a central, accessible location for such information to be kept. In fact, two especially successful research days stand out in my mind because of vertical files on local families, one in the city of Wilmington, Delaware, and one in the very small town of Alto, Texas.

Special Reference Materials

Libraries contain many kinds of reference materials. Some, such as encyclopedias and dictionaries, are particularly useful for finding specific information on a given subject. Bibliographies, on the other hand, help locate books and materials that aid in your search. Two groups of these bibliographic sources are especially helpful to genealogists and historians. The first group is references that help you find materials in individual libraries: library catalogs and union catalogs. The second group assists you in finding materials on a given subject: subject bibliographies, and indexes and abstracts.

Library Catalogs. One of the most helpful bibliographic sources in any library is, of course, the card catalog, or library catalog, as it more properly called now that it is often on computer rather than on cards. This library catalog is a type of bibliography that lists, ideally, all the materials in a given library, or division of a library, by subject, author, and title. As more libraries are converting their catalogs to computer, patrons are often faced with an out-of-date card catalog, sometimes still in use, and an incomplete computerized catalog that contains only a portion of the materials in the library. In addition, the computerized systems often require patrons to think very creatively to find materials on a given subject. If you cannot find what you need using a subject search, ask whether the system can do a keyword search. Nevertheless, patrons should consult both card and computer catalogs when possible and ask for help from a librarian when necessary.

Some library catalogs have been published as reference guides not only to in-house patrons but also to those who live elsewhere and may wish to visit, request a copy of something, or borrow materials on interlibrary loan. Catalogs may cover an entire library or a particular collection within the library. Examples of such published catalogs are the following:

Daughters of the American Revolution, Library Catalog (Washington, DC: National Society of the DAR, 1982-; vol 2, additions; vol. 3 lists book additions from 1985-1991). Note that the DAR Library does not participate in interlibrary loan.

Denver Public Library, Catalog of the Western History Department (Boston: G.K. Hall & Co., 1970), 7 vols. plus supplements.

Descriptive Inventory of the Archives of the State of Illinois, by Victoria Irons and Patricia C. Brennan (Springfield, IL: Illinois State Archives, 1978).

Dictionary Catalog of the Local History and Genealogy Division of the New York Public Library (Boston: G.K. Hall & Co., 1974), 18 vols.

Some subject bibliographies for large collections may be considered catalogs in the broad sense because they list books available in a particular place even though these books deal with only one collection of the overall holdings. Some examples include the following:

Bibliographic Guide to Black Studies (Boston: G.K. Hall & Co., annual), supplements to *Dictionary Catalog* of New York Public Library's Schomburg Collection, below. The company also publishes Bibliographic Guides in North American History, Maps and Atlases, and Microform Publications.

The Black Experience: A Guide to Afro-American Resources in the Florida State Archives (Tallahassee, FL: Florida Department of State, Division of Library and Information Services, Bureau of Archives and Records Management, 1988, reprinted 1991).

Dictionary Catalog of the Schomburg Collection of Negro Literature and History in the New York Public Library (Boston: G.K. Hall & Co., 1962, supplements 1967 & 1972), 9 vols.

Genealogical Material and Local Histories in the St. Louis Public Library, by Georgia Gambrill (St. Louis: St. Louis Public Library, 1966, supplement 1971).

A Genealogist's Guide to the Allen County Public Library, by Karen B. Cavanaugh (Watermill, IN: Allen County Public Library, 1989).

Genealogy: A Guide to the University of California Berkeley Library, by Barbara Lee Hill, Patricia A. Davison, ed. (Berkeley, CA: The Library Associates, The General Library, 1984).

Guide to Civil War Records in the North Carolina

Archives (Raleigh, NC: North Carolina Archives, 1966).

Guide to Genealogical Notes and Charts in the Archives Branch, Virginia State Library and Archives, Lyndon H. Hart III, comp. (Richmond, VA: Virginia State Library, 1988).

Guide to Local and Family History at The Newberry Library, by Peggy Tuck Sinko (Salt Lake City: Ancestry Publishing, 1987). (The Newberry Library is in Chicago.)

Local History and Genealogy Resources of the California State Library, Gary E. Strong, ed. (Sacramento, CA: California State Library Foundation, 1991).

Preliminary Guide to Pre-1904 County Records in the Archives Branch, Virginia State Library and Archives, Suzanne S. Ray, et al., comp. (Richmond, VA: Virginia State Library, 1987).

Preliminary Guide to Pre-1904 Municipal Records in the Archives Branch, Virginia State Library and Archives, Lyndon H. Hart and J. Christian Kolbe, comp. (Richmond, VA: Virginia State Library, 1987).

Virginia Genealogy: A Guide to Resources in the University of Virginia Library (Charlottesville, VA: University of Virginia Press, 1983).

Many libraries have finding aids that are mini-catalogs showing the library's holdings on a particular subject, such as military records, immigration and passenger lists, census records, county records, or periodicals. In libraries with open stacks and microform files, many finding aids provide the call numbers and location within the library. Finding aids are most often found at reference areas in the library. They may be published, in notebook binders, or on microfiche. Ask for information about finding aids at the reference desk.

Browsing, fortunately, is permitted in many libraries. It may not be time-efficient, but it can help make up for gaps in the cataloguing system or holes in the searcher's work list for the day. Besides, it is fun and often rewarding. Appendix B of this book lists Dewey Decimal and Library of Congress call numbers for many of the materials that genealogists use. These are given to help you browse. This wandering in the stacks does not take the place of using the library catalog but can help you find things you may not know to look for and might not find otherwise. I still remember the delight I felt while browsing in one university library. While hurrying down an aisle of history books with a call number in hand, looking for something else, I spotted a book of eighteenth-century passenger lists that I had not seen before. Thank goodness for titles on the spines of books. On a lark, I decided to pause long enough to inspect its index and found, much to my surprise, the only ancestor of my own that I have ever found on a passenger list.

Union Catalogs. Another type of bibliography that identifies holdings of particular libraries is union catalogs. These are combined lists of holdings from two or more libraries. This kind of reference can help you find out which libraries own which materials. One such series, the *National Union Catalog* (NUC) (Washington, DC: Library of Congress) lists thousands of books on many subjects in hundreds of libraries. The catalog is most useful for identifying the locations of specific books or works of specific authors, and books are listed alphabetically by author. A separate series lists the same books by subject. Since 1983 this catalog has been issued in microfiche.

More than seven hundred volumes comprise the *National Union Catalog Pre-1956 Imprints*. These books are also arranged alphabetically by author, and the process of using them is the same as for the *National Union Catalog*. When I wanted to find a family history written by a Blakeney in 1928, I pulled the volume covering the *Bl* part of the alphabet. I found the author's full name, correct title, publication information, the Library of Congress card number, and the coded names of other reporting libraries that own the book. The volumes on *Locations* are supplements for both the NUC and *Pre-1956 Imprints*, arranged by Library of Congress card numbers, listing additional libraries that own the books having Library of Congress numbers. (In other words, books without Library of Congress numbers will not be listed in the *Locations* supplements.)

The *National Union Catalog of Manuscript Collections*, or NUCMC (pronounced *nuck-muck*) is probably of greater use to genealogists. It is a series of books describing the contents and location of various manuscript collections around the country. These manuscript collections are often family and business papers that have been given to a library or archives. The contents can include letters, diaries, business ledgers, genealogy notes, Bibles, deeds, memorabilia, and other documents pertaining to a family, business, town, county, school, church, or organization. Because families and businesses do not exist in a vacuum, their papers are likely to include information on or mention of their relatives, friends, neighbors, and business associates. Cluster genealogy becomes important again when you are looking for manuscript collections that may include an elusive ancestor. The ancestor may not have saved letters and documents, but one of his neighbors or cousins might have.

Publication of NUCMC began in 1962, covering cataloguing done from 1959-1961. New volumes are published annually, when possible, to include newly contributed or newly reported collections. Because of the massive nature of the project, there is a time lapse between reporting and publication. The 1991 volume, for example, was issued in the spring of 1993.

Cumulative indexes to date cover these years: 1959-1962, 1963-1966, 1967-1969, 1970-1974, 1975-1979, 1980-1984, 1985, and 1986-1989. In these indexes, the searcher can look for these topics:

1. Surnames to find references to individuals or families.

2. State, city, and county names to find manuscript records pertaining to that locality. Under state names are subheadings such as newspapers, churches, family and personal papers, maps, slavery, vital records, genealogy, organizations and societies, and legal affairs, with further subheadings such as lawyers' and judges' papers.

3. General subject headings such as religious denominations or names of ethnic groups.

4. Specific companies, organizations and institutions, universities and schools, churches, ships, or occupations.

5. Types of records (wills, deeds, etc.), genealogy, and other subject headings. For example, under the topic *Blacksmithing* are references to that occupation in various states, as reflected in the manuscript collections being reported.

Each topic, name, or subheading listed in the index will have a coded number beside it, as in *Emily Ann Steenberg Mitchell (1826-1847) 84-1720*. In parentheses are the life dates of the person named. The *84* refers to the catalog of 1984, and *1720* refers to item number 1720 in that year's list. Turning to the 1984 volume, one finds MS 84-1720 at the head of the entry and the title of the collection: *Mitchell and Barnes family papers, 1791-1911*. This collection, the gift of a family member in 1977, is housed in the Cornell University Library, Department of Manuscripts and Archives, Ithaca, New York. The description of the collection tells that it is chiefly correspondence, legal

documents, daybooks, photos, and clippings. The letters include some to Emily (Minnie) Ann Mitchell, daughter of William L. (1825-1904) and Emily Ann Steenberg Mitchell (1826-1847). The entry lists names and life dates of other family members who were correspondents and the New York counties represented in the collection. Some entries will also tell you whether the collection has a catalog of its own at the repository to help locate specific items quickly.

A useful resource when using NUCMC is a two-volume *Index to Personal Names in the National Union Catalog of Manuscript Collections, 1959-1984* (Alexandria: Chadwyck-Healey, 1988), Vol. 1 — A-K, Vol. 2 — L-Z. The entries in this index are the same as those in the main indexes, but isolate the personal names from place and institutional names and topical references.

If you are planning a visit to a particular city and want to find out about manuscript collections in that city that have been reported in these catalogs, use the Geographical Guide to Repositories at the front of the most recent volume. This reference is alphabetical by state and lists each reporting repository and the year(s) of its reports. You can then refer to the catalog of the year(s) listed, in the alphabetical list of repositories, and find the number of each collection that repository has reported. If a listing in the Geographical Guide sent you to the volume for 1974, and that volume showed 74-1200-1237 with the name of the repository you want to visit, then you would know that items 1200-1237 in the 1974 catalog are descriptions of collections housed in that repository. You can read these descriptions to determine whether you need to plan time during your visit to study them.

Another reference at the front of the NUCMC volumes is a General Guide to Repositories by subject area and by type of repository. Genealogists would probably be most interested in the repositories listed under the subjects *Religion*, *Ethnic Groups*, and *Regional History*. The types of repositories include, for example, college and university libraries, historical societies, museums, public libraries, special libraries, and religious institutions. Under *city archives* in the 1975-1990 list are only three repositories: Baltimore, Maryland; Camden, South Carolina; and Charleston, South Carolina. The only two listed under *county archives* in the same volume are Bexar County, Texas, and Saratoga County, New York. This does not mean that these are the only three cities and two counties with archives collections. It means that these are the only ones reporting descriptions of special collections between 1975 and 1990. Furthermore, NUCMC usually does not report official records housed in archives or courthouses if those records were created there or would ordinarily be found there. The collections reported are those found in more-or-less unexpected places.

Most manuscript collections are limited to use within the repository. You should contact the staff to find out if any of the collection or its catalog are available on interlibrary loan. If they are not, you have a perfect excuse for a vacation.

Another kind of union list of particular interest to genealogists is *American Newspapers, 1821-1936*, Winifred Gregory, ed. (New York: Wilson, 1937, reprint by Kraus Reprint Corp. of Millwood, New York, 1967). This huge volume reports in detail the newspapers held by nearly six thousand repositories in the United States and Canada. As in most books of this kind, the repositories are listed by abbreviations, which are explained at the beginning of the book. The entries themselves are arranged alphabetically by state, within the state by city, and under each city, by title. Under each newspaper title is its frequency, i.e., weekly or daily, its dates of publication, any changes in its name, and which repositories have which dates. For example, I wanted to find out who has copies of the *New York Evening Post* from 1821. The entry shows that existing 1821 copies of this newspaper are scattered among such places as the New York Public Library, New York Historical Society, American Antiquarian Society, Lehigh University, and others.

You also may wish to consult the union catalog *Newspapers in Microform: United States, 1948-1983* (Washington, DC: Library of Congress, 1984). In addition, many states now have or are preparing union lists of newspapers published in their state. See chapter seven for further discussion of newspapers and these finding aids.

The *Union List of Serials in the Libraries of the United States and Canada*, Edna Brown Titus, ed. (New York: H.W. Wilson Co., 1965), lists thousands of periodical publications by state and city. For example, to find out about the *New Orleans Advocate*, I consulted the serials union list and discovered that it was "a weekly journal devoted to Christianity, our country, and literature," published from 1866 to at least 1869, and that Ohio Wesleyan University owns copies.

Union lists on computerized databases are very useful tools for finding materials if a searcher has access to them. The first was OCLC, which began in 1967.

Others include RLIN and Western Library Network (WLN). The original purpose of such computerized systems was to provide uniform cataloguing. A valuable by-product is advanced, efficient assistance with interlibrary loan.

Subject Bibliographies. Whereas library catalogs and union catalogs focus on sources in particular libraries, subject bibliographies as well as indexes and abstracts help identify sources on specific subjects. These reference materials do not always tell you where to find a particular book or article, but they tell you that it exists. When limited to the description of all or part of a particular collection, these guides may also be considered a special kind of library catalog or finding aid. Examples of subject bibliographies useful to genealogists are the following:

The American Colonies in the Seventeenth Century, Alden T. Vaughan, comp. (New York: Appleton-Century-Crofts, Meredith Corporation, 1971).

A Bibliography of American Autobiographies, Louis Kaplan, comp. (Madison, WI: University of Wisconsin Press, 1961). Includes subject index.

A Bibliography of American County Histories, William P. Filby (Baltimore: Genealogical Publishing Company, 1985).

Confederate Imprints: A Check List Based Principally on the Collection of the Boston Athenaeum, Marjorie Lyle Crandall, comp. (Boston: The Boston Athenaeum, 1955), 2 vols.

Confederate Imprints: A Bibliography of Southern Publications from Secession to Surrender (an expansion and revision of Crandall and Harwell, earlier works), T. Michael Parrish and Robert M. Willingham, Jr. (Austin, TX: Jenkins Publishing Co., n.d.).

Documents of the American Revolution, 1770-1783 (Colonial Office Series), K.G. Davies, ed. (Shannon, Ireland: Irish University Press, 1972-1981), 21 vols. Records in the Colonial Office of the Public Records Office, London. Indexed. Calendar and abstracts of documents, 1770-1776. Transcripts of documents, 1775-1783.

Genealogies in the Library of Congress: A Bibliography, Marion J. Kaminkow, ed. (Washington, DC: Library of Congress, 1972, 2 vols., Vol 3 — Supplement, 1972-1976. Reprints of all 3 vols. by Magna Carta Book Co., Baltimore).

Goldentree Bibliographies in American History (Arlington Heights, IL: Harlan Davidson/Forum

Press, 1973). John Hope Franklin compiled the volume on African-American history. John Shy prepared the one on the American Revolution.

Guide to American Indian Documents in the Congressional Serial Set: 1817-1899, Stephen L. Johnson (New York: Clearwater Publishing Co., 1977).

A Guide to Manuscripts Relating to American History in British Depositories, Grace C. Griffin (Washington, DC: Library of Congress, 1946).

Guide to Reprints (Englewood Cliffs, CO: Microcard Editions, 1967-1976; from 1977, published by Guide to Reprints, Inc., P.O. Box 249, Kent, CT 06757). A guide to reprints of books and journals, as reported by publishers; listed alphabetically by author.

More Confederate Imprints (Richmond, VA: Virginia State Library, 1957), 2 vols.

Revolutionary America, 1763-1789: A Bibliography (Washington D.C.: Library of Congress, 1984, 2 vols.) A guide to sources in the Library of Congress.

Travels in the Old South: A Bibliography (1527-1860) and *Travels in the New South: A Bibliography (1865-1955)*, by Thomas D. Clark and *Travels in the Confederate States: A Bibliography (1861-1865)*, by E. Merton Coulter (Norman, OK: University of Oklahoma Press, 1956-1959, 1962, and 1948).

United States Local Histories in the Library of Congress: A Bibliography, Marion J. Kaminkow (Washington, DC: Library of Congress, 1975, 5 vols. Reprint by Magna Carta Book Company, Baltimore, with supplement, 1986).

See chapter nine for bibliographies concerning African-American history and genealogy.

Bibliographies on various aspects of United States history have Library of Congress call numbers in the Z1236-plus range. The American Revolution bibliographies are catalogued under Z1238, and Civil War bibliographies, under Z1242. From Z1251 to about Z1360 are the works on each state, in alphabetical order. For example, Colorado is Z1263; Minnesota is Z1299; and Vermont is Z1343. Bibliographies pertaining to specific ethnic groups are under Z1361. Sometimes you can find very useful materials by browsing in this area of a library.

Books in Print. The kinds of bibliographies mentioned above help searchers find sources in a particular libary or subject area. *Books in Print* (New Providence, NJ: R.R. Bowker, annually) is another kind of resource, one that lists by author, title, or subject books currently available as well as books taken out of print (OP) and those that are out of stock indefinitely (OSI). To find books of genealogical value and interest, look in the subject volumes under state, county, and city names as well as topics such as census, history, genealogy, records, registers, pension, Afro-American, slavery, free Negroes, American Indians, tribal names, and ethnic group names. Publishers' names, addresses, and phone numbers are in the Publishers volume.

The OP-OSI volume lists out-of-print works by title and author but also includes (1) retailers (not a comprehensive list) who sell out-of-print, used, and rare books, along with subjects in which they specialize, such as local or state history, Civil War, the South, or genealogy, (2) search services for finding specific out-of-print publications, and (3) on-demand publishers who can make hard copies or microcopies of out-of-print works, depending on availability and copyright limitations. In libraries, these volumes are usually found in special reference sections or at the reference desk.

Indexes and Abstracts. Indexes and abstracts form another kind of bibliographic source. One of the best-known examples of such an index, though of limited genealogical use, is *Reader's Guide to Periodical Literature* (New York: H.W. Wilson), in publication since 1900. A searcher can look up periodical articles by author, title, or subject and learn the name and issue of the periodical in which the article may be found. This index covers mostly popular magazines and few of the ones genealogists find most useful. However, the subject heading *Genealogy* can lead readers to interesting articles in such magazines as *Life, Hobbies, Ms., House and Garden*, and *Essence*. For older articles, consult *Nineteenth Century Reader's Guide to Periodical Literature, 1890-1899* (New York [now Bronx]: H.W. Wilson, 1944) and *Poole's Index to Periodical Literature, 1802-1906* (Gloucester, MA: Peter Smith, 1963 reprint).

Indexes to Historical and Genealogical Periodicals. A helpful reference that includes both index and abstracts is *America: History and Life* (Santa Barbara, CA: ABC-Clio Information Services). This series began in 1964. From 1955 through 1963, the same kind of information appeared in *Historical Abstracts*, by the same publisher, which is now an index for subjects other than American history. However, *America: His-*

tory and Life now has a Volume Zero that contains an index and more than six thousand abstracts from the years 1954-1963.

Until 1989, each annual edition was divided into four separate publications: (A) abstracts of articles, (B) book reviews, (C) abstracts of dissertations, and (D) index by author, subject, or title. Beginning with Volume 26 (1989), five issues appear each year. Issues 1-3 contain abstracts, reviews, and dissertation citations plus an index to these. Issue 4 contains only abstracts, reviews, and citations, with no index, because it is followed shortly by the annual cumulative subject and author index, with other reference tables. Five-year indexes began in 1964.

Articles mentioned in the index volumes 1-25 have code numbers such as 22A2591. The *22A* means Volume 22, Part A (abstracts of articles), and *2591* is the abstract number. The abstract gives the name, volume, and page numbers of the periodcial in which to find the article.

In this *America: History and Life* index, look first for the names of ancestors or places pertinent to their lives. This is not an every-name index but an index to people, places, and topics that are the subjects of books, articles, or dissertations. Each of these publications is listed under at least four subject headings. For example, in Volume 29 (1992), an article about M. LaRue Harrison was listed under the headings *Arkansas Cavalry*; *First Arkansas, Northwestern*; *Civil War*; and *Unionists*, in addition to his name. Under each heading, the reference was *1219a*. You would look for entry 1219 in Volume 29 for the abstract and journal information needed to find the article. This article is by Diane Neal and Thomas W. Kremm, "An Experiment in Collective Security: The Union Army's Use of Armed Colonies in Arkansas," in *Military History of the Southwest*, Vol. 2, No. 2 (1990), p 169-181.

The *Combined Retrospective Index Set to Journals in History, 1838-1974* [CRIS/History] (Annadel N. Wile, ed., Washington, DC: Carrollton Press, Inc., 1977) is a nine-volume set of indexes covering some 342 subject categories, found in articles in over 240 journals, with two additional volumes of author indexes. The first four volumes deal with world history. Volumes five to nine index first the chronological periods of United States history and then topics in United States history, in alphabetical order, from Agriculture, Antebellum South, and Black History, to individual states, and the West. Most articles appear several times, under different keywords or subject categories. Each reference

gives a journal number with volume and page number where the article can be found. The end pages of each index volume list all these journal numbers and identify the journal names. In our library, the staff has been nice enough to add call numbers beside each journal owned by the library. Many of these journals are publications of state historical societies, universities, and professional associations. Titles include *Quaker History*, *Ohio History*, *Filson Club History Quarterly* (Kentucky), *South Atlantic Quarterly*, *William and Mary Quarterly*, *Virginia Magazine of History and Biography*, *New Jersey History*, *Church History*, and the *Register of the Kentucky Historical Society*.

Of special interest to genealogists is Volume 6, the Biography and Genealogy index. This massive index lists surnames alphabetically, many with given names. This also is not an every-name index but an index to people who are the subjects of articles. References given the same finding information as in the other volumes: journal, volume, and page number where you can find the article. Remember that the index covers periodicals through 1974.

An *American History Periodical Index* was prepared between 1958 and 1968 by Russell L. Knor of River Grove, Illinois, and Joseph A. Huebner of Chicago. These eleven volumes are a "comprehensive cumulation index" of forty-eight quarterlies and journals, largely the historical society journals from most of the states. An amazing accomplishment, this index covers each periodical from its first volume. Because this work was mimeographed rather than printed, its distribution may not be widespread.

Writings on American History is a bibliography that has been published almost annually since 1902. Until 1962, it included books and articles, including many family histories. Since 1962 it has focused only on articles. It groups entries by historical time period, state, and topic, including *genealogy* in some volumes. Volumes are indexed by author and subject. (Its publication history is complicated, including at various times the Government Printing Office, the American Historical Association, KTO Press, the Library of Congress, and Kraus, but the volumes are shelved together in the American History reference section or stacks.)

The extensive *Virginia Historical Index*, often called the Swem Index (by Earl Gregg Swem of the College of William and Mary, originally published 1934, reprint by Peter Smith, Magnolia, MA, 1965) offers comprehensive coverage of a small but important group of periodicals. All are Virginia publications.

William and Mary Quarterly Historical Magazine,
Series 1 and 2 (1892-1930) (most of these volumes available from Kraus Reprint).

Calendar of Virginia State Papers and other manuscript papers in the State Library (1652-1869) (available from Kraus Reprint).

Tyler's Quarterly Historical and Genealogical Magazine (1919-1929) (available from Kraus Reprint).

William Walter Hening's Statutes at Large (1619-1792 laws of Virginia).

Virginia Magzine of History and Biography (1893-1930) (available from Kraus Reprint).

Virginia Historical Register and Literary Advertiser (1848-1853) (available from Reprint Co. Publishers).

Lower Norfolk County Virginia Antiquary (1895-1906).

Many libraries, especially larger or older ones, have these publications, which are a real treasure store for genealogists working in Virginia, Kentucky, West Virginia, and even Maryland and other states. The Swem index is quite comprehensive, including family, individual, business, and place names; events; topic headings such as journals, churches, courts, Indians, academies, marriages, divorce, free Negroes; and a myriad of historical and cultural topics such as clothing, furniture, and even ink powder. Because index entries are spelled as they appear in the text, the searcher should look under variant spellings. In libraries where I have used this index, it is catalogued and shelved with Virginia materials (975.5 or F221).

Several indexes exist for multiple genealogical periodicals, in addition to Swem's *Virginia Historical Index.* One is Donald Lines Jacobus's *Index to Genealogical Periodicals* (New Haven, CT: D.L. Jacobus), a three-volume index to over fifty journals and quarterlies that did not have their own comprehensive indexes:

Volume 1 (1932): issues through 1931.
Volume 2 (1947): 1932-1946, including Revolutionary War and Family Records sections.
Volume 3 (1953): 1947-1952.

The three volumes were combined into one easier-to-use book by Carl Boyer and reissued in 1983. This revised edition is divided into name and place indexes, which give the name of the periodical, volume, and page number where the article may be found.

Maud Quigley of Grand Rapids, Michigan, indexed some ninety periodicals received by the Grand Rapids Public Library into three books (Grand Rapids, MI: Western Michigan Genealogical Society, 1981):

1. *Index to Family Names in Genealogical Periodicals Plus Addenda,*
2. *Index to Hard-to-Find Information in Genealogical Periodicals,* and
3. *Index to Michigan Research Found in Genealogical Periodicals.*

The hard-to-find information in the second volume includes military subjects, migrations, ship passengers, maps and trails, ethnic and religious groups, and headings for individual states. The list of periodicals in each volume tells which years are covered by the index for each journal. The index gives the name of the periodical with volume and issue number, not the page, for each reference.

The *Periodical Source Index* (PERSI) is a project of the Allen County Public Library of Fort Wayne, Indiana, and is available in print or in microfiche. Its basic eight-volume set, published between 1988 and 1990, indexes over two thousand periodicals of the United States and Canada between 1847 and 1985. Annual indexes began in 1986 to cover genealogy and local history publications of each new year. The journals indexed are those received by the Allen County Library, excluding family-name periodicals. Of the basic set, half the volumes index place names; the other half, surnames. (PERSI is not an every-name index.) The place-name indexes for the United States are alphabetical by state, then by county. Many subjects and record types are covered in the indexes, including cemeteries, directories, passenger lists, histories and biographies, naturalizations, maps, obituaries, wills and deeds; and census, church, court, land, military, tax, voter, and probate records. Entries give the volume and year of the journal in which the item appears. The alphabetical list of journal codes appears at the end of the each book. If you need an article from a periodical that your library does not have, you can obtain a copy from the Allen County Library.

Another major index is *Genealogical Periodical Annual Index: Key to the Genealogical Literature,* Laird C. Towle, ed. (Bowie, MD: Heritage Books, annual since 1962). It indexes over 270 periodicals whose publishers subscribe to the service and includes surname, locality, and topical categories. References give the volume, issue number, and beginning page number where the particular article or item may be found, and the periodical list includes addresses of each publisher. If you do not have access to the periodical you need, you can try interlibrary loan or write to its publisher and ask to purchase that issue. Back copies of the GPAI are still in print and available for purchase from Heritage Books.

The *Index to Genealogical Periodical Literature, 1960-1977*, by Kip Sperry (Detroit: Gale Research, 1979, now out of print), is in many libraries. It indexes articles about general and ethnic sources, research procedures, bibliographies, maps, and the like, not persons and places.

Major genealogical and historical periodicals that have published their own comprehensive indexes include the following examples:

Topical Index to National Genealogical Society Quarterly, Volume 1-50 (1912-1962), Carleton E. Fisher, comp. (Arlington, VA: National Genealogical Society, 1964).

The New England Historical and Genealogical Register, Index, Volume 1-50 (Baltimore: Genealogical Publishing Company, 1972 reprint of 1907 original published by the New England Historic Genealogical Society, 4-volume index of persons and subjects). In 1989, Mrs. Jean D. Worden of San Dimas, California, privately published a subject index for volumes 51-142 (1897-1988) of the *New England Historical and Genealogical Register*.

Fifty Year Index to the Mississippi Valley Historical Review, 1914-1964 (Bloomington, IN: Organization of American Historians, 1973).

Genealogical Guide: Master Index of Genealogy in the Daughters of the American Revolution Magazine, Volumes 1-84, 1892-1950 (Washington, DC: DAR Magazine, 1951). An index to volumes 85-89 (1950-1955) was issued in 1956.

Newspaper indexes and other reference materials are discussed in chapter seven.

Computerized Periodical Indexes. Computerized periodical indexes are now in use in many university libraries and businesses and in some public libraries. Most of them deal with financial, legal, business, management, and scientific subject areas, but some do include newspapers and historical journals. At this time, the limitations of these databases outweigh their advantages for most genealogists. First, they are expensive subscription services. Fee structures vary but include annual or monthly fees, which are prohibitive

to the casual or infrequent *individual* user. Those with online availability charge per-use fees in addition to the subscription fees to join the online service through which one can access the index. Second, because of the cost of using the indexes, the *institutions* that do subscribe usually limit their use to staff or students and usually for business-related or academic purposes, not for personal genealogical searches. Third, the periodicals and newspapers that are indexed or abstracted in these databases usually include issues dating back only to the late 1980s when the services began. The companies with whom I have talked admit that they have limited plans or no plans to go into back issues.

For those who have access to them, computerized indexes do include items that could benefit a genealogical search. First, *America: History and Life* is available on CD-ROM or online access through DIALOG. Second, one of the companies that provides several databases is UMI (University Microfilms). Their *Newspaper Abstracts* covers newspapers (including obituaries) from 1989 forward for larger cities such as New York, San Francisco, Boston, Atlanta, Detroit, Houston, Denver, Los Angeles, St. Louis, and Washington. Their *Periodical Abstracts* index covers more than fifteen hundred periodicals in many subject areas. Included are journals of some interest to genealogists, such as *American Heritage, American Historical Review, American History Illustrated, American Indian Quarterly, Canadian Journal of History, Church History, Civil War History, Journal of American History, Journal of Military History, Pacific Historical Review, Southwestern Historical Quarterly, Western Historical Quarterly*, and *William and Mary Quarterly*. The company has several products available, with index only or with text. The services are available as online databases through DIALOG or on CD-ROM.

Another marketer of computerized indexes is Information Access Company, which has both index and full-text databases on CD-ROM or online. Several products are indexes of popular magazines, and the newspaper index covers several large national papers. The *Government Publications Index* covers the Government Printing Office's *Monthly Catalog*, dating back to 1976. *Academic Index* contains indexing and abstracts for more than fifteen hundred periodicals — most of the ones listed above plus such others as *American Jewish History, American West, The Journal of Negro History*, and *Social History*.

For those who need a particular article from a periodical and cannot find it locally or through interlibrary loan, UMI has an Article Clearinghouse, which can sell you copies of articles from thousands of periodicals and newspapers. (They take care of copyright fees and royalties.) There is a base fee with additional fees for fax or rush delivery. Quickest service is for articles published since 1988, but pre-1988 articles are available on many titles. This service is also available for dissertations and master theses. (See Appendix E for address.)

Government Documents

The United States government generates thousands of records each year, and an amazing number of these deal with history, or individuals and events that *will be* history. Many government publications are useful references for genealogists and historians.

Monthly Catalog and Government Publications. The *Monthly Catalog of United States Government Publications* (Washington, DC: Government Printing Office, since 1895) is the index for finding reports, pamphlets, maps, books, manuals, and other publications of the government. The *Catalog* allows a searcher to look for material by author, title, subject, title keyword, series, and various document numbers. Each index reference gives you a number by which you can look up more complete information in the books of entries. For example, *91-22354* means entry number 22354 in the 1991 volumes. That entry will tell you such information as the department or agency issuing the document, whether it is for sale at a government bookstore, whether it is a depository item, and a Government Printing Office number. This is the number under which the document is usually catalogued in the stacks of government documents depositories. The listing begins with a letter that indicates the department issuing the document: *A* for the Department of Agriculture, *I* for the Department of the Interior, *LC* for Library of Congress, *C* for Department of Commerce, and so forth.

Since the *Monthly Catalog* has been published since 1895, it is helpful that cumulative indexes have been prepared, both by the Government Printing Office and by several commercial publishers. Cumulative indexes from 1976 to the present are available on CD-ROM in many libraries.

For genealogists, the most useful items found through the use of the *Monthly Catalog* are maps, histories, National Archives and Library of Congress reference books, and bibliographies of many kinds. Try

looking up place names connected with your ancestor.

The following are examples of publications that could be helpful to genealogists and historians. The first three were published by the Center of Military History, United States Army, Washington, DC.

Commanding Generals and Chiefs of Staff, 1775-1991: Portraits and Biographical Sketches, by William Gardner Bell, 1992.

The Continental Army, by Robert K. Wright, Jr., 1983, part of the Army Lineage series.

The Inspectors General of the United States Army, 1777-1903, by David A. Clary and Joseph W.A. Whitehorne, 1987.

Journals of the Continental Congress, 1774-1789 (Washington, DC: Government Printing Office, 1904-1937), 34 vols. Indexed.

The United States Army in the World War, 1917-1919. 17 vols. (Washington, DC: Government Printing Office, 1948).

Where to Write for Vital Records (Hyattsville, MD: U.S. Department of Health and Human Services, Public Health Service, 1990 or later edition).

United States Serial Set and Indexes. The U.S. Serial Set Indexes (Bethesda: Congressional Information Service, Inc.—not a government agency) are tools to help searchers access many of the Congressional documents generated between 1789 and 1969 from both the House of Representatives and the Senate. These materials do contain information on ancestors. The indexes fall into twelve parts:

Part I—1789-1857	Part VII—1909-1915
Part II—1857-1879	Part VIII—1915-1925
Part III—1879-1889	Part IX—1925-1934
Part IV—1889-1897	Part X—1935-1946
Part V—1897-1903	Part XI—1947-1958
Part VI—1903-1909	Part XII—1959-1969

Each of these parts contains three volumes: Part 1, Subject Index A-K; Part 2, Subject Index L-Z; and Part 3, Finding Lists. The Finding Lists contain an index of names of individuals and organizations receiving private relief and related actions of Congress. Use the Finding Lists to look for ancestors' names. However, these are not every-name indexes to the texts of the documents.

Use the Subject Indexes especially to find documents pertaining to your research area. Look under the state, territory, or other locality name. The index gives the titles of documents, but the titles are not always descriptive of all the material that may be found there. Good examples are the various census records of the islands of St. George and St. Paul in Alaska, which are included in various other reports and indexed without any suggestion of a census. Be alert to titles that mention petitions, name lists, depositions, or other indications that groups of names may be in the text. Some longer documents have their own indexes. Be sure to check the end of the document for such an index.

The coded numbers that accompany each name in the index refer the searcher to the related document. *H.rp.539 (31-1) 585* tells that the information is found in House Report number 539 (from the thirty-first Congress, first session) and may be found in Serial Volume 585. *S.doc.* means Senate document. *H.misdoc.* means House miscellaneous document, and *S.exdoc.* or *H.exdoc.* means an executive document from the corresponding legislative body. Refer also to the user guide at the beginning of each book. The serial number is the key to finding the document quickly, but all the information is necessary once you find the correct serial volume. Some libraries have these volumes in book form; some, in microform.

The *S.doc. 37(17-1)59* to my surprise concerned my ancestor Sterling Orgain, a Tennessee merchant and partner in the firm of Moore and Orgain. From previous research I knew that Alfred Moore and Orgain were brothers-in-law, married to sisters. The document concerning them was indexed in the Finding Lists under both names and yielded an interesting set of events. On 17 September 1818, the two men purchased from one Morris Lindsay an account against the federal government for $120 for blacksmith work. Lindsay had made 120 pairs of horseshoes for the Tennessee volunteer mounted gunmen involved in the Seminole War. Peter Hagner of the Third Auditor's Office, Treasury Department, had refused the claim on the grounds that these soldiers, under an act of 2 January 1795, were given an allowance of forty cents a day to cover their costs, including the use of their horses, arms, and other needs. The government therefore was not responsible for their horseshoes. Orgain and Moore bought the account and re-submitted it as a petition to the Senate for payment. The Senate Claims Committee twice rejected it as well. Finally, in February 1824, the petition was presented a third time and was referred to the Military Affairs Committee. This group differed with the auditor's "most rigid construction" of the 1795 law, saying they could not conceive

that the soldiers were intended by the law to shoe their own horses during their service. "[Nor] can the committee believe that the soldier who defends his country, and fights its battles, should be deprived of his well earned reward, by deductions of this kind, without an express provision to that effect, for it is well known, that shoeing horses and providing those shoes, has uniformly constituted an expenditure of the quartermaster's department." Presenting the supporting evidence and precedence for authorizing such payments, the committee begged leave to present to the Congress a bill for paying the account. That bill passed in May 1824, nearly six years after the original work was done.

Two additional aids for finding information are:

1. *Digested Summary and Alphabetical List of Private Claims Which Have Been Presented to the House of Representatives from the First to the Thirty-First Congress, Exhibiting the Action of Congress on Each Claim with References to the Journals, Reports, Bills, &c, Elucidating its Progress.* Originally compiled by order of the House of Representatives. (Baltimore: Genealogical Publishing Co., reprint, 1970.) Although the bulk of this book deals with claims arising from the Revolutionary War, the volume includes private claims from post-Revolutionary years.

2. *List of Private Claims Brought Before the Senate (Fourteenth through Thirtieth Congress, 1815-1849),* Washington, DC, 1849, Vol. 2, Serial 534. Names are alphabetical.

The company that publishes the Serial Set, Congressional Information Service, also publishes historical indexes to other government materials:

1. *United States Congressional Committee Hearings Index,* early 1800s to 1969.
2. *Unpublished United States Senate Committee Hearings Index,* 1823-1964. Index to personal names. Mostly twentieth-century material.
3. *Unpublished United States House of Representatives Committee Hearings Index,* 1837-1946.
4. *United States Congressional Committee Prints Index,* 1789-1969.
5. *Presidential Executive Orders and Proclamations,* 1789-1983.
6. *United States Supreme Court Records and Briefs,* 1897 to present.
7. *United States Statutes at Large,* 1789 to present.

8. *Congressional Record and Predecessors*, 1789 to present.
9. *United States Congressional Journals*, 1789-1978.

These indexes in book form and the documents themselves are usually found in library documents or reference sections. User guides in each volume explain the coded references.

The *Congressional Record*, the *House Journal*, and the *Senate Journal* are reports of the proceedings of each session of Congress. The Journals are the official documents published at the end of the Session to provide a history of bills, resolutions and procedural matters. They do not include debates. The *Congressional Record* is a daily report published during each session. It includes texts of bills, debates, votes, and anything else that happens on the floor of either house, as well as material added by members for publication that may or may not be related to the business at hand. Apart from an ancestor who was a member of either house and his participation in its proceedings, the genealogist would probably be most interested in the private acts for relief of individuals. The serial set usually is a more comprehensive coverage of these matters than the *Record* or *Journals* because the facts and documents of the case are reproduced in the serial volumes. (See page 127, Public Statutes at Large.)

PART II — LAW LIBRARIES

Law libraries specialize in information pertaining to the legal profession: laws, court decisions, and other reference materials such as professional directories. These collections contain much genealogical information that on the whole has not been abstracted for genealogists but is there for the searching. Universities with law schools have law libraries that are usually open to the public. In addition, many counties have a law library in or near the courthouse.

State Laws

Books of state statutes make up a sizable section of law libraries. Many volumes of these laws have indexes of varying degrees of usefulness, from mere calendars of titles to actual surname, place name, and subject listings. The Swem *Virginia Historical Index* includes Hening's Statutes of Virginia (1619-1792) in its listings, although this index is more likely to be found with history reference materials in a public or university library than in a law library. A very good cumulative

index to H.P.N. Gammel's editions of the laws of Texas is the *Analytical Index to the Laws of Texas, 1823-1905* (Cadwell Walton Raines, Austin: Von Boeckmann-Jones Co., Printers, 1906, reprint by Fred B. Rothman and Company, 1987). This index contains individual names as well as topics, such as relief acts, memorials and petitions, free Africans, adoption, legalizing (certain marriages), legitimating (children), and name changes. Another such index is *A Complete Index to the Names of Persons, Places, and Subjects Mentioned in Littell's Laws of Kentucky* (W.T. Smith, 1931). Such cumulative indexes are quick ways to look for ancestors, extended family, or specific businesses. One working on city or county history would also find such indexes valuable since legislative action did involve city and county boundaries, courts, professional and license fees, officers, businesses, roads and bridges, schools, and other concerns.

Of greatest interest to genealogists is the fact that our state legislatures, like their national counterpart, in almost every session have enacted laws that addressed the needs or wishes of individual citizens in such matters as payment for services rendered to the state, name changes, land titles, financial aid, property and inheritance questions, adoption, marriage, and divorce. These *private acts* or *relief acts* are sometimes indexed separately by subject and name; sometimes they are indexed along with the *public acts*.

In early years, state laws approved name changes. The Mississippi legislature, in January and February 1840, allowed two men to change their names. William Mitchell of Lawrence County became William Mitchell Rayman, and George Washington Grant of Leake County became George Washington Grant Thompson, since he was the son of James J. Thompson. The reader is naturally curious about the circumstances leading to these changes, and often the reason was inheritance, although the records do not always explain. Neither do the published statutes always identify the resident county of the persons named. That information would perhaps be found in the petition that initiated the proceeding.

The same Mississippi legislative session did declare Mariah E. Marley, natural child of Samuel Marley of Yazoo County, to be his legitimate child, entitled to the rights of any other children of whole blood, including the *right to inherit* from her father's estate should he die intestate. The Alabama General Assembly on 9 January 1835 authorized Louisa Blankenship to change her name to McAllister, under which she could inherit property bequeathed to her in the will of Edmund McAllister, deceased, of Lawrence County, on the condition that she would take the name McAllister. Some name changes were also granted in divorce decrees.

State legislatures also addressed the issues of marriage and legitimate children. The first legislature of the state of Texas on April 1846 legalized the marriage of Samuel M. Parry and Elizabeth Neese "as though at the time of the celebration of said marriage no legal disability existed thereto" and made their children, Samuel, Mary, Catharine, Rosand, John, William, David, and Martha, legitimate. Such information furnishes a searcher with a good list of children's and parents' names and the knowledge that these children were all living in 1846. This act does not specify the county of residence or whether Neese was Elizabeth's maiden name or name by a previous marriage.

Adoption was another concern handled by state legislatures. A good example from Texas was the March 1848 act that authorized the name of Zachary Taylor Long, infant (can mean *infant* or simply *young, a minor*) son of Andrew Long, to be changed to Zachary Taylor Winfree and the child to be adopted by Jacob F. Winfree and made "capable of inheriting in the same manner as if the said infant were the lawful child" of J.F. Winfree.

Another special kind of law was for aid and relief of persons in need. The Texas legislature, for example, on 10 April 1901, voted that Mary E. Batchelor, widow of James W. Batchelor, continuing unmarried and in indigent circumstances, was entitled to a pension of $150 a year during her lifetime, to take effect ninety days after adjournment of the session.

In some states, mostly in the years prior to the Civil War, the state legislature had some jurisdiction over divorce. Often the chancery or equity court in each county or district could review the case and issue a decree recommending the dissolution of the marriage, and the legislature had the right of final approval. In some cases, the parties could appeal directly to the legislature. The Alabama Assembly in January and February 1854, granted sixty divorces, and all but two of the cases originated in the Chancery Courts throughout the state. Apart from complete divorce, one option was divorce from bed and board, a legal separation. In January 1834, Laura Bell and Susan Pool, both of Mobile County, Alabama, received this kind of divorce by act of the state legislature. These divorce records found in the laws of the state can be especially useful when a searcher faces a burned courthouse in the county.

In many states women's rights were severely limited, especially in the matter of property rights. The Alabama act for the relief of Elizabeth Jewell, 20 Dec 1837, approved for her the right to acquire, hold, and dispose of separate property as if she were a *feme sole* (single female) and declared that her separate property was not liable for payment of any debts of her husband, Thomas Jewell.

Although many searchers will find the laws enacted by state legislatures of limited genealogical usefulness in searching for their own ancestors, the family historian who wants to know more about the life and times of a given ancestral family will probably want to read laws of the state on crime and punishment, marriage and divorce, taxation, inheritance, women's rights (or the lack of rights), slavery and freedmen, professional and business licensing, and so forth.

Of course, appropriation bills still come before legislatures to determine the budget of the state government. An ancestor who worked for the state would have had his or her salary determined ultimately by the legislature. For example, the list published in the laws of Texas for the Special Session of August 1901, gives the semi-annual salary of each employee, not by name but by job title. The nurses at the Confederate Home were allowed $144 each. Apart from salaries, the governor's office received a six-month appropriation of $18 for ice. Comparing the final enactment with the Senate version published in the *Senate Journal*, shows that one item denied was a request from the Department of Agriculture, Insurance, Statistics, and History for $100 to purchase a "typewriter machine." However, the Senate allowed $5 per month rent for typewriters for the Senate clerks. Is this genealogy? If your ancestors were the employees affected by these decisions, the information adds detail and spice to your family history. If your ancestors lived in the state and paid the taxes that supported these appropriations, you may find this part of state history enlightening and fascinating. If you live in the state currently, you may find that things have not changed very much!

A number of law libraries and university libraries have the entire collection of state and territorial laws, called session laws, on microfiche or in book form. Current publishers of Session Laws include William S. Hein and Company of Buffalo; Law Library Microform Consortium of Hawaii; and UMI of Ann Arbor, Michigan. (See Appendix E for addresses.) If your local library does not have the session laws for your state, perhaps this could be a project for special donations.

A series of laws useful when studying the colonial period of U.S. history is the Colony Laws of North America Series (John D. Cushing, ed., Wilmington, DE: Michael Glazier, Inc., 1978). Sixteen volumes represent the earliest printed laws for Delaware, Georgia, Maryland, Massachusetts, the Pilgrims of New Plimouth (*sic*), New York, New Hampshire, New Haven and Connecticut, New Jersey, North Carolina, Pennsylvania, Rhode Island and Providence Plantations, South Carolina, and Virginia. The volumes are facsimile reproductions of original printed sources.

Public Statutes at Large of the United States

Laws and resolutions passed by the United States Congress as well as ratified treaties to which the United States is a party are collected in the series called *Public Statutes at Large of the United States of America*, from 1789 to the present. For genealogists, again the most valuable part of these publications is the Private Acts passed during each session. Just as citizens of the states appealed to their state legislatures for relief, so citizens of the country called on the Congress for help with personal claims and concerns.

The great majority of these private acts of Congress concern pensions for military service, but some address other concerns. A bill passed on 28 May 1830 for the relief of John Moffitt directed the Treasury Department to ascertain the value of Continental Loan Office Certificate number 104 issued to John Moffitt by the Loan Commissioners of South Carolina and to pay him the sum due on the certificate, excluding interest. An outgrowth of any war is the need for support of families of servicemen killed in the war. An 11 August 1790 act approved an annuity in the amount of seven years' half-pay of a lieutenant colonel to be paid to Frances Eleanor Laurens, the orphan daughter of the late Lieutenant Colonel John Laurens, who was killed while in the service of the United States.[9]

The private acts of Congress fortunately are included in the indexes of the *Public Statutes*. The first eight volumes of the *Public Statutes* cover the period from 1789 to 1845. Volume 6 is devoted entirely to the private acts approved during those years, with an index. The private acts from 1845-1900 are published after the public statutes in each volume and are included in the general index to that volume. Each volume covers one Congress, both sessions. Since 1875, the U.S. Government Printing Office has published the

Public Statutes, beginning with the forty-third Congress (1873-1875). In 1901 and succeeding years, the public and private acts were separated into two volumes, and Part II of each pair covers the private acts. The Serial Set is the place to find documents supporting the action; therefore, individuals who are the recipients of these acts are indexed also in the Serial Set Finding Lists.

Appellate Courts

All reported cases from the federal courts between 1754 and 1941 are indexed in volumes 66-70 of the *Federal Digest* (St. Paul, MN: West Publishing Co.). The reported cases are usually those appealed to a higher court and cases before the Court of Claims. Volumes 66-68 index cases alphabetically by the name of the plaintiff; volumes 69-70, by the name of the defendant. In listing each case, the index gives an abbreviation for the name for the lower court (for example, *CC* for circuit court, *DC* for district court) and the book that reports the case. (A chart at the front of Volume 2 translates the various abbreviations for the court names.) The book reference *127USRep96*, for example, sends the searcher to Volume 127, page 96, of the series called *U.S. Reports*, coded *USRep*. The following digests are covered by the index:

> *Appeals Cases in the District of Columbia* (AppDC)
> *Circuit Courts of Appeals Reports* (CCA)
> *Court of Claims Reports* (CtCl)
> *Court of Customs Appeals Reports* (CtCustApp)
> *Custom and Patent Appeals Reports* (CCPA)
> *District of Columbia Court Reports* (DC)
> *Federal Cases* (FedCas)
> *Federal Reporter* (F)
> *Federal Supplement* (FSupp)
> *Supreme Court Reporter* (SCt)
> Lawyers' Edition of the *U.S. Supreme Court Reports* (LEd)
> *U.S. Reports* (USRep)

These publications, including *Federal Digest*, are most often found in law libraries but are sometimes included with U.S. documents (although they are not government documents) or special collections in university and research libraries. Larger law firms also maintain libraries, but access may be restricted to their own employees.

These appellate cases contain much genealogical information concerning relationships, dates, and events in people's lives. Some of that data may be available in family and local sources; but especially in counties with burned courthouses, the same information may be found only in such legal digests. The testimony in the following example even mentions that the recorder's office where a deed in question was deposited burned before 1806. This case was *Lewis et al. vs. Baird et al.* from the Circuit Court for the District of Ohio, July 1842, Federal Case number 8316 (15Fed-Cas457). It contains the following genealogical material:

1. The ancestor of the complainants, General Robert Lawson, served in the Virginia Continental Line in the Revoluntionary War and received a warrant for ten thousand acres of land.

2. His wife, Sarah, of Fayette County, Kentucky, died in Virginia in 1809. Lawson himself died in Richmond, Virginia, four years before his wife's death.

3. Testimony mentions John O'Bannon, who died in January 1812, and Lawson's son-in-law George T. Cotten.

4. James McKinley, a witness, in 1796 lived on the farm of Daniel Feagins, who had two sons, Fielding and Edward Feagins, and who lived near Germantown, Mason County, Kentucky, in 1796.

The case of *Clare vs. Providence and Stonington Steamship Company of Rhode Island* from the U.S. Circuit Court for the Southern District of New York, 14 May 1888, presents the suit of Almire R. Clare of Rhode Island, administratrix and widow of Charles C. Clare, who died intestate about 11 June 1880, while a passenger aboard a steamship in route from New York City to Stonington, Connecticut. A collision of ships occurred, and Mr. Clare was missing. A friend found and identified his body later at the morgue. A son Charles who was with his father on board survived the collision. The widow, left with four minor children, sued the steamship company for $5,000 plus interest accrued since her husband's death. The appeals court denied her plea, saying she could not prove that her husband drowned as a result of the collision (127US45).

To gain the most from these reports, one must use cluster genealogy because much of the genealogical information given is for people other than those named in the title of the case. A good example is the *Lewis vs. Baird* case discussed above. Another example is the case of *Young et al. vs. Dunn et al.* from the Circuit Court for the Eastern District of Texas, 1882. A letter that was probated as a will of James A. *Caldwell*,

dated 21 March 1842 and addressed to S.C. *Colville*, names Jane *McFarland*, wife of Jacob McFarland, as Caldwell's "only blood relation, now in Texas" (10F717). Caldwell, Colville, and McFarland are not parties to the lawsuit and therefore are not listed in the index.

Some case reports reprint the entire will of an ancestor, as occurred with the will of Samuel DeVaughn of the District of Columbia, who died 5 July 1867, and the will of Mary Vermilya, who died in 1824 in Hudson County, New Jersey (17SCt461 and 10F857, 33F201).

One case, *Aaron Bradshaw vs. Nehemiah B. Ashley*, contains a citation of genealogical data from another case, *Mitchell vs. Mitchell* (1851) from Maryland, involving land of one Francis J. Mitchell (died 1825), his son James D. Mitchell, and James' widow Elizabeth. The Mitchell case was simply cited as part of the argument in the Bradshaw case; thus, the Mitchell dispute does not appear in the *Federal Digest* index to cases.

American Digest System and National Reporter System

West Publishing Company also has a comprehensive program of digests that cover primarily appellate court opinions from state as well as federal jurisdictions. The American Digest System began with a set of books called the *Century Digest*, literally the *American Digest, Century Edition*, which covered cases from 1658 to 1896. The volumes are arranged alphabetically by legal topics but cover all reported American case law during that period. These books are indexed in the second set, the *First Decennial Digest*, which covers cases reported between 1897 and 1906. Thereafter, each ten-year period has its own *Decennial Digest:*

Second Decennial Digest (1907-1916)
Third Decennial Digest (1916-1926)
Fourth Decennial Digest (1926-1936)
Fifth Decennial Digest (1936-1946)
Sixth Decennial Digest (1946-1956)
Seventh Decennial Digest (1956-1966)
Eighth Decennial Digest (1966-1976)
Ninth Decennial Digest, Pt 1 (1976-1981), *Pt 2* (1981-1986)
Tenth Decennial Digest, Pt 1 (1986-1991), with Part 2 in progress in monthly and quarterly cumulations.

The genealogist looking for cases involving family members can look in the *Table of Cases* under the name of the plaintiff. Cases after 1976 are also indexed by defendant. The volumes called *Table of Cases* are usually the last books in each set. Volumes 21-25 of the *First Decennial Digest* cover both that set and the *Century Digest*. The searcher should consult the explanations and abbreviations to understand how to access the cases, but the principle is basically this: volume number, abbreviation of the digest in which the case appears, topic number under which to find the case mentioned if it appears in one of the Decennial Digests, or the page number in a book of case reports. The slightly different numbering in the *Century Digest* is cross-referenced in the *First* and *Second Decennial Digests*. References such as 51Miss128 and Cooke179 (Tenn) refer to case reports from the states: Volume 51, page 128 of the Mississippi Reports and page 179 of Cooke's Tennessee Reports. A citation such as 48C War27 tells the searcher to go to Volume 48 of the *Century Digest*, the topical heading *war* and its subdivision 27. A table of abbreviations at the front of the volume will clarify the names of the series given in the reference.

Smaller digests, also published by West, cover each region of the country and each state individually except Delaware, Nevada, and Utah. The Dakotas are combined in one digest, as are Virginia and West Virginia. These sets contain references to cases decided in the state courts and reported in the National Reporter System. The reports are for decisions issued by appellate courts in the states. The cases are also included in the American Digest System (Decennial Digests) discussed above. The regional digests with the states they cover are listed in the following chart. (Many states have other digests and reporters as well.)

Regional Digests

Atlantic Digest (1764 to present): Connecticut, Delaware, District of Columbia (Court of Appeals), Maine, Maryland, New Hampshire, New Jersey, Pennsylvania, Rhode Island, Vermont. See Federal Digest for Circuit Court for District of Columbia.

North Eastern Reporter (discontinued in 1972): Illinois, Indiana, Massachusetts, New York, Ohio. Use Decennial Digest for cases after 1972.

North Western Digest: Iowa, Michigan, Minnesota, Nebraska, North Dakota, South Dakota, Wisconsin.

Pacific Digest: Alaska, Arizona, California, Colorado, Hawaii, Idaho, Kansas, Montana, Nevada, New Mexico, Oklahoma, Oregon, Utah, Washington, Wyoming.

South Eastern Digest (1729 to present): Georgia, North Carolina, South Carolina, Virginia, West Virginia.

Southern Digest (1809 to 1989): Alabama, Florida, Louisiana, Mississippi. Use Decennial Digests for years after 1989.

South Western Reporter (discontinued): Arkansas, Kentucky, Missouri, Tennessee, Texas. Each state has its own Digest now.

New York Supplement and California Reporter are separate reporters for the most litigious states and include some lower court decisions.

Military Law Reporter covering military appellate courts began in the mid-1970s.

These digests refer the searcher to the various regional or state *reports* or *digests*, which are the cases and decisions themselves, i.e., the reports of the cases, in the same format as the discussion above on the Decennial Digests.

Legal Databases

Massive computerized databases of legal, business, scientific, and news information are now available from various subscription services. These databases cover many subjects with the latest news and information from newspapers, periodicals, business and professional journals, and legal reports, generally from the 1980s forward. Two of the most well known that include the legal field are Westlaw from West Publishing Company (P.O. Box 64833, St. Paul, MN 55164-9752) and Lexis—Nexis from Mead Data Central (P.O. Box 933, Dayton, OH 45401). For the most part these services are available to businesses who subscribe to them and in law libraries for students, faculty, and lawyers.

However, Mead Data Central offers the same service to the public through Nexis Express. For genealogists, the most exciting aspect of the service is the capability to search texts of legal cases for ancestors who do not appear in the published plaintiff and defendant indexes. Equally exciting is the fact that the database covers cases that are published in the many reports and digests, even those that extend back into the eighteenth century. You can request a search that is quite specific, i.e., one name in one state for a narrow date range, or a broader search for extended family in a region of states for any time since the beginning of the case reports. The results of the search can be faxed or mailed to you. The results include the full text of case reports that are found. Remember these are mostly appellate cases that have been reported in the *Reporter* and *Digest* system. No database includes all cases ever tried.

Yes, there is a fee for using the service, but it is much more economical than spending days in a law library. The fee is based on the amount of professional and research time used in the search and the printing, faxing, or postage. If the search finds nothing, the fee still applies but of course is smaller because of less time or printing used. In this case, you have still saved yourself the effort of looking. You can contact Nexis Express at (800)843-6476.

Legal Directories

Several directories of persons in the legal profession began publication in the late nineteenth century. The *Lawyers Directory* by the Sharp and Alleman Company of Philadelphia has been published under various titles since 1883. Martindale's *American Law Directory* (New York: G.B. Martindale) began in 1868 with annual editions. J.H. Hubbell's *Legal Directory* (New York: Hubbell Legal Directory Co.), also an annual publication, began in 1870. The Martindale and Hubbell volumes listed lawyers in the United States, Canada, and some European countries; United States bankers (one or more per city); real estate agents (Martindale, 1874); United States consuls living abroad (Hubbell, 1929); and other groups pertinent to the legal business, a description of the court system in each state, and a synopsis of its laws. These two companies merged in 1931 and continue as a New Providence, New Jersey company, Martindale-Hubbell Law Directory, Inc. The 1993 edition was the first to list lawyers alphabetically throughout the country. Earlier volumes were listed alphabetically by state and towns within it.

The Martindale directory of 1920 told me that my grandfather H.O. Metcalfe had been admitted to the Texas bar in 1913, made between $2,000 and $5,000 annually, and had high recommendations for ability and promptness. Mr. C.E. Mead, with whom he worked, was a very capable lawyer who had been in the profession since 1890. The 1924 and subsequent directories correctly reported my grandfather's birth year as 1887. Space in the biographical section or business card section could be purchased by those lawyers

who wanted their schooling, professional memberships, or specializations advertised.

In addition, directories of law professors and other legal professionals contain biographical information.

Other Reference Material

Law libraries also contain sections on foreign law, maritime law, specialized topics such as social security, family law, and commercial law; general books on legal history; biographies; reference tools such as the *Encyclopedia of Associations* (Denise S. Akey, ed., Detroit: Gale Research Co.) and Congressional directories and biographical lists; and legal research guides to various states.

Legal encyclopedias covering many topics in statutory and case law include these:

> *American Jurisprudence 2d.* (Rochester, NY: Lawyers Co-Operative Publishing Co., 1962).
> *Corpus Juris*, William Mack and Donald J. Kiser, eds. (New York: American Law Book Co., 1932).
> *Corpus Juris Secundum*, Francis J. Ludes and Harold J. Gilbert, eds. (Brooklyn: American Law Book Company, 1953).

PART III – FAMILY HISTORY LIBRARY AND CENTERS

The Church of Jesus Christ of Latter-day Saints, sometimes abbreviated LDS, maintains the largest genealogical library in the world in Salt Lake City and some twelve hundred branch libraries throughout the world. As with many libraries, some materials are available on interlibrary loan and some are not. To get a more complete idea of the size and scope of this library, consult *The Library: A Guide to the LDS Family History Library*, Johni Cerny and Wendy Elliott, eds. (Salt Lake City: Ancestry, 1988.)

The materials for loan are available through the Family History Center branches and can be borrowed for a period of three weeks, six months, or indefinitely. Fees vary for the three time periods. The FHL Catalog is available on microfiche and on CD-ROM. The catalog tells you which county and state records, censuses, church and cemetery records, and a host of other materials are available on loan or in Salt Lake City. These materials come to the centers on microfilm or microfiche.

In addition, Family History Centers and their patrons have available for use several computerized programs on CD-ROM. The first is the Ancestral File, a compilation of descendancy reports, family group sheets, and pedigree charts submitted by church members, nonmembers, and genealogical organizations specifically to this collection, which is updated periodically. Although living persons may be named in the file's alphabetical surname list, vital information is provided for deceased persons only. This information includes birth, marriage, and death dates and places; spouses' and children's names; and the names and addresses of those who submitted the information.

The Family History Department of the LDS Church does not attempt to verify the accuracy of the information; therefore, caution is necessary for searchers using such databases. Some find very valuable information, but conflicting details appear frequently. One ancestor may be listed several times by several would-be searchers, with different vital dates, different birthplaces, or other information. Finding an ancestor or someone with the same name in the file is not proof of anything.

Searchers can use the file without charge. Its greatest value is helping descendants find others who are working on the same family, and it may supply new details about ancestors who are in the file. Variant spellings and similar names appear in the surname lists in an attempt to identify each family member who has been submitted.

Persons interested in submitting reliable data to this collection may write to FamilySearch Support Unit, 4 WW, 50 East North Temple Street, Salt Lake City, UT 84150. For further details on submitting information, call the FamilySearch Support Unit at (801)240-2584.

The Family History Centers also receive quarterly updates on the Family Registry, which is another research tool. It is an alphabetical list of people who submit queries on ancestors and another list of the ancestors. The service is free of charge to those submitting and to those using the information. As a searcher, you can look up your own surname to find other searchers by the same name, or you can look up an ancestor to find another person working on the same family.

This database again requires care in the use of its information, for it is recorded *as submitted* by other searchers. In the March 1992 update I found my ancestor Daniel Croom listed by three different people. One of them had the same dates that I have for the ancestor, but a different birthplace. (I believe, along with other cousins, that he was born in England, but this reference said Ireland. A second person showed him born in Scotland.) The third submitter agreed with the

Scotland birthplace but gave a birthdate some fifteen to twenty years too late to fit with existing evidence, and a death date of 1733 instead of 1735. This mistake could be a typographical error by the person entering the information but is a good illustration of the discrepancies one must be alert for. The one who gave a 1733 death date for Daniel apparently has not seen his will, written on 3 November 1734, or the probate record of 20 May 1735 in Goochland County, Virginia. Perhaps someone believes there were two men named Daniel Croom living in Virginia in the early 1700s.

An older microfilm collection that some Family History Centers have is called Family Group Sheets. The set is made up of family group sheets submitted by church members prior to about 1969 and not duplicated on the other database collections. A supplement to the original file is also in some centers.

The International Genealogical Index (IGI) is an alphabetical list by surnames and region taken largely from group sheets processed through the Temple of the LDS Church. Other extracted vital records are included as well. One can find in this file birth, marriage, and death information, parents' names, and other family data on deceased persons from more than ninety countries. This collection is published both on microfiche and on CD-ROM and is updated periodically. Each entry has a reference number that allows you to find the "input source" and get a copy of the individual record. Assistance is available from the center volunteers.

Each branch Family History Center usually maintains a collection of microfilm or microfiche on indefinite or permanent loan. These are placed in the center by patrons and by local societies. The materials usually include some items pertaining to the local or regional area. For example, the Houston East Stake FHC in Texas has a large collection of Mexican vital records and the entire 1920 census for Texas, but also has helpful passenger lists and Canadian records as well. The Houston Texas Stake FHC has an extensive microfiche collection of Scottish Old Parochial Registers and other European records.

Other collections that centers may have include the *Periodical Source Index* (PERSI), the *U.S. Social Security Death Index*, and *U.S. Military Personnel Who Died in Korea or Vietnam*.

PART IV—INTERLIBRARY LOAN

Interlibrary loan is an important part of research. Loan

through other libraries is usually handled by the library reference departments, which also have many of the directories and other materials that searchers use time and time again. Thus, the reference librarians are an important asset to any searcher. They are not there to do research for you but to point you toward references, to offer suggestions, to answer questions, and to handle interlibrary loan. One habit that gives genealogists a bad reputation in libraries and public records repositories is being unprepared before asking questions, thus expecting too much assistance from the staff, who have many patrons to help and their own work to do. In the case of interlibrary loan, the sending and receiving librarians can work more effectively for you if you provide accurate title, author, and publication information, and page numbers if applicable. It is your job to get that information before requesting interlibrary loan.

OCLC is one subscription service that libraries may join for the purpose of uniform cataloguing and for interlibrary loan. The system contains a large database of titles from libraries throughout the country and is the source of much interlibrary loan material, primarily books. A subscription service called EPIC can perform subject searches on the OCLC database. If your library participates in OCLC or another catalog database, you have access to millions of books.

In the area of genealogy, however, few libraries loan materials. Those that do loan genealogical materials, sometimes with limitations and restrictions, include a number of universities. Some public or state libraries will loan to other libraries within their own state. (It is not important that the borrower know the lending policy of each library, for you probably would not be using the OCLC system yourself or contacting the library that holds the material you would like to borrow. Usually only the reference or interlibrary loan librarians have access to the system. I have found these resource people to be very helpful and conscientious in their efforts to acquire the materials we patrons need.) The fee you pay for such interlibrary loan is minimal and well worth the cost.

Interlibrary loan is also possible through various genealogical and historical institutions. Several independent lending, i.e., rental, libraries are listed with their addresses and brief descriptions in Appendix C on Archives, Libraries, and Rental Libraries. Chapters two, three, and seven show various public, university, and historical society libraries that participate in interlibrary loan of certain parts of their collections. Some of these institutions have published descriptions of their loan materials. One such booklet is *Searching for Your Ancestors on Microfilm*, by Virginia Rogers Smith and Judith Dinkel Smith (Baton Rouge: State Library of Louisiana, 1992), a booklet of microfilm available on loan from the Louisiana Section of the State Library. The loan collection includes much National Archives microfilm, Louisiana newspapers, and parish and state records.

Footnotes are on page 175.

CHAPTER NINE

Focus on African-American Genealogy

Genealogists searching any ethnic, racial, or nationality group will have in common certain sources that are basic to genealogical research, such as census records; land, estate, tax, marriage, and vital records; cemetery and church records; newspapers; and so forth. Before 1865, however, African-American genealogy acquires a particular difficulty because of the existence of slavery and the relative scarcity of records concerning individual slaves. Certainly information can be found on many of them and on freedmen, even if it seems buried in obscure places. Patience and perseverance are the keys to this kind of research. Besides sources that everyone has in common, some special ethnic sources do exist and may be helpful. In addition to family sources, libraries and archives offer many possibilities for the researcher.

AFRICAN-AMERICANS IN BASIC RECORDS

Sources that all genealogists have in common are useful for finding ancestors after the Civil War, as well as freedmen and some slaves before 1865. The examples in this section demonstrate the kinds of information that can be found in these basic sources, especially on slaves and free Negroes, to encourage searchers to broaden their use of such sources.

Church Records and Census Records

These are two basic sources of great help to genealogists of any ethnic group. As an illustration, consider the information they have yielded about a particular black family of West Tennessee. The Presbyterian Church in Bolivar, Hardeman County, Tennessee, was organized in November 1852, and its records show membership and baptism for some blacks before the Civil War. Rose, a "servant" of E.G. Coleman, was baptized and admitted to membership on 21 November 1858. The next year, on 19 June 1859, her four sons were baptized: Moses Elijah, Lewis Pleasant, Joe Stevens, and Thomas Henry. The church record does not indicate the ages of any of these but is valuable in identifying the children's mother and the slave owner's name. It is not uncommon for southern churches before the Civil War to show blacks on the membership rolls, even when the majority of the members were white.

The 1870 census indicates that this African-American family did keep its former master's name after the Civil War. The head of household was Pleasant Coleman, mulatto, age 40, born in Virginia. Rose was age 40, born in North Carolina. Five children were in the family: Thomas (17), Lewis (16), Moses (14), Elvira (12), and Adaline (10), all recorded as black and all born in Tennessee. The other son, Joe Stevens Coleman (?), is not yet accounted for in 1870. Comparing this information with the slave census schedule of 1860, one finds that the slave population at Coleman's farm in 1860 could accommodate all of this family, including the youngest, for there was a four-month-old female slave in that census. (The slave schedule does not name the slaves.) Post-Civil War deed records in the same county indicate land records in the name of Pleasant Coleman, Moses Coleman, and Thomas Coleman in the 1880s.

1790-1810 Censuses. Federal census records before 1870 vary greatly in their usefulness for tracing slave or free ancestors. The 1790-1810 federal censuses named free heads of household (white, black, Indian, or people of mixed blood) but gave only the total number of slaves or free persons other than white living in each household. For example, in the Cheraw District of South Carolina in 1790, ten households of free persons other than white were identified in the census. Listed one after the other, therefore probably living very close together, were the free households of William Hatcher (Negro with three free persons), Patty Braveboy (two free persons), Sam Braveboy (four free persons), and Dick Knight (seven free persons). None of these families included slaves.

The 1790 census is set up with two columns for white males (over 16 and under 16), one column for white females, one column for "all other free persons," and one column for slaves. Some of these Cheraw District residents were identified by the racial designation *negro* or *mulatoe* (*sic*) but also by the fact that the first three columns in the census (the ones for whites) were blank. A white head of household would have been marked in the first column (males over 16) or third column (white females). In these families, the only column checked was the one for "all other free persons," meaning "other than white." Therefore, all the persons in these households were "free persons other than white," including the head of household in the count. When Dick Knight's family lists seven "other free persons," the census means "Dick Knight and six others who are not white."

1820-1840 Censuses. The census of 1820 was the first to ask for free blacks by age groups, but slaves were listed only as a total number within each household. The censuses of 1830 and 1840 used virtually the same forms, with both free Negroes and slaves grouped in age brackets, as were whites.

African-American historian Carter G. Woodson made a thorough study of the census of 1830 since he felt it was taken at a high point of free Negro culture, especially in the South.[10] During the five years after that census, laws and practices in the South began making life much more difficult for free Negroes and many migrated north. One phenomenon of the 1830 census was that some 3,815 free blacks in twenty states, two territories, and the District of Columbia were slaveowners. These were most numerous in Louisiana (966), Virginia (951), Maryland (654), and South Carolina (484). Free Bob of Lafayette County was the only black slaveowner in Arkansas Territory, and there was only one each in Ohio and Connecticut. Other states where free Negroes owned slaves were Alabama (48), Delaware (9), District of Columbia (132), Florida Territory (15), Georgia (61), Illinois (7), Kentucky (121), Mississippi (17), Missouri (4), New Hampshire (3), New Jersey (16), New York (21), North Carolina (193), Pennsylvania (23), Rhode Island (3), and Tennessee (68). Only in Michigan Territory and the states of Indiana, Maine, Massachusetts, and Vermont were there no free black owners of slaves.

At least two of these slave owners were listed with white wives, Jacob of Read and Syphe of Matthews in Nansemond County, Virginia. Others, such as James Meggs and Joseph Stapleton of Clarke County, Alabama, each owned one slave. This information suggests that they may have purchased their wives. Men who set out to purchase their own freedom and that of their family members often bought their wives first and freed them so that additional children born into the family would be born free. By law, the child received the status of its mother.

Among the black slave owners in 1830 were clusters of families with the same surname. For example, in Mobile County, Alabama, seven were named Chastang. In Natchitoches Parish, Louisiana, thirteen were named Meytoier. This fact does not prove that these men and women were related, but a searcher of either surname would want to be aware of these clusters and study the families with the possibility of kinship in mind.

Another phenomenon that appears in these early censuses is the presence of households where all are listed as slaves. Carter G. Woodson included the 1830 cases in his book *Free Negro Owners of Slaves in the United States in 1830* as a separate section titled *Absentee Ownership of Slaves in the United States in 1830*. Some of these may have been slaves who were hired out to earn their livings. In the District of Columbia, for example, Peter McCoy was listed in the head of household column with a household totaling one person, who was a slave. The census did not make clear whether Peter McCoy was the slave owner or the slave himself who happened to be living alone. If he were the slave owner, one would expect to find him listed not far away with his own household. However, the name is listed only once in the District of Columbia index and appears only once on that page. It seems likely, therefore, that the slave was the one named as head of household. Other sources may help answer the question.

In Madison County, Alabama, Pleasant Merrill, overseer for Major Gones, was listed as head of a household of seventeen slaves. No free persons were listed in the household. However, Pleasant Merrill was not one of the slaves. He and his young wife were enumerated in the previous household as whites. The owner may have lived elsewhere, but the overseer was nearby.

A more common situation occurred in Conecuh County, Alabama. The head of household column read "Starke H. Boyakin's slaves." Twenty-four slaves made up the entire household. No free persons of any race were listed living with them. This entry clearly suggests that the owner lived elsewhere or had died. In a clearer example in Richmond, Virginia, the household marked "Peyton Randolph's estate" showed two slaves living apart from any owner. Neither of these examples clarifies who might have been in charge at each location, a trusted slave or a person in the next household.

1850 and 1860 Censuses. The 1850 census was the first to list all persons in free households by name, giving age, sex, race, occupation, and birthplace for each. The 1860 census gives the same type of information. In some counties, the enumerators gave more information than was asked for, and these additions can be very helpful to genealogists. Chatham County, Georgia, was one of these censuses. The enumerator not only listed the town or county of birth for everyone, instead of just the state or country, but also gave very specific information on some of the children's ages. For example, Amanda Rose was a 34-year-old mulatto seamstress, born in Savannah (in Chatham County). Her family included William Hood (15, a bricklayer, born in Savannah), Theodore Rose (8 years and 8 months old, born in Savannah), and Leonora Rose (5 years and 8 months old, born in Savannah). Giving the ages of children in months helps pinpoint birthdates. William Hood's age was given as 15 in June 1860. According to the instructions on the census, the age given was to be the age as of the last birthday. William, therefore, had turned 15 but was not yet 16. His birth, then, could have occurred after June 1 in 1844 or in the first half of 1845, if the age given in the census was actually correct. Theodore, on the other hand, had already passed his eighth birthday and was eight months into his ninth year. Assuming the age given was correct, one could figure he was probably born in September 1851. He would have turned eight in September 1859. By June 1860, he would have completed eight more months toward his ninth birthday. The same reasoning would suggest that Leonora was born in September 1854.

Near this family in Savannah lived Sarah Candy, age 72, a black woman living alone who earned her living by washing and ironing. She gave her birthplace as Africa.

Separate slave schedules for 1850 and 1860 list slave owners by name in each county and slaves by age and sex, but not by name. However, the Bowie County, Texas, enumerator in 1850 gave more than the instructions called for and listed the names of all the slaves in the county. That is the only county I have found

where slaves were named. By 1870, with slavery dead, all persons were listed by name.

Censuses from 1870 Forward. The censuses from 1870 forward present the same problems to searchers of any racial or ethnic group. Many families were not enumerated, for many reasons. Some individuals in families were left out, probably unintentionally. Mistakes occurred in names, ages, birthplaces, and other pieces of information. In spite of these problems, federal census records are valuable sources readily available to searchers.

In these later censuses, enumerators still made "mistakes" for which genealogists are grateful. Remember that relationships are not asked for in the 1870 census. Yet, two examples occur in the Jasper County, Mississippi, 1870 census where the enumerator gives us that information anyway. In the black family headed by Crawford (age 58) and Adeline (52) Kelly, there were eleven younger family members between the ages of 24 and 1, listed in order from oldest to youngest as children in a family usually were. One would want to ask if the youngest were really children of a 52-year-old woman. However, after the baby, four more Kellys were listed, ranging in age from four years to one month. The enumerator bracketed these and marked them *Grandchildren*. (Perhaps Adeline, therefore, really was the mother of the one-year-old, or perhaps Adeline was not really 52 years old.)

The second example was from the same neighborhood, in the black family of Manuel (28) and Jane (25) Heidelberg. Besides their four young children, a Sarah McDonald (16) was living with them. Under the column for Sarah's occupation, the enumerator wrote "living with brother-in-law." Normally Manuel would be Sarah's brother-in-law in one of two ways. The most likely was that Manuel was the husband of Sarah's sister. The other is that Sarah was the wife of Manuel's brother. It is conceivable that brothers could have different surnames, but there was no indication given that Sarah was then or had been married. Nevertheless, the information helps the genealogist narrow the search, knowing that a relationship existed.

Local Censuses and County Records

Some states took state and school censuses between the federal decennial censuses. These are sometimes valuable sources for locating a household in a particular place at a given time, and some of these list each household member by name and age. State census records are discussed in chapter three. State archives or historical societies, county courthouses, or county or local school offices sometimes have the school censuses.

While Texas was still a province of Mexico, the government took town censuses in Nacogdoches and San Antonio in 1830. The surviving parts of these records list names and ages of each person in the household, and a few slaves are included. In the Nacogdoches household of Batis Andre Bacoqui, for example, were slaves Jacobo (34, male) and Aseli (35, female).[11]

Courthouse records of deeds and bills of sale also identify slaves and sometimes give information that may be helpful clues for further searching. Such records in Hardeman County, Tennessee, show E.G. Coleman's purchase of Jane, about *18 years old* in 1850, of sound mind and body; and Albert, a *carpenter* about *26 years old* in 1851 (Deed Book K, 285; N, 501).

The San Augustine County, Texas, deed records contain a bill of sale dated 25 October 1837, for the slave Easther, *age 38*, from B.F. Gates of *Adams County, Mississippi*, to Almanzon Huston of San Augustine. This additional information about Gates' residence might be a clue for further search on Easther (Deed Book D, 21).

Fayette County, Tennessee, deeds give some genealogical information on one particular slave family. In July 1843, a deed of trust of John L. Day and Thomas Patton mentioned the slave woman Mary, age 30, and *her child* Jane, age 2. Eighteen months later, in January 1845, Patton gave to his daughter Sarah Jane Day (wife of John L.) Mary and *her children* Penny, Jane, and Leanna (Deed Book I, 475; L, 434).

County will books and probate records also contain slave information. The will of Edmond Jones of Madison County, Tennessee, written in July 1835, and amended in February 1836, distributed his slaves among his children. To the advantage of the searcher, he, like so many other slave owners, named his slaves in the document. Additionally helpful is the naming of a few relationships in this will: Sam, *his wife* Dicy, and *their child* Isham went to Thomas M. Jones; Aggy and *her child* Paul, to John Edmund Jones. The 1856 estate inventory of Margaret Turley in Caldwell County, Kentucky, names the slave woman Sitha, about *42 years old*, and *her child* Ellen (Inventory Book I, 18). Likewise, the 1794 inventory of the estate of Richard Phillips of Amelia County, Virginia, lists his fifteen slaves by name, including Judy and *her child* Queen (Will Book 5, p 79).

Marriage records, especially in the South immediately after the Civil War, reflect the marriages of freed men and women. For some years and in various ways, these brides and grooms were often identified as black. Some counties used separate record books for blacks and whites. Some used the abbreviation *col'd* or *col* (colored) or *fmc* (free man of color) and *fwc* (free woman of color) beside the names. This practice may help searchers identify the correct ancestor and the correct date, since many counties had black and white residents of the same names.

An example of separate marriage books is the Hardeman County, Tennessee, Freedmen's Marriage Records, 1865-1870. Racial designation is found only with the names of the men who joined the grooms in signing the marriage bonds. When George W. Morgan got his marriage bond in December 1868, prior to marrying Martha J. Coleman, his surety was Ike Napier, *col'd*. However, before Thornton Alexander married Lizzie Blaylock in April 1868, the surety on his bond was Jessee *(sic)* Blalock, a white farmer of the county.

Birth and death records are usually twentieth-century sources in most states and cities. Older ones are often found in county courthouses, or in city or state health or vital statistics bureaus. These are discussed in chapter five. Divorce records are court records, usually found in the offices of state district courts, circuit courts, or superior courts, in the county where the plaintiff resided.

City Directories

City directories before and after the Civil War included African-American residents. Some entries give only name, address, and occupation, and older directories often give racial designation as *c.* or *col'd* or *colored*. In addition, the Stockton, California, 1865 directory also notes the former residence of each person. Thus, the searcher learns that Virgil Campbell (*colored*) was pastor of the M(ethodist) E(piscopal) Church, lived on Commerce Street below Washington, and came from Arkansas. A.L. Newby was a black cook who lived on Sutter, between Washington and Lafayette, and came from Connecticut. The Boyd's Delaware State Directory of 1859-1860 showed many free black residents, including a number of widows. One Charlotte Bailey, *widow of Daniel*, was a cook who lived at 604 E. 5th. Two entries that showed the same address suggest that Rosana Furron, widow of William, and Harriet Hopkins, widow of James, may have lived together at 12th Street at the corner of Tatnall. The genealogist would want to investigate whether the two ladies might have been related.

State government records often contain information on African-Americans before and after the Civil War. Two such sources are memorials and petitions to the state legislature and laws and acts of the legislature.

State Government Records

Memorials and petitions are sources usually found in state archives collections because they were sent to the state government for special considerations. Often finding aids or indexes are available in the archives to help the searcher determine whether an ancestor or relative filed such a petition or request. Sometimes the papers contain genealogical information, and sometimes their primary value is simply identifying an ancestor in a particular place at a particular time. These petitions may be signed by many people subscribing to a special request, or they may concern the needs of one individual or family.

One such petition in Texas in 1870 was signed by 445 men of the three-county area of Falls, Robertson, and Limestone. Sixty of the signers were identified as "free men of color." This designation could be helpful to a searcher, especially one working on the Wilson surname, for eleven Wilsons appear on the list. Three of the men were named George Wilson. Two were black, Senior and Junior (perhaps father and son), and one was white. Besides the three Georges, six more Wilson men were identified as black and two others were apparently white. Such a set of names becomes a checklist to use in searching other county records and the census for genealogical information and relationships. Although this kind of petition itself contains no specific genealogical data, its primary value lies in placing these 445 men in that area on or about 28 June 1870. It offers some consolation for the searcher who discovers that his ancestor did sign the petition and yet was not enumerated in the census of that same summer. Whether he remained in the area or moved on later that year, he was there at least long enough to be considered a citizen of one of the three counties named.

A more personal kind of petition, which asks special help from the legislature, often does contain genealogical information. Such a plea from Zylpha Husk is in the Texas Archives. A free black woman living in Harris County, Republic of Texas, in December 1841, Zylpha stated that she was a native of Georgia, about 27 years old, and had come to Texas about five years before and to Houston about 1839. Living with her was her daughter, Emily, about 13 years old. The Congress of the Republic of Texas had passed a law on 5 February 1840 requiring free blacks to leave Texas by 1 January 1842. Just before this deadline, Zylpha petitioned the Congress of the Republic for permission to remain, as she "would not know where to go if driven hence." Attached were the signatures of a number of prominent citizens supporting her request and testifying that she had conducted herself well and earned her living by honest industry as a washerwoman. No specific action on this request appears in the laws passed by the Congress of the Republic. However, in December 1842, President Sam Houston issued a proclamation allowing free Negroes to remain for two years after 5 February 1843 (Gammell's *Laws of Texas*, 2, p 879). He stated that the change was made in response to the many "honest and industrious" free persons who had been in the Republic for years and were anxious to remain.

A slightly different petition for special consideration concerned an African-American woman of Houston, Texas, named Liley, or Delilah, "one of the best cooks in the republick (*sic*) of Texas," "honorable," "trustworthy," of "good conduct . . . [and] good moral character." She had "by her industry" earned enough money to purchase her freedom from her mistress, Cynthia Ewing, who was asking the legislature to "pass a law to Emancipate her." The petition, dated 1 Nov 1847, was signed by some eighty men and women who supported her request. (The acts of the legislature do not reflect how the request was handled.) The document gives residence information and insight into her talent and character. For these reasons, it is a valuable source.

State legislatures sometimes approve acts for the relief or benefit of individuals, sometimes as a response to a petition or memorial. The *private acts*, found with other laws of the state, contain genealogical information on some slaves and free Negroes, especially since a number of states regulated their activities and their manumission. One such act from the Alabama legislature, on 19 January 1854, freed John Bell, a slave of William R. King, deceased, with the assent of the heirs. The report gives no further information on Bell or the King family, but the searcher would want to find the William R. King in the 1850 census, the slave schedule of 1850, or county records, especially probate, and any newspaper mentions of Bell in that area of the state. This act lets the searcher know to look for Bell and any family in the free population schedules of 1860 and public records from 1854 forward. It also identifies the slaveowner and narrows the search for further information on Bell prior to 1854.

The 1831 Alabama legislature authorized John Robinson, a "free man of color," to free his wife, Ann, a slave, and her two children, Lelia Ann and LaFayette, upon posting a $500 bond with the Madison County court. The 1830 census of Madison County shows John Robinson (age 24-36) as a free Negro with a household of seven persons, four of them slaves. These four include three children under 10 and an older woman, more of the age to be Robinson's mother than his wife. The woman closer to his own age is listed as free already, along with another child under 10. Madison County is one Alabama county that has not had a destructive fire. Therefore, courthouse records may yield more information on Robinson's purchase and emancipation of his wife and children, his dealings with the county court, and the identification of his household.

Court Records

Court records in county courthouses or federal district courthouses can contain much genealogy. These records can be found in court docket books, court minute books, and court case files in the court clerk's office. Federal court records more than thirty years old are sent to the National Archives branch that services the state in which the court is located. These branches are listed in Appendix D of this book. The kinds of genealogical information found in court cases are illustrated below and in chapter eight.

Court records, including appellate records, do contain information for black genealogists. An example is Warren Hall's case against the U.S. and Mary Roach, reported in the U.S. Court of Claims *Reports* (11CtC1197). Although this court is not an appellate court, the reports are published and available in law libraries. Hall's case provided this genealogical information:

1. Hall's mother was an Indian and his father, African.
2. His mother was a free woman in Alexandria, Virginia, at the time of his birth; therefore, he was entitled by law to her status.
3. However, he was later sold as a slave in New Orleans and from 1844-1864 was a slave on the

Bachelor Bend plantation of Benjamin Roach's father in Mississippi.

Appellate courts at the state or federal level can contain similar information from cases appealed from lower courts. One case that contains considerable genealogical information was argued before the Texas Supreme Court during its Demember term of 1847 (2 Texas Reports 342). The case of *Robert M. Jones vs. Laney et al. by their next friend James Colbert* was an appeal from Lamar County. The case report gives the family's history. Laney was born in 1811, a slave of James Gunn in the Chickasaw Nation, now Mississippi. Gunn was an Indian with an Indian wife living in the Chickasaw Nation. In 1814, when Laney was 2 years and 9 months old, Gunn freed her in writing and recorded the action at the Chickasaw agency. Laney continued living with her mother, still a slave of Gunn, until Gunn's death in 1823. After 1823, but before going to live with Susan Colbert, a Chickasaw woman, Laney had two children, who, with her grandchildren, were the other defendants in the court case. In 1842, Colbert, Laney, and her family as free persons moved to the Choctaw Nation, where they lived together until November 1846.

The slaveowner, Gunn, did have a will in which he named several slaves and then left the balance of his slaves to his daughter, Rhoda, without designating their names. Rhoda and her husband, Joseph B. Potts, and the widow, Molly Gunn, sold these slaves to Robert M. Jones, of Indian descent, then living in the Choctaw Nation. The Gunn heirs and Jones considered Laney one of the slaves included in the sale and claimed they did not know of Gunn's manumission of Laney. Jones went to court to get Laney and her children as his slaves by right of purchase. The state Supreme Court affirmed the judgment of the trial court that Laney and her family were indeed free as proven by the written document of manumission, which Gunn had voluntarily executed. The searcher who finds such a case would want to go to the original trial court for any additional information, such as the names of Laney's children and grandchildren.

How does the researcher find these cases? One approach is to find a copy of *Judicial Cases Concerning American Slavery and the Negro*, by Helen Tunnicliff Catterall, ed. (Washington, DC: Carnegie Institute, 1926-1937, 5 vols. Reprint by Negro Universities Press, 1968). These books are abstracts of reported cases from the high courts of states and countries. Each abstract contains the case name, the volume and page number of the digest in which the case report can be found, and the date of the case. The indexes include case numbers and some individuals mentioned in the cases. The five volumes are organized by the state in which the case originated, according to this table:

Volume 1: Cases from courts of England, Virginia, West Virginia, Kentucky.

Volume 2: Cases from courts of North Carolina, South Carolina, Tennessee.

Volume 3: Cases from courts of Georgia, Florida, Alabama, Mississippi, Louisiana.

Volume 4: Cases from courts of New England (Connecticut, Rhode Island, Massachusetts, Vermont, New Hampshire, Maine), Middle States (Delaware, Maryland, New Jersey, New York, Pennsylvania), and the District of Columbia.

Volume 5: Cases from courts of states north of the Ohio River and west of the Mississippi River (Arkansas, California, Illinois, Indiana, Iowa, Kansas, Michigan, Missouri, Nebraska, Ohio, Texas, and Wisconsin), Canada and Jamaica.

If you do not have access to this set, you have at least two other choices. First, if you know that a lawsuit took place within the family you are searching, you can look in the Table of Cases, under the name of the plaintiff, in the *First Decennial Digest* (Volume 25) or subsequent Decennial Digests. These tables are indexes that refer you to the case reports where you can find more about the case. The problem with this approach is that you have to know the plaintiff's name. See chapter eight for more discussion of the Decennial Digests and how to use them.

The more general approach is to conduct a survey in the following books. The references are to the topical, or *key word*, heading of Slavery. They contain a short statement about each reported case during the given time period in federal and state appellate courts pertaining to slavery.

Century Digest, Vol. 44, beginning column 851, about 165 pages of cases before 1896.

First Decennial Digest, Vol. 18, p 423-439, some 17 pages of cases 1896-1906.

Second Decennial Digest, Vol. 20, p 1148-1152, 5 pages of cases 1906-1916.

Third Decennial Digest, Vol. 24, p 1473-1476, 4 pages of cases 1916-1926.

Fourth Decennial Digest, Vol. 28, p 483-485, 3 pages of cases 1926-1936.

Fifth Decennial Digest, Vol. 39, p 1976-1978, 3 pages of cases 1936-1946.

Sixth Decennial Digest, Vol. 27, p 425, one case between 1946 and 1956.

Seventh Decennial Digest, Vol. 27, p 1442, reference to a few early cases and laws.

This very large subject is divided into subtopics, such as "who is a slave," fugitive slaves, manumission, crimes by or against slaves, property rights of slaves, hiring of and regulation of slaves. Each subtopic cites cases involving that matter of law. For example, topic 46 concerns the registry of slaves. Cases cited were all Pennsylvania cases arising out of the state laws requiring and detailing the registry of slaves (1780, 1782, 1788). Topics 7 and 8, concerning who were slaves, capsule cases from various states. Cases are listed in outline form under each topic, as in [a], [b], [c], etc. The synopsis of each case gives the state in which it originated, the year of the appeal, an abstract of the case and the decision, the name of the case, and the reference to where the case report may be found. The following is a sample citation and its translation into layman's language:

> *[n] Mo 1827 — The children of a negro slave, in Illinois, born after the ordinance of 1787 abolishing slavery, are entitled to their freedom. Merry v Tiffin. 1Mo725.*
>
> *[n in the outline] case heard in Missouri in 1827, using the ordinance of 1787 which prohibited slavery in the Northwest Territory, which included Illinois. Case name:* Merry versus Tiffin. *Report found in Vol. 1 of Missouri Reports, original page 725.*

The searcher then finds the Missouri Reports, cases heard by the Missouri Supreme Court, Volume 1. The case actually has two defendants, Tiffin and Menard, and was appealed from the St. Louis Circuit Court's May term, 1827. The man named John (no surname given), age 36, was born of a slave mother but after 1787. He had been held as a slave from the time of his birth. As the synopsis shows in the citation above, the court agreed that John was indeed entitled to his freedom, as were others in the same circumstances. If this case report shows surnames, slave names, or localities in which you are interested, you would want to pursue the more detailed information in the records of the St.

Louis Circuit Court for the May term, 1827.

The genealogical information in a case may concern people who are not the plaintiff or defendant. This is another reason for searching for cases based on locality rather than case name. An example is a federal case capsuled in the Slavery topic of the First Decennial Digest (Vol. 44, topic 40-41, fugitive slaves). The case name was *U.S. vs. Lewis L. Weld*, from the First Judicial District, at Leavenworth, Territory of Kansas, January 1859. The circumstances of the case are involved with the federal fugitive slave law of 18 September 1850 and Lewis L. Weld, who aided a slave in his escape. The *genealogical* information concerns the slave Peter Fisher, alias Charles Fisher, alias Charley Fisher, a slave in Kentucky and property of John O. and Anna Bell Hutchison, young children of Rain C. Hutchison. Fisher escaped and made his way to Kansas, followed by Hutchison, who had him arrested as a fugitive. Fisher escaped again, with the aid of Lewis L. Weld, who was indicted by the grand jury for his part in the escape. In April 1860, Supreme Court of Kansas (in *Pacific States Reports*, Book 24, subtitled Kansas Supreme Court Reports, Vol I) voided the indictment.

Voter Registration Lists

In the southern states after the Civil War, voter registration lists made between 1867 and 1869 may be the first public records of former slaves. Like petitions and memorials, many of the surviving registers are housed in state archives. Check with the state of your research interest to learn whether these have been microfilmed and are available on interlibrary loan. Again, some of these records distinguish black voters with a variety of designations. Several examples from these voter registers will show their value. In Austin County, Texas, Thomas Hawkins registered to vote in August 1867. He stated that he had lived for 45 years in the state and 20 years in Austin County. He gave his birthplace as Guinea, Africa. In November 1869, Harry Bartin and Bob Kerkindoll registered to vote in Robertson County, Texas. Both said they had been in Texas 40 years. Bartin, born in South Carolina, had also been in the county 40 years (meaning, in the area that became that county in 1837). Kerkindoll, who came to the county only two years before, gave Kentucky as his birthplace.

Newpapers

Newspapers are often helpful sources for marriage and death information, for local activities in which an an-

cestor may have participated, and for advertisements and legal notices that may have concerned an ancestor. Newspapers prior to 1865 also contained notices of slaves for sale or runaway slaves. In the attempt to make a sale or find a runaway slave, the owner often included information about the slave's appearance, age, occupation, or other talents.

African-American newspapers did exist before the Civil War. In 1969-1970, the Negro Universities Press, now part of Greenwood Publishing Group, Inc., reprinted two series of these along with some early twentieth-century black periodicals. The two series include the following publications, with the dates of the issues that were reprinted.

Series I
Alexander's Magazine (1905-1909)
Colored America Magazine (1900-1909)
Competitor (1920-1921)
Crisis: A Record of the Darker Races (1910-1940)
Douglas' Monthly (1858-1863)
Half-Century Magazine (1916-1925)
Messenger: World's Greatest Negro Monthly (1917-1928)
National Anti-Slavery Standard (1840-1870)
National Era (1847-1860)
National Principia (1858-1866)
Negro Quarterly: A Review of Negro Life and Culture (1942-1943)
Opportunity: A Journal of Negro Life (1923-1939)
Quarterly Review of Higher Education Among Negroes (1933-1960)
Race Relations: A Monthly Summary of Events and Trends (1943-1948)
Radical Abolitionist (1855-1858)
Southern Frontier (1940-1945)
Voice of the Negro (1904-1907)

Series II
African Observer (1827-1828)
American Anti-Slavery Reporter (1834)
American Jubilee (1854-1855)
Anti-Slavery Examiner (1836-1845)
Anti-Slavery Record (1835-1837)
Anti-Slavery Tracts (1855-1861)
Brown American (1936-1945)
Color Line (1946-1947)
Education (1935-1936)
Fire!! (1926)
Harlem Quarterly (1949-1950)
National Negro Health News (1933-1950)

National Negro Voice (1941)
Negro Music Journal (1902-1903)
Negro Story (1944-1946)
New Challenge (1934-1937)
The Non-Slaveholder (1846-1854)
Race (1935-1936)
Slavery in America (1836-1837)

The *National Era* was published in Washington, D.C., and reported at length on national politics and political personalities. However, it did print marriage and death notices, presumably from its readers and subscribers, although the paper does not say whether the people in the announcements were black or white. The notices come from New York, Maryland, Pennsylvania, and even as far away as Illinois and Ohio.

Charles Blockson's chapter, "Black American Records and Research," in *Ethnic Genealogy* (Jessie Carney Smith, ed., Westport, CT: Greenwood Press, 1983) gives a list of African-American newspapers and a bibliography of books about them.

SPECIAL SOURCES FOR AFRICAN-AMERICAN GENEALOGY

Registers of Slaves or Free Negroes

One useful source of black history is the registers or certificates of free blacks required by some states at various times before the Civil War. At the same time, a few states required slave registration. Surviving records can be found in some county courthouses, state libraries, archives, or historical societies. The Maryland Archives, for example has the Prince George's County Certificates of Freedom, 1806-1852, and at least one manumission book from Anne Arundel County, which includes certificates of freedom, 1810-1864. The South Carolina Archives has filmed the Charleston Free Negro Tax Books, about 1811-1860, on two rolls of microfilm. The Indiana State Library has some Indiana free Negro registers and a few Pennsylvania slave registers. The National Archives has some manumission records in Record Group 21. Other registers may be found in the Virginia State Library, Virginia Historical Society, South Caroliniana Library, University of Missouri at Columbia, North Carolina Archives, Georgia Archives, and Georgia Historical Society. Records that have been published include the following:

Entitled! Free Papers in Appalachia Concerning Antebellum Freeborn Negroes and Emancipated Blacks of Montgomery County, Virginia, by Richard B. Dickenson, Varney R. Nell, ed. (Arlington, Virginia: National Genealogical Society, 1981).

Register of Free Blacks, Rockingham County, Virginia, 1807-1859, compiled by Dorothy A. Boyd-Rush (Bowie, MD: Heritage Books, 1992).

Register of Free Negroes: Northampton County, Virginia, 1853-1861, compiled by Frances Bibbins Latimer (Bowie, MD: Heritage Books, 1992).

Alexandria County, Virginia, Free Negro Registers, 1797-1861, compiled by Dorothy S. Provine (Bowie, MD: Heritage Books, 1990).

Register of Black, Mulatto and Poor Persons in Four Ohio Counties, 1791-1861, Joan Turpin, comp. (Bowie, MD: Heritage Press, 1985). Clinton, Highland, Logan, Ross counties.

Register of Blacks in Ohio Counties, 1804-1861: Ross County, 1804-1855; Clinton County, 1838-1861; Logan County, 1824-1857; Highland County, 1828-1843 (Columbus, OH: Ohio Historical Society, 1971).

Register of Free Negroes and also of Dower Slaves, Brunswick County, Virginia, 1803-1850, by Frances Holloway Wynne (Fairfax, VA: the author, 1983).

Registers of Blacks in the Miami Valley [Ohio]: A Name Abstract 1804-1857, by Stephen E. Haller and Robert H. Smith (Dayton, OH: Wright State University, 1977).

Registers of Blacks in the Miami Valley [Ohio], 1804-1857 (Dayton, OH: Wright State University, 1977). Microfilm of original records.

The information in these registers varies, but may include manumission records that originated in that county or elsewhere, affidavits that testified to someone's free status, registration of free persons as they moved into a new county, and evidence of free status from wills and deeds. The *Alexandria County, Virginia, Free Negro Registers 1797-1864* (Dorothy S. Provine, Bowie, MD: Heritage Books, 1990) contains much valuable information. Registration number 11 (p 2) tells the background of Nicholas Cammel, who in 1805 was about 35 years old. He was born in St. Pierre, Martinique, and came to Virginia in 1793. Registration number 73 (p 13) contains an affidavit of Susan Peade, wife of James Peade, who swore that she knew the mother of Kitty Harris, a free black woman. Kitty's mother was a white woman of Fairfax County, Virginia, near Occoquan; therefore, Kitty was born free. (A newborn child carried the status of its mother.) The free man Elick registered his status in entry number 27 (p 5) with evidence that he was freed by the will of Peter Hellen of Calvert County, Maryland, in 1814.

Indexes to Deposit Ledgers of Branches of Freedman's Savings and Trust Company

In the National Archives under the records of the Office of the Comptroller of the Currency, Records Group 101, are indexes to Deposit Ledgers of some branches of the Freedman's Savings and Trust Company, 1865-1874. They are indexes only, incomplete and undated, and the deposit ledgers themselves remain unlocated, either missing or destroyed. The microfilmed indexes, grouped by state and city, are alphabetical by the first letter of the surname, but not in strict alphabetical order. Thus, all of the New Bern, North Carolina, indexes are together. If there are several volumes for a city, there are, therefore, several sets of *As* to look through in searching for a surname beginning with *A*.

The lack of dates is not so great a problem when the searcher knows that the Freedman's Savings and Trust Company did business from 1865 to 1874. The company was established for deposits by or on behalf of freed slaves or their descendants. Although thirty-three branches were established, the indexes exist for twenty-six of them. The set of microfilm (M817) contains five rolls:

1. Huntsville, Alabama; Little Rock, Arkansas; Washington, D.C.
2. Jacksonville and Tallahassee, Florida; Augusta and Savannah, Georgia; Lexington and Louisville, Kentucky.
3. New Orleans and Shreveport, Louisiana; Baltimore; Natchez and Vicksburg, Mississippi; St. Louis, Missouri; New York City.
4. New Bern, Raleigh, and Wilmington, North Carolina; Philadelphia; Beaufort and Charleston, South Carolina.
5. Memphis and Nashville, Tennessee; Norfolk and Richmond, Virginia; and unidentified.

How can these indexes help a searcher? First, they help to establish a particular ancestor in a particular place, sometime between 1865 and 1874. For example, when William Cowper appears in several New Orleans ledgers, you know that he was in the city over a period of months, perhaps several years.

Second, some of the records give the full names of the depositors. It is often difficult to find what name a middle initial stood for. This may be one source of the complete name. Examples from the New Orleans ledgers are Eli Mansfield Goodwin, Ann Gracie Hamilton, Alfred Samuel Jervis, and Peter Israel Jones; from Shreveport, Alonzo Gustavus Longuire and Silas Flenoy Priestly.

Third, occasionally names of both husband and wife are given. Some of these are implied husband-wife relationships, such as Eliza and William Grey and Eliza A. and Nelson Mack of Baltimore. Sometimes the relationship is stated, as in these New Orleans entries: Butler Alexander and his wife, Harriet, and John C. McKennon and wife, Delilah. This information can help identify couples whose marriages may not have been recorded or spouses who may have no other records.

Fourth, other identifying evidence may add to the searcher's information about an ancestor:

1. Thomas Trusty, *Sr.*, of New York City;
2. *Major* E.F. Townsend and *Private* James Lewis of Vicksburg;
3. J. Walpool's *grocery* in Shreveport;
4. In New Orleans, *Rev.* Henry Green, *Widow* Elizabeth Gabriel, and Elizabeth James *alias* Wilson. The term *alias* did not always mean what it implies today but can indicate a married name and a maiden name, or sometimes two married names.

In the years after the Civil War, a number of organizations sprang up, formed by or for the benefit of freed slaves. A number of these organizations had accounts in the Freedman's Savings and Trust Company. You will not find an ancestor's name connected with the organizations in these account ledger indexes, but you will get a flavor of the times and ideas for further searching if records or newspaper accounts of these organizations still exist. Such accounts in New Orleans included the Union Band No. 1, the Lutheran Benevolent Society, The Louisiana Association for the Benefit of Destitute Colored Orphans, Jeremiah Good Samaritans, the Colored Laboring Men, the First African Baptist Association, and St. James Chapel of the A(frican) M(ethodist) E(piscopal) Church. Organizational accounts in Baltimore included the Good Intent Building Association No. 1, the Chosen Sons and Daughters of the True Israelites, the Fifth Ward Pioneer Club, nine Jacob's Well chapters, the Grand Rising Sons of Faith, the Independent Sons and Daughters of A. Lincoln, the John Wesley Sabbath School, Long Shoreman's Association No. 2, the Davis Tabernacle No. 4 of the

Brothers and Sisters of Moses, a number of churches, and King Melchisedek's Pasture No. 7. Shreveport's accounts included the Ladies Drayman's Association and the Colored Brass Band. New York City's branch had accounts from a number of trade associations and lodges as well as the Enharmonic Singing Association.

These account ledger indexes tell us that in these towns and cities, black churches were being established, that people in certain occupations were banding together for mutual aid (coachmen, laborers, woolmen, lady draymen, longshoremen, etc.), that there was a growing concern for education among blacks, that people were seeking social and fraternal outlets, and that poverty was a problem that private organizations were trying to address.

Registers of Signatures of Depositors in the Freedmen's Savings and Trust Company

The National Archives microfilm series M816 is records of account holders from twenty-nine branches of the Freedmen's Savings and Trust Company. Most of the branches represented in this set are the same as those in the Indexes to Deposit Ledgers discussed above. However, the Jacksonville, Florida, branch is not included in the signature registers. Genealogists will be grateful that four cities not included in the Indexes to Deposit Ledgers do have some surviving signature registers: Mobile, Alabama; Atlanta, Georgia; Columbus, Mississippi; and Lynchburg, Virginia.

These signature registers provide much more genealogical information than the deposit ledgers and, in some cases, have death certificates of the account holders attached. In some organizational accounts in Philadelphia, names and signatures of officers appear in the registers.

Most of the registers contain personal and family information, just as we provide beneficiary information today. Additional information was sometimes included, such as the wife's maiden name, depositor's age, names of people who could draw on the account, or names of military units in which the depositor had participated during the Civil War. Some widows who had no children of their own named brothers or sisters, along with nieces and nephews. Such a "beneficiary" designation of course may suggest the maiden name of the depositor. Some account holders named their former masters and plantations. Others indicated that they had been free before the war.

Almost every entry contains some genealogical information, but some depositors gave more informa-

tion than others. The following record is one of the more complete entries.[12]

> Depositor: Graham Bell Date: 2 October 1866, some notes added 31 March 1869.
> Occupation: 1866, carriage driver; 1869, dining room servant. Residence specified. Born in 1845, Mississippi. In 1866, age 21 years, 4 months, 3 weeks. Came to Louisiana 1852. No master's name given.
> Father's name Sam, died in Mississippi. Mother's name Nancy Turner. Stepfather's name William Turner. Wife's name Mary E. Bell. Wife's mother—Nancy Bright.
> Children: "Lewis 5 Bell" (age 5?, added in 1869?) and Ida Victoria (added with "8 mos.")
> "Children dead Spencer Jackson and John." Brother Sam in New Orleans. (Brother) Allen dead. (Brother) Ben? dead. Sister Maria wife of Henry Stewart in Natchez. Mother had 8 children.

Other records of the company housed in the National Archives include letters to and from the commissioners, dividend payment records, loan and real estate ledgers, financial and accounting records, a record of bonds filed for lost passbooks, and records of the liquidation of the company between 1881 and about 1920. One additional set of microfilm is M874, Journal of the Board of Trustees and Minutes of Committees and Inspectors of the company.

Bureau of Refugees, Freedmen, and Abandoned Lands

Congress created the Bureau of Refugees, Freedmen, and Abandoned Lands in 1865 as a part of the War Department to aid former slaves in coping with the realities of life after the Civil War. Until its termination in 1872, the Bureau dealt with many aspects of work, education, health care, family life, adjustment to freedom, political and community participation, race relations, and day-to-day necessities.

Records of the Bureau headquarters (Record Group 105) contain letters and records to and from the Commissioner, Superintendent of Education, quartermaster, and other officials. Some of the microfilmed records (not all the records) are in series M752 (Commissioner's letters and registers), M742 (Selected Commissioner's records), and M803 (Education Division). Some of the Commissioner's records contain freedmen's marriage records.

On the state and local levels were the district or field offices, with an assistant commissioner over the activities in the state, his quartermaster and other officers, superintendents of education, and local agents around the state. Field offices were located in the District of Columbia, Kentucky, Maryland, and the former Confederate states—Alabama, Arkansas, Florida, Georgia, Louisiana, Mississippi, North and South Carolina, Tennessee, Texas, and Virginia. Bordering states of Missouri and Kansas fell under the Arkansas office. Delaware and West Virginia were served by both the District of Columbia and Maryland offices. Although a number of field office records have been filmed, much more is available for study only at the National Archives. These records also contain marriage records, labor contracts, records of relief of indigent persons, leases of abandoned lands, and files of the many other activities of the Bureau.

Microfilmed Bureau records include these series: (The first number is Records of the Assistant Commissioner for that state. The second number refers to Records of the state Superintendent of Education.)

Alabama—M809, M180.
Arkansas—M979, M980.
District of Columbia—M1055, M1056.
Georgia—M798, M799.
Louisiana—M1027, M1026.
Mississippi—M826.
North Carolina—M843, M844.
South Carolina—M869.
Tennessee—M999, M1000, Selected Record of Field Office, T142.
Texas—M821, M822.
Virginia—M1048, M1053.

One section of these records that contains genealogical information is the indentures of apprenticeship. A good illustration comes from Hardeman, Tennessee, where E.G. Coleman, a white farmer, signed the documents to bind seven young orphans into his care. The indentures furnish the following information about the children, as of 6 January 1866:[13]

1. Louis Cross, turned 10 on 5 March last (his birthdate—5 March 1855)
2. Fillis Cross, turned 8 on 26 April last (her birthdate—26 April 1857)
3. Aaron Cross, turned 6 on 20 August last (his birthdate—20 August 1859)
4. Isham Cross, turned 4 on 24 September last

(his birthdate—24 September 1861)
5. Margaret Cross*, turned 5 on 28 October last (her birthdate—28 October 1860)
6. Jane Cross*, turned 8 on 6 April last (her birthdate—6 April 1859)
7. Alice Cross*, will turn 10 next February 15 (her birthdate—15 February 1856)
   *orphan scratched out and note added: abandoned by her mother 1862.

There were children of at least two different mothers, and the documents do not say anything more about the mothers or name the former slave owner. In some indentures, a child was bound out with the consent of the mother, as when six-year-old Abe Lincoln was bound to G.W. Swinebroad of Hardeman County, Tennessee, in February 1866. In these and most other cases, boys were indentured until the age of 21, and girls, until age 18. The employer agreed to teach them, in these cases, farming and housekeeping, and provide clothes and money ($100 to males, $75 to females) at the end of the term. The employer also had to sign a bond with two other men as sureties that he would honestly and fairly abide by the terms of the indenture. Each indenture was cosigned by a Bureau agent.

Other National Archives Records
Among the many kinds of military records in the National Archives are several groups that pertain specifically to African-American service personnel. The primary group is the M589 set—Index to Compiled Service Records of Volunteer Union Soldiers Who Served With United States Colored Troops. The ninety-eight rolls of microfilm are arranged alphabetically by surname. These help identify the soldier's unit and state from which he served.

The M858 series of microfilm, The Negro in the Military Service of the United States, 1639-1886, reproduces documents relating to military participation of blacks as well as reports concerning slaves, fugitives, and prisoners of war.

Although not exclusively an African-American source, the General Index to Pension Files, 1861-1934 (T288), includes black pensioners. This is a massive index, arranged alphabetically.

District of Columbia records relating to slaves are found in several National Archives record groups. Microfilm group M433 contains Records of the District Court for the District of Columbia Relating to Slaves,

1851-1863. Records from 1862-1863 of the Board of Commissioners for the emancipation of slaves in the District of Columbia are microfilmed in series M520.

The National Archives microfilmed materials may be purchased through the National Archives or Scholarly Resources. Many may be rented from the AGLL or the FHL. The microfilm is also available for use at the Archives in Washington, at various Archives branches, and at other research libraries. (Addresses are in Appendices C, D, E.)

To give you an idea of the scope of some of the National Archives materials relating to African-American history and genealogy, consult *Black History: A Guide to Civilian Records in the National Archives*, compiled by Debra L. Newman (Washington, DC: National Archives Trust Fund Board, 1984). Many Archives materials are not on microfilm and require much time and patience to study. The records also vary considerably in their genealogical content but certainly have great historical value.

Slave Narratives

During the Great Depression of the 1930s, the Writers Project of the Works Progress Administration conducted numerous interviews with former slaves. The typescripts of these stories and reminiscenses fill forty-one volumes: Series 1 and 2, originally published in 1941 and reprinted in 1972 by Greenwood Publishing, under the title *The American Slave: A Composite Autobiography*, and Supplemental Series 1 and 2, published in 1978-1979. The set covers the following topics and states, which were the residences of the former slaves when they were interviewed in the 1930s, not always the states where they were born or grew up.

Series 1 (Volumes 1-7) and Series 2 (Volumes 8-19)
Volume 1 — From Sundown to Sunup: The Making of the Black Community
Volume 2 — South Carolina Narratives, parts 1 and 2
Volume 3 — South Carolina Narratives, parts 3 and 4
Volume 4 — Texas Narratives, parts 1 and 2
Volume 5 — Texas Narratives, parts 3 and 4
Volume 6 — Alabama and Indiana Narratives
Volume 7 — Oklahoma and Mississippi Narratives
Volume 8 — Arkansas Narratives, parts 1 and 2
Volume 9 — Arkansas Narratives, parts 3 and 4
Volume 10 — Arkansas Narratives, parts 5 and 6

Volume 11 — Arkansas Narratives, part 7, and Missouri Narratives
Volume 12 — Georgia Narratives, parts 1 and 2
Volume 13 — Georgia Narratives, parts 3 and 4
Volume 14 — North Carolina Narratives, parts 1 and 2
Volume 15 — North Carolina Narratives, parts 3 and 4
Volume 16 — Narratives from Kansas, Kentucky, Maryland, Ohio, Virginia, Tennessee
Volume 17 — Florida Narratives
Volume 18 — Unwritten History of Slavery (from Fisk University)
Volume 19 — *God Struck Me Dead* (from Fisk University)

Supplemental Series
Volume 1 — Alabama Narratives
Volume 2 — Arkansas, Colorado, Minnesota, Missouri, Oregon, and Washington Narratives
Volumes 3-4 — Georgia Narratives, parts 1 and 2
Volume 5 — Indiana, Ohio Narratives
Volumes 6-10 — Mississippi Narratives, parts 1, 2, 3, 4, and 5
Volume 11 — North Carolina and South Carolina Narratives
Volume 12 — Oklahoma Narratives

Supplemental Series 2
Volume 1 — Alabama, Arizona, Arkansas, District of Columbia, Florida, Georgia, Indiana, Kansas, Maryland, Nebraska, New York, North Carolina, South Carolina, Oklahoma, Rhode Island, Washington Narratives
Volumes 2-10 — Texas Narratives

These narratives are the reports of the WPA writers' interviews with men and women who had been free Negroes before the Civil War, but mostly with elderly former slaves, some 65 to 70 years after emancipation. Naturally, those who remembered life during slavery were older than 75 years when they were interviewed, and many reported their ages in the 90s. Many of the interviews used standardized questions about slave life, housing, clothing, food, work, holidays, songs, religious life, weddings, funerals, and superstitions. The genealogist naturally wishes that more attention had been paid to family history in the interviews, but many of them contain good information and provide fascinating reading.

The interview with Mrs. Susan Dale Sanders of Louisville, Kentucky, contained this genealogical information of both black and white families (from Series 2, Volume 16, Kentucky section, p 43-45):

1. Susan was born near Taylorsville, Spencer County, Kentucky, lived there until four or five years ago when she moved to Louisville. (Interview not dated; many were mid-1930s.)

2. Her mother (not named) was raised from infancy by her master, Reuben Dale, a "good ole baptist." He let the slaves go to church. (Church records might give more information.)

3. Susan's father was Will Allen, a slave of Colonel Jack Allen, who permitted him to stay at Dale's farm and work at Allen's.

4. Susan was one of seven children born to this couple. The boys were Harry and Peter. They joined the army and fought in the Civil War.

5. Susan was named for Susan Dale Lovell, Reuben Dale's daughter who lived down the road from his farm.

6. Will Allen died after the war was over and before Susan married.

7. Susan Dale married William Sanders and had six children.

8. William Sanders had fought in the war and was "wounded in the body," but lived a long time after the war. His widow was receiving a veteran's pension. (Look for pension application.)

Will Oats of Mercer County, Kentucky, gave his interviewer information that could be a great help to searchers of this family, especially since the brothers used different surnames (Series 2, Volume 16, Kentucky section p 18-19).

1. Will Oats was born in 1854 in Wayne County, "up Spring Valley." He said he was 84 at the time of the interview. He moved to Mercer County after he was grown.

2. His parents were Betty Oats and Will Garddard of North Carolina. He grew up living with his mother, grandmother, and siblings.

3. His three sisters were living at the time of the interview: Lucy Wilson and Frances Phillips of Ohio and Alice Branton of Mercer County.

4. His two brothers, also still living, were Jim Coffey and Lige Coffey of Harrodsburg, Kentucky. (Lige is a common nickname for Elijah.)

5. His masters were Lewis Oats and his sister.

6. His grandmother (unnamed) walked from Monti-cello (where they lived?) to Camp Nelson when the war closed to get their "free papers." She bought a little land and house where they all went to live. (Deed records or Freedmen's Bureau records might give more information.)

Both white and black searchers would do well to consult these volumes, because they contain extemely valuable clues and information from men and women who knew the people they talked about. These books are sources of cluster genealogy of the black *and* white families who lived on the same land, their neighbors, and relatives.

Negro Year Book
Between 1912 and 1952, Tuskegee Institute (now University) issued the *Negro Year Book*, which contains biographical and professional information on African-Americans in business, agriculture, religion, science, government, education, civil rights, health professions, military, journalism, the arts, and literature, as well as a directory of national organizations and news items on current issues. The Depression and War years saw some gaps in publication, but these books contain much useful information.

LIBRARY COLLECTIONS
Public, private, and university libraries are discussed in chapter eight. However, this section is added to illustrate the application of some of the sources to African-American genealogy and history.

A very important contribution to this field is the *Journal of Negro History*, founded by Carter G. Woodson in 1916 and published by the Association for the Study of Negro (now African-American) Life and History, Inc., in Washington, D.C. Volume 1 of this quarterly publication contains articles that illustrate the value of this periodical for genealogists and historians. The founder wrote the lead article for the first issue, "The Negro of Cincinnati Prior to the Civil War." He mentioned that when the war began in 1861, the nation had about 3.5 million slaves and about 135,000 free Negroes. John H. Russell also wrote for Volume 1, Number 3, "Colored Freemen as Slave Owners in Virginia." A fifty-three-page section of Volume 1, Number 2, "Eighteenth Century Slaves as Advertised by Their Masters," reprints numerous newspapers advertisements about runaway slaves from Boston to Charleston. Many of these notices gives the name and physical description of the slave as well as his or her trade or talent. It is conceivable that some modern searchers could identify ancestors as far back as the eighteenth century with the help of such notices and other standard sources.

One well-documented and fascinating article in a much more recent issue concerned a slave named Free Frank McWhorter of Kentucky and Illinois, his business enterprises, and his amazing efforts to purchase freedom for many family members.[14] Reading such articles gives searchers further ideas of sources and methods of research. An index to volumes 1-53 (1916-1968) was published in 1970.

A companion publication from the same association is the *Negro History Bulletin*, which contains some articles of biographical and genealogical interest. An example is "Willis A. Hodges; Freedom Pioneer [1815-1890]," by Williard B. Gatewood, Jr., in Volume 43 (1980), p 12-13, 16.

The *America: History and Life* indexes discussed in chapter eight are found in the reference sections in larger libraries. By looking under specific names, places, and subject headings, one can find a number of articles pertaining to many aspects of African-American biography, history, and ultimately, genealogy. For example, in Volume 29, Number 1 (1992) listed under the topics Blacks, Chaplains, Civil War, and the names William T. Sherman, Henry M. Turner, and William Waring is an article about two black Union army chaplains (Waring and Turner) and Sherman's march through South Carolina in 1865.[15] The listings in the index refer the reader to abstract 1224 earlier in that volume. There the reader finds a brief description of the article as well as the author, title, and journal information necessary to find the article itself.

Likewise, the *Combined Retrospective Index Set* (CRIS) for history has whole sections dealing with black history, slavery, Negroes, the Civil War, the antebellum South, the period of Reconstruction after the Civil War, and other topics useful for finding African-American history and biography. Volume 6 of the set is an index devoted to biography and genealogy. See chapter eight for further discussion of this set of reference materials.

General reading and looking at indexes in many different books can reveal interesting and useful information. One such item on a North Carolina man named Lawrence Ward appeared in *Hood's Texas Brigade: A Compendium* by Harold B. Simpson (Hillsboro, TX: Hill Junior College Press, 1977, p 466). Ward was a slave and a cook with the Rowan County Artillery, offi-

cially known as Company D, First Regiment, North Carolina Artillery, and also called Reilly's Battery, which was assigned to Hood's Texas Brigade. He was with others in the unit as a Union prisoner of war at Plymouth, Virginia, on 31 October 1864.

Among reference materials in any library are directories. In addition to the directories listed in the appendix, such as the *Encyclopedia of Associations*, a useful publication for identifying African-American groups pursuing history and genealogy is *Minority Organizations: A National Directory* (Garrett Park, MD: Garrett Park Press, 4th ed., 1992). Among others, the directory includes the following:

1. African-American Genealogy Group, 7th and Arch Street, Philadelphia, PA 19106.

2. African-American Family History Association, P.O. Box 115268, Atlanta, GA 30310.

3. Afro-American Genealogical and Historical Society of Chicago, 740 East 56th Place, Chicago, IL 60637.

4. Afro-American Genealogical and Historical Society, Inc., P.O. Box 73086, Washington, DC 20056.

5. Association for the Study of Afro-American Life and History, Inc., 1407 14th Street NW, Washington, DC 20005. Publishes *Journal of Negro History* and *Negro History Bulletin*.

General Bibliography

It would be a monumental task to compile a bibliography of all books written on slaves or free blacks before the Civil War and on black history after the war. However, the genealogist can find a number of helpful books in university, public, and private research libraries. The following list is given as a brief sample of the kinds of books available. More recent books and those still in print will be listed in publishers' catalogs and in *Books in Print* under subject headings such as Afro-American, Blacks, Free Negroes, or Free Blacks, or place names. *Books in Print* is available for reference in most libraries.

Some of these books are histories containing some genealogical information. However, the genealogist who is also a historian compiles a much more complete family history and stands a better chance of finding pertinent information than one who limits the search to birth, marriage, and death dates.

Three books by Daniel F. Littlefield, Jr. (Westport, CT: Greenwood Press): *Africans and Seminoles: From Removal to Emancipation* (1977); *Africans and Creeks: From the Colonial Period to the Civil War* (1979); *The Chickasaw Freedmen:*

A People Without a Country (1980).

Antebellum Black Newspapers: Indices to New York Freedom's Journal (1827-1829), *The Rights of All (1829)*, *The Weekly Advocate (1837)*, and *The Colored American (1837-1841)*, by Donald M. Jacobs, ed. (Westport, CT: Greenwood Press, 1976).

Black Baltimore, 1820-1870, by Ralph Clayton (Bowie, MD: Heritage Books, 1987).

Black Higher Education in Kentucky, 1879-1930: The History of Simmons University, by Lawrence H. Williams (Lewiston, NY: The Edwin Mellen Press, 1986).

Black History: A Guide to Civilian Records in the National Archives, Debra L. Newman, comp. (Washington, DC: National Archives Trust Fund Board, 1984).

Black Legislators in Louisiana During Reconstruction, by Charles Vincent (Baton Rouge: Louisiana State University Press, 1976).

The Black Presence in the Era of the American Revolution, by Sidney Kaplan and Emma Nogrady Kaplan (Amherst, MA: University of Massachusetts Press, 1989).

Black Yankees: The Development of an Afro-American Subculture in Eighteenth Century New England, by William D. Piersen (Amherst, MA: University of Massachusetts Press, 1988).

Blacks in Selected Newspapers, Censuses and Other Sources: An Index to Names and Subjects, James de T. Abajian, comp. (Boston: G.K. Hall, 1977, 3 vols.).

Blacks of Pickaway County, Ohio, in the Nineteenth Century, by James Buchanan (Bowie, MD: Heritage Books, 1988).

Blacks Who Stole Themselves: Advertisements for Runaways in the Pennsylvania Gazette, 1728-1790, by Billy G. Smith and Richard Wojtowicz (Philadelphia: University of Pennsylvania Press, 1989).

California Black Pioneers: A Brief Historical Survey, by Kenneth G. Goode (Santa Barbara, CA: McNally & Loftin Publishers, 1974). Mentions many individuals.

The Confederate Negro: Virginia's Craftsmen and Military Laborers, 1861-1865, by James H. Brewer (Durham, NC: Duke University Press, 1969).

A Different Story: A Black History of Fredericksburg, Stafford and Spotsylvania, VA, by Ruth Coder Fitzgerald (Bowie, MD: Heritage Books, 1979).

First Hundred Years: A History of Arizona Blacks, by Richard E. Harris (Apache Junction, AZ: Relmo Publishers, 1983).

Free Black Heads of Household in the New York State Federal Census 1790-1830, by Alice Eichholz and James M. Rose (Detroit: Gale Research, 1981).

The Free Blacks in Urban America, 1800-1850: The Shadow of the Dream, by Leonard P. Curry (Chicago: University of Chicago Press, 1981).

Free Blacks in a Slave Society, Paul Finkelman, ed. (New York: Garland Publishing, 1989). A collection of articles from various periodicals on free Negroes in Charleston and South Carolina, North Carolina, Savannah and Georgia, New Orleans and Louisiana, Delaware, Virginia, Alabama, Mississippi, and Florida. Part of a series with other volumes entitled *Fugitive Slaves; Slavery in the North and the West; Slavery, Revolutionary America, and the New Nation; Antislavery; Religion and Slavery*; and others.

Free Blacks of Anne Arundel County, MD, 1850, Ralph Clayton, comp. (Bowie, MD: Heritage Books, 1987).

Free Blacks, Slaves, and Slaveowners in Civil and Criminal Courts: The Pamphlet Literature, 2 vols., Paul Finkelman, ed. (New York: Garland Publishers, 1988).

Free But Not Equal; The Midwest and the Negro During the Civil War, by V. Jacque Voegeli (Chicago: University of Chicago Press, 1967).

Free Coloreds in the Slave Societies of St. Kitts and Grenada, 1763-1833, by Edward L. Cox (Knoxville: University of Tennessee Press, 1984).

Free Negro Family: A Study of Family Origins Before the Civil War, by E. Franklin Frazier (Salem, NH: Ayer Co. Publishers, 1968, reprint of 1932 original).

Free Negro Heads of Families in the United States in 1830, Carter G. Woodson, comp. (Washington, DC: Association for the Study of Negro Life and History, 1925).

The Free Negro in Antebellum Louisiana, by H.E. Sterkx (Cranberry, NJ: Farleigh Dickinson University Press, 1972).

The Free Negro in North Carolina, 1790-1860, by John Hope Franklin (New York: W.W. Norton and Co., 1971, reprint of 1942 original).

The Free Negro in Virginia, 1619 to 1865, by John H. Russell (New York; AMS Press, reprint of 1913 original).

Free Negro Labor and Property Holding in Virginia, 1830-1860, by Luther Porter Jackson (New York: Appleton-Century Co., Inc., 1942).

Free Negro Owners of Slaves in the United States in 1830 Together With Absentee Ownership of Slaves in the United States in 1930, by Carter G. Woodson (Westport, CT: Negro Universities Press, 1968, reprint of 1924 original).

Free Negroes in the District of Columbia, 1790-1846, by Letitia Woods Brown (New York: Oxford University Press, 1972). Includes lists of free Negroes from primary sources, including District of Columbia Negro taxpayers, 1824-25, and an excellent bibliography.

The Freedmen's Bureau in South Carolina, 1865-1872, by Martin Abbott (Chapel Hill, NC: University of North Carolina Press, 1967).

A Heritage Discovered: Blacks in Rhode Island, by Rowena Stewart (Providence, RI: Black Heritage Society, 1978).

The History of Negro Servitude in Illinois and of the Slavery Agitation in That State, 1719-1864, by Norman Dwight Harris (Westport, CT: Greenwood Press, reprint of 1904 original).

In Search of Canaan: Black Migration to Kansas, 1879-1880, by Robert G. Athearn (Lawrence, KS: The Regents Press of Kansas, 1978).

Index to "The Journal of The Afro-American Historical and Genealogical Society Quarterly" Issues of 1980-1990, compiled by Barbara D. Walker (Bowie, MD: Heritage Books, 1992).

Life Behind a Veil: Blacks in Louisville, Kentucky, 1865-1930, by George C. Wright (Baton Rouge: Louisiana State University Press, 1985).

List of Black Servicemen Compiled From the War Department Collection of Revolutionary War Records, Debra L. Newman, comp. (Washington, DC: National Archives and Records Service, 1974).

List of Free Black Heads of Families in the First Census of the United States, 1790, Debra L. Newman, comp. (Washington, DC: National Archives and Records Service, 1973).

List of Inhabitants of Colonial New York: Excerpted from The Documentary History of the State of New York, by Edmund B. O'Callaghan (Baltimore: Genealogical Publishing Company, 1979, reprint from 1849-1851 original). Includes 1755 census of slaves. Some counties, statistical; some name slaves.

Many Thousands Gone: The Ex-Slaves' Accounts of Their Bondage and Freedom, by Charles H. Nichols (Bloomington, IN: Indiana University Press, 1969). Slave narratives.

Minutes of the Proceedings of the National Negro Conventions, 1830-1864, Howard H. Bell, ed., (Salem, NH: Ayer Co. Publishers, 1970).

North of Slavery: The Negro in the Free States, 1790-1860, by Leon F. Litwack (Chicago: University of Chicago Press, 1965).

A Peculiar Paradise: A History of Blacks in Oregon, 1788-1940, by Elizabeth McLagan (Portland, OR: Georgian Press, 1980).

Pennsylvania's Black History, by Charles L. Blockson (Philadelphia: Portfolio Associates, 1975).

The Philadelphia Negro: A Social Study, by W.E.B. DuBois (New York: Benjamin Blom, 1967, reprint of original 1897 volume).

Philadelphia's Black Elite, 1787-1848, by Julie Winch (Philadelphia: Temple University Press, 1988).

Register of Negro Slaves and Masters for 1805-1807, Knox County, Indiana Territory, by June Barekman (Chicago: Barackman (*sic*) Family Association, 1970).

Selected Documents Pertaining to Black Workers Among the Records of the Department of Labor and its Component Bureaus, 1902-1969, by Debra L. Newman (Washington, DC: National Archives and Records Service, 1977).

Slave Genealogy: A Research Guide With Case Studies, by David H. Streets (Bowie, MD: Heritage Books, 1986).

Slaves Without Masters: The Free Negro in the Antebellum South, by Ira Berlin (New York: Oxford University Press, 1981, reprint of 1974 edition from Pantheon Books).

A World in Shadow: The Free Black in Antebellum South Carolina, by Marina Wikramanayake (Columbia, SC: University of South Carolina Press, 1973).

Subject Bibliographies

Subject bibliographies help the genealogist identify books and other materials that might prove helpful. Useful bibliographies particularly for African-American history and genealogy include these:

Bibliographic Guide to Black Studies (Boston: G.K. Hall & Company, an annual supplement to the *Dictionary Catalog of the Schomburg Collection* below, represents only holdings of the New York Public Library).

Bibliography of Louisiana Books and Pamphlets in the T.P. Thompson Collection of the University of Alabama, Donald E. Thompson, comp. (University, AL: University of Alabama Press, 1947).

Black Access: A Bibliography of Afro-American Bibliographies, by Richard Newman (Westport, CT: Greenwood Press, 1984). Subject index and chronological index. Lists many library catalogs and guides.

Black Genealogy: An Annotated Bibliography, by Edith Green Sanders (Atlanta: Atlanta Public Library, Samuel Williams Special Collections, 1978). Catalog of materials in the Williams Collection.

Black Index: Afro-Americana in Selected Periodicals, 1907-1949, by Richard Newman (New York: Garland Publishing, 1981). Indexed by subject, place, and author.

Black Journals of the United States, by Walter C. Daniel (Westport, CT: Greenwood Press, 1982).

Blacks and Their Contribution to the American West: A Bibliography and Union List of Library Holdings Through 1970, by James de T. Abajian (Boston: G.K. Hall, 1977).

Blacks in the American Armed Forces, 1776-1983: A Bibliography, by Lenwood G. Davis and George Hill (Westport, CT: Greenwood Press, 1985).

Blacks in the American West: A Working Bibliography, by Lenwood G. Davis (Chicago: CPL Bibliographies, 1976).

Blacks in the Pacific Northwest 1789-1974: A Bibliography of Published Works and Unpublished Source Materials on the Life and Contributions of Black People on the Pacific Northwest, Nos. 767-768 (Chicago: CPL Bibliographies, 1975).

Blacks in the State of Ohio, 1800-1976: A Preliminary Survey, Nos. 1208-1209, by Lenwood G. Davis (Chicago: CPL Bibliographies, 1977).

Catalogue of the Charles L. Blockson Afro-American Collection, Charles L. Blockson, ed. (Philadelphia: Temple University Press, 1990). Over thirty thousand entries. The collection is now housed at Temple University.

The Chicago Afro-American Union Analytic Catalog: An Index to Materials on the Afro-American in the Principal Libraries of Chicago, by G.K. Hall Branch of Chicago Public Library (Boston: G.K. Hall & Company, 1972).

Data Relating to Negro Military Personnel in the Nineteenth Century, by Aloha South (Washington, DC: National Archives and Records Service, 1973).

Dictionary Catalog of the Negro Collection of Fisk University Library, by Fisk University (Boston: G.K. Hall & Company, 1974).

Dictionary Catalog of the Schomberg Collection of Negro Literature and History in the New York Public Library (Boston: G.K. Hall & Company, 1962, supplements 1967 and 1972).

Guide to Manuscripts and Archives in the Negro Collection of Trevor Arnett Library, Atlanta University (Atlanta: Trevor Arnett Library, 1971).

Newspapers and Periodicals By and About Black People: Southeastern Library Holdings, by North Carolina Central University School of Library Science (Boston: G.K. Hall & Company, 1978). Listings from Alabama, Georgia, North Carolina, South Carolina, Tennessee, and Virginia.

Books on African-American Genealogy

Books pertaining to African-American genealogy and sources include these:

Afro-American Genealogy Sourcebook, by Tommie M. Young (New York: Garland Publishers, 1987, went out of print in 1992).

Black Genesis, by James Rose and Alice Eichholz (Detroit: Gale Research Co., 1978).

Black Genealogy, by Charles L. Blockson (Englewood Cliffs, NJ: Prentice-Hall, 1977).

Directory of Afro-American Resources, by Walter Schatz, ed. (New York: R.R. Bowker Company, 1970).

Ethnic Genealogy: A Research Guide, edited by Jessie Carney Smith, with a chapter on African-American research by Charles L. Blockson. (Westport, CT: Greenwood Press, 1983). Extensive bibliography included.

OTHER SOURCES AVAILABLE IN ARCHIVES, LIBRARIES, AND HISTORICAL SOCIETIES

Archives holdings of public records and manuscript

collections (private, family, organization, or business records) contain sources helpful to historians and genealogists. In the United States, the national and state governments and some local governments have some form of archives collection that houses public records pertaining to the administration of the government. The records they contain may vary considerably from place to place. Local archives may include such items as city council minutes and ordinances, municipal court records, police and fire department records, civil service employee records, school tax and administrative records, and property tax rolls. County records may also include information from sheriffs' files, the poorhouse, or other agencies. At the state and national levels, the archival records cover legislative, executive, and judicial branches of government and agencies within those branches.

Few of the public records pertain exclusively to black history or genealogy, or to any other ethnic group. Black history and genealogy are part of the whole history of the area that the records cover. Some of the repositories that house such public records have indexes, card files, or other finding aids to help searchers know what is there and how to access the material.

Manuscript collections from the private sector may contain diaries, scrapbooks, family Bibles, and letters from individuals and families; ledgers, account books, and journals from plantations or other businesses; cemetery and funeral home records; and minutes, membership lists, and other records of churches and fraternal organizations. Remember that a number of the slave narratives, manumission papers, and indentures of apprenticeship give exact birthdates of people who were born as slaves. These records suggest that someone was keeping slave birth records on some of the farms and plantations. One lady said that when she married, she was given a Bible with her family's dates that the mistress had recorded. It is conceivable that some of these Bible records or plantation birth records can be found in manuscript collections.

Manuscript items are seldom indexed comprehensively, but can contain good information about the people in that family, business, or organization, and their associates. Consult Tommie Morton Young's *Afro-American Genealogy Sourcebook* (New York: Garland Publishing, Inc., 1987) for a lengthy and very specific bibliography of black history and genealogy sources. In addition, Ira Berlin's *Slaves Without Masters: The Free Negro in the Antebellum South* (Oxford:

Oxford University Press, 1981, paperback edition of original 1974 Pantheon edition) includes an extensive bibliography of manuscript sources consulted in the preparation of that book. The *National Union Catalog of Manuscript Collections* (see chapters seven and eight) is another resource for finding family, business, plantation, and organization records. As time passes, more people have access to OCLC, RLIN, and NIDS databases as locators of manuscript materials.

The list below is a compilation of information supplied mostly by the institutions named. This list is a further attempt to help searchers know where to go in search of black history and genealogy. The items mentioned are in addition to basic research materials such as land, marriage, probate, court, vital, deed, and census records, general population indexes and biographical files, which many of these institutions have. Institutions that are not mentioned may well have similar materials. You should inquire within your research area.

Alabama Archives—African-American newspapers.

Arizona Department of Library, Archives, and Public Records—*Arizona Informant* from 1971.

Arizona Historical Society—*Arizona Informant, Arizona's Negro Journal, Black Heritage.*

Arkansas History Commission—Index to black soldiers in Union service during the Civil War. Arkansas records of the Bureau of Refugees, Freedmen and Abandoned Lands (1865-1871), including records of the superintendent of education, field office records, and records of the assistant commissioner. Slave narratives. Slave Schedules, 1850-1860.

Arkansas, Southwest Arkansas Regional Archives—Index to 1870 black population of Hempstead County. Books on black history. Slave Schedules, 1850-1860.

California State Library—Some African-American newspapers for California.

California, University of California at Berkeley, Bancroft Library—At least eight African-American newspapers.

Colorado Historical Society—Colorado newspapers, city directories, manuscript collection.

Connecticut State Library—Books on black history and slavery in Connecticut. Barbour Index to Connecticut vital records which includes race with names.

Delaware Archives—"Too numerous to list." Includes legislative papers, petitions on slavery and blacks.

Delaware Historical Society—African-American newspapers, 1970-1985, including *Delaware Spectator*. Records of Delaware Abolition Society 1801-1807. Slavery collection. Society for the Encouragement of Free Labor papers 1826-1828. Papers of several African School societies 1809-1861. Private papers, diaries, account books.

District of Columbia, Historical Society of Washington, D.C.—Columbian Harmony Society publications: burials, marriages, funeral home records, etc.

District of Columbia, Library of Congress—Manuscript collections, Carter G. Woodson collection, papers of American Colonization Society, etc.

Florida State Archives—*The Black Experience: A Guide to Afro-American Resources in the Florida State Archives* (Tallahassee: Florida Archives, 1988, reprinted 1991). An excellent and extensive survey of black history in state and local records, manuscript collections, photographic collection, and the state library's Florida Collection. Includes records of state institutions and agencies, state censuses, Spanish archives, courts; the Photographic Collection; the Florida Collection; and private papers of families, businesses, schools, organizations, and churches.

Georgia Archives—Atlanta city directories from 1876. Voters lists during Reconstruction. Vertical file of family, church, cemetery records. Manuscript collections. County registers of slaves and free Negroes.

Georgia Historical Society—Registers of free persons of color for Chatham County, 1817-1865.

Illinois State Archives—Some county registers of indenture or servitude. Three collections (Hammes, J. Nick Perrin, and Kaskaskia Manuscripts) that include some slave and servant records.

Illinois—In Louisiana State Archives, *Servants and Slave Records of St. Clair County, IL, 1720-1863*, by David E. Richards, on microfiche.

Indiana Historical Society—Manuscript collections of key African-American public figures and organizations. Indianapolis *Recorder* collection and others. For greater detail, inquire with the program archivist for Afro-American history at the historical society library.

Indiana State Archives—Free Negro registers for Switzerland, Clark, Franklin, Ohio counties. Indi-

ana African-American soldiers from Civil War, Spanish-American War, twentieth-century wars. Records of Indiana State Board of Colonization, 1852-1865. Veterans' enrollments of 1886, 1890, 1894. Bibliography of printed sources as well. Check with individual counties for additional Free Negro registers.

Indiana State Library, Genealogy Division—Bibliography of printed sources for African-American research includes some regional and state materials. Indianapolis and Fort Wayne African-American newspapers. City directories, Indianapolis newspaper index. Some Indiana and Pennsylvania slave and free Negro registers.

Iowa Historical Society, Des Moines—Des Moines *Iowa Bystander*, scattered issues.

Iowa Historical Society, Iowa City—Des Moines *Iowa Bystander*, 1894-1976.

Kentucky Department of Libraries and Archives, Public Records Divison, Archives—State records (examples): Cabinet for Human Resources (Colored Section of Child Welfare Division, Kentucky Home Society for Colored Children 1936-1938, Negro Services-Negro Survey, Negro Health Services 1939-1940); enlistment records of African-American soldiers in World War I; Board of Medical Licensure—applications include late nineteenth and early twentieth century African-American physicians; Governors' Papers—correspondence files of 1830-1861 include letters relating to fugitive slaves. County Records (examples): school census enumerations, indenture of apprenticeship books, slave lists, manumission reports, emancipation bonds, voter registration books, veterans' discharges, tax assessment books (sometimes separate Negro tax lists).

Kentucky, Filson Club—Jefferson County, Kentucky, marriage records 1908-1915.

Louisiana, New Orleans Public Library—City archives, including petitions for emancipation 1835-1846. Registers of Free Coloured Persons Enabled to Remain in the State 1840-1864.

Louisiana, Southern University Library—Black history and archives.

Louisiana State Library, Louisiana Section—New Orleans *Daily Creole* (1856-1957), New Orleans *Weekly Pelican* (1886-1889), New Orleans city directories (1805-1901), slave narratives.

Louisiana State University—Private papers, including Metoyer families. Slavery collection.

Louisiana, Tulane University—Family papers, including some plantation records. Pontchartrain Railroad Company minute book.

Maine Historical Society—Abyssinian Church records.

Maryland Archives—Some manumission records and free Negro registers.

Maryland, Enoch Pratt Free Library—African-American history collection.

Maryland Historical Society—Maryland Colonization Society papers. Private papers, account books. Anne Arundel County almshouse minute book.

Massachusetts, New England Historic Genealogical Society—Periodicals, manuscript collection.

Michigan State Archives—Bibliography on African-American sources includes state record groups of attorney general, civil rights, civil service, Civil War, commerce, corrections, education, governors, military, etc. Archives of labor history and urban affairs at Wayne State University, Detroit, MI 48202.

Michigan State Library—Detroit *Plaindealer*, 1889-1893, Michigan and other city directories.

Mississippi Archives—Mississippi Freedmen's Bureau papers, slave narratives, extensive collection of marriage records 1865-1926, Mississippi newspapers. Legislative and governors' papers. Some family papers.

Missouri Historical Society, St. Louis—St. Louis African-American newspaper clipping collection of Charles Turner, 1889-1919. Dexter P. Tiffany Collection includes slave sale receipts, manumission papers (indexed in archival card catalog), and St. Louis free Negro bonds and registers.

Missouri, University of Missouri, Western Historical Collection—County free Negro registers. Manuscript collections.

Nebraska Historical Society—Variety of sources including some newspapers.

New Mexico, Albuquerque Public Library—One local, recent black newspaper.

New York Genealogical and Biographical Society—Published books and periodicals relating to African-American history and genealogy.

New York Public Library—Special division of the library, Schomburg Center for Research in Black Culture, 515 Malcolm X Blvd., New York, NY 10037. Phone: (212)491-2200.

North Carolina Division of Archives—Cohabitation records of counties, 1866-1868, in which some 20,000 former slave couples registered their marriages. Some post-Civil War marriage books separated blacks and whites. County slave papers, dealing with sales, court cases, emancipation bonds, depositions concerning runaway slaves, apprenticeship records, slave work permits, etc., of twenty-five counties. Some include free Negroes. Miscellaneous records of twenty-nine other counties include some slave papers. Records of the Division of Negro Education 1900-1961, Department of Public Welfare 1925-1960, Winston-Salem State University 1899-1928. Twenty-eight collections of private papers of the antebellum period that contain information about blacks. Collections of personal or institutional papers specifically about blacks and a slave collection 1748-1856. Records of North Carolina Freedmen's Bureau 1865-1870. The Negro in the Military Service of the United States, 1639-1886. Black newspapers of the late nineteenth century. Some black family Bible records. Records of the Good Samaritan Hospital, Charlotte 1891-1960.

North Carolina, Duke University—Manuscript collections.

North Carolina, University of North Carolina, Southern History Collection—Family papers. Papers of North Carolina Manumission Society.

Ohio Historical Society—*Selected Bibliography of Black History Sources at the Ohio Historical Society*. Special Enumeration of Blacks Immigrating to Ohio, 1861-1863. *Palladium of Liberty* (Ohio's first black newspaper).

Ohio State Library and Archives—Check library catalog under Afro-American—state name—county name—genealogy. Ohio city directories.

Ohio, Western Reserve Historical Society—Newspaper *Call and Post*, Freedmen's Bureau records. Church, organization, business, cultural records. Consult their African-American Archives.

Ohio, Indiana State Library—Registers of Blacks in the Miami Valley (Ohio), 1807-1857.

Oregon Historical Society—Some African-American organization papers and newspapers.

Pennsylvania Historical Society—Published materials on black history in general, several African-American newspapers. Abolition Society of Delaware minute books 1801-1819. Papers of Pennsylvania Society for Promoting the Abolition of Slavery.

Rhode Island Historical Society—Consult their "Guide to African-American Sources in the Manuscript Divison," unpublished guide.

South Carolina Archives—Sumter County 1865 Capitation and Dog Tax Book, 1867 tax returns, 1868 voter registrations, 1869 militia enrollments, South Carolina military participation. Freedman's Bureau records, including marriage and divorce records 1866-1868, and registers of signatures of depositors in South Carolina branches of Freedman's Savings and Trust Company, etc. Magistrates and Freeholders Court (about 1793-1865), criminal case records involving slaves and free Negroes, and some manumission records. Guardianship records of free Negroes. County manumission books. Free Negro tax books of Charleston 1811-1864. Legislative papers relating to slavery and free Negroes. Consult *Black Slaveowners: Free Black Slave Masters in South Carolina, 1790-1860* by Larry Koger. Church records, including First Baptist Church, Columbia, which had African-American members before the Civil War. Consult *African Methodism in South Carolina: A Bicentennial Focus* by Bishop Frederick C. James. Plantation records.

South Carolina Historical Society—Plantation records. Charleston Almshouse records. Manuscript collections.

South Carolina Library, Columbia—Plantation records. Some African-American newspapers. Charleston free Negro registers.

Tennessee State Library and Archives—Basic sources. Also Confederate pensions for black servants in the Civil War. Family papers, legislative papers.

Texas Archives—Voter registrations 1867-1869.

Virginia Historical Society—Some African-American newspapers. Some slave and free Negro registers. Some records of the Virginia Colonization Society.

Virginia State Library—County registers of free Negroes. County records of the Overseer of the Poor. Family papers. City records. Legislative and governors' papers.

Virginia, University of Virginia—Family papers, city records.

Washington, D.C.—See District of Columbia.

Wisconsin, University of Wisconsin at Milwaukee—Manuscript collections, including records of Milwaukee Urban League 1919-1979, and Milwaukee Branch of NAACP 1917-1970.

Footnotes are on page 175.

CHAPTER TEN

Native American Genealogy

Native Americans have long been in the land that became the United States, but their written history is comparatively short. Prior to the nineteenth century, actual genealogical information was seldom recorded. Since the first European contact, numerous private and government records have named individual Indian men in connection with trade, treaties, and tribal leadership. Until the mid-nineteenth century, however, few of these records mentioned their wives and families, other than as statistics. In fact, the censuses of southeastern Indians prior to their removal to Oklahoma in the 1830s were among the first records to go beyond the chiefs to name other heads of household.

Native American genealogists whose ancestors remained with or identified with their tribal group into the twentieth century have a good possibility of finding ancestoral records in a number of government-generated documents. However, those Americans who suspect they have an Indian ancestor and want to trace that line have a more difficult task.

Many Americans have family traditions that tell of an Indian ancestor but do not tell who, where, or when. One of my friends is in the fourth generation of a Southern family with such a tradition, and many of the relatives in each generation have had physical characteristics that support that tradition. However, no family records contain evidence of which ancestor might be the Indian, or which couple might be of mixed blood. The leading candidates are being studied, but they did not remain identified with any tribal group and do not show up in many basic genealogical records. This scenario recurs time and time again among American families. We all know that there was a time when families of mixed blood preferred to keep the fact quiet, and after a generation or two, it was forgotten. Often the opposite is true now. Many people are proud to claim Indian ancestors or wish they had some. And those who have a clue to their most recent Indian ancestor, and therefore to their Indian

line, wish they could *find* them in the records.

The search for Indian ancestors follows the same principles as any other genealogical search. Thus, before beginning, you must know an approximate time frame for the most recent Indian ancestor and the tribe or geographical area of residence. Without a tribal name, you have to find the geographical area where the person was at a given time and study the history of that area for tribal possibilities. If you know the tribe's name from family tradition or from records, your search is automatically narrowed to the geographic area where that tribe lived.

EARLY RECORDS

Prior to the establishment of the United States federal government, contact with Native Americans was the concern of the armies, governments, and missions mostly of Spain, France, and Britain. In addition, some colonial period records relating to Indians can be found in archives collections in the original states. Most of these records are historical rather than genealogical.

However, two examples illustrate the genealogical information that is sometimes available. The geographical area in this case is the region of northern Mexico and the Big Bend area of Texas known to Spaniards as La Junta de los Rios del Norte y Conchos, a large area around the junction of the Rio Grande with the Rio Conchos. Henrique Rede Madrid has translated a Spanish report that contains early census records of the area: *Expedition to La Junta de los Rios, 1747-1748: Captain Commander Joseph de Ydoiaga's Report to the Viceroy of New Spain* (Austin, TX: Texas Historical Commission, Office of the State Archaeologist, Special Report 33, 1992). As he traveled, Ydoiaga took censuses in the La Junta region, recording names of heads of household with marital status and number of children, and unmarried women and bachelors, noting Christian baptism for some. The residents were Indians as well as persons of mixed Indian and Spanish ancestry. Maps in the book help identify the location of the villages, some of which correspond to communities in the same location today.

In the Archives of the Big Bend at Sul Ross University (Alpine, Texas) are presidio and church records from the La Junta region. Although the presidio and church were on the south side of the Rio Grande, they served the north (Texas) side as well. The La Junta church records, 1775-1857, from present Ojinaga in Mexico, contain baptism and marriage registrations. The baptism records give name of child, baptism date, some with the age of the child at the time of the sacrament, parents' names and place of origin, and sometimes godparents' names. Between 1807 and the 1820s, a number of Apache Indian children were baptized there. Soldiers at the presidio had to petition the commanding officer for permission to marry local women, and the records often reflect names of parents of both bride and groom. Selected records have been published in "Settlement and Settlers at La Junta de los Rios, 1759-1822," by Oakah L. Jones, in the *Journal of Big Bend Studies* (Alpine, TX: Sul Ross University, 3, January 1991, p 43-70).

FEDERAL RECORDS

As the United States extended its sovereignty over western lands beyond the original thirteen states, Indians of course appeared in federal records. The difficulty is finding and documenting the individual Indians, especially women.

Nontribal Indians in Census Records

Since the earliest contact, intermarriage between Indians and other ethnic groups has occurred, especially between Indian women and white men. Unfortunately for genealogists, many of these marriages took place on the fringes of settled areas or completely away from a European-style civilization. Therefore, many of these unions were common law or performed according to Indian custom, and no official record was ever made. (This lack of marriage record, of course, was not limited to mixed marriages. As in any case when a wife of unknown background is found, the search for her maiden name and family will have to be done with the cluster techniques, multiple sources, patience, and perseverance that are discussed elsewhere in this book. Besides, if she or her husband was an Indian, the fact is not always made clear in the existing records.

An Indian not living in a tribal situation was considered by the government as part of the general popula-

tion, as illustrated in the instructions for census takers in 1880:

> *Indians not in tribal relations, whether full-bloods or half-breeds, who are found mingled with the white population, residing in white families, engaged as servants or laborers, or living in huts or wigwams on the outskirts of towns or settlements are to be regarded as a part of the ordinary population of the country for the constitutional purpose of the apportionment of Representatives among the States, and are to be embraced in the [general population] enumeration.*

Such Indians who "mingled with the white population" do appear occasionally in the basic records, such as censuses. For example, the 1840 census of Attala County, Mississippi, contains a number of Indian families, labeled as such and enumerated in the columns for free persons of color. Heads of household include those with English names, such as Fisher Durant, John Smith, and Charles Westly; Indian names, such as Comotohana and Chunkchoo; single names, such as George and Washington; and other names, such as Doctor Jack and Choctaw Wallace. At Franklin, Macon County, North Carolina, in 1860 were families all born "in the Cherokee Nation, North Carolina." A few used English names, such as Jim Wood Pecker and wife, Sally, with apparent sons Willie, John, and David. Eight families were recorded with the surname Connahuk and Indian given names, including Gay hihigh, Aka, and Chew way laka. They were identified as Indians in the column for *color*, even though the printed choices were only white, black, or mulatto.

As white frontiersmen married into Indian tribes, their offspring often kept their fathers' surnames. Some Indians transliterated their Indian name into English and used it as a surname. Others adopted European surnames related to physical characteristics, accomplishments, or occupation, much in the manner of Europeans in the Middle Ages.

Indians with only one name are often listed in the census indexes as though *Indian* were their surname. Those with at least two names are indexed by the surname or the Indian name that seemed to the census taker or indexer to be a surname.

The 1870 census was the first to include *Indian* as one of the categories of *color* (race) to be designated by the enumerators. Jasper County, Mississippi, was home to a number of Indians living among the whites and blacks. Those with English names included John Marsh and Wife, Betsy, both born in Mississippi and married in December 1869. As in some white and black households, genealogical information sometimes creeps into these records, unasked for but appreciated. In the household of Indians Tom and Susey Parker was Molly Parker, age 60, identified as "living with son." In the case of one young Indian family with no surname, John, Susy, and infant Nancy, the other person in the household was Oliver Deace, identified as "living with brother." One must ask whether John and Suzy ever took the surname Deace and what its significance was.

Although Indians in what became Oklahoma were not enumerated in the general population schedules of the nineteenth century, the 1860 slave schedule for the "Indian lands west of Arkansas" acts as a partial Indian census, at least for the considerable number who were slave owners. This enumeration appears at the end of the slave schedule for Arkansas, M653, roll 54. In the Cherokee Nation, the majority of slave owners were Indians, often marked *Ind.* after their names, such as Eagle, James Johnson, John Glass, Rachel Rider, Pigeon Halfbreed, and Chief John Ross. In the Choctaw and Creek nations, a number were listed by Indian name: Cah notamah, Nu kia chee, Ben a hantubbee, Nocosille of New Yorker, and Tick Funke of Tuckaparche. A few in the Creek Nation were listed by only one name, such as Polly, a Seminole, and Hope, a Negro. Comparing the slave owner list with the general population schedule of the same area, which included only whites and free blacks, helps distinguish the slave owners who were Indians with English names. In the Chickasaw Nation, Georgia Ann Love in the general population schedule was marked as wife of a native, who was not named. In the corresponding slave schedule, Samuel Love was listed as a slave owner. One would want to find other records to answer the question of whether this Samuel was Georgia's husband, as suggested in these censuses.

In 1880 the Census Bureau instructed enumerators to take a special census of Indians on reservations, using 1 October 1879-1880 as the census year. In addition, persons who died after 1 October 1880 were to be included, but children born after 1 October 1880 were to be omitted. Apparently, partial enumerations were made only for Indians living near military posts in Washington, Oregon, California, and the Dakotas. Contact the National Archives and regional branches in those areas for availability. At this writing, the re-

cords apparently have not been microfilmed.

In 1900 and 1910, the census also included a special Indian schedule for enumerating Indians on and off reservations. Every family composed primarily of Indians was to be reported on the special schedule. Indians living in predominantly white or black households were to be included in the general population schedule. These Indian schedules are usually found on the microfilm with the general population, at the end of the county in which the families resided.

Records of Tribal Indians

For historical reasons, the records of Indians who remained in tribal situations are basically divided into two distinct categories: (1) the southeastern tribes (the Five Civilized Tribes), most of whom were removed to what is now Oklahoma, and (2) the Indians who were wards of the federal government, living on reservations, some of whom were also removed to Oklahoma. Nearly all the records were processed through the Office of Indian Affairs (OIA), established in 1824 within the War Department. The office was created to exercise jurisdiction over Indian matters and became the Bureau of Indian Affairs (BIA) in 1947 within the Department of the Interior. Aside from BIA files, records were generated as the Indians confronted other areas of federal jurisdiction, such as the army and the courts. In addition, certain tribes allied themselves with the Confederate cause during the Civil War. Records of all these activities are housed in the National Archives or its regional branches. Many are available on microfilm for <u>use</u> at research libraries, for <u>purchase</u> from the Archives or Scholarly Resources, or for <u>rent</u> from the FHL or AGLL.

The Five Civilized Tribes. The Five Civilized Tribes (Cherokee, Creek, Choctaw, Chickasaw, and Seminole) lived in the southeast before their removal to the area that became Indian Territory and then Oklahoma. They were self-governing nations until 1906, just prior to Oklahoma statehood. Each tribe had its own agent from the Office of Indian Affairs until the Union Agency was set up in Muskogee about 1874 In the early 1900s, that agency became an area office of the OIA, later BIA.

Before 1896, these nations had jurisdiction over their own citizenship and over non-Indians who were allowed to live and work in tribal territory. Those non-Indians who did not abide by the rules the tribes established were considered intruders and became the subjects of numerous records. In preparation for the allotment of tribal lands to individual Indians, the federal government assumed the task of identifying eligible tribe members. In 1896, the Dawes Commission, headed by Senator Henry Dawes, was authorized to receive applications for enrollment in addition to persons already on tribal rolls. The enrollment applications contain much genealogical information, are microfilmed, and are listed on page 160.

Tucked into government documents are sometimes gems of information that provide genealogists with vital clues or answers. The problem is finding them since many collections are not indexed or completely catalogued. One such record is a twelve-page Register of persons who wish reservation under the Treaty of July 8, 1817. It is a list of eastern Cherokees, some of whom agreed to move west to Arkansas, and others who asked to take advantage of a government policy that would give them 640 acres of reserved land during their lifetimes but revert to the state on the death or abandonment of the grantee.

The register does not contain much concrete genealogical information, but it does give the name of the reservee, the number in the family, and a general idea of the family's residence on the rivers of north Alabama, north Georgia, east Tennessee, and western North Carolina. This is an early list, made in 1817 and 1819, before the removal records, and thus can be helpful in identifying and locating some heads of household for the first time. Included are females, such as Elizabeth Walker, a native, and Ca hu can, a widow, and a number of men who used Indian or translated names: Wey-chutta, The Musk Rat, and The Old Mouse. The register is also valuable for its inclusion of a number of white men, such as James Lasley, Parker Collin, and Thomas Cordery, who were married to Cherokee women and who signed up in the right of their wives. The wives are not named, but the list is evidence that these white men had Indian wives at this particular time and gives a clue to their place of residence. The register appears in transcription in several books cited in the following bibliography, including *Cherokee Roots, Cherokee Reservees*, and *Cherokee Emigration Rolls*. The microfilm of the original can be found in M208, Records of the Cherokee Indian Agency in Tennessee, 1801-1835, among other items on roll 13. The index and the register are separated by other material.

Among the largest collections of records of the Five Civilized Tribes are those at the National Archives, the Fort Worth, Texas, regional branch of the National Archives, the Oklahoma Historical Society, and the Western History Collection at the University of Oklahoma. Microfilmed National Archives records dealing with Indians of the Five Civilized Tribes include those listed below. See also M1011, M234, M595 (for eastern Cherokee, Choctaw, and Seminole) in the next section. Records held and microfilmed by the Ft. Worth regional Archives are designated with the *7RA* prefix. Both the National Archives and the Ft. Worth regional branch have additional manuscript records of a similar nature that have not been microfilmed. These include census rolls of Indians and freedmen, claims, school records, payment rolls, enrollment records, and land allotment records (1899-1914). In addition, the Atlanta regional Archives branch holds some eastern Cherokee agency records (1886-1952) and some from the Seminole agency. The Oklahoma Historical Society also holds some national/tribal records such as tax lists, censuses, and marks and brand registrations. The University of Oklahoma Western History Collection holds the Cherokee Nation papers, which include censuses and government records of various kinds, and numerous Indian Pioneer interviews conducted by the WPA in the 1930s.

The following are some of the microfilmed records on the Five Civilized Tribes.

1. **Cherokee**
   a. Records of the Cherokee Indian Agency in Tennessee, 1801-1835 (M208).
   b. Cherokee Nation census rolls: 1852 Drennen roll (7RA01). 1867 Tompkins roll of Cherokee citizens and freedmen and 1867 census (7RA04). Index to Tompkins roll (7RA51, roll 1). 1880 census and index (7RA07). 1883 census and payroll (7RA29). 1883 census (7RA56). 1886 census (7RA58). 1890 census (7RA08 and 7RA60). Old Settler roll, 1895, with index to payment roll, 1896 (T985). 1896 census (7RA19). Index to 1896, except freedmen (7RA71).
   c. Rolls of the Eastern Cherokee: 1835 with index (T496). 1848 Mullay roll, 1851 Siler roll, 1852 Chapman roll (7RA06). See also *i* below.
   d. Selected letters received by Office of Indian Affairs relating to Cherokee of North Carolina, 1851-1905 (M1059).
   e. Eastern Cherokee Applications of the U.S. Court of Claims, 1906-1909 (M1104, 348 rolls). Grievances of the Cherokees against the gov-

ernment arising from treaties were taken to the Court of Claims, which decided in favor of the eastern Cherokee. The Interior Department had to identify those persons entitled to share in the distribution of the settlement funds. Guion Miller compiled the roll. He reported in 1909 that nearly 46,000 applications had come in, representing about 90,000 persons, of whom about 30,000 were approved.

f. Records Relating to the Enrollment of the Eastern Cherokee, by Guion Miller, 1908-1910 (M685). Includes copies of earlier rolls (Chapman, Drennan, Old Settler, and the Hester roll of 1884) with indexes.

g. Cherokee Citizenship Commission docket books, 1880-1884, 1887-1889, list of rejected claimants, 1878-1880, and persons admitted to citizenship (7RA25). Decisions of U.S. Court on Cherokee citizenship (7RA98).

h. Payroll of Delaware-Cherokee, 1896, and Shawnee-Cherokee census, 1896 and 1904 (7RA26). 1867 Delaware-Cherokee list and index (7RA73). Delaware, Shawnee, and North Carolina Cherokees, 1867-1881 (7RA74). Payroll, per capita, Delaware, 1904 (7RA26). Index to Delaware-Cherokees (7RA81).

i. Cherokee payment rolls; Lipe roll, 1880 (7RA33). 1883 roll (7RA57). 1890 roll (7RA59). Starr roll and index, 1894 (7RA38). Old Settlers roll, 1896 (7RA34). 1902 payment to destitute Cherokees and payment to intermarried whites 1909-1910 (7RA80). 1912 and duplicate per capita payroll (7RA81). Equalization payment rolls, 1910-1915 (7RA82).

j. Cherokee Freedmen, various indexes and rolls, 1880-1897 (7RA51). Lists (7RA53, roll 8). 1893 census (7RA54).

k. Intruder cases and indexes, 1901-1909 (7RA53). 1893 census of intruders (7RA55).

l. Indexes: Cherokees by intermarriage, Delaware-Cherokees, new born freedmen, new born Cherokees by blood (7RA81, roll 1).

m. Register of Cherokee students, 1881-1882 (7RA91).

2. Creek

a. Censuses: 1832, Parsons and Abbott roll (T275). Old Settlers roll, 1857 (7RA23). Citizens and Freedmen (Dunn roll), 1867 (7RA05). Creek Freedmen, 1867 (7RA44). Creek Freedmen with index, 1869 (7RA05). 1882 (7RA43). 1890 and 1895 (7RA12, roll 1). Colbert roll, 1896 (7RA12, roll 2, and 7RA69).

b. Records of the Creek Trading House, 1795-1816 (M4).

c. Payrolls: 1858-1859 (7RA23). 1867 (7RA44). 1869 for Creek Freedmen as of 1867 (7RA44). 1890 (7RA46). 1895 (7RA12, roll 2). 1896 (7RA12, roll 1). Loyal Creek payment roll, 1904 (7RA31).

d. Authenticated tribal roll, 1890 (7RA41).

e. Intruder cases and indexes (7RA53).

f. Applicants for citizenship, 1895-1896, and citizenship commission docket book, 1895 (7RA68). Lists and index of Creek applicants admitted to citizenship, 1896 (7RA42).

3. Choctaw

a. Records of the Choctaw Trading House, 1803-1824 (T500).

b. Choctaw and Chickasaw allotment ledgers, including Mississippi Choctaw, with index (7RA153).

c. Choctaws paid by Chickasaws under Treaty of 22 June 1855 (7RA09).

d. Payrolls: 1893 index to payroll and orphans list (7RA64). Index to same (7RA65). Townsite fund payment roll with index, 1904 (7RA83). Choctaw-Chickasaw townsite fund payroll with index, 1906 (7RA84). $20 payment roll, 1908 with index (7RA88). Equalization payroll and index, 1910 (7RA89). $50 payment roll and index, 1911 (7RA90). $300 payment roll and index, 1916 (7RA93). $100 payment roll and index, 1917 (7RA94).

e. Records of Choctaw-Chickasaw citizenship court, 1902-1904 with index (7RA27).

f. Records of intruders in Choctaw-Chickasaw Nations, 1900-1901, and list of U.S. citizens living unlawfully in Pickens County, Chickasaw Nation (7RA53, roll 8). Indexes to Choctaw intruder cases (7RA53).

g. Census records: 1885 index (7RA62). 1896 census with index (7RA02). 1896 census (SW16). Chocktaw-Chickasaw freedmen rolls, 1885 (7RA63). Census of these freedmen, 1896 (7RA66).

h. Mississippi Choctaw townsite payroll and index, 1908 (7RA107), 1911 (7RA108).

i. Records relating to identification of Mississippi Choctaw (7RA116).

4. Chickasaw

a. Records of Treasury Department (RG56), correspondence concerning administration of trust funds for the Chickasaw and others, 1834-1872 (M749).

b. Annuity roll, 1878 (7RA21).

c. Census rolls, 1897 with index (7RA21)

d. List of intruders, not dated (7RA21). Indexes to intruder cases and intruders (7RA53).

e. Index to $40 townsite fund payroll, 1904 (7RA97). Supplement to previous payroll, 1906, with indexes (7RA84). Payment roll, 1908 (7RA100). Equalization payment roll, 1910 (7RA101). Chickasaw incompetent payroll, 1903 (7RA96).

5. Seminole

Allotment schedules for 1901 and 1902, payment and census rolls 1868, 1895-1897 (7RA20).

6. Enrollment

a. Applications for enrollment of the Commission to the Five Civilized Tribes, 1898-1914 (M1301). Includes doubtful and refused applications. 468 rolls of microfilm, arranged by tribe.

b. Enrollment cards (also called census cards) for the Five Civilized Tribes, 1898-1914 (M1186). Categories: citizen by blood, by marriage, newborn, minor citizens by blood, freedmen, newborn freedmen, minor freedmen. Includes Delaware Indians adopted by the Cherokee. "Straight" cards indicated application was approved. D cards were considered doubtful applications and later transferred to Straight or Rejected cards. Information includes name, age, sex, relationship to head of household, enrollment number if approved, parents' names, degree of Indian blood, and sometimes notes about births, deaths, etc. Arranged by field number (census card number, different from enrollment number). Roll 1 is index to final rolls. Descriptive pamphlet available from the National Archives.

c. Final rolls (Dawes rolls) of citizens and freedmen of the Five Civilized Tribes in Indian Territory, 1907, 1914 (T529 and 7RA3). Includes approved and disapproved names; Mississippi Choctaw and Delaware Cherokee; roll (enrollment) number and census card numbers.

d. Index to Choctaw R cards (7RA147).

e. Index to Cherokee rejected and doubtful Dawes enrollment cards (7RA24).

Records of Reservation Indians. The National Archives hold numerous records relating to Indian reservations and their inhabitants, although few of the materials pertain to eastern Indians. (Some eastern Indians are under the authority of state governments.) In addition, the regional Archives branches also hold some Indian records pertinent to reservations, tribes, agencies, and BIA field offices in their region. For example, the Kansas City branch holds records of the Sioux and the Consolidated Chippewa. Contact the branches for agency and field office records, which include such materials as land allotment registers, annuity payment rolls, marriage and vital statistics registers, heirship records, registers of families, student records, school censuses, and records of agency employees. A chart that may help you find such records is a table of BIA field offices, their records and which branch archives holds them: *Guide to Genealogical Research in the National Archives* (Washington, DC: National Archives, revised edition 1985), p 163-167. The microfilm listed below are National Archives publications. Contact the National Archives for the descriptive pamphlets that are available for many of the publications (M or T numbers).

1. **Indian Census Rolls, 1884-1940** (M595). Roll by roll listing found in *American Indians: A Select Catalog of National Archives Microfilm Publications* (Washington, DC: National Archives, 1984). Records submitted by agents or superintendents in compliance with an 1884 law. Not all agencies reported each year. Includes schools, seminaries, and only those persons who maintained a formal affiliation with a tribe. Series organized by agency or institution. Does not include the Five Civilized Tribes in Indian Territory; does include Mississippi Choctaw and eastern Cherokee. Descriptive pamphlet available. Very important resource.

2. **Records of Superintendencies of Indian Affairs.** Until the 1870s, superintendents were responsible for Indian affairs in a broad area, could include a number of tribes, and for the agencies within their jurisdiction. Agents were the government employees assigned to one or more tribes,

under the jurisdiction of a superintendent, and after the 1870s, reporting directly to the Commissioner of Indian Affairs. Agents distributed money and supplies, carried out treaty provisions, and concerned themselves with education within the tribe. By the early 1900s, agents were being called superintendents. The following records include reports, correspondence, contracts.

a. Records of the Arizona Superintendency, 1863-1873 (M734).

b. Records of the Central Superintendency, 1813-1878 (M856).

c. Records of the Dakota Superintendency, 1861-1870, 1877-1878; of the Wyoming Superintendency, 1870 (M1016).

d. Records of the Idaho Superintendency, 1863-1870 (M832).

e. Records of the Michigan Superintendency, 1814-1851 (M1).

f. Records of the Minnesota Superintendency, 1849-1856 (M842).

g. Records of the Montana Superintendency, 1867-1873 (M833).

h. Records of the Nevada Superintendency, 1869-1870 (M837).

i. Records of the New Mexico Superintendency, 1849-1880 (T21).

j. Records of the Northern Superintendency, 1851-1876 (M1166).

k. Records of the Oregon Superintendency, 1848-1873 (M2).

l. Miscellaneous letters sent by Pueblo Indian Agency, 1874-1891 (M941).

m. Records of the Southern Superintendency, 1832-1870; of the Western Superintendency (to conform with Wyoming above), 1832-1851 (M640).

n. Records of the Utah Superintendency, 1853-1870 (M834).

o. Records of the Washington Superintendency, 1853-1874 (M5).

p. Records of the Wisconsin Superintendency, 1836-1848; of the Green Bay Subagency, 1850 (M951).

q. Superintendents' annual reports, statistical and narrative, 1907-1938 (M1011). Includes Five Civilized Tribes. All but Roll 1 arranged alphabetically by institution or agency.

3. **Historical sketches of field units** and subject

headings used in M18, 1824-1880 (T1105).

4. **Correspondence.**

a. Letters received by Office of Indian Affairs, 1824-1881 (M234). Arranged by agency or superintendency or by topic, such as annuity goods and emigration, then by registry number. Registers for these letters (M18) give registry number (after mid-1836), name of writer, date written and received, agency or jurisdiction under which it was filed, and summary. Letters sent by Office of Indian Affairs, 1824-1881 (M21). Some indexing by addressee.

b. Letters received by Secretary of War on Indian Affairs, 1800-1823 (M271). (Primarily southern Indians and the Seneca in New York.) Each year is alphabetical by writer. Letters sent by Secretary of War on Indian Affairs, 1800-1824 (M15). 6 rolls, indexed.

c. Letters received by superintendents of Indian trade, 1806-1824 (T58). Letters sent by superintendents of Indian trade, 1807-1823 (M16). Indexed by addressee.

d. Letters received by Indian Division of Department of the Interior, 1849-1880 (M825). Letters sent by same division, 1849-1903, and indexes through 1897 (M606).

e. Letterbook of the Natchitoches-Sulphur Fork Factory (trading post), 1809-1821 (T1029).

f. Letters of the Arkansas Trading House, 1805-1810 (M142).

5. **Miscellaneous records and reports.**

a. Records relating to investigations of the Ft. Phil Kearney or Fetterman Massacre 1866-1867 (M91). BIA records.

b. Special files, 1807-1904 (M574). Correspondence, reports, affidavits, etc., primarily relating to claims and investigations. Consult descriptive pamphlet on the series for specifics.

c. Report books, 1838-1885 (M348). Copies of reports to Congress, President, and other officials. Original report books, 1849-1880 (M825).

d. Records relating to the enrollment of Flathead Indians, 1903-1908 (M1350).

e. Reports of inspection of field jurisdictions, Office of Indian Affairs, 1873-1900 (M1070). Rolls alphabetical by agency, superintendency, or institution.

f. Chetimachas Indians, Louisiana, federal court records (7RA12).

g. Osage annuity rolls, 1878-1909 (7RA35).

h. Miami annuity payment roll, 1895, and census list, 1881 (V236).

Apart from these agency and tribal records, historical records of various tribes are found in the *Territorial Papers of the United States*, and *Territorial Papers of the Departments of State and Interior*, the *New American State Papers: Indian Affairs* (Volumes 3 and 4—Northwest, Volumes 6-13—Southeast), and the Gales and Seaton *American State Papers: Indian Affairs*.

Court records sometimes are helpful in providing genealogical information about individuals. (Chapter eight discusses court records in greater detail.) One such case came before the Ohio Supreme Court in December 1843. (*Lane vs. Baker*, 12 Ohio Supreme Court Reporter, p 237) Thomas Lane, who lived in Silvercreek, Greene County, sent his son John Eldridge Lane and his other two children to school on 25 January 1841. They were not allowed to stay at school because it was said that they were Indian children, not white. The issue in the case was the degree of Indian blood, which was determined to be less than one-half. The court decided in Lane's favor that the children be considered white. The original court records would give more thorough discussion than the printed report, including perhaps the names of the other children and the identity of the Indian ancestor(s).

Military records from the National Archives contain information about Indians who have served as soldiers. (Compiled service records and other evidences of service are discussed in chapter four.) The most pertinent sources are these:

1. Registers of enlistments in the U.S. Army, 1798-1914 (M233). Roll 70—Indian Scouts, 1866-1877. Roll 71—Indian Scouts, 1878-1914.

2. Compiled service records of military units in volunteer Union organizations (Civil War) (M594). Roll 225 includes Indian Home Guards.

3. Compiled service records of confederate soldiers (M258). Rolls 77-91 are units of Cherokee, Choctaw, Chickasaw, Creek, Osage, and Seminole soldiers. *American Indians: A Select Catalog of National Archives Microfilm Publications* lists contents of each roll.

4. Compiled records showing service of military units in Confederate organizations (M861). Roll 74 contains information on the Indian units.

BIBLIOGRAPHY—A SAMPLING

This bibliography includes several how-to books on Indian genealogy, transcriptions of original records, bibliographies, reference books, and a few general histories.

Africans and Creeks: From the Colonial Period to the Civil War, by Daniel F. Littlefield, Jr. (Westport, CT: Greenwood Press, 1979).

American Indians: A Select Catalog of National Archives Microfilm Publications (Washington, DC: National Archives, 1984). Roll-by-roll listings to help you order or use the film.

American Indian Archival Material: A Guide to Holdings in the Southwest, by Ron Chepesiuk and Arnold Shankman (Westport, CT: Greenwood Press, 1982). Depositories by state with description of holdings.

Atlas of Great Lakes Indian History, Helen Hornbeck Tanner, ed. (Norman, OK: University of Oklahoma Press, for Newberry Library, 1987).

Bibliography of the Osage, by Terry P. Wilson (Metuchen, NJ: Scarecrow Press, 1986). No. 6 of Native American Bibliography Series.

Bibliography of the Sioux, by Jack W. Marken and Herbert T. Hoover (Metuchen, NJ: Scarecrow Press, 1980). No. 1 of Native American Bibliography Series.

Biographical and Historical Index of American Indians and Persons Involved in Indian Affairs, United States Department of the Interior (Boston: G.K. Hall, 1966), 8 vols. Lists books, articles, documents, and where they are found.

Black Indian Genealogy Research: African-American Ancestors Among the Five Civilized Tribes, by Angela Y. Walton-Raji (Bowie, MD: Heritage Books, 1993).

Cartographic Records in the National Archives of the United States Relating to American Indians, Laura E. Kelsay, comp. (Washington, DC: National Archives, 1974, Reference Information Paper No.71).

Cherokee Advocate Newspaper Extracts, by Dorothy Tincup Mauldin (Tulsa, OK: Oklahoma Yesterday Publications, current), 7 vols. Corresponds to microfilm rolls at Oklahoma Historical Society, 1844-1906.

Cherokee Blood: Cherokee Indian Genealogy Based on Records of the U.S. Court of Claims, by Shirley Hoskins (Chattanooga, TN: the author, 1982). Based on Eastern Cherokee claims applications, 1906-1909.

Cherokee By Blood; Records of Eastern Cherokee Ancestry in the U.S. Court of Claims, 1906-1910, by Jerry Wright Jordan (Bowie, MD: Heritage Books, 1987-1992), 8 vols.

Cherokee Emigration Rolls 1817-1835, by Jack D. Baker (Oklahoma City, OK: Baker Publishing Co., 1977).

The Cherokee Freedmen: From Emancipation to American Citizenship, by Daniel F. Littlefield, Jr. (Westport, CT: Greenwood Press, 1978).

Cherokee Reservees, by David K. Hampton (Oklahoma City, OK: Jack Baker Publishing, 1979).

Cherokee Roots, by Bob Blankenship (Bowie, MD: Heritage Books, 1992, reprint of 1978 original), 2 vols. Volume 1—Eastern Cherokee rolls, 1817-1924; Volume 2—Western Cherokee rolls, 1851-1909.

Colonial Records of South Carolina: Documents Relating to Indian Affairs, William L. McDowell, Jr., ed. (Columbia, SC: South Carolina Archives, 1958 [Vol. 1], 1970 [Vol. 2]). Volume 1, 1750-1754. Voume 2, 1754-1765.

Cherokee Roll: Indians by Blood, B.J. and Dianne D. Graves, comps. (Houston: G and S Publishers, 1989). From Microfilm T529, Final rolls of the Five Civilized Tribes, roll 2.

A Complete Roll of All Choctaw Claimants and Their Heirs: Existing under the Treaties between the United States and the Choctaw Nation as far as shown by the Records of the United States and the Choctaw Nation, Joe R. Goss, comp. (Conway, AR: Oldbuck Press, 1992, reprint of 1889 original).

The Confederate Cherokees: John Drew's Regiment of Mounted Rifles, by W. Craig Gaines (Baton Rouge: Louisiana State University Press, 1989). Has muster rolls of 1861.

Dictionary Catalog of the Edward E. Ayer Collection of Americana and American Indians in the Newberry Library, the Newberry Library (Boston: G.K. Hall, 1961), 16 vols.

Ethnic Genealogy: A Research Guide, Jessie Carney Smith, ed. (Westport, CT: Greenwood Press, 1983). Chapter 7, "American Indian Records and Research," by Jimmy B. Parker, dealing mostly with reservation Indians. Extensive bibliography.

Exploring Your Cherokee Ancestry, by Tom Moo-

ney (Tahlequah, OK: Cherokee National Historical Society, 1990).

Guide to American Indian Documents in the Congressional Serial Set, 1817-1899, by Steven L. Johnson (New York: Clearwater Publishing Company, 1977).

Guide to American Indian Resource Materials in Great Plains Repositories, Joseph C. Svoboda, comp. (Lincoln, NE: Center for Great Plains Studies, University of Nebraska-Lincoln, 1983).

Guide to Catholic Indian Mission and School Records in Mid-West Repositories, by Philip C. Bantin with Mark G. Thiel (Milwaukee: Marquette University Libraries, Department of Special Collections and University Archives, 1984).

A Guide to Cherokee Documents in Foreign Archives, by William S. Anderson and James A. Lewis (Metuchen, NJ: Scarecrow Press, 1983). No. 4 in Native American Bibliography Series.

A Guide to Cherokee Documents in the Northeastern United States, by Paul Kutsche (Metuchen, NJ: Scarecrow Press, 1986). No. 7 in Native American Bibliography Series.

A Guide to the Indian Tribes of the Pacific Northwest, Robert H. Ruby and John A. Brown, eds. (Norman, OK: University of Oklahoma Press, 1992 revised edition).

A Guide to Manuscripts Relating to the American Indian, by J.E. Freeman and M.D. Smith, with supplement (1982) by D. Kendall (Philadelphia: American Philosophical Society, 1966).

Guide to Records in the National Archives Relating to American Indians, by Edward E. Hill (Washington, DC: National Archives, 1984).

Guide to Sources of Indian Genealogy, by Charles Butler Barr (Independence, MO: the author, 1989).

Handbook of American Indians North of Mexico, Frederick Webb Hodge, ed. (Washington, DC: Government Printing Office, as Bureau of American Ethnology, Bulletin 30, 1907-1910), 2 vols. Standard reference on tribes, alternate names, locations, bibliography. Reprint by Scholarly Press, Grosse Pointe, MI, 1968, and Greenwood Press, Westport, CT, 1969.

Handbook of North American Indians, William G. Sturtevant, ed. (Washington, DC: Government Printing Office for the Smithsonian, 1978-).

How to Research American Indian Blood Lines: A Manual on Indian Genealogical Research, by

Cecelia Svinth Carpenter (South Prairie, WA: Meico Associates, 1984).

In Pursuit of the Past: An Anthropological and Bibliographic Guide to Maryland and Delaware, by Frank W. Porter III (Metuchen, NJ: Scarecrow Press, 1986). No. 8 of Native American Bibliography Series.

The Indian Tribes of North America, by John R. Swanton (Washington, DC: Government Printing Office, as Bureau of American Ethnology, Bulletin 145, 1952, reprint by Smithsonian).

The Indian Tribes of the Southeastern United States, by John R. Swanton (Washington, DC: Government Printing Office, as Bureau of American Ethnology, Bulletin 137, 1946, reprint by Greenwood Press, Westport, CT). History and bibliography.

Indians of the Great Basin: A Critical Bibliography, by Omer C. Stewart (Bloomington, IN: Indiana University Press, 1982).

Introductory Guide to Indian-Related Records (to 1876) in the North Carolina State Archives, by Donna Spindel (Raleigh, NC: North Carolina Division of Archives and History, 1977).

The Intruders: The Illegal Residents of the Cherokee Nation, 1866-1907, by Nancy Hope Sober (Ponca City, OK: Cherokee Books, 1991).

The Iroquois in the Civil War: From Battlefield to Reservation, by Laurence M. Hauptman (Syracuse, NY: Syracuse University Press, 1993).

List of Cartographic Records of the Bureau of Indian Affairs, Laura E. Kelsay, comp. (Washington, DC: National Archives, 1954. Special List No. 13).

Native American Periodicals and Newspapers, 1828-1982, James P. Danky, ed. (Westport, CT: Greenwood Press, 1984).

Native Americans: An Annotated Bibliography, by Frederick E. Hoxie and Harvey Markowitz (Pasadena, CA: Salem Press, 1991). Part of Magill Bibliographies.

Ottawa and Chippewa Indians of Michigan, 1870-1909, by Raymond C. Lantz (Bowie, MD: Heritage Books, 1991). Ottawa and Chippewa Indi- ans of Michigan, 1855-1868, Including Some Swan Creek and Black River of the Sac and Fox Agency for the Years 1857, 1858, and 1865, same author and publisher, 1992.

Our Native Americans and Their Records of Genealogical Value, by E. Kay Kirkham (Logan, UT: Everton Publishers, 1980), 2 vols.

The Papers of Chief John Ross, Gary E. Moulton, ed. (Norman, OK: University of Oklahoma Press, 1985). Volume 1, 1807-1839. Volume 2, 1840-1866. Indexed.

Potawatomi Indians of Michigan, 1843-1904, Including some Ottawa and Chippewa, 1843-1866, and Potawatomi of Indiana, 1869 and 1885, by Raymond C. Lantz (Bowie, MD: Heritage Books, 1992).

Records of the Bureau of Indian Affairs, Edward E. Hill, comp. (Washington, DC: National Archives, 1965), 2 vols. Preliminary Inventory No. 163.

Reference Encyclopedia of the American Indian, Barry T. Klein, ed. (New York: Todd Publications, 4th ed., 1986). Volume 1—Agencies, reservations, libraries with Indian materials, museums, associations, bibliography, schools, tribes. Volume 2—Who's Who.

Sioux Personal Property Claims From the Original Ledger, Ruth Brown, transcriber (Medford, OR: Rogue Valley Genealogical Society, Inc., 1987). Payments to Sioux Indians and heirs for ponies seized in 1876 at various agencies, claims filed pursuant to acts of 1889 and 1891.

Those Who Cried, The 16,000: A Record of the Individual Cherokees Listed in the United States Official Census of the Cherokee Nation Conducted in 1835, James W. Tyner, ed. (n.p.: Chi-ga-u, Inc., 1974). Cherokees in Alabama, North Carolina, Georgia, Tennessee.

1823 Census of the Creek Indians, by Jeanne Robey Felldin and Charlotte Magee Tucker (Tomball, TX: Genealogical Publications, 1978). Facsimile of census taken by Parsons and Abbott.

1860 Federal Census, Indian Lands West of Arkansas, by Dorothy Tincup Mauldin (Tulsa, OK: Oklahoma Yesterday Publications, current). Facsimile reprint with surname index.

CHAPTER ELEVEN

Immigration and Naturalization

IMMIGRATION

Immigration to what is now the United States has taken place for at least fifteen thousand years, for American Indians were immigrants too. However, written records of immigrants cover only about five hundred years, and the bulk of those, only about two hundred to two hundred fifty years.

From the Colonial period, few immigrant arrival records exist, for there was no uniform or widespread registration. However, at various times, colonies required foreign, i.e., non-British, newcomers to swear allegiance to the English crown, as in eighteenth-century Pennsylvania. In the absence of official passenger lists, these oaths are evidence of arrival in the colony.

The Pennsylvania State Archives houses a large set of Philadelphia arrival records that cover almost a century and are published as *Pennsylvania German Pioneers: A Publication of the Original Lists of Arrivals in the Port of Philadelphia from 1727 to 1808*, by Ralph Beaver Strassburger, William John Hinke, ed. (Norristown, PA: Pennsylvania German Society, 1934, 3 vols; reprint of Vols. 1 and 3 by Genealogical Publishing Company, Baltimore, 1966). List number 156C (in Volume 1, p 444) was dated 12 September 1750: "Foreigners on ship Priscilla, Capt William Wilson from Rotterdam and Cowes did this day take and subscribe the usual oaths." The list contains seventy-four names representing 210 passengers, including my own Johann Peter Muth.

Early arrivals in various colonies have been published, both in periodicals and in books such as these:

Cavaliers and Pioneers: Abstracts of Virginia Land Patents and Grants, 1632-1800, Nell Marion Nugent, comp. (Baltimore: Genealogical Publishing Company, 1974-1979, reprint), 3 vols.

A Compilation of Original Lists of Protestant Immigrants to South Carolina, 1763-1773, by Janie Revill (Baltimore: Genealogical Publishing Company, 1968, reprint of 1939 original).

Early Virginia Immigrants, 1623-1666, by George Cabell Greer (Richmond, VA: W.C. Hill Printing Company, 1912 reprint 1960 by Genealogical Publishing Company, Baltimore).

The Early Settlers of Maryland, Gust Skordas, comp. (Baltimore: Genealogical Publishing Company, 1968).

Emigrants to Pennsylvania, 1641-1819, Michael Tepper, ed. (Baltimore: Genealogical Publishing Company, 1975). Passenger lists from the *Pennsylvania Magazine of History and Biography*.

Immigrants to the Middle Colonies, Michael Tepper, ed. (Baltimore: Genealogical Publishing Company, 1978). Passenger lists from the *New York Genealogical and Biographical Record*.

Except for some baggage and cargo manifests, few actual passenger lists were kept until federal law required them in 1819. The first mandatory lists were made by ship captains for the collector of customs at the first port where an arriving ship stopped. For a time, quarterly reports from the customs officials went to the State Department, which then reported to Congress. Some of these can be found in Congressional documents. These customs passenger lists continued to be kept throughout much of the nineteenth century. Later lists were made under the authority of the Immigration and Naturalization Service. The largest ports of entry for many years were New York, Philadelphia, Baltimore, Boston, and New Orleans, although numerous smaller ports also had incoming passengers, both aliens and returning citizens. New Orleans passenger lists include at least one member of the Preuss family who settled in Houston during the 1870s and 1880s. The German (Prussian) Emil Preuss, age 21, arrived from Bremen on the S.S. *Nurnberg* on 11 November 1880. He reported his occupation as laborer and his destination as Galveston.

One kind of customhouse record was the slave manifest. These lists identify the vessel and date of arrival as well as the name, age, and sex of slaves and the name and address of the consignee. The National Archives has some of these records (RG36) for Philadelphia (1790-1840), New Orleans (1819-1852), Mobile (1822-1860), and Savannah (1801-1860).

Although a number of bibliographies of passenger lists have been published, one of the most helpful tools in immigration research, and a good place to start is P. William Filby's *Passenger and Immigration Lists Index* (PILI), cited in the bibliography beginning on page 171. This multivolume bibliography and index now includes more than two million names from published passenger lists, naturalization records, and claims for headrights. Besides the name of the immigrant, each entry gives age, place and year of arrival, sometimes family members accompanying the immigrant, and the source and page number of the information. For example, John Dick was 46 when he came into Georgia in 1775 with his wife, Mary (33), his daughter, Jane (12), and child, Grizel (4). James Cato was 28 when he came to Maryland, also in 1775. The source of these entries is identified in the "Bibliography of Sources Indexed" in each volume so that the searcher can find the source and any other details given there, such as ship name or place of naturalization.

The companion *Passenger and Immigration Lists Bibliography, 1538-1900* annotates over 2,550 published sources of the information in the PILI. This bibliography also aids the searcher by indexing ethnic groups, destinations and arrival ports, and states. For example, under Vermont in the index, one finds an entry for naturalizations in Franklin County, nineteenth century, with the source where this information can be found. The sources in the *Bibliography* have the same code numbers that they have in PILI.

Original passenger lists can be tedious and frustrating to examine because many are not indexed and many are incomplete. One source of passenger lists that people enjoy using is the database of arrivals at the port of Galveston, Texas, 1836-1921, at the city's Texas Seaport Museum. As the major Gulf port of entry west of New Orleans, Galveston received thousands of immigrants bound for Texas and much of the central portion of the nation. The records in the database have come from the National Archives, the Texas State Archives, other contemporary documents, and records contributed by descendants of arriving immigrants. By typing into the system the surnames of interest, visitors can find name, arrival date, country of origin (or embarkation), and destination of more than 115,000 immigrants.

Evidence of origin or arrival is also sometimes found in newspapers, obituaries, voter registration lists, militia muster rolls, family Bibles, church records, land records, and census records. Federal censuses from 1850 forward and some state censuses ask for birthplace of each person. The 1900, 1910, and 1920 censuses ask the year of immigration and whether the person is a naturalized citizen. As with any census information these details may be omitted, incomplete, or incorrect, but sometimes they provide just the right clue.

Existing passenger lists are not centralized in a few convenient repositories. However, publication has made thousands of them accessible to searchers. The following are microfilmed passenger lists available for use at research libraries, including the National Archives and the regional branches (film pertaining to their region), for purchase from the National Archives or Scholarly Resources, or for rent from AGLL or FHL. Roll-by-roll listings are in *Immigrant and Passenger Arrivals: A Select Catalog of National Archives Microfilm Publications* (Washington, DC: National Archives, 2d edition, 1991). The lists themselves are chronological. The indexes are alphabetical or by Soundex code. (See chapter two for explanation of Soundex.) Note that some of the lists include crew members on the vessels.

1. About sixty-five smaller Atlantic, Gulf, and Great Lakes ports.
   a. Index, 1820-1874 (M334). Lists, 1820-1873 (*sic*) (M575).
   b. Index to passenger lists of vessels arriving at ports in Alabama, Florida, Georgia, South Carolina, 1890-1924 (T517).

2. Baltimore, Maryland
   a. Index (Soundex) to federal passenger lists, 1820-1897 (M327). Index to passenger lists submitted to city under state law, 1833-1866 (M326), included the following. Passenger lists, 1820-1891 (M255).
   b. Quarterly abstracts of passenger lists, 1820-1866 (M596).
   c. Passenger lists, 1891-1909 (T844). 1897-1952 (T520).
   d. Passenger lists, 1954-1957 (M1477).

3. Boston, Massachusetts

a. Passenger lists, 1820-1891 (M277). Index to passenger lists, 1848-1891 (M265).

b. Passenger lists, 1891-1943 (T843). Index to lists, 1902-1906 (T521). Index, 1906-1920 (T617). Book indexes, 1899-1940 (T790).

c. Crew lists of vessels arriving 1917-1943 (T938).

4. Detroit, Michigan
   a. Card manifests (alphabetical) of persons entering through Detroit, 1906-1954 (M1478).
   b. Passenger lists, 1946-1957 (M1479).

5. Galveston, Texas
   a. Index, 1846-1871 (M334). Lists, 1846-1871 (M575, roll 3).
   b. Index, 1896-1906 (M1357). Index, 1906-1951 (M1358). Lists, 1896-1951 (M1359), including arrivals at Houston, Brownsville, Port Arthur, Sabine, and Texas City. Lists between 1871 and 1896 are missing.

6. Gulfport and Pascagoula, Mississippi
   Index to passengers arriving at Gulfport, 1904-1954 and at Pascagoula 1903-1935 (T523).

7. Key West, Florida
   Passenger lists of vessels arriving 1898-1945 (T940).

8. New Bedford, Massachusetts
   a. Index, 1826-1852 (M334). Lists 1826-1852 (M575).
   b. Index, 1902-1954 (T522). Lists, 1902-1942 (T944).
   c. Crew lists on vessels arriving 1917-1943 (T942).

9. New Orleans, Louisiana
   a. Customs Service passenger lists, 1813-1866 (V116). Roll 1 includes partial index, 1839-1861.
   b. Quarterly abstracts of lists, 1820-1875 (M272). Chronological.
   c. Index to passenger lists before 1900 (T527). Lists, 1820-1902 (M259).
   d. Index to passenger lists, 1900-1952 (T618). Lists, 1903-1945 (T905).
   e. Crew lists on vessels arriving 1910-1945 (T939).

10. New York, New York
    a. Index to passenger lists, 1820-1846 (M261). Lists, 1820-1897 (M237).
    b. Index to passenger lists, 1897-1902 (T519). Index (Soundex) to lists, 1902-1943 (T621). Lists, 1897-1957 (T715, nearly 8,900 rolls).

c. Book indexes to passenger lists, 1906-1942, grouped by year and shipping line (T612).

d. Index (Soundex) to passenger lists, 1944-1948 (M1417).

11. Philadelphia, Pennsylvania
    a. Index to passenger lists, 1800-1906 (M360). Lists, 1800-1882 (M425).
    b. Index (Soundex) to passenger lists 1883-1948 (T526). Book indexes, 1906-1926 (T791). Lists, 1883-1945 (T840).

12. Portland, Maine
    a. Index to passenger lists for Portland and Falmouth, 1820-1868 (M334). Lists, 1820-1868, Portland and Falmouth (M575, rolls 9-14).
    b. Index to passenger lists, 1893-1954 (T524). Book indexes, 1907-1930 (T793). Lists, 1893-1943 (T1151).

13. Providence, Rhode Island
    a. Index to passenger lists, 1820-1867 (M334). Lists, 1820-1867 (M575, rolls 15-16).
    b. Index to passengers, 1911-1954 (T518). Book indexes, 1911-1934 (T792). Lists, 1911-1943 (T1188).

14. St. Albans District, Vermont
    a. Index (Soundex) to Canadian border entries through St. Albans, 1895-1924 (M1461).
    b. Index to Canadian border entries through small ports in Vermont, 1895-1924 (M1462).
    c. Index (Soundex) to entries into St. Albans, Vermont, through Candian Pacific and Atlantic ports, 1924-1952 (M1463).
    d. Manifests of passengers arriving in the St. Albans, Vermont, district through Canadian Pacific and Atlantic ports, 1895-1954 (M1464).
    e. Manifests of passengers arriving in the St. Albans, Vermont, district through Canadian Pacific ports, 1929-1949 (M1465).

15. San Francisco, California
    a. Index to passenger lists, 1893-1934 (M1389). Lists, 1893-1953 (M1410).
    b. Passenger lists, 1954-1957 (M1411).
    c. Customs passenger lists, 1903-1918 (M1412).
    d. Registers of Chinese laborers arriving at San Francisco, 1882-1888 (M1413), 1888-1914 (M1414). Lists of Chinese applying for admission to U.S. through San Francisco, 1903-1947 (M1476).

e. Alien crew lists on vessels arriving 1896-1921 (M1436). Crew lists, 1905-1954 (M1416).

f. Passengers on vessels arriving from Hawaii, 1902-1907 (M1440).

g. Passengers on vessels arriving from insular possessions, 1907-1911 (M1438).

16. Savannah, Georgia
    a. Index to passenger lists, 1820-1868 (M334). Lists, 1820-1868 (M575, roll 16).
    b. Passenger lists, 1906-1945 (T943).

17. Seattle, Washington, and other Washington ports
    a. Lists of Chinese arriving 1882-1916 (M1364).
    b. Passenger lists, 1890-1957 (M1383). 1949-1954 (M1398).
    c. Crew lists on vessels arriving 1903-1917 (M1399).
    d. Certificates of head tax paid by aliens arriving from foreign contiguous territory, 1917-1924 (M1365).

NATURALIZATION

Naturalization is the process by which immigrants become citizens of the United States. During the colonial period, each colony established its own process of naturalizing foreigners as citizens of that colony. State and county records reflect these actions. Because English subjects coming to the colonies, of course, were not foreigners, no naturalization process was needed.

After the founding of the United States government, Congress devised a two-step procedure, which remained basically the same until 1941, when the first step was dropped. That first step was a declaration of one's intention to become a citizen, followed usually two to seven years later, depending on the current law, by a petition for naturalization. Any court of record (federal, state, or county) had the authority to accept and approve or reject the documents, and each court kept its own records of the proceedings. (Thus, no centralized depository contains these records.) After 1906, federal circuit (abolished 1911) or district courts usually handled the proceedings, but many still went through state and county courts. Records may be found in volumes labeled as declarations of intent, civil court minutes, oaths of allegiance, certificates of naturalization, or naturalization minutes.

Of course, immigrants were not required to apply for citizenship, and many never did so. Some filed only the declaration and never completed the process. The immigrant could file the declaration at any time, and many took the step within the first several years after their arrival. The petition for naturalization could be filed usually after five years' residence in the country and one year of residence in the state. Until 1922, wives and minor children automatically became citizens with their husband/father. After 1922, women were required to file for their own citizenship.

Records of naturalization are scattered through the files of hundreds of courts. Many county and state courts still hold their own records, and clerks can direct searchers to the appropriate volumes and files. Court records not still held by the court can often be found in state archives or historical societies. The county records inventories conducted by the WPA in the 1930s may also help locate these proceedings. Federal court records are usually housed in the National Archives regional branch that services the state where the court is located (see Appendix D). The regional branches can answer more specific questions about their holdings.

If you know which court an ancestor used to file his declaration or petition and know the location of the records of that court, your search is considerably shortened. The two documents did not have to be filed in the same court, but petitions often have supporting evidence of where the declaration was filed.

If you do not know which court the ancestor used, you may still be saved from searching records of many courts. If you can determine from census or other records an approximate date of naturalization or know where the immigrant was living during the first five to fifteen years after arrival in this country, you can often narrow the search. The 1870 census used column 19 to record male *citizens* age 21 or older. The 1900, 1910, and 1920 all ask whether each adult male was naturalized or alien, and the 1920 form asks for the year of naturalization. Although the immigrant had several choices of court to use, many localities concentrated their naturalization proceedings in one or two courts, and many courts used separate record books for these records. Of course, if the family kept the certificate of naturalization issued to the new citizen, that document can furnish the name of the court where the proceedings took place. If an immigrant ancestor bought land under the Pre-emption Act of 1841 or the Homestead Act of 1862, evidence of his declaration of intention and naturalization should be with the land-entry case files at the National Archives.

If your immigrant ancestor was naturalized after 1906, a copy of the file was sent to the Bureau of Immigration and Naturalization. You can request a copy on form G-639 available from Immigration and Naturalization Service (INS) offices. Mail the form to the INS, Freedom of Information, 425 I Street, Room 5304, Washington, DC 20536.

To begin the process of naturalization an immigrant filed the "first papers," a declaration of intention to become a citizen. A rather typical nineteenth century declaration, filed on 14 February 1890 in Jeff Davis County, Texas, gives only basic but potentially helpful information about the applicant. He was Claude Albert Smith, born 6 November 1866 in Ipswich, Suffolk County, England. He stated that he had arrived at the port of New York on 21 April 1888 and that his occupation was ranchman.

After 1906, such documents were more standardized and detailed in the information they provided. The following declaration was subscribed and sworn in the office of the clerk of the state district court, Fort Bend County, Texas, 24 January 1916:

I, Steve Walchik, aged 36 years, occupation farmer, do declare on oath that my personal description is: color, white; complexion, Light; height, 5 feet 6 inches; weight, 135 pounds; color of hair, light; color of eyes, grey; other visible distinctive marks, none. I was born in Moravia Austria on the 28 day of January, anno Domini 1880; I now reside at Sugarland, Ft. Bend County, Texas. I emigrated to the United States of America from Bremen Germany on the vessel Koeln; my last foreign residence was Moravia Austria. [note added between lines] My wife's name is Johana she lives with me at Sugarland, Ft. Bend County, Texas. It is my bona fide intention to renounce forever all allegiance and fidelity to any foreign prince, potentate, state, or sovereignty, and particularly to Francis Joseph Emperor of Austria and Apostolic King of Hungary of whom I am now a subject; I arrived at the port of Galveston in the state of Texas on or about the 30th day of June anno Domini 1902; I am not an anarchist; I am not a polygamist nor a believer in the practice of polygamy; and it is my intention in good faith to become a citizen of the United States of America and to permanently reside therein: SO HELP ME GOD. Signed: Steve Walchik.

The following naturalization record from the earliest years contains much less genealogical information

than later, especially twentieth-century, records.

United States. South Carolina. To all to whom these presents may come Greeting Whereas at a Federal District Court, held in the city of Charleston under the jurisdiction of the United States of America this eighth day of February Anno Domini 1798 and in the twenty second year of the Independence and Sovereignty of the said States Alexander McFarlane late of Nova Scotia came into the said court and made application to be made a citizen of these our said States, and having complied with all the conditions and requisites of the acts of Congress in such case made and provided, for establishing a uniform rule of naturalization, and the Oath to support the Constitution of the United States of America, and to renounce all allegiance and fidelity to any Foreign Prince, Potentate State or Sovereignty whatever, being administered unto him in open Court before the Honorable Thomas Bee Esquire Federal District Judge of the same he the said Alexander McFarlane is by virtue thereof and the premises declared and enrolled a citizen of the said States. In Testimony whereof I have fixed the seal of the said court to these presents, at the City of Charleston in the District aforesaid the day and year above mentioned. Thomas Hals, Fedl. Dist. Clerk of Register. (Seal) Recorded 9th February 1798.

By contrast, a more recent petition for naturalization, dated 9 August 1907, contains much more genealogical information. The applicant was Sidney Augustus Marsh, a retail lumber dealer of Wharton, Texas, who sailed from Antwerp, Belgium, in August 1889, arrived at New York thereafter on a ship whose name he did not remember, and was in Texas by December 1889. His petition gives this additonal information:

Born 7 September 1865, London, England. Wife Silvia Jane (Moody) Marsh, born in Dover, England. Seven living children: (1) Mabel, b 2 December 1887, London, (2) Dora, b 19 June 1889, London, (3) Lucille, b 19 December 1894, Wharton, Texas, (4) Estelle, b 19 July 1896, Wharton, (5) Dulce, b 19 February 1898, Wharton, (6) Henry, b 13 October 1902, Wharton, (7) Audry, b 26 November 1903, Wharton. Declara-

tion of intention to become citizen, filed 29 March 1892, Wharton.

The affidavits on his character and residence were signed by J.P. Taylor, a local rice farmer, and Tom Brooks, a Wharton merchant. Marsh swore his oath of allegiance and was admitted to citizenship 5 December 1907. (Petition No. 4, Vol 1, Petition and Record, 1907-1912, District Court of Wharton County, Texas).

The following microfilm publications are some of the naturalization records available at the National Archives and the appropriate regional branches. They may be purchased from the National Archives or Scholarly Resources. They may also be rented from FHL. Research libraries may also have them for use.

1. Alaska. Index to naturalization records of U.S. district courts of the Territory of Alaska, 1900-1929 (M1241).

2. California. Selected indexes to naturalization records of U.S. circuit and district courts of the northern district of California, 1852-1928 (T1220).

3. Colorado. Naturalization records of the U.S. district courts of Colorado, 1877-1952 (M1192).

4. Maryland. Index to naturalization petitions to U.S. circuit and district courts of Maryland, 1797-1951 (M1168).

5. Montana. Index to naturalization records of Montana territorial and federal courts, 1869-1929 (M1236).

6. New England. Index to New England naturalization petitions, 1791-1906 (M1299).

7. Oregon. Index to naturalization records of the U.S. circuit and district courts of Oregon, 1859-1956 (M1242).

8. Pennsylvania. Index to registers of declarations of intent and petitions for naturalization of U.S. circuit and district courts of the western district of Pennsylvania, 1820-1906 (M1208). Index to naturalization petitions in U.S. circuit and district courts of the eastern district of Pennsylvania, 1795-1951 (M1248).

9. South Carolina. Record of admissions to citizenship in the district of South Carolina, 1790-1906 (M1183).

10. Washington. Indexes to naturalization records of U.S. district courts, western district of Washington, northern division (Seattle), 1890-1952 (M1232). Index to naturalization records of King County territorial and superior courts, 1864-1889, 1906-1928 (M1233). Index to the same in Thurston County, 1850-1974 (M1234). Index to the same in Snohomish County, 1876-1974 (M1235). Index to the same in Pierce County, 1853-

1923 (M1238). Index to naturalization records of the U.S. district court, western district of Washington, southern division (Tacoma), 1890-1953 (M1237).

NAME CHANGES

Numerous examples exist of immigrants or their descendants who changed their names by translating, anglicizing, or simplifying the original or by choosing a different name. The translations occurred when Verdi became Green, Koenig became King, Schmidt changed to Smith, and Le Blanc became White. Anglicizing may have been simply a matter of a spelling change based on the way people pronounced the name or the way English-speaking recorders happened to write it down. In this way, for example, the German *Rhine* sometimes was recorded as *Ryan*. Such examples, of course, tell the genealogist that finding an ancestor recorded as Michael Ryan does not automatically give the searcher Irish roots. Simplification of the name so that it was easier for Americans to pronounce and spell also has numerous examples: *Heidt* became *Hite*; *Tighe* became *Tie*; *O'Donnell* became simply *Donald* or *Donaldson*; *Morganari* changed to *Morgan*; and at least one *Preuss* was recorded as *Price*.

Texan Jimmy Dalla's family came to this country about 1909 from the Austrian Tyrol, now part of Italy. Their surname was Dalla Valla. As early as 1911, newspaper accounts were using the name in its original form and in the shortened form, which the family gradually adopted, *Dalla*. Bill Brohaugh's immigrant family were Olsens from an area in Norway called Brohaug. They found so many Olsens already in their new home that they began distinguishing themselves as the Olsens from Brohaug. Eventually, they dropped the *Olsen* altogether and became (with a slight spelling change) *Brohaugh*.

Steve DeAlmeida's immigrant ancestors were Carl and Anna Alice (Gunnison) Gumerson, from Goteborg, Sweden. When the widow Gumerson married the Portuguese Manuel DeAlmeida in the United States in 1884, her son Carl Edward simply assumed his stepfather's surname. Thus a Swede has a Portuguese surname.

Houstonian Mary Argiropoulos tells that when her father Elias Blahothanasi reached Ellis Island from Greece about 1903, the authorities there changed his name to Louis N. Pappas.

These four families have preserved their immigrants' stories, and those traditions may be the only evidence of the name changes that were made. Like thousands of others, they do not seem to have gone through any official channels in assuming their new identity.

Some names are changed through court action, and court records can help identify those cases. Some immigrants or their descendants used the state legislatures for name changes. Two examples come from the Laws of Delaware, Private Acts of 1899, when Joseph F. Zinieuries changed his name to Joseph F. Emory, and Michael Ostrowsky shortened his name to Michael Ostro. The New York legislature on 27 March 1848 enabled Johan Hinnerich August von Rethwisch to become John Washington. If his descendants do not have family records that show his original name, the legislative record gives them a pleasant surprise.

Naturalization was another process through which names were changed. A good example is the young Greek Spiridon Kalivospheris who immigrated from Sparta in the first decade of the twentieth century and told his son Jerry this story of how his name was changed. When the traveling judge came through Marion, Ohio, in 1910 and naturalized three new citizens, two from Germany and one from Greece, he changed all three names on the spot. Young Spiridon was told his new name would be Spiro Kaler, and so he remained. When his younger brothers joined him in this country, he made them change their names to Kaler as well.

ETHNIC SOCIETIES

A number of ethnic historical and genealogical societies exist in the United States. These are only examples of some societies:

Dutch Family Heritage Society, 2463 Ledgewood Drive, West Jordan, UT 84084-5738.

German-Texan Heritage Society, P.O. Box 684171, Austin, TX 78768-4171.

Immigrant Genealogical Society, P.O. Box 7369, Burbank, CA 91510-7369.

The Vesterheim Genealogical Center, division of Norwegian-American Museum, 415 Main Street, Madison, WI 53703-3116.

Others may be identified through the *Encyclopedia of Associations* and other reference books listed in Appendix C.

BIBLIOGRAPHY — A SAMPLING

American Naturalization Processes and Procedures, 1790-1985, by John J. Newman (Indianapolis: Indiana Historical Society, 1985).

American Passenger Arrival Records: A Guide to the Records of Immigrants Arriving at American Ports by Sail and Steam, by Michael Tepper (Baltimore: Genealogical Publishing Company, 1988). Excellent background for understanding and locating the records.

Bonded Passengers to America, Peter Wilson Coldham (Baltimore: Genealogical Publishing Company, 1983), 9 volumes in 3. Includes earlier volumes, *English Convicts in Colonial America* (New Orleans: Polyanthos Press, 1974, 1976), 2 vols.

Czech Immigration Passenger Lists, 1848-1879, Leo Baca, comp. (Hallettsville, TX: Old Homestead Publishing Company, 1983).

Dutch Immigrants in the United States Passenger Manifests, 1820-1880: An Alphabetical Listing by Household Heads and Independent Persons, Robert P. Swierenga, comp. (Wilmington, DE: Scholarly Resources, 1983), 2 vols.

Emigrants from England, 1773-1776, by Gerald Fothergill (Boston: New England Historic Genealogical Society, 1913, reprint 1977 by Genealogical Publishing Company, Baltimore).

Encyclopedia Directory of Ethnic Organizations in the United States, by Lubomyr R. Wynar (Littleton, CO: Libraries Unlimited Inc., 1975).

The Famine Immigrants: Lists of Irish Immigrants Arriving at the Port of New York, 1846-1851, Ira A. Glazier and Michael Tepper, ed. (Baltimore: Genealogical Publishing Company, 1983-1986), 7 vols.

Germans to America: Lists of Passengers Arriving at United States Ports, Ira A. Glazier and P. William Filby, eds. (Wilmington, DE: Scholarly Resources, 1988-). 32 volumes by 1993. Volume 1 begins with 1850. Volume 32 goes through September, 1876.

Hamilton County, Ohio Citizenship Records Abstracts, 1837-1916, by University of Cincinnati (Bowie, MD: Heritage Books, 1991). Covers more than 25,000 people.

Harvard Encyclopedia of American Ethnic Groups, Stephen Thernstrom, ed. (Cambridge, MA: Belknap Press of Harvard University Press, 1980).

Immigrant and Passenger Arrivals: A Select Catalog of National Archives Microfilm Publications (Washington, DC: National Archives, 2d edition, 1991).

Immigration and Ethnicity: A Guide to Information Services, John D. Buenker et. al., eds. (Detroit: Gale Research, 1977). Includes lists of centers, repositories, societies, journals.

Italians to America: Lists of Passengers Arriving at United States Ports, 1880-1899, Ira A. Glazier and P. William Filby, eds. (Wilmington, DE: Scholarly Resources, 1992-). Volumes 1-4 cover New York, 1880-1890.

The Immigrant Experience: An Annotated Bibliography, by Paul D. Mageli (Pasadena, CA: Salem Press, 1991), part of Magill Bibliographies.

Locating Your Immigrant Ancestor, by James C. and Lili Lee Neagles (Logan, UT: Everton Publishers, 2d ed., 1986).

Migration, Emigration, Immigration: Principally to the United States and in the United States, by Olga K. Miller (Logan, UT: Everton Publishers, 1974, Volume 2 — 1981). Primarily a bibliography.

Naturalization Laws (1918-1972), Gilman G. Udell, comp. (Washington, DC: Government Printing Office, 1972).

New World Immigrants: A Consolidation of Ship Passenger Lists and Associated Data from Periodical Literature, Michael Tepper, ed. (Baltimore: Genealogical Publishing Company, 1979), 2 vols.

Passenger and Immigration Lists Index: A Guide to Published Arrival Records of about 500,000 Passengers Who Came to the United States and Canada in the Seventeenth, Eighteenth, and Nineteenth Centuries, by P. William Filby (Detroit: Gale Research, 1981). 3 vols. 12th annual supplement, 1993. Indexes published passenger, naturalization, and other immigration records. Cumulative supplements, 1982-1985, 1986-1990. Very valuable reference source. Over 2 million names indexed. Preliminary Edition, 1980.

Passenger and Immigration Lists Bibliography 1538-1900, P. William Filby, ed (Detroit; Gale Research, 2d ed., 1988). Entries list over 2,500 published passenger and naturalization lists. Companion to *Index* listed above.

Passenger Arrivals at the Port of Baltimore, 1820-1834: From Customs Passenger Lists, Michael Tepper, ed. (Baltimore: Genealogical Publishing Company, 1982).

Passengers and Ships Prior to 1684, Walter L. Sheppard, comp. (Baltimore: Genealogical Publishing Company, 1970). Early Pennsylvania.

Port Arrivals and Immigrants to the City of Boston, 1715-1716, 1762-1769, William H. Whitmore, comp. (Baltimore: Genealogical Publishing Company, 1973).

San Francisco Ship Passenger Lists, 1850-1864, by Louis J. Rasmussen (Baltimore: Genealogical Publishing Company, 1978).

Swedish Passenger Arrivals in New York, 1820-1850, by Nils W. Olsson (Chicago: Swedish Pioneer Historial Society, 1967).

CHAPTER TWELVE

Long-Distance Genealogy

Many genealogists have a research library near enough that they can travel to and from in a day and have a good part of the day for research. Others must depend on rental libraries and purchased materials between overnight trips to a research facility. Few of us live within easy reach of the Family History Library or the Library of Congress and the National Archives in Washington. And no one finds all the material that could benefit a search in any one location. We all depend on a variety of sources in a variety of locations.

This book has been an effort to encourage genealogists to branch out in their search, to try new avenues of sources. It is obvious that such branching out gives us the potential of finding much more about our ancestral families. What one source does not have, another one may.

In addition, genealogists need to build their own libraries at home and in their local public libraries. Libraries that are available to you can hardly buy all the books or subscribe to all periodicals that could benefit *your* search. Therefore, genealogists need to buy books (and perhaps share with the local library) and subscribe to periodicals relative to their own searches. The sources mentioned in this chapter address these concerns further.

BOOKSELLERS

It is beyond the scope of this book to try to identify all booksellers who sell genealogical materials. One reason for the appendix of publishers is to give you direct access to people who publish them so that you can get catalogs and order by mail. Many of those in the appendix also sell books by other publishers. The list of booksellers given here is but a sampling of those with whom you can also deal by mail.

Barnette's Family Tree Book Company, 1001 West Loop North, Houston, TX 77055. Phone: (713)684-4633.

Blair's Book Service, Rt. 2 Box 186-A, Woodstock, VA 22664-6542. Phone: (703)459-2090. BBS (703)459-5898.

Claitors Laws Books, P.O. Box 3333, Baton Rouge, LA 70821.

Frontier Press, 15 Quintana Drive, Suite 159, Galveston, TX 77554. Phone: (409)740-0138.

Genealogy Books and Consultation, 1217 Oakdale, Houston, TX 77004. Phone: (713)522-7444.

Genealogy House, 3148 Kentucky Avenue South, St. Louis Park, MN 95426.

Genealogy Unlimited, Inc., P.O. Box 537, Orem, UT 84059-0537. Phone: (801)226-8971.

Hearthstone Bookshop, 5735-A Telegraph Rd., Alexandria, VA 22303. Phone orders: (703)960-0086.

Higginson Book Company, 14 Derby Square, Salem, MA 01970. Phone: (508)745-7170. Mostly family histories.

Jonathan Sheppard Books, P.O. Box 2020, Empire State Plaza Station, Albany, NY 12220.

Tuttle Antiquarian Books, Inc., P.O. Box 541, Rutland, VT 05702. Phone: (802)773-8229.

SOCIETIES AND PERIODICALS

Why join genealogical societies? One reason is gaining access to research aids and sources pertaining to your area of research. (Participation in your local society, even outside your research area, can be beneficial too.) Many local, county, and state societies publish some kind of periodical or journal that contains abstracts of records and newspapers, entries from diaries, letters to or from residents about the people or events in the local area, tombstone transcriptions, and other helpful source materials. The publications also may contain articles about researching in the state or about genealogical scholarship, book reviews, and notices of seminars. Of course, not all genealogical periodicals are published by societies. One very fine private one that is dedicated to research and sharing records of the state is *The South Carolina Magazine of Ancestral Research* (Brent Holcomb, ed., P.O. Box 21766, Columbia, SC 29221).

A second reason for joining a society in your research area is for networking with others working in the same research area. Some societies publish membership lists with the surnames that each person researches. This allows members to contact each other directly, share information, and meet distant cousins.

Queries

Another method of networking among genealogists is through queries. The purpose of queries is to find information on elusive ancestors by making contact with other searchers who are working on the same surname or family. Almost every genealogical periodical contains a section of queries, and some specialize in them. Everton's *Genealogical Helper* is a periodical not produced by a society but full of queries. These are three periodicals primarily dedicated to queries.

Lost and Found Newsletter, P.O. Box 207, Wathena, KS 66090.

The National Queries Forum, P.O. Box 593, Santa Cruz, CA 95061-0593.

Southern Queries Magazine, P.O. Box 726, Durham, NC 27702-0726. For Southern-descended researchers wherever they live. *South* in its broad definition: former Confederacy, Delaware, District of Columbia, Maryland, West Virginia, Kentucky, Missouri, Oklahoma. Indexed. Six issues a year.

Other ways of networking and distributing queries are through genealogy columns in newspapers and computer bulletin boards. A source to help identify which newspapers have genealogy columns is *News-paper Genealogical Column Directory*, by Anita Cheek Milner (Bowie, MD: Heritage Books, 1992, 5th ed.), which is organized by state and county.

The National Genealogical Society (Arlington, Virginia) sponsors a public bulletin board, National Genealogy Conference, that can be accessed through affiliates in many cities across the country. A number of others exist through libraries, other genealogical societies, and software manufacturers. Because most of these bulletin boards to date do not offer actual online searching of primary records, they are not a prime concern of this book. One that does have some actual database searching available is located at the Atchison (Kansas) Public Library. Most of them, however, are sources for networking and sharing of information on software. In this respect, many genealogists find them helpful.

Finding Societies and Periodicals

It is fairly easy to find societies in your research area.

1. Consult directories of societies and associations in the reference section of your public library. Examples include *Encyclopedia of Associations; Regional, State and Local Organizations* (Detroit: Gale Research, latest edition) and *Meyer's Directory of Genealogical Societies in the USA and Canada*, Mary Keysor Meyer, comp. (Mt. Airy, MD: by Meyer, latest edition).

2. Consult the extensive list of genealogical societies and libraries that appears each summer in Everton's *Genealogical Helper*. This periodical is available in hundreds of libraries.

3. Consult *The Standard Periodical Directory* (New York: Oxbridge Communications, Inc., latest edition). U.S. and Canadian periodicals, including ethnic, genealogical, historical.

4. Look at the collection of periodicals in a major research library.

FOOTNOTES

Chapter 2

[1] Netti Schreiner-Yantis and Florene Speakman Love, comp., *The 1787 Census of Virginia* (Springfield, VA: Genealogical Books in Print, 1987), Vol. 1, p 329-330.

[2] Abstracts from the *Eastern Clarion, Mississippi Genealogical Exchange*, XVI, 66.

[3] Walter P. Webb, ed., *Handbook of Texas* (Austin, TX: Texas State Historical Association, 1952) I, p 869.

Chapter 4

[4] *Military Service Records: A Select Catalog of National Archives Microfilm Publications* (Washington, DC: National Archives Trust Fund Board, 1985), p 1; *Military Service Records in the National Archives of the United States*, General Information Leaflet No. 7 (Washington, DC: National Archives and Records Administration, 1985), p 2, 5-6.

[5] National Archives Microfilm M999, Records of the Assistant Commissioner for the State of Tennessee, Bureau of Refugees, Freedmen, and Abandoned Lands, Roll 26, part 2, *Descriptions of Abandoned Property and Its Former Owner*, Volume 32 (Tennessee), p 6.

Chapter 5

[6] Pollyanna Creekmore, *Early Tennessee Taxpayers 1778-1839* (Easley, SC, now Greenville, SC: Southern Historical Press, 1980, reprint 1988), p 163. This title implies a wider range of coverage than actually is the case. Washington County (1778 and 1787), Greene County (1783), Carter and Sullivan (1796), and Grainger (1799) are the only eighteenth-century lists included. The other lists range from 1801 to 1818 and then skip to Cocke County (1839).

Chapter 6

[7] Letter to the author from Mrs. Marie M. Barnett, Librarian, Grand Lodge of Virginia, Richmond, Virginia, 31 January 1992.

Chapter 7

[8] Published at least four times. (1) Originally *Atlas to Accompany the Official Records of the Union and Confederate Armies*, Washington, DC: Government Printing Office, 1891. (2) *The Official Atlas of the Civil War*, New York: T. Yoseloff, 1958. (3) *The Official Military Atlas of the Civil War*, New York: Arno Press, 1978. (4) *The Official Military Atlas of the Civil War*, New York: Fairfax Press, 1983.

Chapter 8

[9] *Public Statutes of the U.S.A.*, Richard Peters, ed. (Boston: Little, Brown and Co., 1862), Vol. 6, p 433, 5.

Chapter 9

[10] Carter G. Woodson, *Free Negro Owners of Slaves in the United States in 1830* (Washington, DC: Association for the Study of Negro Life and History, 1925).

[11] Gifford E. White, *1830 Citizens of Texas* (Austin, TX: Eakin Press, 1983), p 117.

[12] National Archives Microfilm M816, Registers of Signatures of Depositors in Branches of the Freedmen's Savings and Trust Company, 1865-1874, Roll 12—New Orleans, 1866-1874, Account Number 66.

[13] National Archives Microfilm M999, Records of the Assistant Commissioner for the State of Tennessee of the Bureau of Refugees, Freedmen, and Abandoned Lands, Roll 20—Indentures of Apprenticeship, 1865-1868, loose papers grouped by county.

[14] Juliet E.K. Walker, "Pioneer Slave Entrepreneurship—Patterns, Processes, and Perspectives: The Case of the Slave Free Frank on the Kentucky Pennyroyal, 1795-1819," *Journal of Negro History*, Volume 68, Number 3 (Summer, 1983): p. 289-308.

[15] Edwin S. Redkey, "They are Invincible," *Civil War Times Illustrated*, 28, Number 2 (1989): p 32-37.

Appendix A

[16] "Allen Family, Bible Record of Archer Allen," *William and Mary Quarterly*, Series 1, 22: p 195.

Dates

JULIAN AND GREGORIAN CALENDARS

The Julian calendar in use in Europe for centuries had twelve months and 365 days with a leap year of 366 days every fourth year, similar to our calendar today. However, it was not accurate enough to stay synchronized with sun time. Man's calendar gradually ran behind the sun's calendar until, in 1582, we were ten days behind the sun. This problem was most evident in calculating the date of Easter, which is determined by the spring equinox, March 21. In 1582, this date on the Julian calendar was March 11. Therefore, Pope Gregory XIII had the calendar corrected, and the day after October 4, 1582 was October 15 instead of October 5. To remain accurate, we now omit three leap-year days every 400 years, on the double-zero years that can *not* be evenly divided by 400: 1700, 1800, 1900, 2100, etc. The other double-zero years, which *can* be evenly divided by 400 (with no remainder),

are leap years: 1600, 2000, 2400. In addition, the Pope changed New Year's Day from March 25 to January 1.

The confusion would have been lessened if all areas had adopted the new calendar at the same time. Spain, Portugal, Poland, France, and most of Italy made the change in 1582. However, November 12 that year in Rome was November 2 in London. Belgium, parts of Holland, and most Catholic German states, including Austria and some Swiss areas, made the change in 1583-84. Hungary had adopted the new calendar by 1587. The Protestant German areas did not officially convert to the Gregorian calendar until 1699 and 1700. Denmark and Norway changed over in 1700, along with parts of Holland. Much of Protestant Switzerland switched in 1701. Much of Eastern Europe and Asia kept the old system or their own calendar until the twentieth century. Ireland, Scotland, England, and her colonies officially used the old system until 1752. By then, the difference between the two systems was 11

READING OLD STYLE AND NEW STYLE DATES

Date as given in an old record	*Date under* Old Style Julian Calendar	*Date under* New Style Gregorian Calendar
12da 5mo*	12 July	12 May
3da 10mo	3 December **	3 October
24 Jany 1702/03†	24 January 1702	24 January 1703
29da 1mo 1703†	29 March 1703	29 Jan 1703
7da 2mo 1728/29	7 February 1728	7 February 1729
1da 11mo 1750 *OS*	1 January 1750	*OS* applies only to Julian Calendar.
11/22 Feb 1731/32	11 February 1731	22 Feb 1732

*You cannot know for sure which month is meant unless you know which calendar was in use.
**Sometimes you will see 7ᵇᵉʳ, 8ᵇᵉʳ, 9ᵇᵉʳ, 10ᵇᵉʳ for the months September, October, November, and December. Remember that *septem, octo, novem,* and *decem* are the Latin numbers 7, 8, 9, and 10, and these were the seventh, eighth, ninth, and tenth months.
†Dual dating of the year applies only to January, February, March. After March 25, the year was the same under both calendars.

FORMULA FOR DETERMINING THE DAY OF THE WEEK

Formula		Example 1 25 Dec 1848	Example 2 19 Oct 1781
Step 1. Begin with the last 2 digits of the year.		48	81
Step 2. Add ¼ of this number, disregarding any remainder.		12	20
Step 3. Add the date in the month.		25	19
Step 4. Add according to the month:			
January	1 (for leap year, 0)		
February	4 (for leap year, 3)		
March or November	4		
April or July	0		
May	2		
June	5		
August	3		
September or December	6	6	
October	1		1
Step 5. Add for the 18th century	4		4
19th century	2	2	
20th century	0		
21st century	6		
Step 6. Total the numbers.		93	125
Step 7. Divide by 7. Check the remainder against the chart to determine the day of the week.		13 with a remainder of 2. Christmas was on Monday.	17 with a remainder of 6. Cornwallis surrendered at Yorktown on Friday.
1 = Sunday	5 = Thursday		
2 = Monday	6 = Friday		
3 = Tuesday	0 = Saturday		
4 = Wednesday			

days, for 1700 had been a leap year in Britain and other areas under the old calendar but not in Rome and areas under the new one. For further information, consult such references as the *World Almanac* (New York: Pharos Books, annual), the *Book of Calendars* (Frank Parise, ed., New York: Facts on File, Inc., 1982), or encyclopedias.

The notation *5/16 May 1710* indicates 5 May 1710 under the old calendar (*OS* for *Old Style*) but 16 May 1710 under the new style (*NS*). Dates between 1 January and 24 March fell into two different years, depending on which calendar was used. Thus, a date in February 1680 under the new calendar was still 1679 under the old system, which did not change to the new year until March 25. Since many people gradually switched to a January 1 New Year's date before the British officially changed calendars, there was ample reason to use a double date: February 22, 1679/80.

Family historians of course need to keep these differences in mind when studying their research finds. According to the Bible record of one Allen family of Virginia, daughter Patty was born on 25 August 1746 and her sister, Obedience, on 1 March 1747. If the dates were recorded correctly in the Bible, the older calendar must have been in use. On the old calendar, the March 1 immediately following Patty's birth was still 1746 because the new year did not begin until March 25. Thus, Obedience was born eighteen months after her older sister and could have written her birthdate *1 March 1747/48.*[16]

Quaker records often referred to months and days by number rather than by secular names, which were derived from pagan gods. Occasionally, other records reflect this same practice.

DATE REFERENCES OFTEN FOUND IN OLD NEWSPAPERS, LETTERS, AND OTHER SOURCES

the 8th instant	means	the 8th of this month
the 28th ultimo	means	the 28th of last month
Tuesday last	means	the most recent Tuesday
Thursday next	means	the nearest Thursday to follow
February last	means	the most recent February
December last	means	the most recent December, even though in a previous year

Footnotes are on page 175.

DAYS OF THE WEEK

Some reference books, such as the *World Almanac* (NY: Pharos Books), have perpetual calendars to help you determine on which day of the week a particular event occurred. However, you can figure it out for yourself with the formula given on page 177. The formula is correct for the Gregorian calendar.

Library Call Numbers

This appendix is given to facilitate browsing in libraries using either of these two numbering systems. Researchers will need to consult the library catalog for more detailed references, for exact titles of interest, and for other areas of the library where pertinent subject matter may be filed. The numbers given are those for history and related topics of interest to genealogists.

DEWEY DECIMAL SYSTEM

909.04	History of ethnic groups
929.1	Works about genealogy
929.2	Family histories
929.3	Genealogy sources: census, county records, etc.
929.4	Names
929.5	Cemetery records
940	European history
970	General history of North American racial, ethnic, and national groups

	970.1	North American native peoples in general
	970.3	Specific North American native people
	970.4	Specific North American native people in specific places in North America

971	Canadian history
972	Middle American and Mexican history
973	United States history

	973.1	Pre-1607
	973.2	Colonial Period, 1507-1775
	973.3	American Revolution and Confederation Period, 1775-1789
	973.4-973.6	Pre-Civil War, 1789-1861
	973.7	Civil War, 1861-1865
	973.8	Reconstruction, 1865-1901
	973.9	After 1901

974	Northeastern States, history

	974.1	Maine
	974.2	New Hampshire
	974.3	Vermont
	974.4	Massachusetts
	974.5	Rhode Island
	974.6	Connecticut
	974.7	New York
	974.8	Pennsylvania
	974.9	New Jersey

975	Southeastern States, history

	975.1	Delaware
	975.2	Maryland
	975.3	District of Columbia
	975.4	West Virginia
	975.5	Virginia
	975.6	North Carolina
	975.7	South Carolina
	975.8	Georgia
	975.9	Florida

976	South Central States and Gulf Coast, history

	976.1	Alabama
	976.2	Mississippi
	976.3	Louisiana
	976.4	Texas
	976.5	not assigned
	976.6	Oklahoma
	976.7	Arkansas
	976.8	Tennessee
	976.9	Kentucky

977	North Central States, history

	977.1	Ohio
	977.2	Indiana
	977.3	Illinois
	977.4	Michigan
	977.5	Wisconsin
	977.6	Minnesota

	977.7	Iowa
	977.8	Missouri
	977.9	not assigned
978		Western States, history
	978.1	Kansas
	978.2	Nebraska
	978.3	South Dakota
	978.4	North Dakota
	978.5	not assigned
	978.6	Montana
	978.7	Wyoming
	978.8	Colorado
	978.9	New Mexico
979		Far Western States, history
	979.1	Arizona
	979.2	Utah
	979.3	Nevada
	979.4	California
	979.5	Oregon
	979.6	Idaho
	979.7	Washington
	979.8	Alaska
	979.9	not assigned
996.9		Hawaii, history
200s		Religion
280s		Church history of specific denominations
281		Eastern Orthodox Church
282		Roman Catholicism
283		Anglican and Episcopalian Churches
284		Lutheran, Calvinistic, Moravian, Huguenot, Arminian, Anabaptist Churches
285		Presbyterian, Reformed, and Congregational Churches
286		Baptist, Disciples of Christ, Adventist Churches
287		Methodist Churches, including African Methodist Episcopal, United Methodist, etc.
289		Church of Christ, Quaker, Mormon, Mennonite, Christian Science, Shaker, Unitarian Churches
296		Judaism
300s		Social Sciences
325		Some Passenger Lists (International Migrations)
305.8		Black Americans, Native Americans, other ethnic groups
340		Laws, Court Cases

LIBRARY OF CONGRESS SYSTEM

CS21		Genealogy
CS71		Family histories, United States
E78		Indians by state and region
E83		Indian Wars
E99		Indians by tribe
E128.9		Afro-Americans in individual counties, cities, towns
E154		U.S. Directories and Gazetteers
E162-E169		U.S. Description and Travel
E178		U.S. History, general
E181		U.S. Military history
E182		U.S. Naval history
E184		U.S. Racial, Ethnic, and some Religious Groups, alphabetically. For example:
	E184.A2	Acadians, Cajuns
	E184.H9	Huguenots
	E184.L88	Luxemburgers
E184.5-E185.98		Afro-Americans, including E185.93 + - Afro-Americans in individual states, alphabetical by state
E186-199		U.S. Colonial Period
E201-298		U.S. Revolution Period
	E263	Revolution in the states, A-W
	E269	Revolution, Participation by groups, for example: E269.N3 Negroes and E269.15 Indians
E301-E453		U.S. 1783-1861, including
	E441-453	Slavery in the U.S. (see also card catalog for locations of other related materials)
E455-E655		Civil War, including subdivisions:
	E548	Registers of Dead and Wounded
E495-537		Civil War (Union) by states:
	E495	Alabama
	E495.5	Arizona
	E496	Arkansas
	E497	California
	E498	Colorado
	E499	Connecticut
	E500	Delaware
	E501	Washington, D.C.
	E502	Florida
	E503	Georgia
	E504	not assigned
	E505	Illinois
	E505.5	Indian Territory

E506	Indiana		E579	Tennessee
E507	Iowa		E580	Texas
E508	Kansas		E581	Virginia
E509	Kentucky		E582	West Virginia
E510	Louisiana	E585	Confederate participation by racial, ethnic, religious groups, including	
E511	Maine			
E512	Maryland		E585.A35	Afro-Americans
E513	Massachusetts		E585.I53	Indians
E514	Michigan		E585.N3	Negroes
E515	Minnesota	E611-612	Confederate Prisons	
E516	Mississippi	E615-616	Union Prisons	
E517	Missouri	E660-738	U.S. history 1865-1900	
E518	Nebraska	E740-	U.S. history, twentieth century	
E519	Nevada			

E520	New Hampshire
E521	New Jersey
E522	New Mexico
E523	New York
E524	North Carolina
E525	Ohio
E526	Oregon
E527	Pennsylvania
E528	Rhode Island
E529	South Carolina
E530	South Dakota
E531	Tennessee
E532	Texas
E532.95	Utah
E533	Vermont
E534	Virginia
E535	Washington state
E536	West Virginia
E537	Wisconsin

| E540 | Union participation by racial, ethnic, religious groups, including E540.N3 - Negroes |
| E545-655 | Civil War (Confederate) by states: |

	E551	Alabama
	E552	Arizona
	E553	Arkansas
	E558	Florida
	E559	Georgia
	E561	Indian Territory
	E564	Kentucky
	E565	Louisiana
	E566	Maryland
	E568	Mississippi
	E569	Missouri
	E571	New Mexico
	E573	North Carolina
	E577	South Carolina

History of the States (Call numbers are organized by regions but are given here alphabetically):

F321-335	Alabama
F901-915	Alaska
F406-420	Arkansas
F806-820	Arizona
F856-870	California
F771-785	Colorado
F91-105	Connecticut
F191-205	District of Columbia
F161-175	Delaware
F306-320	Florida
F281-295	Georgia
D620-629	Hawaii
F741-755	Idaho
F536-550	Illinois
F521-535	Indiana
F616-630	Iowa
F676-690	Kansas
F446-460	Kentucky
F366-380	Louisiana
F16-30	Maine
F176-190	Maryland
F61-75	Massachusetts
F561-575	Michigan
F601-615	Minnesota
F336-350	Mississippi
F461-475	Missouri
F726-740	Montana
F661-675	Nebraska
F836-850	Nevada
F31-45	New Hampshire
F131-145	New Jersey
F791-805	New Mexico
F116-130	New York
F251-265	North Carolina

F631-645	North Dakota		F301	West Florida
F486-500	Ohio		F351-355	Mississippi Valley and Middle West
F691-705	Oklahoma		F396	Old Southwest and Lower Mississippi Valley
F871-885	Oregon		F476-485	Old Northwest
F146-160	Pennsylvania		F516-520	Ohio River and Valley
F76-90	Rhode Island		F551-556	Great Lake region
F266-280	South Carolina		F591-596	Trans-Mississippi West
F646-660	South Dakota		F597	Northwest, Upper Mississippi Valley
F431-445	Tennessee		F598	Missouri River and Valley
F381-395	Texas		F721	Rocky Mountain states
F821-835	Utah		F786-788	New Southwest
F46-60	Vermont		F851-852	Pacific Northwest and Alaska
F221-235	Virginia		F970	Territories, Possessions
F886-900	Washington		PN4840-4899	American Newspapers
F236-260	West Virginia			
F576-590	Wisconsin			
F756-770	Wyoming			

History of Regions:

F1-15	New England
F106	Atlantic Coast, Mid-Atlantic states
F296	Gulf states

PN4883	Native American/Indian Newspapers
PN4884-4885	Foreign Language Press, alphabetically, for example:
PN4885.N6	Norwegian-American newspapers and periodicals

Archives, Libraries, and Rental Libraries

Listed below are addresses for major archives and libraries with genealogical materials in each state. In addition are included rental libraries and those institutions that loan or sell microform copies of censuses, newspapers, and other sources.

Consult the following sources for additional libraries, institutions, and organizations that may aid in your search:

American Library Directory (New Providence, NJ: R.R. Bowker, latest edition). Alphabetical by state, city, library name. Gives brief description of emphasis or collections.

Directory of American Libraries with Genealogical or Local History Collections, P. William Filby, comp. (Wilmington, DE: Scholarly Resources, 1988).

Directory of Archives and Manuscript Repositories in the United States (Washington, D.C.: National Historical Publications and Records Commission, National Archives and Records Service, General Service Administration, latest edition. Second edition, 1988, by Oryx Press in Phoenix, AZ.)

A Directory of Historical Organizations in the United States and Canada, Mary Bray Wheeler, ed., (Nashville: American Association for State and Local History, latest edition). The association may be contacted at 172 Second Avenue North, Suite 202, Nashville, TN 37201.

Encyclopedia of Associations: A Guide to National and International Organizations, Denise S. Akey, ed. (Detroit, MI: Gale Research Inc., annual). Multivolume. These volumes divide associations into categories. The categories of greatest interest to genealogists include number 6—Cultural Organizations, number 10—Fraternal and Ethnic Associations, number 11—Religious Institutions, number 12—Veterans, Hereditary, and Patriotic Societies, and number 13—Hobby and Avocational Groups. The index is organized alphabetically by name of association or keyword, and there is some cross-referencing. The number given with each name in the index is the entry number of that group in the main listing, not a page number.

Encyclopedia of Associations: Regional, State, and Local Organizations (Detroit, MI: Gale Research Inc., latest edition [1992-1993, 3rd ed.]). 5 vols. by region. Little overlap with the *National/International* vols. above.

The Genealogical Helper (Logan, UT: The Everton Publishers, Inc.) Each July-August issue carries a directory of genealogical societies, libraries, and periodicals.

Meyer's Directory of Genealogical Societies in the U.S.A. and Canada, Mary K. Meyer, ed. (Mt. Airy, MD: 1988, 7th ed.).

The Official Museum Directory (Washington, DC: American Association of Museums, latest edition).

LENDING LIBRARIES AND PURCHASE OF MICROFILM

American Genealogical Lending Library (AGLL), P.O. Box 244, Bountiful, UT 84011. (801)298-5358. Microfilm *Territorial Papers*, census records, county records, local histories, cemetery records, much National Archives microfilm, some periodicals. Annual membership fee for rental privileges and discount on purchases. Some film that is available for rent may also be purchased.

Duke University, Perkins Library, Durham, NC 27706-2597. For interlibrary loan of microfilm census schedules that they have, contact their Newspapers and Microforms Dept. For purchase of these same films, contact University of North Carolina, Wilson Library, Special Collections, Chapel Hill, NC 27514.

Family History Library (FHL), 35 North West Temple Street, Salt Lake City, UT 84150. Rental through one of their branch history centers, located nationwide.

Look in your telephone directory under Church of Jesus Christ of Latter-day Saints. Individual Family History Centers will be listed under the church heading. Each branch has a catalog and order forms. Visitors may use FHL materials at the main library as well.

Genealogical Center Library, P.O. Box 71343, Marietta, GA 30007-1343. Rents books only. Has a sizable collection including some materials from almost every state. Largest number of materials for Alabama, Arkansas, Connecticut, Georgia, Illinois, Indiana, Kentucky, Maryland, Massachusetts, Missouri, New York, North Carolina, Ohio, Oklahoma, Pennsylvania, South Carolina, Tennessee, Texas, and Virginia. Reasonable annual membership fee.

National Archives, Pennsylvania Avenue at Eighth Street NW, Washington, DC 20408. Purchase of microfilm that it holds. No interlibrary loan. Researchers may visit and use their materials in person.

National Archives Microfilm Rental Program, P.O. Box 30, Annapolis Junction, MD 20701-0030. (301)604-3699. Rental of federal population census schedules (not the supplemental schedules) and selected American Revolutionary war records on microfilm.

National Genealogical Society, 4527 Seventeenth Street North, Arlington, VA 22207-2363. Lends selected books from its library to members. Inquire about current catalog price.

New England Historic Genealogical Society, 101 Newbury, Boston, MA 02116. Large library of books and manuscripts open to visitors. Collection especially strong on New England, but includes Canadian, European, and American materials. Loans to members.

Scholarly Resources, Inc., 104 Greenhill Ave., Wilmington, DE 19805-1897. (800)772-8937. The authorized distributor of National Archives microfilm (sales, not loan). See Appendix of Publishers for detailed description of this company.

MAJOR LIBRARIES AND ARCHIVES

Alabama

Alabama Department of Archives and History, 624 Washington Avenue, Montgomery, AL 36130-0100.

Birmingham-Jefferson County Public Library, Southern History Collection, 2020 Park Place (mailing address 2100 Park Place), Birmingham, AL 35203.

Mobile Public Library, 701 Government Street, Mobile, AL 36602-1499.

Samford University Library, 800 Lakeshore Drive, Birmingham, AL 35229.

Alaska

Alaska Archives and Records Management, 141 Willoughby Avenue, Juneau, AK 99801-1720.

Alaska Historical Library and Museum, State Office Building, P.O. Box G, Juneau, AK 99811-0571.

Alaska State Library and Archives, P.O. Box 110571, Juneau, AK 99811-0571.

Arizona

Arizona Historical Society Research Library, 949 E. Second Street, Tucson, AZ 85719.

Arizona Department of Library, Archives and Public Records, 1700 W. Washington, Phoenix, AZ 85007.

Phoenix Public Library, 12 E. McDowell, Phoenix, AZ 85004.

Arkansas

Arkansas History Commission, Archives, One Capitol Mall, Little Rock, AR 72201.

Arkansas State Library, One Capitol Mall, Little Rock, AR 72201.

Pine Bluff-Jefferson County Library, 200 E. Eighth Avenue, Pine Bluff, AR 71601.

Southwest Arkansas Regional Archives, Old Washington Historic State Park, Washington, AR 71862.

University of Arkansas Library, Special Collections, Fayetteville, AR 72701.

University of Arkansas Library, Special Collections, 2801 S. University, Little Rock, AR 72204.

California

California State Archives Library (interim address until 1995), 201 N. Sunrise Avenue, Roseville, CA 95661.

California State Archives (address after early 1995), 1020 "O" Street, Sacramento, CA 95814.

California State Library, 914 Capitol Mall, P.O. Box 942837, Sacramento, CA 94237-0001.

California Historical Society Library, 2099 Pacific Avenue, San Francisco, CA 94109-2235.

Sutro Library, Branch of California State Library, 480 Winston Drive, San Francisco, CA 94132.

Bancroft Library, University of California at Berkeley, Berkeley, CA 94720.

California Genealogical Society Library, 300 Brannan Street, San Francisco, CA 94142.

Los Angeles Public Library, 630 W. Fifth Street, Los Angeles, CA 90071-2097.

San Diego Historical Society, 1649 El Prado, Balboa Park, P.O. Box 81825, San Diego, CA 92138.

San Francisco Public Library, Civic Center, San Francisco, CA 94102.

Colorado

Colorado Historical Society Library, 1300 Broadway, Denver, CO 80203.

Colorado State Archives and Public Records, 1313 Sherman Street, Denver, CO 80203.

Denver Public Library, Genealogy Section, 1357 Broadway, Denver, CO 80203.

Connecticut

Connecticut Historical Society Library, One Elizabeth Street, Hartford, CT 06105.

Connecticut State Library, 231 Capitol Avenue, Hartford, CT 06106.

Godfrey Memorial Library, 134 Newfield Street, Middletown, CT 06457.

New Haven Colony Historical Society Library, 114 Whitney Avenue, New Haven, CT 06510-1025.

Pequot Library, 720 Pequot Avenue, Southport, CT 06490-1496.

Delaware

Historical Society of Delaware Library, 505 Market Street Mall, Wilmington, DE 19801.

Delaware Bureau of Archives and Records Management, Hall of Records, P.O. Box 1401, Dover, DE 19903.

University of Delaware Library, Newark, DE 19717-3267.

Delaware State College, Jason Library, History Room, Dover, DE 19901. Call for appointment: (302)739-5111.

Wilmington Public Library, 10th and Market Street, Wilmington, DE 19801.

District of Columbia

Library of Congress, Independence Avenue at First Street SE, Washington, DC 20540.

National Archives, Pennsylvania Avenue at Eighth Street NW, Washington, DC 20408.

Historical Society of Washington, D.C., 1307 New Hampshire Avenue NW, Washington, DC 20036.

Daughters of the American Revolution, Library, 1776 D Street NW, Washington, DC 20006-5392.

Florida

Division of Library and Information Services, State Library, Florida Collection, R.A. Gray Building, 500 Bronough, Tallahassee, FL 32399-0250.

Florida Bureau of Archives and Records Management, Florida State Archives, R.A. Gray Building, Tallahassee, FL 32399-0250.

Florida State University, Strozier Library, Tallahassee, FL 32306-2047.

Miami-Dade County Public Library, 101 W. Flagler Street, Miami, FL 33130-1523.

Orange County Library, 101 E. Central, Orlando, FL 32801.

University of Florida, Yonge Library of Florida History, Library East, Gainesville, FL 32611.

Georgia

Georgia Department of Archives and History, 330 Capitol Avenue SE, Atlanta, GA 30334.

Georgia Historical Society Library, 501 Whitaker Street, Savannah, GA 31499.

Atlanta Historical Society Library, 3101 Andrews Drive NW, Atlanta, GA 30305.

Atlanta Public Library, One Margaret Mitchell Square NW, Atlanta, GA 30303-1089.

Emory University, Woodruff Library, 1364 Clifton Road NE, Atlanta, GA 30322.

University of Georgia, Little Memorial Library, Athens, GA 30602.

Washington Memorial Library, 1180 Washington Avenue, Macon, GA 31201-1794.

Hawaii

Hawaii State Archives, Iolani Palace Grounds, Honolulu, HI 96813.

Hawaii State Library, 478 S. King Street, Honolulu, HI 96813.

Hawaiian Historical Society, 560 Kawaiahao Street, Honolulu, HI 96813.

Maui Historical Society, 2375 A Main Street, P.O. Box 1018, Wailuku, Maui, HI 96793.

Bishop Museum Library, 1525 Bernice Street, P.O. Box 19000-A, Honolulu, HI 96817-0916.

DAR Memorial Library, 1914 Makiki Heights Drive, Honolulu, HI 96822.

University of Hawaii at Manoa, Hamilton Library, 2550 The Mall, Honolulu, HI 96822.

Idaho

Idaho State Historical Society, Library and Archives, 450 N. Fourth Street, Boise, ID 83702.

Idaho State Historical Society, Genealogy Department, 450 N. Fourth Street, Boise, ID 83702.

Idaho State Archives, 325 W. State Street, Boise, ID 83702.

Boise State University Library, 1910 University Drive, Boise, ID 83725.

Ricks College, McKay Library, 525 S. Center, Rexburg, ID 83460-0405.

Illinois

Illinois State Archives, Archives Building, Springfield, IL 62756.

Illinois State Historical Library, Old State Capitol, 501 S. Second, Springfield, IL 62701.

Chicago Historical Society, North Avenue and Clark Street, Chicago, IL 60614-6099.

Newberry Library, 60 W. Walton Street, Chicago, IL 60610-3394.

Indiana

Indiana Historical Society Library, 315 W. Ohio Street, Indianapolis, IN 46202-3299.

Indiana State Library, Genealogy Division, 140 N. Senate Avenue, Indianapolis, IN 46204-2296.

Indiana State Archives, 140 N. Senate Avenue, Room 117, Indianapolis, IN 46204-2215.

Allen County Public Library, Historical Genealogy Department, 900 Webster Street, P.O. Box 2270, Fort Wayne, IN 46801-2270.

Iowa

Iowa State Library, E. 12th and Grand Avenue, Des Moines, IA 50319. (law, medicine, state documents)

Iowa Genealogical Society Library, 6000 Douglas Avenue, Suite 145, P.O. Box 7735, Des Moines, IA 50322.

State Historical Society of Iowa Library, 402 Iowa Avenue, Iowa City, IA 52240-5391.

State Historical Society of Iowa, Library Archives Bureau, Capitol Complex, 600 E. Locust, Des Moines, IA 50319.

Sioux City Public Library, Aalfs Library, 529 Pierce Street, Sioux City, IA 51101-1203.

Kansas

Kansas State Historical Society, Library and Archives, Memorial Building, 120 W. 10th, Topeka, KS 66612-1291.

Wichita Public Library, 223 S. Main, Wichita, KS 67202.

Kentucky

Kentucky Department for Libraries and Archives, Public Records Division, 300 Coffee Tree Rd., P.O. Box 537, Frankfort, KY 40602-0537.

Kentucky Historical Society Library, Old Capitol Annex, 300 W. Broadway, Box H, Frankfort, KY 40602-2108.

Filson Club, 1310 S. Third Street, Louisville, KY 40208.

Owensboro-Daviess County Public Library, 450 Griffith Avenue, Owensboro, KY 42301.

University of Kentucky, King Library North, Periodicals/Newspapers/Microtexts Collection, Lexington, KY 40506-0391.

Western Kentucky University, Kentucky Library, Bowling Green, KY 42101.

Louisiana

State Library of Louisiana, P.O. Box 131, 760 Riverside Mall, Baton Rouge, LA 70821-0131.

Louisiana Office of Secretary of State, Archives and History Library, 3851 Essen Lane, P.O. Box 94125, Baton Rouge, LA 70804.

Historic New Orleans Collection Library, 533 Royal Street, New Orleans, LA 70130.

Louisiana State University, Middleton Library, BA/Doc Department, Baton Rouge, LA 70803.

Louisiana State University, Hill Memorial Library, Special Collections, Baton Rouge, LA 70803.

New Orleans Public Library, 219 Loyola Avenue, New Orleans, LA 70140.

Shreve Memorial Library, 424 Texas Street, P.O. Box 21523, Shreveport, LA 71120.

Southern University, Cade Library, Southern Branch Post Office, Baton Rouge, LA 70813.

Tulane University, Howard-Tilton Library, Special Collections, 6823 St. Charles Avenue, New Orleans, LA 70118.

Maine

Maine State Library and Archives, State House Station 64, LMA Building, Augusta, ME 04333-0064.

Maine Historical Society Library, 485 Congress Street, Portland, ME 04101.

University of Maine, Fogler Libray, Orono, ME 04469.

Maryland

Maryland State Archives Library, 350 Rowe Boulevard, Annapolis, MD 21401.

Maryland Historical Society Library, 201 W. Monument Street, Baltimore, MD 21201.

Enoch Pratt Free Library, Maryland Room, 400 Cathedral Street, Baltimore, MD 21201.

University of Maryland, College Park Campus, McKeldin Library, Maryland Room, College Park, MD 20740.

Massachusetts

Massachusetts State Archives, State House, Beacon Hill, Boston, MA 02133.

State Library of Massachusetts, 341 State House, Beacon Hill, Boston, MA 02133-1099.

Massachusetts Historical Society, 1154 Boylston Street, Boston, MA 02215. (No genealogy collection as such)

New England Historic Genealogical Society Library, 101 Newbury Street, Boston, MA 02116.

American Antiquarian Society, 185 Salisbury Street, Worchester, MA 01609.

Boston Public Library, Genealogy Department, Copley Square, Boston, MA 02116.

Michigan

Library of Michigan, 717 W. Allegan, P.O. Box 30007, Lansing, MI 48909.

Michigan Department of State, State Archives, 717 W. Allegan, Lansing, MI 48909.

Detroit Public Library, 5201 Woodward Avenue, Detroit, MI 48202.

Minnesota

Minnesota Historical Society Research Center, 345 Kellogg Boulevard West, St. Paul, MN 55102-1900. (Library and state archives)

Iron Range Research Center, Highway 169 West, P.O. Box 392, Chisholm, MN 55719-0392.

Minneapolis Public Library, Minnesota History Collection, 300 Nicollet Mall, Minneapolis, MN 55401-1992.

Mississippi

Mississippi State Department of Archives and History, 100 S. State Street, P.O. Box 571, Jackson, MS 39205.

University of Southern Mississippi, McCain Library and Archives, P.O. Box 5148, Southern Station, Hattiesburg, MS 39406-5148.

Missouri

State Historical Society of Missouri, University Library Building, 1020 Lowry Street, Columbia, MO 65201-7298.

Missouri State Library, 600 W. Main Street, P.O. Box 387, Jefferson City, MO 65102-0387.

Missouri Historical Society, 225 S. Skinker Boulevard, P.O. Box 11940, St. Louis, MO 63112-0940.

Missouri Office of Secretary of State, State Archives, 600 W. Main Street, Jefferson City, MO 65102.

University of Missouri, Western History Manuscript Collection, 23 Ellis Library, Columbia, MO 65201.

Montana

Montana Historical Society Library and Archives, 225 N. Roberts, Helena, MT 59620-9990.

Montana State Library, 1515 E. Sixth Avenue, Helena, MT 59620. (State documents)

Nebraska

Nebraska State Historical Society Library, 1500 R Street, P.O. Box 82554, Lincoln, NE 68501.

Omaha Public Library, Clark Library, 215 S. 15th Street, Omaha, NE 68102-1004.

Nevada

Nevada Historical Society Museum, Research Library, 1650 N. Virginia Street, Reno, NV 89503-1799.

Nevada State Library and Archives, 100 Stewart Street, Carson City, NV 89710.

University of Nevada-Reno, University Library, Reno, NV 89557.

University of Nevada-Las Vegas, Dickinson Library, 4505 Maryland Parkway, Las Vegas, NV 89154-0001.

New Hampshire

New Hampshire Historical Society, 30 Park Street, Concord, NH 03301-6384.

New Hampshire State Library, 20 Park Street, Concord, NH 03301.

New Hampshire Records and Archives Center, 71 S. Fruit Street, Concord, NH 03301-2410.

New Jersey

New Jersey Historical Society Library, 230 Broadway, Newark, NJ 07104.

New Jersey Department of Education, State Library, 185 W. State Street, CN 520, Trenton, NJ 06825-0520.

New Jersey Department of State, State Archives, 185 W. State Street, Trenton, NJ 06825-0520.

Farleigh Dickinson University, Messler Library, 207 Montross Avenue, Rutherford, NJ 07070-2299.

Joint Free Public Library of Morristown and Morris Township, One Miller Road, Morristown, NJ 07960.

Newark Public Library, New Jersey Department, 5 Washington Street, P.O. Box 630, Newark, NJ 07101-0630.

Rutgers University, Alexander Library, Special Collections, 169 College Avenue, College Avenue Campus, New Brunswick, NJ 08903.

New Mexico

New Mexico State Library, 325 Don Gaspar, Santa Fe, NM 87503-1629.

Commission of Public Records, New Mexico Archives, 404 Montezuma Street, Santa Fe, NM 87503.

Library of the Museum of New Mexico, 110 Washington Avenue, P.O. Box 2087, Santa Fe, NM 87504-2087. (Historical, not really genealogical)

Albuquerque Public Library, Special Collections, 423 Central Avenue NE, Albuquerque, NM 87102.

New York

New York State Library, Cultural Education Center, Empire State Plaza, Albany, NY 12230.

New York Historical Society Library, 170 Central Park West, New York, NY 10024-5194.

New York Genealogical and Biographical Society Library, 122 E. 58th Street, New York 10022-1939.

New York Public Library, Genealogy and Special Collections, Fifth Avenue at 42nd Street, New York, NY 10018.

North Carolina

North Carolina Division of Archives and History, 109 E. Jones Street, Raleigh, NC 27611.

North Carolina State Library, 109 E. Jones Street, Raleigh, NC 27611.

Duke University, Perkins Library, Durham, NC 27706.

Forsyth County Public Library, North Carolina Room, 660 W. Fifth Street, Winston-Salem, NC 27101.

Public Library of Charlotte and Mecklenburg County, 310 N. Tryon Street, Charlotte, NC 28202-2176.

University of North Carolina, Wilson Library, Special Collections, Chapel Hill, NC 27514.

North Dakota

North Dakota State Library, Liberty Memorial Building, 604 E. Boulevard Avenue, Bismarck, ND 58505.

State Historical Society of North Dakota, State Archives and Historical Research Library, 612 E. Boulevard Avenue, North Dakota Heritage Center, Bismarck, ND 58505-0830.

North Dakota State University Library, North Dakota Institute for Regional Studies, SU Station, P.O. Box 5599, Fargo, ND 58105-5599.

Ohio

State Library of Ohio, Archives, State Office Building, 65 S. Front Street, Room 510, Columbus, OH 43266-0334.

Ohio Historical Society Archives Library, 1982 Velma Avenue, Columbus, OH 43211-2497.

Western Reserve Historical Society, 10825 East Boulevard, Cleveland, OH 44106.

Bowling Green State University, Center for Archival Collections, Fifth Floor, Jerome Library, Bowling Green, OH 43403.

Cincinnati Historical Society Library, 1301 Western Avenue, Cincinnati, OH 45203.

Cincinnati Public Library, Genealogy Department, 800 Vine Street, Cincinnati, OH 45202.

Rutherford B. Hays Presidential Center Library, 1337 Hayes Avenue, Spiegel Grove, Fremont, OH 43420-2796.

Oklahoma

Oklahoma Historical Society Library, Historical Building, 2100 N. Lincoln Boulevard, Oklahoma City, OK 73105-4997.

Oklahoma Division of Archives and Records, 109 State Capitol, Oklahoma City, OK 73105.

Rudisill North Regional Library, 1520 N. Hartford, Tulsa, OK 74106.

University of Oklahoma, Western History Collection, 630 Parrington Oval, Room 452, Norman, OK 73019.

Oregon

Oregon Historical Society Library, 1230 SW Park Avenue, Portland, OR 97205.

Oregon State Library, 250 Winter Street NE, Salem, OR 97310.

Oregon State Archives, 800 Summer Street NE, Salem, OR 97310.

Genealogical Forum of Oregon, 1410 SW Morrison Street #812, Portland, OR 97205.

University of Oregon Library, Newspaper Microfilming Project, Eugene, OR 97403.

Pennsylvania

Pennsylvania State Archives, Third and North Street, P.O. Box 1026, Harrisburg, PA 17108-1026.

Pennsylvania State Library, P.O. Box 1601, Walnut Street and Commonwealth Avenue, Harrisburg, PA 17105.

Carnegie Library of Pittsburgh, Pennsylvania Department, 4400 Forbes Avenue, Pittsburgh, PA 15213-4080.

Historical Society of Pennsylvania Library, 1300 Locust Street, Philadelphia, PA 19107.

Historical Society of Western Pennsylvania, 4338 Bigelow Boulevard, Pittsburgh, PA 15213-2695.

Temple University, Paley Library, Berks and 13th Street, Philadelphia, PA 19122.

Rhode Island

Rhode Island Historical Society Library, 121 Hope Street, Providence, RI 02906.

Rhode Island State Archives, 337 Westminster, Providence, RI 02903.

Rhode Island State Library, State House, 82 Smith Street, Providence, RI 02903.

Providence Public Library, 225 Washington Street, Providence, RI 02903-3283.

South Carolina

South Carolina Department of Archives and History, Capitol Station, P.O. Box 11669, Columbia, SC 29211-1669.

South Carolina Library, University of South Carolina, Columbia, SC 29208.

South Carolina Historical Society Library, Fireproof Building, 100 Meeting Street, Charleston, SC 29401-2299.

Charleston Library Society, 164 King Street, Charleston, SC 29401.

York County Library, P.O. Box 10032, 138 E. Black Street, Rock Hill, SC 29731.

South Dakota

South Dakota State Historical Society, Library and State Archives, 900 Governors Drive, Pierre, SD 57501-2217.

South Dakota State Library, 800 Governors Drive, Pierre, SD 57501-2294.

Aberdeen Public Library, 519 S. Kline Street, Aberdeen, SD 57401-4495.

Tennessee

Tennessee State Library and Archives, 403 Seventh Avenue North, Nashville, TN 37243-0312.

Chattanooga-Hamilton County Library, 1001 Broad Street, Chattanooga, TN 37402.

Knoxville-Knox County Public Library, 500 W. Church Avenue, Knoxville, TN 37902.

Memphis-Shelby County Public Library, 1850 Peabody Avenue, Memphis, TN 38104.

Memphis State University Library, Southern Avenue, Memphis, TN 38152.

Texas

Texas State Library, Archives Division, 1200 Brazos Street, P.O. Box 12927, Capitol Station, Austin, TX 78711.

Texas State Library, 1200 Brazos Street, P.O. Box 12927, Capitol Station, Austin, TX 78711.

Barker Center for American History, University of Texas, SRH 2.109, Austin, TX 78713-7330.

Clayton Center for Genealogical Research, 5300 Caroline, Houston, TX 77004.

Confederate Research Center, Hill Junior College, Hillsboro, TX 76645.

Dallas Public Library, 1515 Young Street, Dallas, TX 75201.

Ft. Worth Public Library, 300 Taylor Street, Ft. Worth, TX 76102-7309.

Utah

Utah State Historical Society Library, 300 Rio Grande, Salt Lake City, UT 84101-1182.

Utah State Archives, Archives Building, State Capitol, Salt Lake City, UT 84114.

Brigham Young University, Lee Library, 3080 HBLL, Provo, UT 84602.

Family History Library, Church of Jesus Christ of Latter-day Saints, 35 NW Temple, Salt Lake City, UT 84150.

Marriott Library, Serials Collection, University of Utah Campus, Salt Lake City, UT 84112.

Vermont

Vermont Department of Libraries, State Library, 109 State Street, Montpelier, VT 05609.

Vermont Historical Society Library, Pavilion Building, 109 State Street, Montpelier, VT 05609-0901.

Office of Secretary of State, Vermont State Archives Library, 109 State Street, Montpelier, VT 05609-1103.

Canfield Memorial Library, Vermontiana Collection, Rt. 7A (Main Street), P.O. Box 267, Arlington, VT 05250-0267.

Rutland Free Library, Center and Court Streets, Rutland, VT 05701.

Virginia

Virginia State Library and Archives, 12th and Capitol Street, Richmond, VA 23219.

Virginia Historical Society Library, 428 North Boulevard, P.O.Box 7311, Richmond, VA 23221-0311.

College of William and Mary, Swem Library, Williamsburg, VA 23185.

Colonial Williamsburg Foundation, Central Library, 415 N. Boundary Street, P.O. Box C, Williamsburg, VA 23187.

Fairfax City Regional Public Library, Virginia Room, 3915 Chain Bridge Road, Fairfax, VA 22030.

Museum of the Confederacy Library, 1201 E. Clay Street, Richmond, VA 23219.

National Genealogical Society, 4527 17th Street North, Arlington, VA 22207-2399.

United Daughters of the Confederacy Library, 328 North Boulevard, Richmond, VA 23220.

University of Virginia, Alderman Library, Special Collections, Charlottesville, VA 22903.

Washington

Washington State Library, Capitol Campus, P.O. Box 42460, Olympia, WA 98504-2460.

Washington State Office of Secretary of State, Division of Archives, 12th and Washington, P.O. Box 9000, Olympia, WA 98504-0418.

Seattle Public Library, Genealogy Section, 1000 Fourth Avenue, Seattle, WA 98104.

Tacoma Public Library, 1102 Tacoma Avenue South, Tacoma, WA 98402-2098.

Washington State Historical Society, Hewitt Library, 315 N. Stadium Way, Tacoma, WA 98403.

West Virginia

West Virginia Archives and History Library, Cultural Center, State Capitol Complex, Charleston, WV 25305.

West Virginia University Library, West Virginia and Regional History Collection, Colson Hall, P.O. Box 6464, Morgantown, WV 26506.

Cabell County Public Library, 455 Ninth Street Plaza, Huntington, WV 25701-1417.

Clarksburg-Harrison Public Library, 404 W. Pike Street, Clarksburg, WV 26301.

Marshall University, Morrow Library, Special Collections, Huntington, WV 25755.

Wisconsin

State Historical Society of Wisconsin Library, 816 State Street, Madison, WI 53706.

Wisconsin Division of Archives and Manuscripts, 816 State Street, Madison, WI 53706.

Milwaukee Public Library, 814 W. Wisconsin Avenue, Milwaukee, WI 53233-2385.

University of Wisconsin at Milwaukee Library, 2311 E. Hartford Avenue, P.O. Box 604, Milwaukee, WI 53201.

Wyoming

Wyoming State Archives and Records Management, Barrett Building, 2301 Central Avenue, Cheyenne, WY 82002.

Wyoming State Library, Supreme Court-Library Building, Cheyenne, WY 82002. (Not really genealogical)

Laramie County Library, 2800 Central Avenue, Cheyenne, WY 82001.

University of Wyoming Library, University Station, P.O. Box 3334, Laramie, WY 82071-3334.

APPENDIX D

National Archives and Branches

National Archives, Pennsylvania Avenue at Eighth Street, NW, Washington, DC 20408. Phone: (202)501-5400. Civil Reference Desk, 501-5395. National coverage and Washington, D.C.

National Archives II, 8601 Adelphi Road, College Park, MD 20740.

REGIONAL BRANCHES OF THE NATIONAL ARCHIVES

Anchorage—National Archives, **Alaska Region**, 654 West Third Avenue, Anchorage, AK 99501. Phone: (907)271-2441. FTS: 868-2441. Serving Alaska.

Atlanta area—National Archives, **Southeast Region**, 1557 St. Joseph Avenue, East Point, GA 30344. Phone: (404)763-7477. FTS: 246-7477. Serving Alabama, Florida, Georgia, Kentucky, Mississippi, North Carolina, South Carolina, Tennessee.

Boston area—National Archives, **New England Region**, 380 Trapelo Road, Waltham, MA 02154. Phone: (617)647-8100. FTS: 839-7100. Serving Connecticut, Maine, Massachusetts, New Hampshire, Rhode Island, Vermont.

Chicago—National Archives, **Great Lakes Region**, 7358 South Pulaski Road, Chicago, IL 60629. Phone: (312)581-7816. FTS: 353-0162. Serving Illinois, Indiana, Michigan, Minnesota, Ohio, Wisconsin.

Denver—National Archives, **Rocky Mountain Region**, Building 48, Denver Federal Center, Denver, CO 80225-0307. Phone: (303)236-0817. FTS: 776-0817. Serving Colorado, Montana, North Dakota, South Dakota, Utah, Wyoming. Also has most New Mexico records although National Archives publicity to date keeps New Mexico in the Southwest Region.

Fort Worth—National Archives, **Southwest Region**, 501 West Felix, P.O. Box 6216, Fort Worth, TX 76115. Phone: (817)334-5525. FTS: 334-5525. Serving Arkansas, Louisiana, New Mexico*, Oklahoma, Texas. *Most New Mexico records are in Denver.

Kansas City—National Archives, **Central Plains Region**, 2312 East Bannister Road, Kansas City, MO 64131. Phone: (816)926-6272. FTS: 926-6272. Serving Iowa, Kansas, Missouri, Nebraska.

Los Angeles area—National Archives, **Pacific Southwest Region**, 24000 Avila Road, P.O. Box 6719, Laguna Niguel, CA 92607-6719. Phone: (714)643-4241. FTS: 796-4241. Serving southern California, Arizona, and Clark County, Nevada.

New York—National Archives, **Northeast Region**, 201 Varick Street, New York, NY 10014. Phone: (212)337-1300. Serving New Jersey, New York, Puerto Rico, Virgin Islands.

Philadelphia—National Archives, **Mid-Atlantic Region**, 9th and Market Streets, Room 1350, Philadelphia, PA 19107. Phone: (215)597-3000. FTS: 597-3000. Serving Delaware, Pennsylvania, Maryland, Virginia, West Virginia.

Pittsfield—National Archives, **Pittsfield Region**, 100 Dan Fox Drive, Pittsfield, MA 01201. Phone: (413)445-6885, ext. 26. A microfilm reading room serving primarily the Northeast but including census and some other records with national coverage.

San Francisco area—National Archives, **Pacific Sierra Region**, 1000 Commodore Drive, San Bruno, CA 94066. Phone: (415)876-9009. FTS: 470-9009. Serving Hawaii, Nevada except Clark County, Northern California, American Samoa, Trust Territory of the Pacific Islands.

Seattle—National Archives, **Pacific Northwest Region**, 6125 Sand Point Way NE, Seattle, WA 98115. Phone: (206)526-6507. FTS: 392-6507. Serving Idaho, Oregon, Washington.

Publishers of Materials of Use to Genealogists

This appendix is provided for the reader's convenience in acquiring publications for private use or for a local library. Included are publishers of many works mentioned in this book, if current addresses could be determined.

Many of these publishers list current titles in *Books in Print* or *Microforms in Print*. In addition to publishers listed in this appendix, numerous historical or genealogical societies, state libraries, and universities publish records, periodicals, local history, and genealogy. Many, but not all of them, are listed in *Books in Print*. The *Genealogical Helper*, the *American Library Directory*, and the *Encyclopedia of Associations* also give names and addresses of hundreds of societies and libraries. Contact the individual publishers, societies, and libraries for their catalogs. Be aware that some of them sell works from other publishers as well as their own.

Some of the publishers listed below also have On-Demand services, by which they can photocopy or microprint out-of-print materials, subject to availability and copyright restrictions. If you find that something you want is out of print, inquire about the possibility of On-Demand service.

ABC-Clio Information Services, 130 Cremona Drive, P.O. Box 1911, Santa Barbara, CA 93116-1911. *America: History and Life*, also on CD-ROM.

Abingdon Press, 201 Eighth Avenue, Nashville, TN 37202. Phone: (615)749-6347.

ABP Abstracts, Rte. 1, Box 158C, Rocky Mount, NC 27803. Phone: (919)443-0231.

Aegean Park Press, P.O. Box 2837, Laguna Hills, CA 92654-0837. Phone: (800)736-3587.

AGES. See Ancestral Genealogical Endexing (*sic*) Schedules, Inc.

American Family Records Association, P.O. Box 15505, Kansas City, MO 64106. Phone: (816)373-6570.

American Historical Books, P.O. Box 3401, Knoxville, TN 37927-3401.

American Theological Library Association, Preservation Board, 820 Church Street, Third Floor, Evanston, IL 60201. Phone: (708)869-7788. Many church records, newspapers, periodicals, various denominations. Microfilm, microfiche. On-Demand publishing.

Americana Unlimited, 1701 North 11th Avenue, P.O. Box 50447, Tucson, AZ 85703. Phone: (602)792-3453.

AMS Press, Inc., 56 East 13th Street, New York City, NY 10003. Phone: (212)777-4700. *Territorial Papers*, 26 volumes in 25. They are sold individually. Also publishes microforms under AMS Film Service. On-Demand publishing.

Ancestral Genealogical Endexing Schedules, Inc., P.O. Box 2127, Salt Lake City, UT 84110. Phone: (800)733-0844. (Formerly Accelerated Indexing Systems, Inc.)

Ancestry, P.O. Box 476, Salt Lake City, UT 84110.

Arkansas Ancestors, 222 McMahan Drive, Hot Springs, AR 71913. Phone: (501)623-6766.

Arkansas Research, P.O. Box 303, Conway, AR 72032.

Association for the Study of Afro-American Life and History, 1407 14th Street NW, Washington, DC 20005. Phone: (202)667-2822. *Journal of Negro History, Negro History Bulletin* and some books.

Ayer Company Publishers, P.O. 958, Salem, NH 03079. Phone: (603)669-5933.

Banner Press, Inc., P.O. Box 20180, Birmingham, AL 35216. Phone: (205)822-4783.

Barefield, Marilyn Davis, 4757 Overwood Circle, Birmingham, AL 35222-4405.

Bell and Howell, Publication Systems Division, Old Mansfield Road, Wooster, OH 44691. Phone: (216)264-6666. Newspapers, periodicals, telephone directories; microform reading equipment. Microfilm, microfiche. Newspaper indexes. On-Demand publishing.

Betterway Publications, 1507 Dana Avenue, Cincinnati, OH 45207. *Unpuzzling Your Past: A Basic Guide to Genealogy.*

R.R. Bowker, 121 Chanlon Rd., New Providence, NJ 07974. *Books in Print. American Library Directory.* Newspaper indexes.

Boyd Publishing Company, P.O. Box 367, Milledgeville, GA 31061. (Georgia, South Carolina and church resources)

Brookhaven Press, 2004 Kramer Street, P.O. Box 2287, LaCrosse, WI 54602-2287. Phone: (608)781-0850. Government documents, newspapers, periodicals, research and reference materials, manuscripts and archival materials. Microfilm, microfiche. On-Demand publishing.

Bucks County Genealogical Society, P.O. Box 1092, Doylestown, PA 18901. Phone: (215)345-1394.

Buffalo and Erie County Historical Society, 25 Nottingham Court, Buffalo, NY 14216-3199. Phone: (716)873-9644.

Bullinger's Guides, Inc., 63 Woodland Avenue, P.O. Box 501, Westwood, NJ 07675. Phone: (201)664-7691. Bullinger's Postal and Shippers Guides for the U.S. and Canada.

Caradium Publishing, 2503 Del Prado Boulevard, Suite 435, Cape Coral, FL 33904. Phone: (813)574-1799. Part of International Locator Co. specializing in adoption search.

Carlberg Press, 1782 Beacon Avenue, Anaheim, CA 92804-4515.

Catoctin Press, 709 E. Main Street, Middletown, MD 21769-7802. Phone: (301)371-6293.

Center for Archival Collections, Fifth Floor, Jerome Library, Bowling Green State University, Bowling Green, OH 43403-0175. Phone: (419)372-2411.

Center for Western Studies, P.O. Box 727, Augustana College, Sioux Falls, SD 57197. Phone: (605)336-4007.

Chadwyck-Healey, Inc., 1101 King Street, Alexandria, VA 22314. Phone: (800)752-0515, or (703)683-4890. *Index to Personal Names in the N.U.C.M.C., 1959-1984.* Microfilm of the Draper Manuscripts and microfiche of Draper calendars.

Clearfield Company, 200 East Eager Street, Baltimore, MD 21202. Phone: (301)625-9004.

Clearwater Publishing Co., 75 Rockefeller Center, New York City, NY 10019.

Closson Press, 1935 Sampson Drive, Apollo, PA 15613-

9258. Phone: (412)337-4482. Mostly Pennsylvania and neighboring states.

Colonial Press, The American Academy of Creative Arts, 1237 Stevens Road SE, Bessemer, AL 35023. Phone: (205)428-2146.

Colorado Historical Society, 1300 Broadway, Denver, CO 80203-2137. Phone: (303)866-2305.

Congressional Information Services, 4520 East-West Highway, Suite 800, Bethesda, MD 20814-3389. Phone: (800)638-8380, or (301)654-1500. *United States Serial Set* and *Indexes, Congressional Record*, other early Congressional documents. State, city government documents. Books, Online, microfiche. On-Demand publishing.

CPL Bibliographies, 1313 E. 60th Street, Merriam Center, Chicago, IL 60637-2897. Phone: (312)947-2160.

Curtis Media Corporation, P.O. Box 2660, Sioux City, IA 51106. Local histories.

Datamics, Inc., 350 Fifth Avenue, No. 3304, New York City, NY 10118.

DeLorme Mapping, P.O. Box 298, Freeport, ME 04032.

Dietz Publishing Company, 109 East Cary Street, Richmond, VA 23219.

W.S. Dawson Co., P.O. Box 62823, Virginia Beach, VA 23466. Phone: (804)499-6271.

Eakin Press, P.O. Drawer 90159, Austin, TX 78709-0159. Phone: (512)288-1771.

Ericson Books, 1614 Redbud, Nacogdoches, TX 75961.

Everton Publishers, P.O. Box 368, Logan, UT 84323-0368. Phone: (800)443-6325. *Genealogical Helper.*

Facts on File, Inc., 460 Park Avenue South, New York, NY 10016.

Family Line Publications, Rear 63 East Main Street, Westminster, MD 21157. Phone: (410)876-6101.

Fulcher, Richard C., Genealogical Research and Publishing, P.O. Box 21, Brentwood, TN 37027. Tennessee materials and families.

Gale Research, Inc., 835 Penobscot Building, Detroit, MI 48226-4094. Phone: (800)877-4253. *Encyclopedia of Associations.*

Garland Publishing, 717 Fifth Avenue, 25th Floor, New York City, NY 10022; or 1000A Sherman Avenue, Hamden, CT 06514. Connecticut Phone: (800)627-6273.

Garrett Park Press, P.O. Box 190B, Garrett Park, MD 20896. *Minority Organizations: A National Directory.*

Genealogical Association of Southwestern Michigan, Dept. C, Box 573, St. Joseph, MI 49085. Phone: (616)429-7914.

Genealogical Books in Print, P.O. Box 394, Maine, NY 13802-0394.

Genealogical Enterprises, 1140 Windsong Lane, Siesta Key, Sarasota, FL 34242.

Genealogical Institute, P.O. Box 22045, Salt Lake City, UT 84122. Phone: (801)257-6174.

Genealogical Publishing Company, 1001 N. Calvert Street, Baltimore, MD 21202. Phone: (301)837-3897. Extensive catalog.

Genealogical Sources Unlimited, 407 Regent Court, Knoxville, TN 37923-5807. Phone: (615)690-7831.

German Texan Heritage Society, P.O. Box 684171, Austin, TX 78768.

(Glazier) Michael Glazier, Inc., 1210A King Street, Wilmington, DE 19801. *Colonial Laws of North America* series.

Godfrey Memorial Library, 134 Newfield Street, Middletown, CT 06457. Phone: (203)346-4375. On-Demand publishing of genealogical research materials.

Government Printing Office, see Superintendent of Documents.

Greenwood Press. See Greenwood Publishing Group, Inc.

Greenwood Publishing Group, Inc., 88 Post Road West, P.O. Box 5007, Westport, CT 06881. Includes Negro Universities Press, Greenwood Press, and others. Phone: (203)226-3571. Publishes *The American Slave: A Composite Autobiography* (41 vols).

Guide to Reprints, Inc., P.O. Box 249, Kent, CT 06757. Phone: (203)927-4588. Since 1977, *Guide to Reprints.*

G.K. Hall and Company, 70 Lincoln Street, Boston, MA 02111. Phone: (800)343-2806.

Hannibal Books, 921 Center Street, Hannibal, MO 63401. Phone: (314)221-2462.

Harlan Davidson Inc./Forum Press, Inc., 3110 N. Arlington Heights Road, Arlington Heights, IL 60004. Phone: (708)253-9720. Goldentree Bibliographies, American Biographical History series, American History series.

(Hein) William S. Hein and Co., Inc., Hein Building, 1285 Main Street, Buffalo, NY 14209-1987. Phone: (800)828-7571, or (716)882-2600. *Session Laws of American States and Territories.* Individual states and years can be purchased. Contact company for price. Also publishes the Congressional Record. Microfiche. Also new and used law books.

Heritage Books, Inc., 1540-E Pointer Ridge Place, Bowie, MD 20716. Phone: (800)398-7709. Extensive catalog.

Heritage Papers, P.O. Box 7776, Athens, GA 30604-7776.

Higginson Book Co., 14 Derby Square, Salem, MA 01970. Phone: (508)745-7170. Concentrates on family histories.

Historic Resources, P.O. Box 329, Bountiful, UT 84011-0329.

Historical Society of Carroll County (Maryland), 210 East Main Street, Westminster, MD 21157. Phone (410)848-6494.

Hoffman, Margaret, P.O. Box 446, Roanoke Rapids, NC 27870.

Holbrook Research Institute, 57 Locust Street, Oxford, MA 01540. New England materials.

(Holcomb) Brent Holcomb, P.O. Box 21766, Columbia, SC 29221. Mostly Carolina materials.

Iberian Publishing, 548 Cedar Creek Drive, Athens, GA 30605-3408.

Immigration Historical Research Center, % University of Minnesota, 826 Berry Street, St. Paul, MN 55114. Phone: (612)373-5581.

Indiana Historical Society, 315 W. Ohio Street, Indianapolis, IN 46202-3299. Phone: (317)232-1882.

Infotech Publications, P.O. Box 86, Bowling Green, MO 63334. Phone: (314)669-5694.

Ingmire Publications, 211 Downshire, San Antonio, TX 78216.

Institute of Texan Cultures, 801 S. Bowie Street, San Antonio, TX 78205-3296.

Iowa Genealogical Society, P.O. Box 7735, Des Moines, IA 50322. Extensive Iowa catalog.

J & W Enterprises, P.O. Box 17706, Shreveport, LA 71138-0706.

Jensen Publications, P.O. Box 441, Pleasant Grove, UT 84062.

Kansas Historical Society, 120 SW Tenth Avenue, Topeka, KS 66612-1291. Phone: (913)296-3251.

Kinseeker Publications, P.O. Box 184, 5697 Old Maple Trail, Grawn, MI 49637. Phone: (616)276-6745.

Kinship, 60 Cedar Heights Road, Rhinebeck, NY 12572. Phone: (914)876-4592.

Kraus Micro and Kraus Reprint, Route 100, Millwood, NY 10546. Phone: (800)223-8323.

Journals, newspapers, government archives, research materials. Microfilm, microfiche. On-Demand publishing. Reprint catalog includes Hasse's *Index of Economic Material in Documents of the States of the U.S.; William and Mary Quarterly,* series 1 and part of 3; *Wisconsin Magazine of History* 1918-1973; *Virginia Magazine of History and Biography* 1893-1930; *Tyler's Quarterly Historical and Genealogical Magazine* (Virginia) 1919-1952; *Indiana Magazine of History* 1905-1978; *Confederate States of America, Congress, Journal 1861-1865*; *Arizona Historical Review* 1928-1936; *Arkansas Historical Quarterly* 1942-1956; Gregory's *American Newspapers 1821-1936*; *American Jewish History* 1893-1977; a series of histories of the thirteen American colonies and a history of the Trans-Appalachian frontier.

Langdon and Langdon Genealogical Research, 132 Langdon Road, Aiken, SC 29801. South Carolina materials.

Law Library Microform Consortium, University of Hawaii, Windward Campus, P.O. Box 1599, Kaneohe, HI 96744. Phone: (808)235-1755. *Territorial Papers*; *Session Laws*; *Martindale, Hubbell, and Martindale-Hubbell Law Directories*. Microfiche.

Library Microfilms, 1115 E. Arques Avenue, Sunnyvale, CA 94086. Phone: (408)736-7444. Library union catalogs & other publications in microform, microform supplies & equipment. On-Demand publishing.

Library of Congress Photoduplication Service, 10 First Street SE, Washington, DC 20540. Phone: (202)707-5640. Requires $10 nonrefundable deposit per item before search can be made. This service amounts to On-Demand publishing, if what you want is available.

Longstreet House, P.O. Box 730, Highstown, NJ 08520. Phone: (609)490-7520. Civil War history.

Louisiana State University Press, Baton Rouge, LA 70893.

Magna Carta Book Company, 5502 Magnolia Avenue, Baltimore, MD 21215.

Maryland State Archives, 350 Rowe Boulevard, Annapolis, MD 21401. Phone: (410)974-3914.

Mauldin, Dorothy Tincup. See Oklahoma Yesterday Publications.

McDowell Publications, 11129 Pleasant Ridge Road, Utica, KY 42376. Calendars to Draper Manuscripts.

Mead Data Central, 9393 Springboro Pike, P.O. Box 933, Dayton, OH 45401. Phone: (800)543-6862, or (513)859-1068. Lexis legal database.

Meyer, Mary Keysor, 5179 Perry Road, Mt. Airy, MD 21771. *Meyer's Directory of Genealogical Societies in the U.S.A. and Canada*.

Microcard Editions, Denver Technological Center, 5500 S. Valentia Way, Englewood, CO 80110. Phone: (303)771-2600. *American Revolution: Source Materials Relating to the Struggle for American Independence, Slavery Source Materials*.

Microfilming Corporation of America, 21 Harristown Road, Glen Rock, NJ 07425. Phone: (201)447-3000. Periodicals by and about North American Indians.

Micro Media, Inc., P.O. Box 95, North Branford, CT 06471. Phone: (203)785-0000. Microfilm and microfiche readers and supplies, reproductions, duplicating, On-Demand publishing, hard copy.

Minnesota Historical Society, 1500 Mississippi Street, St. Paul, MN 55101. Phone: (612)296-6980.

Mountain Press, P.O. Box 400, Signal Mountain, TN 37377-0400.

National Archives Trust Fund, Public Sales, Washington, DC 20408. Phone: (202)501-5240. Military, census, supplemental schedules, territorial papers, laws, passenger lists, etc. Microfilm. Printed guide books and pamphlets. Film may also be purchased through Scholarly Resources (see entry on page 196).

National Genealogical Society, 4527 Seventeenth Street North, Arlington, VA 22207-2399. Phone: (703)525-0050.

National Historical Publishing Co., 209 Greeson Hollow Road, P.O. Box 539, Waynesboro, TN 38485.

National Society Daughters of the American Revolution, 1776 D Street NW, Washington, DC 20006-5392. Phone: (202)879-3229.

Nebraska Historical Society, P.O. Box 28554, Lincoln, NE 68501. Phone: (402)741-4772.

Negro Universities Press. See Greenwood Publishing Group, Inc.

New Hampshire Publishing Co., P.O. Box 70, 441 Route 16, Somersworth, NH 03878. Phone: (603)692-4196.

New York Public Library, Fifth Avenue at 42nd Street, New York City, NY 10018-2288. Phone: (212)930-0814. Photographic service, microfilm, microfiche.

North Carolina Archives, Historical Publications, 109 E. Jones Street, Raleigh, NC 27601-2807. Phone: (919)733-7442.

Ohio Genealogical Society, P.O. Box 2625, 34 Sturges Avenue, Mansfield, OH 44906-0625. Phone: (419)522-9077.

Ohio Historical Society, 1982 Velma, Columbus, OH 43211-2497.

Oklahoma Yesterday Publications, 8745 E. 9th Street, Tulsa, OK 74112-4815. Phone: (918)835-4118.

Mostly publications on Oklahoma and the Five Civilized Tribes.

Oregon Historical Society, 1230 SW Park Avenue, Portland, OR 97205.

The Overmountain Press, P.O. Box 1261, Johnson City, TN 37605. Phone: (800)992-2691.

Oxford University Press, 2001 Evans Road, Cary, NC 27513.

Pavilion Press, P.O. Box 250, Douglas, MI 49406. Phone: (616)857-2781.

Pelican Publishers, P.O. Box 3110, Gretna, LA 70054.

Pergamon Microforms International. Pergamon Press, Maxwell House, Fairview Park, Elmsford, NY 10523. Phone: (914)592-7700.

Pharos Books, a Scripps-Howard Company, 200 Park Avenue, New York City, NY 10166. *World Almanac.*

Picton Press, P.O. Box 1111, Camden, ME 04843. Phone: (207)236-6565. Historical and genealogical materials, concentrating on New England but including other areas.

Precision Indexing, a division of American Genealogical Lending Library, P.O. Box 303, Bountiful, UT 84011. Phone: (801)298-5468.

Princeton Microfilm Corp., 43 Highstown Rd., P.O. Box 235, Princeton Junction, NJ 08550. Phone: (800)257-9052, or (609)452-2066. *Journal of Negro History,* etc. On-Demand publishing.

The Reprint Company Publishers, 601 Hillcrest Offices, P.O. Box 5401, Spartanburg, SC 29304. Phone: (803)582-0732. Concentrates on Southern history and genealogy; has some Mid-Atlantic and New England titles. *Virginia Historical Register* reprint of 1853 vols. Distributor for South Carolina Historical Society and R.J. Taylor, Jr., Foundation.

Research Publications Inc., 12 Lunar Drive, Woodbridge, CT 06525. Phone: (800)444-0799, or (203)397-2600. *City Directories of the United States.*

Rothman, Fred B., and Co., 10368 W. Centennial Rd., Littleton, CO 80127. Phone: (800)457-1986. *Raine's Analytical Index to Laws of Texas, 1821-1905.* Some hard copy *Session Laws.* Some On-Demand publishing.

Roxbury Data Interface, P.O. Box 1100, Verdi, NV 89439. Phone: (702)673-6797.

Salem Press, P.O. Box 50062, Pasadena, CA 91105. Magill Bibliographies.

Saur, K.G., Verlag, subsidiary of R.R. Bowker, 245 W. 17th Street, New York City, NY 10011. Phone: (800)521-8110, or (312)337-7023. *Microforms in Print.*

Scholarly Resources, Inc., 104 Greenhill Avenue, Wilmington, DE 19805-1897. Phone: (800)772-8937. A publisher, not a research company. *The* authorized distributor of National Archives microfilm. Film copies made from National Archives masters. Catalogs available for all released federal censuses and the supplemental schedules in the National Archives, American Indian records, black studies, diplomatic records, immigrant and passenger arrival records, military service records. Has information flyers on National Archives microfilm for each state. Also publishes *New American State Papers, 1789-1860* (and other books), some newspapers (microfilm). Microfilm On-Demand publishing.

Schweitzer, George K., 407 Ascot Court, Knoxville, TN 37923-5807.

Sistler, Byron, and Associates, 1712 Natchez Trace, P.O. Box 120934, Nashville, TN 37212. Phone: (615)297-3085, or for orders (800)578-9475. Tennessee, Kentucky, North Carolina, and Virginia materials.

Peter Smith Pub., Inc., 6 Lexington Avenue, Magnolia, MA 01930. Phone: (508)525-3562. *Virginia Historical Index* (Swem).

South Carolina Archives, 1430 Senate Street, P.O. Box 11669, Capitol Station, Columbia, SC 29211-1669.

South Carolina Historical Society, Fireproof Building, 100 Meeting Street, Charleston, SC 29401-2299. Phone: (803)723-3225.

Southern Baptist Convention Historical Library and Archives, 901 Commerce Street, Suite 400, Nashville, TN 37203-3620. Phone: (615)244-0344. Many Baptist records, periodicals.

Southern Historical Press, P.O. Box 1267, Greenville, SC 29602-1267. Phone: (803)233-2346.

Southern University Press, 130 South 19th Street, Birmingham, AL 35233. Phone: (205)933-0345.

Southwest Pennsylvania Genealogical Services, P.O. Box 253, Laughlintown, PA 15655. Phone: (412)238-3176.

Summit Publications, P.O. Box 222, Munroe Falls, OH 44262.

Superintendent of Documents, Government Printing Office, Washington, DC 20402-9325. Phone: (202)783-3238.

(Taylor) R.J. Taylor, Jr., Foundation. See The Reprint Company Publishers.

T.L.C. Genealogy Books, P.O. Box 403369, Miami

Beach, FL 33140-1369. Abstracts of records from Kentucky, Maryland, Mississippi, Missouri, New Jersey, North Carolina, Ohio, Pennsylvania, Virginia, West Virginia, and Wisconsin. Includes tax lists, deed and will books, court order books.

Torch Publications, 7825 Fay Avenue, Suite 200, La Jolla, CA 92037. Phone: (619)456-3595.

University Microfilms, Inc., 300 N. Zeeb Road, Ann Arbor, MI 48106-1346. (A Bell and Howell Company) Phone: (800)521-0600, or (313)761-4700. *Session Laws of American States and Territories. American Periodicals, 1741-1900: An Index to the Microfilm Collections*. Research collections on microfiche: Regimental Histories of the Civil War, Military History Collections, extensive Genealogy and Local History project, Cityfiche [City Directories], Phonefiche [Telephone Directories], Personal Papers. Research Collections on microfilm; Newspapers and Serials. Research collections mailing address: Research Collections/Box 35, P.O. Box 1346, Ann Arbor, MI 48106-9866. Books-On-Demand publishing. Query for availability and rates. Article clearinghouse from UMI/Data Courier, 620 South Third Street, Louisville, KY 40202-2475. Phone: (800) 626-2823, or (502)583-4111. (For dissertations (800)521-3042).

University of Alabama Press, P.O. Box 870380, Tuscaloosa, AL 35487-0380.

University of Chicago Press, 5801 S. Ellis Avenue, Fourth Floor, Chicago, IL 60637. Phone: (312)702-7700. Orders for On-Demand to 11030 S. Langley Avenue, Chicago, IL 60628. Phone: (800)621-2736 or (312)568-1550. On-Demand publishing.

University of Florida Libraries, Interlibrary Loan Office, Gainesville, FL 32611. Florida, Caribbean, Latin American newspapers. Microfilm.

University of Georgia Press, Terrell Hall, Athens, GA 30602.

University of North Carolina, Southern Historical Collection, Wilson Library, CB 3926, Chapel Hill, NC 27599. Phone: (919)962-1345. Supplemental census schedules, etc.

University of North Carolina Press, P.O. Box 2288, Chapel Hill, NC 27515-2288. Phone: (919)966-3561.

University of North Dakota, Fritz Library, Grand Forks, ND 58201. Phone: (701)777-2617.

University of Oklahoma Press, P.O. Box 787, Norman, OK 73070-0787. Phone: (800)627-7377.

University of Oregon Library, 1501 Kincaid, Eugene, OR 97403-1299. Phone: (503)346-3080.

University of Pennsylvania Press, 418 Service Drive, Blockley Hall, 13th Floor, Philadelphia, PA 19104-6097. Phone: (215)898-6261.

University of South Carolina Press, 1716 College Street, Columbia, SC 29208. Phone: (800)763-0089.

University of Southwestern Louisiana, Center for Louisiana Studies, P.O. Box 40831, USL, Lafayette, LA 70504-0831. Street address: 302 East Saint Mary Boulevard, Lafayette, LA 70504. Phone: (318)231-6027.

University of Tennessee Press, 293 Communications Building, Knoxville, TN 37996-0325. Phone: (615)974-3321.

University of Texas Press, P.O. Box 7819, Austin, TX 78713-7819.

University of Washington Press, P.O. Box 50096, Seattle, WA 98145-5096.

University of Wisconsin Library, 728 State Street, Madison, WI 53706. Phone: (608)262-1193. Contact Interlibrary Loan Dept for On-Demand publishing.

University Press of Mississippi, 3825 Ridgewood Road, Jackson, MS 39211-6492.

University Press of Virginia, P.O. Box 3608, University Station, Charlottesville, VA 22903. Phone: (804)924-3468.

University Presses of Florida, 15 Northwest 15th Street, Gainesville, FL 32611.

West Publishing Co., 610 Opperman Drive, P.O. Box 64833, St. Paul, MN 55164-9752. Law books of all kinds and Westlaw legal database.

Western Reserve Historical Society, 10825 East Boulevard, Cleveland, OH 44106.

Westland Publications, P.O. Box 117, McNeal, AZ 85617-0117. Phone: (602)642-3500.

H.W. Wilson Co., 950 University Avenue, Bronx, NY 10452. Phone: (800)367-6770.

Ye Olde Genealogy Shoppe, P.O. Box 39128, Indianapolis, IN 46239.

Federal Census, 1790-1930

WHICH CENSUS REPORTS...?

age, sex, race of each individual in household	1850 forward
agricultural schedules	1850-1880
attendance in school	1850 forward
months attending school	1900
birthdate (month/year) of each person	1900
month of birth if born within the year	1870-1880
birthplace of each person	1850 forward
deaf, dumb, or blind	1850-1890, 1910
defective, dependent, delinquent schedules (DDD)	1880
pauper or convict	1850-1860
prisoner, convict, homeless child, pauper	1890
disabled: crippled, maimed, bed-ridden, or other disability	1880
crippled, maimed, deformed	1890
employer, self-employed, or wage earner	1910-1930
months unemployed	1880-1900
whether person worked yesterday or number on unemployment schedule	1930
home or farm as residence	1890-1910, 1930
home owned or rented	1890-1930
home owned free of mortgage	1890-1920
value of home or monthly rent	1930
farm owned or rented	1890
farm owned free of mortgage	1890
illness, current, or temporary disability	1880
chronic or acute illness,	

length of time afflicted	1890
immigration year	1900-1930
number of years in U.S.	1890-1900
industry/manufacturing schedules	1820, 1850-1880
insane, idiot	1850-1880
defective in mind	1890
language, native	1890, 1910-1930
native language of parents	1920
speaks English	1890-1930
male, eligible/not eligible to vote	1870
marital status	1880 forward
age at first marriage	1930
married within the [census] year	1850-1890
month of marriage, within the [census] year	1870
number of years of present marriage	1900-1910
mortality schedules	1850-1880
mother of how many children, # living	1890-1910
name of each individual in household	1850 forward
name of head of household only	1790-1840
naturalized citizen or first papers	1890-1930
year of naturalization	1920
occupation	1850 forward
parents, whether foreign-born	1870
birthplace of parents	1880 forward
radio set in home	1930
reading and writing, whether able to read or write	1890-1930
persons unable to read and/or write	1850-1880
relationship to head of household	1880 forward
slaves by age, sex, color, etc.	1850-1860
number and age groups of slaves owned	1790-1860
social statistics schedules	1850-1880

Soundex	1880 forward, mostly	cial schedule	1890
street address of family	1880 forward	Civil War veteran, Union or Confederate, or widow	1890
value of real estate owned	1850-1870	Civil War veteran, Union or	
value of personal estate	1860-1870	Confederate	1910
veterans: pensioners	1840	veteran of U.S. military or	
Union vets and widows, spe-		naval forces, which war	1930

Roman and Arabic Numerals

Many researchers find references in arabic numerals to books that are labeled with roman numerals. This chart will help translate one system to the other. The roman system is a combination of several basic numerals: I for one, V for five, X for ten, L for fifty, C for one hundred, D for five hundred, and M for one thousand. Combining these in logical sequence provides the intervening numbers: one less than five (IV) for four, one more than five (VI) for six, one less than ten (IX) for nine, ten plus four (XIV) for fourteen, ten less than fifty (XL) for forty, and one hundred less than one thousand (CM) for nine hundred, and so forth.

Roman	Arabic	Roman	Arabic
I	1	XIV	14
II	2	XV	15
III	3	XVI	16
IV	4	XVII	17
V	5	XVIII	18
VI	6	XIX	19
VII	7	XX	20
VIII	8	XXI	21
IX	9	XXIV	24
X	10	XXV	25
XI	11	XXVI	26
XII	12	XXIX	29
XIII	13	XXX	30

Roman	Arabic	Roman	Arabic
XXXV	35	CM	900
XL	40	M	1,000
XLV	45	MC	1,100
L	50	MD	1,500
LV	55	MDCCC	1,800
LX	60	MCM	1,900
LXV	65	MM	2,000
LXX	70	MMC	2,100
LXXX	80	MMM	3,000
XC	90	$\bar{\text{MV}}$	4,000
XCV	95	$\bar{\text{V}}$	5,000
C	100		
CII	102		
CV	105		
CX	110	*Dates* (often found in
CL	150	copyright dates of older
CXC	190	publications)
CC	200		
CCX	210	MDCCLXXVI	1776
CCC	300	MDCCCLXIV	1864
CD	400	MCMX	1910
D	500	MCMXL	1940
DC	600	MCMLI	1951
DCC	700	MCMLXVIII	1968
DCCC	800	MCMLXX	1970

Sample Census Forms and Family Group Sheet

1790 CENSUS

Township or Local Community _____ County _____ State _____

Enumerator _____ Date Census Taken _____ Enumerator District # _____

Page	Name of Head of Family	Free White Males 16 years & upwards including heads of families	Free White Males under 16 years	Free White Females including heads of families	All Other Free Persons	Slaves	Dwellings / Other information

1800 or 1810 CENSUS

Local Community _____ State _____

County _____ Enumerator District # _____

Date Census Taken _____ Supervisor District # _____

Enumerator _____

Written Page No.	Printed Page No.	Name of Head of Family	Free White Males					Free White Females					All other free persons except Indians not taxed	Slaves
			under 10	of 10 & under 16	of 16 & under 26	of 26 & under 45	of 45 & up	under 10	of 10 & under 16	of 16 & under 26	of 26 & under 45	of 45 & up		
					including heads of families					including heads of families				

1820 CENSUS

Local Community _____ State _____

Enumerator _____ Enumerator District # _____

County _____ Supervisor District # _____

Date Census Taken _____

Written Page No.	Printed Page No.	Name of Head of Family	Free White Males						Free White Females						Foreigners Not Naturalized	Persons engaged in Agriculture	Persons engaged in Commerce	Persons engaged in Manufacture	Free Colored Persons									All other persons	Slaves
			to 10	10 to 16	*16 to 18	16 to 26	26 to 45	45 & up	to 10	10 to 16	16 to 26	26 to 45	45 & up					Males to 14	14 to 26	26 to 45	45 & up	Females to 14	14 to 26	26 to 45	45 & up		

* Those males between 16 & 18 will all be repeated in the column of those between 16 and 26.

1830 or 1840 CENSUS   Part 1

Local Community ——————

Enumerator ——————

County ——————

Date Census Taken ——————

State ——————

Enumerator District # ——————

Supervisor District # ——————

Written Page No.	Printed Page No.	Name of Head of Family	Free White Persons (including heads of families)																														
			Males													Females																
			under 5	5–10	10–15	15–20	20–30	30–40	40–50	50–60	60–70	70–80	80–90	90–100	100& over	under 5	5–10	10–15	15–20	20–30	30–40	40–50	50–60	60–70	70–80	80–90	90–100	100& over

1830 CENSUS Part 2

Local Community _____ State _____

Enumerator _____ Date Census Taken _____ Enumerator District # _____ Supervisor District # _____

Written Page No.	Printed Page No.	Name of Head of Family (from previous page)	Slaves — Males under 10	10–24	24–36	36–55	55–100	100 & up	Slaves — Females under 10	10–24	24–36	36–55	55–100	100 & up	Free Colored Persons — Males under 10	10–24	24–36	36–55	55–100	100 & up	Free Colored Persons — Females under 10	10–24	24–36	36–55	55–100	100 & up	TOTAL	White Persons included in the foregoing who are — deaf & dumb under 14	deaf & dumb 14–25	deaf & dumb 25 & up	blind	foreigners not naturalized	Slaves & Colored Persons included in the foregoing who are — deaf & dumb under 14	deaf & dumb 14–25	deaf & dumb 25 & up	blind

1840 CENSUS Part 2

Local Community _____

Enumerator _____

State _____

County _____

Date Census Taken _____

Enumerator District # _____

Supervisor District # _____

Written Page No.	Printed Page No.	Name of Head of Family (Previous Page)	Slaves												Free Colored Persons													TOTAL	Number of Persons employed in each family in						Revolutionary or Military Service Pensioners in the foregoing	
			Males						Females						Males						Females								Mining	Agriculture	Commerce	Manufacturing & Trades	Ocean Navigation	Canal, Lake, River Navigat'n	Learned Prof'ns & Engineers	Name	Age
			under 10	10-24	24-36	36-55	55-100	100 & up	under 10	10-24	24-36	36-55	55-100	100 & up	under 10	10-24	24-36	36-55	55-100	100 & up	under 10	10-24	24-36	36-55	55-100	100 & up										

1850 CENSUS

Post Office or
Local Community ——————

Enumerator ——————

County —————— State ——————

Date Census Taken —————— Enumerator District #

Supervisor District #

Written Page No.	Printed Page No.	Dwelling in order of visitation	Family Number in order of visitation	Name of every person whose usual place of abode on 1 June 1850 was with this family	Description			Profession, Occupation, or Trade of each Male over 15	Value of of Real Estate Owned	Place of Birth naming state, territory, or country	Married within the year	In School within the year	Persons over 20 unable to read & write	If deaf & dumb, blind, insane, idiot, pauper or convict
					Age	Sex	Color							
		1	2	3	4	5	6	7	8	9	10	11	12	13

1860 CENSUS

Post Office or
Local Community —————————————

Enumerator —————————————

County —————————————   State —————————————

Date Census Taken —————————————   Enumerator District # —————————————

Supervisor District # —————————————

Written Page No.	Printed Page No.	Dwelling Number	Family Number	Name of every person whose usual place of abode on 1 June 1860 was with this family	Description			Profession, Occupation, or Trade of each person over 15	Value of Real Estate Owned	Value of Personal Estate Owned	Place of Birth naming state, territory or country	Married within the year	In school within the year	Persons over 20 unable to read & write	Deaf & dumb, blind, insane, idiotic, pauper, or convict
					Age	Sex	Color								
		1	2	3	4	5	6	7	8	9	10	11	12	13	14

1850 or 1860 CENSUS   Schedule 2 — Slaves

Local Community _____   State _____

Enumerator _____   County _____   Date Census Taken _____

Written Page No.	Printed Page No.	Names of Slave Owners (1)	Number of Slaves (2)	Description — Age (3)	Sex (4)	Color (5)	Fugitives from the State (6)	Number Manumitted (7)	Deaf & dumb, blind, insane or idiotic (8)	Number of Slave Houses (9)
		1								
		2								
		3								
		4								
		5								
		6								
		7								
		8								
		9								
		10								
		11								
		12								
		13								
		14								

Names of Slave Owners (1)	Number of Slaves (2)	Description — Age (3)	Sex (4)	Color (5)	Fugitives from the State (6)	Number Manumitted (7)	Deaf & dumb, blind, insane or idiotic (8)	Number of Slave Houses (9)
1								
2								
3								
4								
5								
6								
7								
8								
9								
10								
11								
12								
13								
14								

1870 CENSUS

Local Community ————
Enumerator ————

State ————
County ————
Date Census Taken ————

Enumerator District # ————
Supervisor District # ————

Written Page No.	Printed Page No.	Dwelling No.	Family No.	Name of every person whose place of abode on 1 June 1870 was in this family	Description			Profession, Occupation, or Trade	Value of		Place of Birth	Parents		Month born within the year	Month married within the year	In school within the year	Cannot read	Cannot write	Deaf & dumb, blind, insane or idiotic	Males eligible to vote	Males not eligible to vote
					Age	Sex	Color		Real Estate Owned	Personal Estate Owned		Father Foreign-born	Mother Foreign-born								
		1	2	3	4	5	6	7	8	9	10	11	12	13	14	15	16	17	18	19	20

1880 CENSUS

Local Community ———————

Enumerator ———————

County ———————

Date Census Taken ———————

State ———————

Supervisor District # ———————

Enumerator District # ———————

Written Page No.	Printed Page No.	Street Name	House Number	Dwelling Number 1	Family Number 2	Name of every person whose place of abode on 1 June 1880 was in this family 3	Color 4	Sex 5	Age 6	Month born if during census year 7	Relationship to head of this household 8	Single 9	Married 10	Widowed / Divorced 11	Married during year 12	Profession, Occupation or Trade 13	Months unemployed this year 14	Currently ill? If so, specify. 15	Blind 16	Deaf & dumb 17	Idiotic 18	Insane 19	Disabled 20	School this year 21	Cannot read 22	Cannot write 23	Birthplace 24	Birthplace of Father 25	Birthplace of Mother 26

Description: Color 4, Sex 5, Age 6

Health: Blind 16, Deaf & dumb 17, Idiotic 18, Insane 19, Disabled 20

1900 CENSUS

Local Community _____
Ward _____
Enumerator _____

State _____
Supervisor District # _____
Enumeration District # _____

County _____
Date Census Taken _____

Written Page No.	Printed Page No.	Street	House Number	Dwelling Number (1)	Family Number (2)	Name of every person whose place of abode on 1 June 1900 was in this family (3)	Relationship to head of family (4)	Color (5)	Sex (6)	Birth Date Month (7)	Birth Date Year (7)	Age (8)	Marital status (9)	# Years married (10)	Mother of how many children? (11)	# of these children living (12)	Birthplace of This Person (13)	Birthplace of This Person's Father (14)	Birthplace of This Person's Mother (15)	Year of Immigration (16)	# Years in U.S. (17)	Naturalized Citizen (18)	Occupation of every person 10 & older (19)	# months not employed (20)	# months in school (21)	Can read (22)	Can write (23)	Speaks English (24)	Owned or rented (25)	Owned free of mortgage (26)	Farm or house (27)	No. of farm schedule (28)

1910 CENSUS

Local Community _____
Ward _____
Enumerator _____
Date Census Taken _____
State _____
Supervisor's District No. _____
County _____
Enumeration District No. _____

Page No.	Street	House No.	1 Dwelling No.	2 Family No.	3 Name of each person whose place of abode on 15 April 1910 was in this family	4 Relationship	5 Sex	6 Color	7 Age	8 Marital Status	9 # Years—Present Marriage	10 Mother of how many children?	11 # living children	Birthplace of 12 This Person	13 Father	14 Mother	15 Year of Immigration	16 Naturalized or alien?	17 Speaks English? If not, give name of language.	18–19 Profession or Occupation & nature of business	20 Employer or Wage Earner or Working on Own Account	21 Out of work 15 April 1910?	22 # weeks out of work in 1909	23 Can read	24 Can write	25 School since 1 September 1909	26 Owned / rented	27 Owned free or mortgaged	28 Farm or house	29 No. of farm schedule	30 Civil War Veteran	31 Blind	32 Deaf & dumb

1920 CENSUS

Local Community _____

Ward _____

Enumerator _____

County _____

Date Census Taken _____

State _____

Supervisor's District No. _____

Enumeration District No. _____

Page No.	Street	House No.	Dwelling No.	Family No.	Name of each person whose place of abode on 1 Jan 1920 was in this family	Relationship	Own or rent home	Owned free or mortgaged	Sex	Color or race	Age	Marital status	Immigration year	Naturalized or alien?	Naturalization year	School since 1 Sept 1919	Can read	Can write	Birthplace of — This person	Birthplace of — Mother tongue	Birthplace of — Father	Birthplace of — Mother tongue	Birthplace of — Mother	Birthplace of — Mother tongue	Speaks English?	Profession or Occupation & nature of business		Employer, wage earner, or self-employed	No. of farm schedule
	1	2	3	4	5	6	7	8	9	10	11	12	13	14	15	16	17	18	19	20	21	22	23	24	25	26	27	28	29

FAMILY GROUP SHEET OF THE _____ FAMILY

Birth date	
Birthplace	Full name of husband _____
Death date	
Death place	His father _____
Burial place	
Occupation	His mother _____
Birth date	
Birthplace	Full name of wife _____
Death date	
Death place	Her father _____
Burial place	
Occupation	Her mother _____
Other spouses	Marriage information

Children of this marriage	Birth date and place	Death date and burial	Marriage date and spouse

Children of this marriage	Birth date and place	Death date and burial	Marriage date and spouse

NOTES AND REFERENCES

INDEX

reference sources, 43, 44, 49, 56, 89-90, 94, 95, 161, 170
Orgain, 124
Organizations, civic and fraternal, 98-99, 111, 113, 116
Orleans Territory, (*See* Louisiana)
Ostro/Ostrowsky, 171
Owen, 74
Owens, 28

P

Panama Canal Zone, 22
Pappas, 170
Parker, 72, 157
Parry, 126
Passenger and Immigration Lists Index (Filby), 166
Passenger lists, 165-166
    microfilm, 54, 166-168
    ordering copies, 54
Passports, 69
Patrick, 91
Patriot War, military service records, 56
Patton, 3, 5, 11, 136
Peade, 141
Pefly, 14
Pegram, 77
Pennsylvania
    African-American sources, 139, 141, 142, 143, 147, 148,
        149, 152, 153-154
    censuses, 8, 12, 14, 18, 22, 35, 41
    city directories, 54
    libraries and archives, 41, 44, 52, 90, 105, 153-154, 165,
        188
    newspapers, 105, 153
    reference sources, 44, 50, 52, 55, 56, 70, 90, 92, 94, 95, 98,
        109, 127, 165, 166, 167, 170, 172
Pension records, (*See* military records)
Pensioners, 1840 census, 12-13
Periodical Source Index (PERSI), 121, 131
Periodicals for genealogists, 173-174
    indexes to historical/genealogical periodicals, 119-123
Perkins, 81
Petitions, legislative, 42, 45-49, 51, 125, 137
Philippines, 20, 22
Phillips, 5, 74, 81, 136, 146
Philpot, 83
Pipen, 12
Pleasants, 31
Polling lists, 81
Pool, 126
Porter, 81
Post Office Department Reports of Site Locations, 110
Potter, 113
Potts, 138
Power of attorney, 77
Prenuptial agreements, 77
Preuss, 4, 84, 165
Priestly, 142

Primary sources, 3
Privacy laws, 59, 70, 91
Private land claims, 66
Private relief claims and acts, 58, 124, 125, 127, 137
Probate records, 78-79, 136
Professional associations and directories, 96-97
Professional licenses, 81
Public land states, 65-66, 78
Public lands, 58, 64-67
Public statutes, U.S., 58, 127
Publishers of genealogical material, 102, 192-197
Puerto Rico, 18, 22

Q

Quail, 15
Quaker dates, 177
Queries in periodicals, 174

R

Rains, 12
Randolph, 81, 135
Rayman, 125
Raynor, 18
Read, 134
Redemptioners, 98
Revolutionary War
    claims, 124
    military service records, 55, 57-58
    pensioners, 12, 64
Reynolds, 81
Rhine, 170
Rhode Island
    African-American sources, 139, 145, 149, 154
    censuses, 8, 12, 18, 20, 35, 41-42
    city directories, 94
    libraries and archives, 42, 90, 105, 154, 189
    newspapers, 105
    reference sources, 44, 48, 50, 56, 90, 94, 95, 109, 127, 167
Richardson, 5, 81
Rider, 157
RLIN, 112, 118, 151
Roach, 138
Robertson, 2, 77
Robinson, 100, 138
Rock, 84, 93
Rose, 135
Ross, 157
Round, 95

S

Safford, 92
Samoa, American, 22
Sanborn Co. fire insurance maps, 94-95, 108
Sanders, 145-146
Schernaildre, 17

Scholarly Resources, 14, 16, 18, 21, 36, 39-41, 45, 49, 55, 145, 157, 166, 170
School records and sources, 91-92, 113, 116, 117
Schwencke, 32
Selby, 101
Seminole Nation, 157, 160, 162
Serial Set, 12, 14-15, 38, 58, 64, 66, 123-125, 163
Severance, 106
Sexton, 19
Shannon, 80
Shaw, 12, 75, 79, 80
Shelby, 4, 15, 26-28, 30, 31, 37, 38, 51, 72, 73, 75, 83, 85, 95, 99
Simpson, 50
Sioux, 160, 162, 164
Slanes, 19
Slaves, 10, 15, 67, 133-141, 144, 145
　census schedules, 13, 135, 157
　narratives/interviews, 145-146
　records, 71, 117, 136-140, 141
　ships, slave manifests, 165-166
Smith, 81, 156, 169
Social Security Administration records, 69-70, 131
Social statistics, census schedules, 14, 33-36
Sorrell, 28
Soundex, 16-18, 20-22, 28-29
South Carolina
　African-American sources, 13, 139, 141, 142, 144, 145, 148, 149, 154
　censuses, 8, 13, 17, 20, 35, 36, 42
　city directories, 105
　libraries and archives, 42, 44, 52, 90, 105, 154, 189
　newspapers, 105
　reference sources, 44, 52, 55, 56, 57, 90, 92, 94, 95, 98, 108, 113, 117, 127, 163, 165, 166, 170, 174
South Dakota
　censuses, 18, 19, 20, 24, 35, 42, 157
　libraries and archives, 42, 44, 52, 90, 105, 189
　newspapers, 105
　reference sources, 44, 49, 52, 56, 90, 95, 109, 161
Southern Claims Commission, 62
Southern states, 13, 14, 24-25, 51, 54, 67, 68-69, 76, 119, 133, 134, 136, 140, 144, 150
Spanish-American War, 22
　service records, 57
Staats, 101
Stanard, 17
Stanton, 101
Stapleton, 134
State censuses, 37-42, 51, 135
State laws, 125-127
Steele, 5, 101
Steenberg, 117
Stevens, 106
Stewart, 45, 143
Subject bibliographies, 118-119, 149-150

Sumter, 113
Supplemental census schedules, 13-16, 33-36
Swem Index, 120-121, 125
Swinebroad, 144
Syferd, 19

T
Talley, 91
Tax lists, 8, 9-11, 42, 68-69, 75-76
Taylor, 8, 83, 170
Tennessee
　African-American sources, 13, 139, 142, 144, 145, 154
　censuses, 9, 13, 17, 20, 35, 42
　city directories, 94
　libraries and archives, 44, 52, 90, 105, 154, 189
　newspapers, 105
　reference sources, 9-11, 44, 48, 49, 52, 56, 57, 60, 90, 94, 95, 113, 157, 158
Territorial papers, 9, 11, 45-49, 53, 108, 162
Texas
　African-American sources, 13, 139, 144, 145, 154
　censuses, 17, 19, 20, 22, 35, 42
　city directories, 94
　libraries and archives, 44, 52, 90, 105, 112, 114, 115, 154, 156, 189
　McLennan County, 15
　newspapers, 105, 106, 122
　reference sources, 44, 51, 52, 56, 57, 64, 66, 90, 93, 94, 95, 97, 108, 113, 117, 125, 126, 155-156
　1830 Citizens of Texas, 8, 42
Thigpen, 15
Thomas, 80
Thompson, 50, 92, 125
Tiffin, 139
Tombstones, 2, 3, 83-84
Townsend, 142
Tract books, 65-66, 78
Trade associations, 96-97
Trusty, 142
Tunnell, 74
Turley, 74, 75-76, 136
Turner, 143, 147

U
Union lists and catalogs, 102, 116-118
Union soldiers service records, 56
United States Geological Survey (USGS), maps, 107
　GNIS database, 110
University sources, 91-92, 117
Utah
　censuses, 18, 24, 35, 36, 42
　city directories, 94
　libraries and archives, 14, 42, 44, 52, 90, 105, 114, 189
　newspapers, 105
　reference sources, 44, 49, 52, 56, 90, 94, 95

More Great Books Full of Great Ideas!

Unpuzzling Your Past: A Basic Guide to Genealogy—Make uncovering your roots easy with this complete genealogical research guide. You'll find everything you need—handy forms, sample letters and worksheets, census extraction forms, a comprehensive resource section, bibliographies and case studies. Plus, updated information on researching courthouse records, federal government resources and computers on genealogy. *#70301/$14.99/176 pages/paperback*

Writing Family Histories and Memoirs—From conducting solid research to writing a compelling book, this guide will help you re-create your past. Polking will help you determine what type of book to write, why you are writing the book and what its scope should be. Plus, you'll find writing samples, a genealogical chart, a publication consent form, memory triggers and more! *#70295/$14.99/272 pages*

Families Writing—Here is a book that details why and how to record words that go straight to the heart—the simple, vital words that will speak to those you care most about and to their descendants many years from now. *#10294/$14.99/198 pages/paperback*

How to Write the Story of Your Life—Leave a record of your life for generations to come! This book makes memoir writing an enjoyable undertaking—even if you have little or no writing experience. Spiced with plenty of encouragement to keep you moving your story towards completion. *#10132/$13.99/230 pages/paperback*

Turning Life into Fiction—Learn how to turn your life, those of friends and family members, and newspaper accounts into fictional novels and short stories. Through insightful commentary and hands-on exercises, you'll hone the essential skills of creating fiction from journal entries, identifying the memories ripest for development, ethically fictionalizing other people's stories, gaining distance from personal experience and much more. *#48000/$17.99/208 pages*

You Can Find More Time for Yourself Every Day—Professionals, working mothers, college students—if you're in a hurry, you need this time-saving guide! Quizzes, tests and charts will show you how to make the most of your minutes! *#70258/$12.99/208 pages/paperback*

Holiday Fun with Dian Thomas—A year-round collection of festive crafts and recipes to make virtually every holiday a special and memorable event. You'll find exciting ideas that turn mere holiday observances into opportunities to exercise imagination and turn the festivity all the way up—from creative Christmas gift-giving to a super Super Bowl party. *#70300/$19.99/144 pages/paperback*

Stephanie Culp's 12-Month Organizer and Project Planner—The projects you're burning to start or yearning to finish will zoom toward accomplishment by using these forms, "To-Do" lists, checklists and calendars. Culp helps you break any project into manageable segments, set deadlines, establish plans and follow them—step by attainable step. *#70274/$12.99/192 pages/paperback*

Kids, Money & Values: Creative Ways to Teach Your Kids About Money—Packed with activities, games and projects! You'll have a lot of fun as you teach your kids good money management habits! *#70238/$10.99/144 pages/10 illus./paperback*

Don't Be A Slave to Housework—Busy people—learn how to get your house in order and keep it that way. From quick clean-ups to hiring help, this book is loaded with advice! *#70273/$10.99/176 pages/paperback*

Raising Happy Kids on a Reasonable Budget—Discover budget-stretching tips for raising happy, healthy children—including specific examples from education and daycare to toys and clothing! *#70184/$10.95/144 pages/paperback*

Step-By-Step Parenting—Learn the secrets to strong bonds among families created out of second marriages. This inspirational guide covers everything from the games step-children play to a step-parent's rights. *#70202/$11.99/224 pages/paperback*

Don Aslett's Clutter-Free! Finally and Forever—Free yourself of unnecessary stuff that chokes your home and clogs your life! If you feel owned by your belongings, you'll discover inedible excuses people use for allowing clutter, how to beat the "no-time" excuse, how to determine what's junk, how to prevent recluttering and much more! *#70306/$12.99/224 pages/50 illus./paperback*

Make Your House Do the Housework—Take advantage of new work-saving products, materials and approaches, to make your house keep itself in order. You'll discover page after page of practical, environmentally friendly new ideas and methods for minimizing home cleaning and maintenance. *#70293/$14.99/208 pages/215 b&w illus./paperback*

Roughing it Easy—Have fun in the great outdoors with these ingenious tips! You'll learn what equipment to take, how to plan, set up a campsite, build a fire, backpack—even how to camp during winter. *#70260/$14.99/256 pages/paperback*

Confessions of a Happily Organized Family—Learn how to make your mornings peaceful, chores more fun and mealtime more relaxing by getting the whole family organized. *#01145/$10.99/248 pages/paperback*

Clutter's Last Stand—You think you're organized, yet closets bulge around you. Get out of clutter denial with loads of practical advice. *#01122/$11.99/280 pages/paperback*

The Organization Map—You *will* defeat disorganization. This effective guide is chock full of tips for time-management, storage solutions and more! *#70224/$12.95/208 pages/paperback*

Into the Mouths of Babes—Discover 175 economical, easy-to-make, vitamin-packed, preservative-free recipes. Plus, you'll find a shopper's guide to whole foods, methods to cope with allergies, a comprehensive prenatal and infant nutrition resource and what not to put into the mouths of babes! *#70276/$9.99/176 pages/paperback*

Streamlining Your Life—Finally, you'll get practical solutions to life's pesky problems and a five-point plan to take care of tedious tasks. *#10238/$11.99/142 pages/paperback*

The Crafts Supply Sourcebook—Turn here to find the materials you need—from specialty tools and the hardest-to-find accessories, to clays, doll parts, patterns, quilting machines and hundreds of other items! Listings organized by area of interest make it quick and easy! *#70253/$16.99/288 pages/25 b&w illus./paperback*

Office Clutter Cure—Discover how to clear out office clutter—overflowing "in" boxes, messy desks and bulging filing cabinets. Don Aslett offers a cure for every kind of office clutter that hinders productivity—even mental clutter like gossip and office politics. *#70296/$9.99/192 pages/175 illus./paperback*